Thomas Plate is a former editor at *New York* magazine, *Newsday* and *Newsweek*, and was recently a visiting editor on the London *Daily Mail*. He is currently working as an editor at the Los Angeles *Herald-Examiner*. He has won a number of awards for writing.

Andrea Darvi, a former Hollywood and TV actress, studied literature at Berkeley and went on to take an honours degree in journalism.

Thomas Plate and Andrea Darvi

SECRET POLICE
The Inside Story of a Network of Terror

First published in Great Britain by
Robert Hale Ltd 1982

Copyright © 1981 by Andrea Darvi and Thomas Plate

Published in Abacus 1983 by Sphere Books Ltd
30–32 Gray's Inn Road, London WC1X 8JL.

Reproduced, printed and bound in Great Britain by
Hazell Watson & Viney Ltd, Aylesbury, Bucks

Contents

Acknowledgments

We would like to thank our sources—some of them put themselves in considerable jeopardy to help us—and James G. Bellows, Lisa Drew, Shaye Areheart, and Theron Raines.

This book is dedicated to the memory of Sarai Ribicoff.

Preface to the British Edition

This book is concerned with internal-security agencies around the world that practice severe repression. It is designed to help all freedom-loving citizens think about the degree of political policing they want and are willing to tolerate.

This is not primarily a book about the milder forms of the phenomenon. The focus is on the bureaucracies of terror—the Iranian SAVAK or the Chilean DINA or the Polish Security Bureau—in an effort to provide a comparative basis for evaluating security and policing problems in democratic countries like Great Britain. We believe that Britons, not to mention Americans, can achieve an invaluable perspective on their own internal-security experiences and needs by evaluating those of other regimes and systems.

This study does not examine all secret police forces, but it does look at many. The three case studies in the first chapter, for example, concern three human beings whose lives brought them into contact with secret police in different parts of the globe—South America, Africa and the Near East.

Their chilling accounts open our study because their stories are both typical and extraordinary. Reading them will reinforce the suspicion that, more and more on this planet, the bizarre has become disturbingly commonplace. But in another sense their stories are atypical: they are about people who survived—or outwitted—the secret police. In our context, this makes these people, and their stories, somewhat unusual.

By design, this is a contemporary study. Almost everything you read here concerns events and institutions of the past decade. Whether we are in the midst of a peculiarly cruel epoch or whether the past decade was a landmark time for the violation of human rights is a question that must be left to future historians. We do not pretend to pass judgment on our times, or even to indict individual regimes, or rulers, or countries. Our intention is, rather, to illustrate a worldwide phenomenon. That phenomenon is secret police whose methods of order-maintenance exceed the boundaries of moral law. The evidence we present shows beyond any doubt that precisely these kinds of secret police are active in many countries around the world—on every continent, in every region, in support of a wide variety of regimes.

We do not argue that the state must not be permitted reasonable means of self-protection. The informed British citizen knows full well that the maintenance of a proper internal-security—and counter-intelligence system—is no simple task. But it is a necessary one, and the effort can prove frustrating. The Maze conundrum in Northern Ireland, which led to complaints of human-rights violations from such respected organizations as Amnesty International, served to demonstrate that, even in the best-intentioned of democracies, the state's right to maintain internal security and the individual's right of free political expression cannot always be readily reconciled.

But, with increasing likelihood, the benefit of the doubt will go to the state. Even in Britain, with its historic democratic tradition and institutions, history seems to be more on the side of order than law. Reviewing controversial police interrogation procedures in Northern Ireland, a Royal Commission in 1972 concluded that the police must be permitted a considerable degree of discretion during interrogation. The payoff from harsh methods of interrogation of suspects, the commission concluded, has proved so important to society as to outweigh the harm caused by intensive interrogations of suspects who ultimately turn out to have been innocent of wrongdoing. In fact, the Parker Committee issued a report that endorsed the employment of interrogation methods that in the

United States, by comparison, would be deemed improper and perhaps even scandalous.* The commission's only major reservation was that the degree of application not exceed bounds absolutely necessary to security needs. But the determination of need should be made solely by the government and security service independent of any external review or accountability. Seven years later, the Bennett Committee, also called upon to review interrogation techniques in Northern Ireland, put the matter bluntly: "Confessions which are 'voluntary' . . . will, however, only be made in an interrogation procedure with the right atmosphere. They will not be made in the atmosphere of a casual conversation or cosy fireside chat . . .". However hard-nosed their conclusions, the Bennett and Parker Committees no doubt spoke for many other governments besides Great Britain's, as the tolerance for political disorder and violent terrorism diminishes apace with the rise of secret police organizations around the world to counter the problem.

With these twin developments arises a related problem, which is the accountability of security services to their governments. The problem is tricky in both democratic and non-democratic systems. In Great Britain, for example, take the issue of MI-5, the lynchpin of the government's internal security network. The question is not simply whether the government has a sufficient degree of control over MI-5. Distressingly, one also has to wonder about MI-5's control over itself. Serious allegations have arisen about security problems within the security system itself. Over the years, these allegations have centred around MI-5 officials; but whatever the exact nature of the suspicion at any given time, the general theme is always the same: that a foreign government knew a great deal more about the daily operations of the country's internal-security service than the British citizen. If operational secrecy from the citizen is necessary to a security service, then the security service certainly owes it to the citizenry to maintain operational secrecy from the enemy. This the British internal security-services may not always have been able to achieve. Under this circumstance, the British citizen may perhaps be forgiven the curiosity to know a bit more about the nature and operation of his security service.

To that end, the Briton may wish to have a broader context with which to evaluate the service in his own country. If our premise, which we plan

---

*To wit, the so-called famous "five techniques": wall-standing, hooding, restricted water-and-bread diet, sleep deprivation and subjecting the suspect to irritating and psychologically disturbing high-frequency noises.

to illustrate, is correct—that secret police in one form or the other are a universal phenomenon with common characteristics—then an understanding of the most repressive secret police agencies will be useful to help assess the nature of the least repressive ones.

How are secret police forces structured and organized? How powerful are they? What are their exact goals as institutions of the state? What kinds of citizens become agents of the secret police? What are their tasks? What kind of behaviour leads to promotion up the ranks? Are the secret police of one country permitted to co-operate with the secret police of another? If not, do they tend to co-operate anyway, on their own? How? Are *all* secret police organizations inherently incompatible with a minimum observance of human rights? Under what circumstances is a hard-core secret police actually a necessary evil? Under what circumstances does a "soft-core" secret police harden into a most repressive one?

We have sought to deal with such fascinating questions by gathering evidence that is both plausible and reliable. To varying degrees of depth, information on many secret police activities has become more available today than ever before. In the past few years there has been an explosion of concern about human rights around the world: an increased dedication of human-rights organizations and human-rights leaders to their cause; and a steady stream of political exiles who have been willing to talk about their experiences. In this environment, information long denied to the journalist has rather suddenly surfaced.

Perhaps for the first time, enough evidence has come to the surface to begin to make some new assessments. One is that secret police forces, whether of the left or the right, tend to be far more alike than different. While the differences among secret police systems can be fascinating, it is equally fascinating that many secret police forces around the world tend to be more or less comparable in organizational structure, operating style, and standard techniques. Even with hugely important cultural and political differences among them, secret police around the world constitute a true generic class.

To be sure, within that class, there is a tremendous variety of secret police behaviour. Not every secret police force engages in torture as a normal interrogation technique; not every secret police force employs the indefinite detention of targeted citizens as a routine matter. Distinctions *are* important. And these distinctions can help British citizens think more clearly about the kind of policing they want—and indeed, even the kind of foreign policy they would support. To put on center stage, as this study does, a considerable amount of evidence about secret police behaviour around the world should make citizens of those countries maintaining the least frightening forms of secret policing not smug about their situation—but wary. The buyer of broadened internal security measures—whether in Britain or the U.S.—had best beware.

The British reader may have problems believing some of the experiences related in this book. Citizens of a democracy like that of the U.S. or Great Britain—but how many others are there, really?—tend to be rather naive about the conditions of freedom, perhaps because they have rather routinely enjoyed more of it than most citizens elsewhere. It is true that the United States and Britain have witnessed substantial degrees of police brutality at various times in their history. And it is true that there have been undeniable abuses by the security services in both Britain and the U.S.A., about which significant and influential segments of the population have justifiably complained. But most of us are likely to find the extreme experiences recounted here quite foreign, literally and figuratively, to our own experiences.

This book is not a leftist—or rightist—tract. It is designed to help inform our thinking about what kind of policing we should have. How should a decent society respond to rising terrorism? What is the proper state response to rising political and economic dislocation? To growing political and economic instability? What, in this context, can we learn from studying foreign secret police? The book you are about to read seeks to illuminate these questions, if not answer them. Optimism is an unadvisable stance on this subject. Secret police behaviour of the most violent sort manifests itself in so many societies that it stands as chilling and eloquent evidence of the potential darkness in human nature. Human nature *is* malleable, and this book is about human nature that has been twisted into what many would regard as inhuman institutions.

The evidence underlying our observations and conclusions was not gathered entirely without risk. "This is a dangerous business," a South African exile now teaching at a major American university warned us in all sincerity. "You must first register with the CIA and tell them what you are doing."

The thought was startling, and puzzling. Surely, the Central Intelligence Agency would have no reason to help. But this is not what our source meant to say. What he meant was that if we declared our intentions to the government, perhaps the CIA would not stand in our way, perhaps no harm—physical or otherwise—would come to us. Since most of our sources had fled from societies in which the press was not at all free to operate as we were, many of them had basic problems in understanding how it could be possible to prepare this kind of book without entailing substantial personal danger.

The important lesson here is that there are few societies in the world where journalists are permitted to do in-depth reporting and research for a politically sensitive book like this. Many exile sources expressed incredulity about our project, because, to their minds, while ours was a wonderful idea for a book, why take such a risk?

We were viewed, at times, as suspicious characters; the experiences of our sources required us to pass a sort of "CIA test." Were we what we said we were—journalists? Or were we really intelligence operatives? But, once we passed the "security clearance," and gained the confidence of our sources, we passed through a fantastic maze of astonishingly well-connected exile networks. They opened up to us in London, New York, and Washington, revealing—from behind otherwise closed doors—highly informed, proud but terrified human beings who, anxious to forget the past, were trying to make new lives for themselves.

In many cases, only their commitment to the cause of human rights prompted them to reopen the old wounds made newly sensitive by our probing questions. These exiles, though now outsiders, had gained considerable inside knowledge about the secret police of their home countries—often through bitter personal experience. In some cases, agents of the same secret police organizations whom they had encountered back home were perhaps no more than listening-distance away when we interviewed them. Or were perhaps infiltrating the human rights organizations where they now worked. The exile knows a great deal about the secret police. His life has often depended on his knowledgeability.

It was the co-operation of many exile circles—and the personal courage of individual exiles—that made this book possible. They provided the one feasible way of approaching this difficult subject. On the basis of their firsthand experiences (which of course were generally unflattering to the governments concerned) we were able to piece together a fair mosaic of who the secret police are and how they operate. The heart of this book therefore comes from interviews that took place in 1979 and 1980, sometimes under difficult and even tense circumstances. Some of the people interviewed were on the run—fugitives from their home countries, where they had been hunted for political violations. We thank them for their help, and we return the favour with absolute assurances of continued anonymity.*

The testimony of some secret police defectors also helped paint the general picture. Alas, there were never very many defectors to interview. Rarely did a secret police agent defect and then live long enough to tell a full story. Indeed, those who did make it to "the other side" tend to be suspect witnesses. Were they really bona fide defectors? Or were they double agents? How does one account for such "sudden" political conversions? In such circumstances, considerable scepticism was necessary in analyzing the testimony. We soon concluded that a book on secret police written exclusively from the perspective of the defector would prove to be not only a very short volume: it would be as suspect as a book relying solely on the testimony of emotionally charged exiles. And only the very highest-level defectors would satisfy: because of the tendency of clandestine institutions to practice bureaucratic compartmentalization, operatives in secret police organizations are generally prevented from viewing—and thereby later describing—the overall organizational picture. The operative is allowed to know only what he needs to know—which may be very little.

And more often than not for us, that perspective was too circumscribed to be all that helpful. By comparison, the testimony of the exile—with his many contacts throughout the exile network—was broader. By virtue of frequent communications with others in his country's exile community, he keeps abreast of all the latest developments—maybe out of concern for relatives back home, out of a basic sense of duty to remain informed, or simply to remain active in the opposition movement to the regime that he fled. He may have an ax to grind, but in time he will tell you all about that ax: what it looks like, how much it weighs, the sharpness and cut of the blade. And often enough, with the benefit of sometimes years of exile behind him, he can put his bitterness and anger into some perspective.

Not relying on the exile alone, we have brought into the picture information provided by (1) some former (and present) government officials concerned with the issues of internal security and counterintelligence, (2) high-level intelligence officers, (3) human-rights organizations and (4) high-level commissions around the world investigating

---

*Please check our bibliography and chapter notes for a sense of the geographical range and authority of these sources. Note also that, for much of the underground material, such as the so-called SAVAK papers, we commissioned translations into English.

the security problems of various countries. The organizations and commissions invariably proved highly reliable sources of information. We not only availed ourselves of the documentation they had accumulated—as you will see in our lengthy chapter notes—but quite often interviewed the human-rights officials and staffers on the commissions for insights that, for one reason or another, never made it into the official file.

It is the authors' belief that this research methodology—that is, the debriefing of political exiles, defectors, academic experts, foreign journalists, and former government officials, as well as the reliance on official and semiofficial reports and investigations—provides the clearest possible set of insights into the subject at hand. On-site reporting, for every country mentioned, would have been far less productive. It would largely have yielded little more than a monotonous repetition of official explanations. Not to mention the fact that, in a number of countries under study, the authors simply would not have been permitted to ask the kinds of questions this book had to ask of the only officials in a position to know the full story.

Just a few years ago, this book might not have been possible to complete. There was just not enough information available to draw the big picture. But now some new fear—and renewed dedication—seems to be in the air. While people are very worried about terrorism and social disorder, they also support a system of human rights that insures freedom from political repression. They intuitively comprehend the enormous trade-off that is involved when personal freedoms are exchanged for a more rigid social order.

Some of our sources told us that they had talked to us far more openly than they ever thought they would. Human-rights organizations report that, for the first time, more and more people seem to be interested in their work. The net effect has been an almost international chemical reaction, resulting in a near explosion of information about what we call the human-rights denial-mechanisms around the world.

This book could not have been written without that explosion of information and concern. It is as if some exiles regard the growing interest in human-rights issues as a way for British and American citizens to save ourselves from what they went through. They worry that unprecedented but nonetheless hardly inconceivable disruptions in economic and political conditions in Britain could produce an extreme form of police behavior that we would characterize as "type-A"; i.e., a DINA or a SAVAK. We share that concern.

Yes, it could happen in Britain—not likely to be sure, but certainly possible. We must not think of the societies in which the secret police are notoriously physically and psychologically brutal as so inherently different that it could only happen there. Precisely because it did happen *there*, it could happen *here*. Complacency is one symptom of the disease of ignorance.

New York City, 1982   THOMAS PLATE
                                                   ANDREA DARVI

ONE

States of Siege

1

They used to have the reputation of coming for you in the middle of the night.

Nowadays they tend to be more open. They may not need the darkness.

It began for the defense attorney not in the middle of the night but in the middle of a crowded elevator.

His office was situated directly opposite the Supreme Court building, where he had worked for five years as a Supreme Court judge and where he was now defending an increasing number of clients on political charges brought by the new dictatorship of General Augusto Pinochet.* It was October 1974—several months after the issuance of Decree Law 521 and the dawning of a new Chilean Government with a restrictive philosophy about political rights.

Decree Law 521 created the Dirección de Inteligencia Nacional.

---

* From 1967 to 1972, he served as a judge pro tem of the Supreme Court (a temporary position filling in for various other justices, sometimes as often as two to four days per week).

In just a few months, much of the world would know it more
familiarly by the acronym DINA.

The defense attorney soon became more involved with DINA
than most. Many of his colleagues feared political cases because of
the regime's growing intolerance—from which not even members of
the bar were immune. But the defense attorney did not shirk clients
accused of political crimes. For such impudence, the defense attorney—not to mention his growing list of clients—came under the
scrutiny of DINA.

Eugenio would have preferred not to have so much business. Like
everyone else, he was frightened, for under the new government,
even a former Supreme Court judge and prominent attorney might
need the services of a defense attorney. The DINA terror was
spreading like an epidemic to which no one was immune.

Eugenio had just left the Supreme Court building, across the boulevard. He had put in a long, tiring, enervating day, for he was
enmeshed in more cases than he could count. Many of his cases involved the unexplained disappearances of clients. They simply
disappeared under circumstances that could at best be described as
suspicious.

Such disappearances were more common now, but as they became
more common, they were becoming less mysterious. It was as if the
operations of the secret police suddenly were somehow less secret.
People were beginning to understand that fellow citizens were simply disappearing off the streets.

It was almost out in the open now: Chile had ceased to be one
kind of civilization, and it was in the process of becoming another
kind. Chile was, as this defense attorney himself had just argued in
open court, becoming a secret-police state.

This was a contention made in public, with apologies to no one,
and with a boldness and persistence that Eugenio knew were sure to
mark him, before long, for a run-in with DINA, the end result of
which no one could predict for sure.

Although a man of very liberal political beliefs, Eugenio was unquestionably above all a patriot who loved Chile and its rich democratic traditions. He loved the intensity of urban life in Santiago, the
bustle of the metropolis, the sometimes comic intensity of its street
life—why, one could hardly make the slightest commotion in his be-
loved downtown Santiago without attracting a crowd. The outbreak
of a shouting match, a fender-bender at a busy intersection, even the

rantings of a street drunk—within minutes, hundreds of Santiagoans would materialize, pushing and shoving for position to catch a glimpse of the action and render an instant personal opinion.

It was through this rush-hour tide of Chilean city life that Eugenio waded as he crossed the boulevard to his office. He was anxious to get to his office, answer the pile of telephone messages that his secretary had said lay on top of his desk, clear up the remaining business, and get home to his wife and children.

Waiting impatiently in the lobby of the office building for the elevator, he ran his mind over a thousand matters, almost forgetting to return the greeting of the elevator boy as he stepped into the elevator car.

The car was packed with men dressed in conservative business suits, but he thought nothing of it. It was, after all, rush hour. Only later, when he had time to reflect on the experience, did he realize that at five o'clock, the elevator car should have been emptying out at the lobby—rather than filling up.

"Señor," one of the men dressed in conservative business suits said, firmly but in a low voice, "we want to talk to you."

At almost any other time, Eugenio would have regarded this as a perfectly reasonable request, but right now, with his workday drawing to a close, he didn't want to talk to anyone. "It is too late," he said, and reaching into his pocket for a business card to give the man, he added, "Call my secretary in the morning."

Suddenly the man who had so politely addressed him was no longer so polite. He grabbed Eugenio brusquely by the arm. And as if on cue, the other men in the elevator squeezed into the two of them, to hide Eugenio from the outside world with layers of agents.

Alert now, Eugenio was under no illusions about what was happening to him. His time had come. It was as simple as that.

Eugenio quickly added up eighteen DINA agents, stuffed inside the increasingly claustrophobic atmosphere of the elevator car. It was, he realized at the time, a meticulous, efficient operation. Before the elevator boy could even move to close the door and take the elevator up to higher floors, the cordon of agents shoved Eugenio out into the lobby. But with the agents in circular formation to shield the short Eugenio from view, they moved quickly across the lobby and out to the street without anyone, except the dumb-struck elevator boy, knowing what was happening.

The DINA car was parked by the curb, only a few dozen yards

from the lobby entrance. There was a driver behind the wheel. The car's motor was idling.

Eugenio, wondering whether these might be his last moments out in the open, made the decision to scream for all he was worth. He wanted to attract a crowd. He was betting on the insatiable curiosity of most Santiagoans. He wanted witnesses.

"I am a lawyer," he shouted out to the street. "I will be arrested like thousands of other Chilean people have been. They will kill me. Help me. You must help me."

But the cordon of agents did not hesitate. They moved grimly forward toward the car. One agent in the pack said, in a low tone of determination and menace, "Shut up, or it will be worse."

The agent's warning only made Eugenio more intent than ever on drawing attention to himself. He felt his only hope was to yell as loudly as he could. He shouted out his name. He screamed: "Look what they are doing to me!"

But the response was meager. A few people stopped to look, but most acted as if they had not heard anything. By Santiago's standards, the little group that he had been able to attract did not deserve to be called a crowd. There was no commotion, only indifference. It was as if people on the street had lost their ability to feel. No one asked the agents any questions. And although several stared directly into the heart of the circle of agents, no one tried to help.

The agents shoved Eugenio into the back seat of a late-model, nondescript Chevrolet, and several crowded into the back seat with him. The car doors shut, while the other agents divided themselves into two groups. One group crowded into a car in front of the Chevrolet, the other into one in back. In moments, the little motorcade spurted off.

The DINA agents in the car seemed as nervous as the Supreme Court justice. The car was moving forward through the rush-hour traffic, but the driver was edgy, erratic.

And Eugenio was determined to be no easy arrest: perhaps, he reminisced years later, it was precisely his very helplessness that propelled him to act so boldly under the threatening circumstances. After all, DINA had already earned quite a reputation for itself; but he was determined that whatever they were going to do to him, he was not going to make their job easy.

As the car careened and swerved through traffic—running lights and practically running down pedestrians—he bombarded the agents with a constant harangue.

"How do you feel when you arrive home and kiss your wife and see your children?" he began. "What will you do for a living when the tyranny stops?" And then, "Have you thought of your victims, women whom you've raped, women who are like your own wives?" And again: "Do you think an attorney like me will ever finish his work? After me, there will be others."

He knew that if he had not been almost certain he was going to disappear from the face of the earth, he would never have had such nerve.

The agents did not bother to reply, but the harangue seemed to be affecting the driver. He steered like a man possessed, who, having lost his cool, was fixated on the single goal of getting this madman they'd arrested out of the populated center of Santiago as fast as he could.

And so he ran every red light, whipped around corners on two wheels rather than four, and didn't care whom or what he hit. After missing a light at one point and plowing into a small car in front of them, he thereupon proceeded to back up into another car. He didn't wait to exchange license numbers for the insurance company. "Keep driving," ordered the supervisor as people on the street started to stop and look. "Don't stop for anyone. Don't answer to anyone."

Eugenio kept up a constant barrage of words. He was fighting fear with invective. At first utterly astonished that they didn't just club him to shut him up, he then grasped at the hope that as a respected attorney, former Supreme Court justice, and prominent citizen, he just might be able to get out of this arrest alive.

But then an agent, pulling out a roll of tape, lurched toward him as if to tape his eyes shut. The taped-over eyes was known as a standard DINA practice when a hood was not used.

But the attorney would have none of it. Eugenio screamed, "I just don't accept that," and reached forward and grabbed the neck of the driver with his hands. "You can kill me but at least one of you will be killed with me because, at the speed we're going, we are going to crash."

Perhaps convinced now that they really had a madman in their midst, the agent retreated and decided not to tape over the jurist's eyes.

The car screeched suddenly to a halt in a well-lit parking lot. They were, the lawyer recognized, behind the main building of the Ministry of Defense, and almost at once the supervising agent rushed out of the car and disappeared into the building.

They waited. Everyone was silent except the jurist, who began his harangue anew: "You know I'm a lawyer and you need a judicial order," he said at one point, to no one in particular inside the car.

Finally, for the first time, one of the agents tried to calm him down.

"Don't worry, we are not going to keep you," the agent said quietly. "We are not going to kill you."

Eugenio was stunned, for two reasons. He was relieved, of course, by the announcement, but he also remembers being shocked, at that moment, by how extraordinarily powerful DINA had become, so powerful that an agent could speak of an arrest or a killing as casually as deciding whether or not to write out a parking ticket.

Fifteen minutes passed before the supervisor came out of the Defense building.

"We are not taking you to Cuatro Álamos," he said, referring to DINA's notorious prison for political targets. "We have gotten instructions to deport you."

"Why are you going to deport me?" he immediately countered.

The supervising DINA agent's answer was stiff and formal: "I have a decree that says you are a danger to national security." However, he kept calling him "Señor," speaking politely and coolly. Whoever the agent had consulted with at the Ministry of Defense must have told him to handle Eugenio with kid gloves.

"I have a last request," Eugenio said, pushing his luck. "I just want to go home and see my wife and children. They don't know where I am or what has happened to me."

"Excuse me, Señor," said the supervisor. "But I have immediate instructions to take you to the airport."

With that, he knew that deportation was irrevocable. He would not be killed, he would be exiled. The supervisor got into the car, the tail car followed, and they all drove for the Santiago airport, which he would now be seeing for the last time. They parked the Chevrolet far from the passenger building and idled the engine while waiting on a remote tarmac. Four agents and a guard stayed with the car and with the jurist, and an agent from the tail car rushed off to the terminal building.

A few minutes passed. Eugenio asked if he could step outside to relieve himself.

The supervising agent, indecisively, said no.

"You can't stop the Chilean people from urinating," Eugenio said tartly.

No one laughed. He hadn't expected laughter, but he continued to play on their indecisiveness. He proposed that if he held a hat over his hand and turned in a direction where no one was in sight, no one would be the wiser.

The agents appeared to consider that proposition seriously. One got out of the car and looked around.

No, that wouldn't be possible, the agent concluded, getting back inside.

"Why not?" Eugenio asked.

"There's a policeman out there," the agent pointed out. "Don't you know that to urinate in the street is illegal?"

"DINA"—thought the former Supreme Court judge sarcastically —"upholder of all laws—small as well as big."

The agent who had run into the passenger building returned to the car with the air that whatever arrangements had been necessary now had been made.

Two agents pushed Eugenio in the direction of an aircraft that had taxied to the far corner of the airport. He later learned that the departure of the plane, a Chilean commercial airline, had been postponed forty minutes in order to accommodate DINA.

Two agents pushed him up the boarding ramp, and following him into the plane, seated him in the first row. It was the only row that was unoccupied.

The plane took off as soon as the agents exited. Seated in a row all to himself in the first-class section of the commercial airliner, he asked a stewardess where he was headed. The stewardess said Buenos Aires. That was the last thing she said to him. Not once during the flight did she ask for his ticket.

Eugenio, living today in political exile in the United States, realizes that he was lucky. Due to his prominence and position of authority, the officials had decided not to kill, torture, or imprison him. Maybe they didn't wish to create a martyr out of him? Who knew what they were thinking? Are the actions of a secret police force ever entirely logical?

2

DINA was a secret police force. It lives today in a new form and with a new acronym, CNI, for National Information Center. In the next story, you will meet agents of the South African security police. They used to be under the overall supervision of BOSS, the national intelligence agency. BOSS then became known in South Africa as DONS. In the story after that, you will see SAVAK in action. SAVAK, the secret police under the regime of the late Shah, lives at this writing in a new form and with a new acronym. It is known as SAVAMA. See Chapter Three for more on the SAVAMA and DONS name changes.

There is a universality to the phenomenon of the secret police that is not entirely understood. No matter the ideological nature of the regime in which they operate, they are more alike than similar. To be sure, there are important differences among them, and some observers tend to be troubled by the generality of the term "secret police." But the term itself is expressly designed to be a general term. It accommodates accumulation rather than discard, inclusion rather than exclusion, comparison on a generic level rather than *sui generis* isolation. "Secret police" is an umbrella term we place over an astonishing and troubling variety of official and semiofficial government conduct.

"Secret police" are official or semiofficial organs of government. They are units of the internal security police of the state, with the mandate to suppress all serious, threatening political opposition to the government in power and with the mission to control all political activity within (and sometimes even beyond) the borders of the nation-state.

Secret police include both strategists and technicians, those who plan the operations as well as those who carry them out. Many governments make a point of organizing their secret police network so that the boys who do the dirty work are kept to one side and the boys who design the overall strategy of internal security are put on the other. But to discuss secret police work in the absence of either branch might be like trying to understand the human body simply by studying the limbs, as if the brain did not count.

It is important to look at the entire structure of the secret police organism. National governments may pointedly advertise a cleavage as broad as the Grand Canyon between the intelligence function (the brain) and the operational section (the body) of the internal security police, but many times the same official or ministry actually has authority over both. For one thing, it makes no sense not to coordinate the two.

Taken together, the intelligence and operational wings of the secret police network often constitute an impressive demonstration of the powers of the state. But while it is essential to understand the full range of these powers, it is also important to understand that the states that require such authority also exhibit profound weaknesses. In effect, they are asking their secret police units to compensate for certain inadequacies of the state.

The late President Eisenhower said it very well indeed. "I would rather try to persuade a man to go along," he wrote, perhaps giving more thought to the philosophical issue of consent than many people suspect, "because once I have persuaded him, he will stick. If I scare him, he will stay just as long as he is scared and then he is gone." Many governments tend to scare more than to persuade.

To scare an entire population, a secret police force does not have to remain secret. It can work quite openly. By 1974, few citizens of Chile had not heard of DINA. In Iran, SAVAK was the best-known acronym among devout Moslems and Christians alike. And is there a single Soviet citizen in the entire U.S.S.R. who does not know of the KGB? What, then, is a secret police force if it is not even secret?

Secrecy per se is not a defining feature of secret police. On the contrary, in some countries, citizens are more aware of the existence of their secret police than the more conventional police. Far more to the point, the defining feature of secret police is the nature of their routine behavior. It is their routine practices, after all, that violate the very psychology (and at times even the anatomy) of human beings in ways that conventional police do not.

It is the nature of the secret police *experience*—not their degree of clandestineness as institutions—that defines these forces. The elements of that experience include: *surveillance* by methods that are illegal oftentimes even under the broad mandates that in theory may tend to govern their activities; *searches,* often without warrants, sometimes conducted civilly, sometimes cruelly, usually disruptively; *arrest* at the time and place and circumstances of the agents' own choosing, without the necessity, should they choose to dispense with whatever formalities might otherwise be required, of judicial warrant or official notice; *interrogation* by any means necessary, including methods of physical and psychological torture that are generally so well defined and known throughout the secret police world that in effect they constitute established, administratively accepted procedures; *detention,* as prolonged as the secret police (possibly but not necessarily in conjunction with the government) deem necessary, often under physically and morally inhumane circumstances. These practices constitute what we will call type-A secret police behavior.

These routine practices of governments—and the secret police representing them—are expressly designed to persuade through scaring. The practice of these techniques does not always have to be exercised, because the option to exercise that power is known to exist. Everyone understands this. In many societies, after all, what secret police do is not even illegal; many societies pass laws authorizing some of these practices. Others simply look the other way as the boundaries of the law are exceeded: many governments openly and rather cheerfully state that they will resort to whatever means may be necessary to curb trouble—whether or not authorizing laws are on the books.

A secret police force does not have to operate in secret to be secret police. Is it possible, then, that the term "secret police" refers not to clandestine activities per se as much as to activities (clandestine or not)—on the part of established police units—that are so intuitively unacceptable that in his heart the average citizen would prefer these practices to remain altogether secret?

In the international police world itself, the term secret police is generally considered a misnomer, if not a left-wing (or right-wing) slander. That certain police activities ought to remain secret is, to be sure, taken entirely for granted. But, to the police mind, a term such as secret police is propagandistic—practically an ideological shibboleth, the language of those who are "antipolice" or antiregime and who want to make the problems of policing even more difficult than they ordinarily are.

To the police mind, policing is a mechanism of government with a variety of instrumentalities that constitute a continuum, so that all police officers and plainclothes agents across the globe may be viewed as inhabiting the same boat. They regard their job as basically impossible; on the best days, it is merely very difficult. And of course, they would defend their practices wholeheartedly: if Iran's SAVAK required certain interrogation techniques as a necessary instrument for maintaining the nation's precarious internal security, then that ought to remain the business of the Iranian authorities.

Whatever they are called, many government security forces are the type-A secret police: that is, those internal security institutions that routinely exhibit the five functions of the hard-core secret police; to wit, surveillance, searches, arrests, interrogation (including torture), and indefinite detention. Within the past decade, perhaps two dozen secret police forces could be placed in this category.

In addition, there are internal-security organizations that are obviously not type-A secret police forces. These include ones in both Western democracies, Communist societies, and Third World countries. Some of these practice several though not all the five functions of the hard-core secret police; these can be labeled type-B. Still others must be regarded as less virulent forms of the phenomenon and therefore could be classified as type-C; for example, the security branch of the Royal Canadian Mounted Police. There are extremely important differences *among* internal security organizations, but taken all together, they add up to a worldwide phenomenon.

3

It was three o'clock in the morning. All the neighbors were sleeping in this poor township of Meadowlands. They came for Malefe very, very quietly.

He was asleep in his bedroom, with papers strewn all over the floor. The last time the South African Security Branch had come, it was also in the dark hours of the morning. Three agents had come and left quietly. Simple questions were asked, direct answers given. Where did you go to school? Where do you work? There were no strong-arm tactics, but of course a file was being worked on. They left after he answered all their questions.

But Malefe did not stop working. The young black activist had become more involved since then: black protest groups, theater clubs, writing. He attended political meetings . . . a lot of them. And when the press had a question, he had an answer. He made no secret of what he thought.

But he knew he was being closely watched. The Security Branch of the South African intelligence network, under the overall direction of the famed Bureau for State Security (later renamed several times) had informers everywhere, and plenty of black ones. Which was another reason why he was so outspoken. Why try to keep a secret from the secret police?

He had surmised that when the Security Branch came again, it would be in the middle of the night. That was the time of a human being's least resistance, the time when there would be the fewest witnesses, the time when you were most likely to have incriminating papers lying carelessly around.

And so it was almost exactly 3 A.M. on a spring night in the early seventies when they knocked, and the young man, deep in sleep, realized at the time that he was reacting too slowly to the knocking to hide the papers.

The agents had sneaked up to the door without even attracting the attention of a neighborhood dog. He knew that if he delayed too much in answering the door, they would assume that he had something to hide. And they were likely to find whatever they were looking for anyway. There wasn't much sense in delaying the inevitable.

When he answered the door, three agents were standing in the entrance. They were three black agents from the Security Branch. They moved into the apartment quietly, but they moved out very quickly. They wanted to get him out of his place as fast as possible.

The car was waiting outside. But a neighborhood dog had caught a scent, and let out a howl. Suddenly, expertly, the three well-trained Security Branch officers changed their act. They began making a lot of noise, slapping their captive on the back in a boisterous and fraternal manner. To anyone who might be watching, it was as if the four had been drinking all night—good fellows for whom the party was not yet over, just one more stop in their all-night revelry.

To the Security Branch plainclothes officers, it was all in a night's work. You go in quietly, so as to avoid gathering a crowd. But almost invariably, predictably, some insomniac neighbor, or some wretched mutt, would catch wind that something unusual was up. Your procedure was simple: if your quiet entrance is detected, exit cheerfully and boisterously, as if you have nothing to hide. Standard security-work operating procedure.

The three black agents put Malefe into the back seat of their car, and they quickly sped away from Meadowlands.

They stopped at the first police station they came to. One of the agents showed his credentials to the desk officer and asked to use the telephone just inside the front entrance. It was a hot night. The door to the station house was open. The car windows were open. Voices were carrying. Malefe was listening intently. The agent, speaking in a voice clearly deferential to some superior at the other end of the line, said simply, "We've got him." The three South African security officers drove the rest of the way to Johannesburg that night. The agents did not bother to blindfold Malefe, whose involvement in writing and theater protest groups and whose candid interviews with the press had finally, brought him under the custody of the Security Branch, in 1972.

"They should have taken me three years before they did," the young man recalled thinking as he looked out the window at the dimly lit suburban towns on the way to the capital.

The drive took a good two hours. When they arrived at John Vorster Square, the headquarters for the security police, the sun was just peeking up over the Johannesburg skyline.

The arresting party was met at headquarters by an officer whom Malefe assumed was the one they had called from the substation two hours earlier, as well as two staff interrogators. Malefe realized instantly that—maybe now, maybe later—there would be beatings. "They should have taken me three years before they did," he thought again—now angry with himself for not having considered leaving South Africa while it was still possible to escape.

The initial interrogation at John Vorster Square by the two staff officers was conducted in an atmosphere of psychological menace, but no torture was applied to him. After one long session, five agents drove him back to his home, in Meadowlands, where they conducted a more thorough search than the initial arresting officers had. They were obviously looking for documents that might serve their purpose in processing his case—by linking him with a larger antigovernment network of black activists. Then, after stuffing a handful of documents in a briefcase, they drove him directly back to John Vorster Square.

And so the young man's imprisonment began. They gave him no idea how long it would last, but the first three years seemed at times unendurable. Between 1972 and 1975, according to this activist now in exile in London, he was tortured repeatedly. Security Branch officers beat him up several times a week, and in their absence they kept him standing in a corner of his cell from 10 A.M. to 4 P.M., day after day.

He was tough up to a point, he recalls, but no one is tough enough to endure torture indefinitely. And there were no limits to the Security Branch officers' persistence. It was only when he forced himself to accept the reality that the Security Branch was prepared to interrogate him indefinitely that he broke down and confessed.

He remembers only that bits and pieces of the language of the confession that he signed when he gave in were preposterously stilted: "Revolutionary uprising. . . ." ". . . people will come from rural areas. . . ." At the height of the torture, when he finally succumbed to their demand to sign the confession, he was not sure he would have the strength to understand and sign the document. But as he read over the document, and they handed him the pen, he seemed to regain strength instantly, as if the decision to confess had a redemptive and replenishing quality, as if he realized as he signed the document that he was going to survive.

The confession did change his life. For, as far as the Security Branch was concerned, his case was over. They had no more interest in him: the Security Branch had gotten what it wanted, and enough time had already been invested in the case; and so the government moved quickly to try the case in court, reach a settlement, and be done with him.

Malefe then had a stroke of wonderful luck. With another prisoner, he worked out what they would say on the witness stand in their self-defense. Communicating with each other through an elaborate but discreet smuggling system, using an unwitting prison guard as the go-between, over a period of months they lined up their testimony so that there would be no discrepancies on the stand.

The trial went off as scheduled; in December of 1975, he and his co-conspirator were tried on six counts of terrorism and smuggling men out of the country for military and guerrilla training in neighboring states.

The trial could not have gone better for Malefe. Not only did his cover story mesh beautifully with his fellow inmate's, but for reasons he was never able to determine, the Security Branch had failed to deliver a key witnesss. Within months—having already served three years—the young man was out of South Africa and living in London.

But the incident surely was no loss for the South African internal security network, of course. For one thing, Malefe, unable to endure torture any longer, did provide a confession. The confession, of course, was not entirely truthful. But the secret police were satisfied. As often as not, a confession is more important to them than the truth.

4

The obvious justification for a secret police force is the security of the state. To what extent is such a force a necessary evil? To use the term "secret police" to describe a universal phenomenon in the world is not necessarily to condemn all aspects of that phenomenon. Are there aspects of secret police behavior worth maintaining? However much we may try to obscure the excessive quality of secret police operations, the acceptance of secret police forces as viable and reasonable work forces for the maintenance of internal security may well be tied to fears of what certain societies might be like without them.

In an epoch in which a wide variety of individuals and groups resort to violence, readily justifying their actions with hardly a second thought, the security of the state is a patriotic goal. The most decent citizens among us are absolutely correct to insist that the state maintain appropriate mechanisms to achieve a measure of internal security. Only the truly democratic or openly pluralistic society agonizes over this matter. In the repressive state of the left or the right, certain institutions are taken for granted. Among them is the internal security police force.

But, in the truly democratic or pluralistic state, the subject of policing will always be intensely debated. After all, can there be a surer sign of an antidemocratic state than agents of the secret police roaming the society in the absence of public debate about the guidelines under which these agents operate?

This is one reason why secret police are important. They are both the final product and an instant index of the society of which they are a part.

To be sure, the secret police should not be the sole standard by which a society ought to be measured. But the reality is that our knowledge about the secret police will surely color our judgment about a society, however necessary it is to avoid ethnocentricity and simplemindedness.

Americans must be especially sensitive to avoid ethnocentric judgments. In many places, history may not be ready for democracy. In
Yugoslavia, which has a thoroughly well-developed and sophisticated secret police system, the centrifugal forces threatening the security of the state are more powerful than Americans might imagine.
Even the internationally admired reformist and critic Milovan Djilas
warned, in an American magazine, about the danger of simplemindedness when thinking about his native land:

"Yugoslavia cannot go at once to democracy. It is not ripe for it.
If the government declared a multiparty system tomorrow, there
would be cows in the streets. Everyone would have his own party—
Cominformists, Croatian nationalists, Serbs. We need something
slow, a process toward democracy. I am in favor of pluralism in the
abstract. But an authoritarian system is better than civil war, and
civil war is better than Russian occupation, to graduate the evils."

A study of secret police systems of varying degrees of extremes,
then, may be a study in necessary evils of varying gradations. It is
precisely the fact that so many societies seem to have concluded that
they are in the throes of a state of internal war (in the Hobbesian
sense) that makes the recourse to the secret police solution an at-
tractive alternative. Ours is hardly a quiet time. That the wars of our
era have tended to be mostly internal rather than international does
not make the insecurities of the affected states any less real or
gravely troubling.

A study of the activities of secret police *within* their states
(largely excluding intelligence units whose franchise involves running missions abroad) is therefore a study of war. Wars within
states, as well as wars between states, necessarily involve measures
that would be considered unacceptable in "normal" times. The di-
mension of a perceived threat is not diminished simply by virtue of
the fact that the enemy cannot be located by an identifying uniform,
in combat formation, across clearly defined borders. International
terrorism, internal subversion, international communism, international fascism—these are the perceived threats to the sovereign
states of our epoch. Arguably, there are times that such threats
sometimes materialize mainly in the eyes of the beholders rather
than in objective reality, but real dangers of these sorts do objectively exist. Even in the most open democracies, of which there are
few, there can be no argument against the need for certain measures
of clandestine intelligence activity to protect society from the ene-

mies of the state. Free societies, as well as closed ones, need to have secret services; otherwise we run the risk that the closed ones will take over the free ones.

Yet even in wars between states, certain standards of behavior are thought important to preserve. Most states, for instance, would proscribe biochemical warfare: even in war-time, when, obviously, normal civilities are not observed, certain humanitarian limits should be adhered to.

So, too, in the exercise of internal security. Perhaps an examination of secret police behavior around the world can help illuminate where and when certain necessary limits have *not* been observed—and therefore why certain limits *must* be established and observed.

The study of secret police is fascinating precisely because it brings us to borders of a different kind—not international boundaries, but new frontiers of excess and inhumanity.

5

The sixty-one-year-old wife of a resident of Tehran who operated a carpet business remembers thinking at the time that it had really gotten out of hand. "Neither the young nor the old," Ozra used to say, "are exempt from the practices of SAVAK."

By the time the seventies dawned, there could not have been a person in Iran who had not heard of the Intelligence and National Security Organization—or, as it was known in practically every household inside Iran and in every student circle outside Iran: SAVAK.

SAVAK seemed to be everywhere, but, for this mother, SAVAK was nearer than to most others. Her eldest son was twenty-seven years old when he, along with thirteen other revolutionaries, had been executed by SAVAK. This was in the very early seventies. Since then, her son had been revered as a revolutionary martyr in those left-wing circles—markedly widened by the mid-seventies—that opposed the Shah.

The mother was no fiery revolutionary herself, but she loved all her sons and held to the belief that even radicals were entitled to have loving, loyal mothers.

And she had friends who were mothers too who held the same staunch views. In the winter of 1976, on the first anniversary of the death of the son of one of her closest friends, Ozra was one of many to attend a special meeting called by the mothers of active *fedayee* (Marxist) guerrillas. There was nothing secret about the get-together. Everyone knew it was being held to commemorate a son's death. And the women went because it afforded them the opportunity to feel that they were not alone.

They gathered together—fifty or sixty mothers strong—at the apartment of the mother whose son's death was being commemorated, on the fourth floor of an apartment building a few blocks from Tehran University.

They began the meeting on time, even though it was both hoped and expected that still more mothers would straggle in. To get the proceedings under way, one of the mothers stood up and began to give a speech, to rally the others into a sense of solidarity under the increasingly grim circumstances of SAVAK's tightening grip.

She had barely begun to speak when there was a knock on the door. She went to the door and opened it, expecting to welcome more mothers. Instead, eleven SAVAK agents introduced themselves and swiftly ordered the mothers to stand up and face the wall.

Then the SAVAK agents conducted a rigorous search of the apartment. In a fury, they went through everything—pocketbooks, papers, drawers, refrigerators—everything. It took the eleven of them a full half hour to cover the apartment.

The mothers stood facing one wall. No one dared to speak, or to look over her shoulder.

The search completed, the agents, as if in unison, turned toward the mothers. An agent announced that they would be taken from the building for questioning, that they would be leaving in groups of five, and that each group would be supervised by a pair of agents.

Ozra was one of the last mothers to be escorted out, which gave her time to think. Carefully taking mental notes on the agents' procedure, she was trying to figure out a way to escape. She was frightened, yes, but not too terrorized to be unable to think.

She realized soon enough that although there were elevators on the fourth floor of the building, the SAVAK agents were escorting the mothers down the stairs. She figured they were leading them out of the building via the basement exit, trying to avoid the elevator traffic. But there were two elevators, and neither of them went as far down as the basement. She assumed there was a SAVAK agent posted at the basement exit, but perhaps there wasn't one at the lobby. Supposing she and a few mothers somehow managed to slip into one of the elevators and slip out through the lobby? Who would see them?

It was, she decided, worth a try.

The agents, she noticed, kept their guns drawn, but they seemed utterly confident that they had these mother hens under control.

She whispered a plan to the mothers on either side of her. An agent noticed the whispering but appeared to think little of it. When the two young SAVAK agents turned to her, the last group of remaining mothers backed off from the wall and left the apartment. The agents followed behind.

But out in the hall, the mothers, instead of turning to the right, in the direction of the stairwell, veered to the left, in the direction of the elevator bank.

"What are you doing?" shouted one of the SAVAK agents, stunned at their unexpected turn.

"I cannot walk down the stairs," she replied calmly. "I must take this elevator. I always take the elevator. I have a pain in my leg." And as if by a miracle, before the utterly stunned SAVAK agents could recover, the doors of the elevator opened wide right before them. It could not have been timed more precisely even if it had been planned.

The mothers stepped gingerly into the elevator, and the doors closed instantly.

It seemed like the longest elevator ride of Mrs. Araghi's life. They had only four floors to go, but in that short stretch of time the mother's mind flashed back over her plan. How could these SAVAK agents be so careless as to leave crucial exits unguarded? No matter how young they were, how could they have been so careless?

Maybe, she thought, those young agents who had gaped open mouthed in amazement as the elevator doors closed in their faces were racing down the stairs to catch up with them when the elevator reached the first floor.

Or maybe they were still standing there, dumfounded.

When the elevator finally stopped on the first floor, none of the mothers knew what to expect.

But when the doors of the elevator opened onto the lobby, the five mothers saw the two young SAVAK agents standing right there in front of them, utterly out of breath from having run down four flights of stairs, their faces expressing more than just annoyance with these wily old women.

But although they had been caught in the act of trying to escape, the mothers behaved as if nothing at all had happened, as if escape had been the farthest thing from their minds.

The agents knew better of course, knew that they had almost been tricked, and when these last five women were being loaded onto the waiting bus filled with the other mothers who had left before them, the agents made a point of telling them they were being taken to the headquarters of the Committee. ·

The Committee was a special internal security group. It was a combined board of SAVAK and other police officials with a special interrogation center created in the mid-seventies to coordinate police activities against dissidents. It was members of the Committee who made the key assessments about the importance of various political targets, deciding how long to detain whom, and what kinds of torture applied to what degree should complement those periods of detention.

When the bus arrived at the Committee building, the SAVAK agents took the mothers into a large hallway, where they were made to wait while those ahead of them were questioned in private rooms.

Upon reaching the hallway, the mothers were brusquely ordered to pull their chadors down over their eyes and faces. The fear among the women swelled as they waited in the hallway. They had all heard terrible stories about SAVAK, or knew people who had suffered at the hands of SAVAK. Some had even lost sons to SAVAK. What might SAVAK do to them?

A single agent escorted each woman up the stairwell at the end of the hall. Blindfolded by their chadors, the women could not see, and some of them stumbled into one another as they moved hesitantly forward. One agent began to shout angrily at them to get them moving faster. A few of the mothers fainted. One vomited. Unlike their sons, they did not have the stomachs to endure even the thought of SAVAK.

When Ozra, silently harping on remembrances of her son's brutal execution by SAVAK five years before, reached the top of the stairs, an agent spoke to her quite calmly, telling her that she could put the chador back in its usual place.

Now that she could see, she noticed she was being led past three large rooms and that in each room one of the mothers was being questioned by an agent. She was ushered to a fourth room, where two SAVAK officials were sitting behind separate desks.

An agent led the woman up to one of the desks, but the interrogator had not quite finished his questioning of another mother, who had preceded her in line. And she could overhear the agent berating the old woman, insisting that she had offered conflicting information to another interrogator and that her lies were going to put her in a great deal of trouble. Ozra, thoroughly chilled by the manner of the agents whom she was watching, decided right then that when her time came, she was going to answer their questions truthfully, as best she could.

Which was exactly what she did: when the interrogators asked her questions ranging from "Who are the members of your family?" to "What are their mailing addresses?" she answered quickly and accurately.

She talked enough for her interrogator to accumulate eight pages from the questioning. Then he asked her if she was illiterate. When she said no, he ordered her to sign a statement pledging that she would not organize or attend any more meetings of this nature. Frightened, relieved, and choked with conflicting emotions, she signed the statement.

But she had to wait until eleven that evening, spending several hours in a large hall doing nothing while under guard, before she was released. She quickly stepped outside of the Committee building in downtown Tehran and hailed a cab. She got into the cab, and with the thought that she was overjoyed to be out without having had to really implicate anyone beyond the immediate group of mothers, who no doubt had had to implicate themselves anyway, she collapsed in the back seat. She knew, after all, why the meeting had been raided and why they had all been taken downtown to the Committee building. They were after another mother who had gone underground with her two sons, both anti-Shah revolutionaries. They had suspected that the mother might be at that meeting. And if she hadn't gone underground so recently, she *would* have been there. SAVAK had come close but not close enough. Its mission was unaccomplished. And that thought made her feel profoundly happy.

6

There are plenty of historical precedents to a DINA- or SAVAK-type secret police force. There was, for example, the secret police organization of ancient Sparta, through which the ruling elite terrorized and controlled the helots . . . or the well-organized secret informant system through which the Julian emperors maintained their rule in Rome . . . or the efficient and effective secret police of the Council of Ten during the Venetian inquisition . . . or the extensive Oprichina of Czar Ivan IV of Russia, the secret police that was so successful in its struggle against the boyars. Political police forces of varying degrees of efficiency and ruthlessness were to be found under the rule of Catherine of Russia and in the empires of Frederick William and Frederick II of Prussia. The Holy Roman emperor Joseph II (1741–90) made use of an extensive personal police force modeled after the highly regarded police of France's Louis XV. Sartine, Louis XV's head of police, defined his territory this way: "Sire, when three people chat in the street, one of them is my man." To rely on a centralized, personalized police force to survey, control, or eliminate organized opposition to a regime was, by the time of the last half of the twentieth century, no novel idea.

The concept of secret police was refined well before recent times. It was defined long before Hermann Goering's Gestapo, or the Italian Arturo Bocchini's OVRA (for Opera Vigilanze Repressione Antifascista), or Stalin's OGPU—later to become the NKVD under Lavrenti Beria (and after Beria's execution in 1953, the KGB).

Indeed, even before the nineteenth century, the concept of a pervasive and all-powerful secret police, functioning as a state within a state, was launched. It was launched, indeed, by the French Revolution itself, that remarkable social upheaval that had as its central concern the rights of man but wound up having a most unintended side effect: helping to inaugurate one of the most effective instruments for the denial of human rights that the world has seen, the modern secret police force. And ironically, the man who might be credited with conceiving and developing the first modern, pervasive secret police organization was, at the onset of his public career, a revolutionary and, at the end of his career, a "liberal."

His name was Joseph Fouché, between 1804 and 1810 Minister of Police under Napoleon. He was the first masterful secret police chief of modern times, successfully pursuing his dream of total police control of the French population.

Fouché's success was attributable to a combination of factors: historical luck, and personal cunning and organizational ability. The historical circumstance was the fact that by the time Fouché came to power, French society had had its fill of revolutionary chaos and was badly in need of some old-fashioned law and order.

Fouché's arrival at this juncture proved to be to his great advantage. He was an absolutely shameless opportunist, as adroit at sniffing the wind as any American clubhouse politician. First plunging into French political life as a revolutionary, he was elected to the Convention in 1792. But when the political winds shifted to the right, so did Fouché. At first a Girondist, he switched to Jacobinism. Seemingly an ardent Jacobin, he heartily supported the Reign of Terror, participating in the 1793 Lyons massacre of the counter-revolutionaries. Then, as the political winds shifted against the Terror, Fouché changed colors, joined the forces of the right, and participated in the plot to overthrow Robespierre. Named Minister of Police in 1799, Fouché then wiped out the Jacobin clubs, helped engineer the coup of 1799, and as Minister of Police under Napoleon, was awarded vast new powers.

But, before long, even Napoleon developed severe apprehensions about the cunning Fouché, who was as brilliant as he was indifferent to ideological consistency. In 1802, Fouché infuriated Napoleon by unexpectedly opposing the move to make Napoleon First Consul for Life. Napoleon summarily sacked him. Fouché, however, beat a terribly clever retreat. He kept in operation—and under his personal control—the extensive spy system he had built up as Minister of Police. And the system provided one very rich dividend: It uncovered a serious plot against Napoleon, which Fouché personally brought to the Emperor's attention. Fouché's comeback was complete: Napoleon reappointed him Minister of Police in 1804, and it wasn't until the second Bourbon restoration that he was forced out of office. At first sent out of the country as ambassador to Saxony, he was soon thereafter adjudged a regicide and exiled to Trieste, where he died in obscurity.

Until then, Fouché had dominated the political scene of France with an authority and perverse cleverness that prefigured the Berias and Goerings of our times. His secret police organization set a precedent against which even contemporary institutions, benefiting from vastly superior technology, must be measured. As the late Tom Bowden, a left-wing British historian, wrote, almost admiringly, in his book *Beyond the Limits of the Law,* Fouché's secret police "not only kept watch on dissidents, the Church, émigrés, foreigners and other state officials, in typical European absolutist fashion, but also became deeply involved in the formation of all policy affecting internal affairs. Fouché, of course, fed into the government machine information which would produce the outcome he desired. He was also not above feeding into the machine erroneous information and imaginative falsehoods, or, where necessary, using the police as agents provocateurs to provoke rebellion which his men could then crush. . . ."

Fouché's concept of the necessary degree of societal control by the police was about as comprehensive as it could be. He was not interested in simply maintaining the status quo; rather, he desired his secret police *to become* the status quo. And so he created a special, *haute police*† to control everything and everybody, which, in the fashion of the secret police of today, kept watch over all sectors of society. Not even the civilian police, in fact, were spared surveillance and infiltration by the *haute police*. And as the penetration of his *haute police* became increasingly thorough, Fouché's secret police kingdom expanded to the point where it is surely accurate to describe it as a kind of state within a state. There was no salon, no brothel, no political club or opposition party that did not contain a Fouché agent or informer. Even Napoleon's inner circle was penetrated. Historians suspect that Napoleon knew as much but figured that he needed Fouché more than he was troubled by him. And Napoleon was troubled by Fouché.

Fouché's police structure, then, became a major decision-making force in the Napoleonic establishment. It was not just a police force —it was a political force. His police not only provided for law and order, they were a cornerstone in that law-and-order structure. Perhaps, as the saying goes, if Fouché had not existed, someone would have had to invent him, for even among the left-wingers of France the desire for order and political perpetuation by means of a police system was growing.

As the Directorate, the ruling council of the revolutionary government of France, put it in a decree issued in 1795, the regime wanted to rely on the police to do more than just investigate crimes and apprehend criminals: "The Executive Directory, convinced that it is easier to maintain public tranquillity than to restore it once it is upset, considers it a matter of the utmost urgency to establish an active and strict police . . . to foil all plots, discover all schemes, con-

† Literally translated, high police.

tain all sedition, cast light on all intrigues, and preserve the peace around the storm of all particular passions." A member of the Directory, who warmly seconded that motion, had this to add: "Our situation requires that a very strict police be established. Every day one of our friends, one of our family, falls to an assassin's bullet. . . . Everyone who was a patriot was in danger. . . . If we had a police we would know if there really were secret meetings in which royalists plot the assassination of the members of the Council; if there are plots in which friends of the Terror wish to sharpen their knives once more . . . [we need] a Ministry charged with giving Paris an active and vigorous police; with it, everything can be known, foreseen, forestalled; carefully placed in public places, it must be able to recognize the agitation and take by surprise any treason which is being prepared."

But if the Directorate never got the political police it wanted, Napoleon did. He had his Fouché, and gave him a relatively free hand. Fouché went to work from there. "The difficulties for the high police [i.e., secret police] are immense," wrote Fouché in his memoirs, "whether it has to operate in the combination of a representative government, so incompatible with whatever is the least arbitrary . . . or whether it acts in behalf of a more concentrated form of government, aristocratic, directorial or despotic. . . ."

Fouché believed that the head of the secret police ought to be a high member of government, unencumbered with the trivial bureaucratic details of conventional policing and responsible to the sovereign ruler only: ". . . I felt that all the powers and abilities of a minister must be absorbed in the high police; the rest might be left [to the lower, civilian police]. My only study was, therefore, to seize with a steady and sure hand all the springs of the secret police, and all the elements composing it. . . .

"I first insisted that, for these essential reasons, the local police of Paris . . . should be placed entirely under my control. . . .

"I found all the constituent elements in the most deplorable state of confusion and decay. The treasury was empty; without money, no police. I soon had money at my command, by making the vice inherent in this great city contribute to the safety of the state. . . .

"I felt that I alone should be the judge of the political state of the interior. . . . This system never failed me, and I was better acquainted with France, veiled in mystery by means of oral and confidential communications, and by wide-grasping conversations. . . . Nothing essential to the safety of the state ever escaped me."

Before long, however, even Napoleon wanted Fouché out of town. He knew too much, had too much power, and was much too clever. All these things made him a dangerous man. And so, after first making him a duke, in 1809, Napoleon sent him out of Paris with a political appointment to some far region. But, once again, Fouché seemed indispensable. In his absence, the high police became heavy-handed, slow-footed, dim-witted. That sure, deft touch was missing. And so, by 1815, Napoleon, slightly desperate, saw fit to bring the master back for a short stint to show everyone how the job of policing France should be done.

By this time, however, Fouché was a changed man. The five years out of power had given him a perspective that he hadn't had before. He had mellowed, becoming even more thoughtful, reformist, philosophical. Given the helm by Napoleon once again, he initiated a wholesale reorganization of the political police, including new programs to improve the quality of the recruits, to raise salaries, and to instill a genuine sense of nonpartisan professionalism in the agents. For instance, the strict guidelines that he issued for police surveillance, he now stipulated, "ought not to extend beyond that demanded by public and private security . . . or to interfere with the free exercise of human activities or civil rights. . . . It is necessary to abandon the errors of a *police d'attaque,* which menaces without guaranteeing and torments without protecting. We must restrict ourselves to the limits of a liberal and positive police."

But, alas, it was the first Fouché—and not the second Fouché—who was to leave the greatest imprint in history. As the famed writer and outspoken anti-Bonapartist Chateaubriand wisely put it, Fouché had created "a monster brought forth in the revolutionary pond by the mating of anarchy and despotism. . . ."‡

Fouché's creation was indeed "a monster" that came to haunt France. Despite its undeniable success in the service of various regimes that without it would probably not have been able to survive, it was helpless in the face of the crises of 1848, 1870, and 1871. Like the SAVAK of Iran under the Shah, Fouché's high police of the eighteenth century became part of the problem, rather than part of the solution. "It was the excessiveness of his 'haute police,'" con-

‡ Chateaubriand wasn't especially fond of Fouché personally, either: ". . . a hyena in human clothes, thief, atheist, and assassin," he once called him.

cluded the historian Bowden in his book, "which, in the long run, led to the destruction of the ordered state which Fouché had pursued so relentlessly. In due course, the people of France reacted against the activities of a police force continually reaching beyond the limits of the law. . . . The irony was doubly intense since it was those who stood as the guarantors of the state who by their excesses caused the state to be overthrown." In other words, the "monster"—the "unleashed" secret police—is not always so easily controlled.

TWO

Models of Efficiency:
Agents at Work

1

The captain and the crew were suspicious. And they certainly should have been. After all, where was the pool? The sun deck? The activities director?

The passenger must have noticed there wasn't even a bar or a decent restaurant on the entire ship. Why go by cargo liner? "And it's more expensive to travel this way," said the captain, calm but suspicious.

But his suspicion didn't bother the lone civilian passenger one bit. For the only thing Romy cared about was that the captain's suspicion would not cause him to change course. He did not care that they suspected he was on the run. They would have had to be naïve not to have their doubts. And if they were at all informed about Philippine politics, they might even have suspected this well-educated passenger of being active in the growing anti-Marcos movement (which in fact he was). No doubt some crew members even knew about LABAN—the militant political group dedicated to the overthrow of the government of Ferdinand Marcos—and wondered if he didn't have something to do with it (which indeed he did).

But Romy Capulong didn't concern himself in the slightest with any of this. He was happy only to see the cargo liner move full steam ahead toward its scheduled destination: Hong Kong.

He didn't need the pools or the restaurants or the shuffleboards. He needed to get as far away from Manila—and as quickly—as possible. This, therefore, was his dream trip. Even if he had to travel via a cargo liner on which he was the only civilian passenger, he couldn't have been happier.

The dramatic escape of Romy Capulong began one fall day in 1979. This founding member and deputy director of LABAN, also a successful patent attorney with a practice in downtown Manila, had given the messenger boy from the law office the keys to his car. He told the boy that in the back seat were stacks of copies of an anti-Marcos newspaper.* He told the office messenger boy exactly where he was having lunch and instructed him to bring him a few copies there. He planned to show them to his luncheon guest, a former law partner and former Philippine senator.

But the messenger boy never came. At about one-thirty in the afternoon, the LABAN official, still waiting at his table at the hotel restaurant just a few blocks from his office for his messenger boy to show up, began to believe that something was wrong. Then Romy Capulong heard himself being paged. Excusing himself momentarily from the luncheon table, he went directly to a house telephone to take the call.

On the phone was his secretary. Her voice was soft, shaky, almost tearful.

Capulong quickly sized up the situation. "What kind of police are they?" he asked, after she explained that plainclothes police were going through everything at the law office.

"Metrocom," she whispered. "There are about eighteen of them. But I can't talk anymore."

* Capulong was instrumental in the printing and distribution of a document, circulating in the Philippine underground, known as "Octopus"; the official subtitle of the document is "Some Are Smarter than Others," a quotation that has become notorious in Philippine business and political circles as the curt answer of Imelda Romualdez Marcos to a question asked during an interview with correspondent Carl Rowan. She was asked to comment on widespread allegations of corruption and unexplained wealth reportedly amassed by relatives and cronies of the First Couple. "Octopus" is a research paper purportedly based mainly on public records (of government offices) that is designed to expose and document the alleged greed and alleged corruption of the martial-law rulers.

The LABAN official figured that his secretary had probably fled to the Xeroxing room, called on the phone extension, and feared the Metrocom agents would see the extension light on and track her down.

At any rate, he knew he was in trouble. Metrocom was an important component of Marcos' security system.

Metrocom roughly stood for Metropolitan Command Intelligence Division of the Philippines Constabulary but to Capulong and others in the anti-Marcos underground it represented far more than the harmless name suggested.

The name "Metrocom" had all too often surfaced in allegations of torture. Political offenders claimed that some of Metrocom's officers were torturers. The charges were so commonplace now that many figured there had to be some truth to them. After all, Metrocom did not bother with petty criminals. Its targets were enemies of the state. Enemies of the state were now defined as opponents of Ferdinand Marcos. Though this LABAN official considered himself an enemy of Marcos and not an enemy of the state, Metrocom was not under orders to make such distinctions. And the enemies of Marcos were growing in number every day. Every day, Metrocom agents had more to do. The situation throughout the Philippines was getting ever more difficult.

Capulong hung up the telephone and walked briskly back to his table. He quickly filled the senator in on what he had just learned.

The senator understood and suggested that they head over to his own law office, where he offered the use of his telephone as well as some advice. Capulong accepted both, first calling his wife, to whom his instructions were urgent and clear. All the documents must be gathered up and moved out of the house. The children must be picked up and moved out of school. The wife and the children must go into hiding at his brother-in-law's house in Pasay City. He would join them there if and when he could.

He then placed calls to a few opposition leaders, risking their phones being tapped. He conferred longest with another well-known senator, who, when martial law was declared in 1972, had been thrown into jail. Released a few years later, he quickly became something of a father figure to those in the anti-Marcos underground. His advice was protective but sharp. "Go into hiding," advised the senator, obviously not mincing words. This senator knew exactly what it was like to be imprisoned as a result of one's political activities in Marcos' Philippines.

Capulong did not hesitate. He dropped out of sight, hiding in the Manila underground. Worried about his wife and office co-workers, he pieced together from occasional phone reports what was happening to them.

When they tried to arrest him at his office and were frustrated at missing him, the Metrocom arresting-team agents took out their frustrations on the office messenger boy, whom they discovered in the parking lot underneath the law office. Questioning the boy about his boss, they worked him over pretty well. And at about the same time, it seemed, another Metrocom team went to Capulong's house, arriving just after his wife had bundled up the LABAN papers and fled but just before the younger son had returned home from school. While conducting a thorough search of the house, the agents interrogated the Capulong boy. "I am just doing my job," the lieutenant in command of the arrest team said. But he was apologetic and polite —never putting a hand on the young son, and never letting the other agents touch him either. They waited at the Capulong residence for hours—giving up and leaving only when they realized Romy Capulong knew he was hot and surely had gone underground.

Piecing all of this together, the LABAN official knew he had to do some quick but careful thinking. This, after all, was 1979, and Metrocom was not staffed by school-crossing guards. He knew that escape from Manila would be tricky and dangerous. He was now a prime Metrocom target, and with the entire Philippine security network probably on red alert, alarm lists with his name in lights would surely be posted before long at every airport and seaport in the country. All the agents had to do was wait for him to make a careless move in public, and it would be all over.

But some of Romy Capulong's friends and associates were to prove themselves helpful and loyal in ways that he never would have expected. For, with their help, a workable escape plan began to fall into place.

A retired military officer helped to lay out the plan. He told Capulong exactly who had to be contacted. And some friends in government service gave him additional reason to have hope. They assured him that the government's computer system at Camp Aguinaldo moved slowly. They said it required at least two days advance notice before it could grind out the alarm notices that could prohibit an exit from the country. This slow-moving system gave Capulong a little time.

Romy Capulong contacted some low-level bureaucrats working in the government. They were sympathetic to the anti-Marcos movement and wanted to help. They told him that there was one pier in the harbor that they believed did not receive those alarm lists, because the pier was used almost solely for cargo liners that ordinarily did not take civilian passengers.

This was obviously the escape hatch, but with a wife and two children still in the country, he needed to be *very* sure. And so he enlisted friends to stake out the pier. Look for plainclothes officers hovering about, Capulong told them. There weren't any, he was told a few days later.

Meanwhile, two close friends also went out on a limb. They struck up a fast friendship with the lone salesgirl at the pier. She was quickly charmed by their friendliness and accepted a date with them at a downtown Manila disco and restaurant. That night, not suspecting why anyone would be so interested in every little detail about her boring job, she revealed practically everything there was to know about that pier. And she could not remember a single civilian passenger leaving Manila from this particular pier. She also could not remember ever working with an alarm list.

With that, Capulong surfaced to buy his ticket. He would not let anyone else do that for him. He looked the clerk at the cargo liner's office in downtown Manila straight in the eye. "There's a convention of patent lawyers in Hong Kong next week," he used as his excuse for taking that particular boat. "I don't want any distractions. I need time to prepare my paper."

Remembering the incident, years later, Capulong said he will never forget the incredulous look on the ticket clerk's face.

The crew members on the cargo liner the next day were also very surprised to see him on that ship. "I need time to write my paper," he said again.

But, for all their doubts, the crew members on the American cargo liner gave him no trouble. It wasn't until the ship docked in Hong Kong that Capulong was asked the first probing questions, when the captain offered him the use of the cargo liner's courtesy van. "Where do you want to go?" he asked; everyone within hearing distance, Capulong noticed, seemed to be listening.

"To the airport," he said unflinchingly. The crew seemed to understand. A junior officer tore off a piece of newspaper that he had been reading, scribbled a few words down, and handed it to Capulong. The note read, "Is there political persecution in the Philippines?"

Romy Capulong silently nodded in the affirmative.

The van took him to the airport. There Capulong purchased a ticket for Seoul. He explained to the ticket agent that he wanted to hook up for a flight to Los Angeles—and, finally, on to New York. His wife and children had left Manila on a commercial flight several days before and would be waiting for him.†

Capulong was sitting at a counter in the Hong Kong airport coffee shop when he suddenly began laughing to himself.

He was trying to picture the anger of that Metrocom arresting team. Word of how the Metrocom foul-up occurred came from his law partner. His law partner had a brother who was a major in the legal branch of the Philippine military. Invoking his brother's name, he struck up a conversation with the commanding officer of the Metrocom team and learned that the agents had arrived on time, but they had arrived at the wrong office building. A building called the San Luis Building was next door to Capulong's office building. But Capulong's office was in the San Luis *Terraces* building. By the time the Metrocom agents realized their mistake, they had lost their man. He had left for lunch. If they had gone to the correct building just five minutes earlier, Capulong wouldn't have made it.

2

The LABAN official was very lucky. One way or the other, secret police usually get their way. With the extraordinary powers of imprisoning, eliminating, deporting, or otherwise expelling their targets, their enemies are usually overmatched. Yet secret police are

† Capulong later explained their escape route in his affidavit for political asylum in the United States: ". . . until they [his family] left in the afternoon of 31 October 1979, our house was under surveillance and my two sons and my wife were being tailed wherever they went by undercover agents of the military. They had to take a circuitous route to shake off this tail on their way to the airport to board the plane for New York by leaving our house in the early hours of the morning, with my two sons in shorts and pretending to go jogging while my wife made it appear she was going to the market, then to church and finally all of them checking in secretly at the Philippine Village Hotel, which was near the airport. They left with only very few personal belongings with them."

also like any government bureaucracy. They are as capable of incompetence as is the post office.

The mistake they made in the Capulong case was by no means uncommon. Secret police forces are *not* perfectly run outfits. Their successes are more often attributable to the powers they wield than to agents' brilliantly performed work. If secret police organizations were to become severely circumscribed by restrictive laws and procedural rules, they would amount to nothing more than run-of-the-mill law-enforcement organizations. As a colonel in the South African Security Branch once put it, the secret police must be placed above the law to function. This point came out in a fascinating exchange that took place at the postmortem inquest into the death of Stephen Biko (Mr. Kentridge was the barrister for the Biko family, forcing an inquiry into the mysterious circumstances surrounding Biko's death; Colonel Goosen was on the stand defending the South African security police):

Mr. Kentridge: "Where'd you get your authority from? Show me a piece of paper that gives you the right to keep a man in chains—or are you people above the law?"

Colonel Goosen: "We have full authority. It is left to my sound discretion."

Mr. Kentridge: "Under what statutory authority?"

Colonel Goosen: "We don't work under statutory authority."

Mr. Kentridge: "You don't work under statutory authority? Thanks very much, Colonel; that's what we have always suspected."

But if the secret police have the powers necessary to do the job, their powers sometimes exceed their talents.

SAVAK, one of the most infamous secret police forces of our time, was powerful and ruthless but not always efficient; and it was sometimes unbelievably clumsy. SAVAK had many operational difficulties common to any large bureaucracy. In cable after cable issued by Tehran Center to agents in the field, these difficulties were repeatedly discussed.

In one typical cable, SAVAK Center, in Tehran, was obviously plagued by the repeated failure of agents to observe even the most fundamental precautions. This cable spelled out in detail the ABCs of self-protective security measures to agents of an organization that had already been in existence for more than a decade:

"On November 18, 1970, adventurist and dissident elements poured explosive material into the gas tank of the vehicle of the company's operations leader in Vienna, and, as a result, the engine exploded and crashed into pieces. However, there was no loss of life. Considering that this danger exists for all the company's representatives and leaders of operations outside the country, please see that security measures and necessary precautions are adhered to when parking a vehicle at a location, and that the possibility of access of the dissidents [to the car] is considered."

So far so good, but six years later, SAVAK was still sending its agents similar messages—but now with an added worry, that in the face of the growing tide of terrorism, SAVAK agents might begin to lose heart:

"On the morning of February 3, 1976, employee Hossein Nahidi of Mashad's SAVAK was martyred by the terrorists. Heavy blows recently received by the terrorists have induced them to take revenge, and it is not unlikely that they will make attacks against the lives of employees outside of the country. Please see that all personnel are warned that, while protecting themselves more is essential, they must remember to carry out their assigned duties more seriously and should keep in mind that under present conditions, with regard to the subversive and terrorist elements, each individual agent has a grave duty to preserve national security. Each agent must endeavor more resolutely to carry out this duty."

The fact that this telegram was apparently fired off to SAVAK's field offices by the head of SAVAK's Third Central Office—who was the operational head of all of SAVAK—clearly suggests that as early as 1976, two years before the Shah fell, SAVAK was a very worried security bureaucracy.

Its fears went hand in hand with other operational problems not always of its own making. SAVAK was one of the largest security bureaucracies in Iran, but it was not the only one. And in the police world, there tends to be as much competition as cooperation. The rivalries among agents of the secret police themselves can complicate their own lives as much as the internal, bureaucratic inadequacies of the organizations to which they belong. Even SAVAK, for all its preeminence, faced bureaucratic snipers, so that there were times when SAVAK agents feared other security agents almost as much as they feared the political opponents of the regime.

The Police Information Service—an innocuous name for an internal security unit of the regular civilian police—had a unit based in Tehran to deal with political targets. One particular Police Information Service captain continually drove SAVAK agents up the wall by edging in on SAVAK cases—and more often than not fouling everybody up. The captain was also a notorious bully and torturer with such a loud and obnoxious manner that few SAVAK agents even wanted to work with him. In fact, SAVAK agents began to wish that the Police Information Service captain would somehow just go away. When SAVAK, therefore, got word of a plan by left-wing guerrillas to assassinate the captain, they actually kept this intelligence information to themselves and put a tail on his car to gleefully observe the guerrillas' work firsthand.

They watched as one night the guerrillas put a bomb in the captain's car, but when the captain got behind the wheel, the bomb didn't ignite as it should have when the ignition was turned on. The SAVAK agents watching the car a block away were probably as disappointed as the guerrillas.

Then, minutes later, three guerrillas, moving out of nowhere, it seemed, drove up to the captain's car and shot him through the open left window. In minutes, agents from the Police Information Service and from SAVAK descended upon the car. (It was almost as if Police Information Service agents had been tailing the SAVAK car that was tailing the captain's car.)

Removing the dead body of the captain, SAVAK and Police Information Service agents fought over how then to move the car, since, they all knew, there was still a bomb strapped somewhere inside. They haggled for about forty-five minutes, conferring back and forth with their superiors in their respective headquarters. Finally, someone in SAVAK headquarters came up with a reasonable compromise. Two agents from SAVAK and one agent from the Police Information Service would take joint control of the car.

And so the three chosen agents got into the car and started it up without any trouble. They then headed for the local SAVAK office, but after about five minutes of driving, the bomb went off, and all three agents were killed.

When news of the terrible blunder filtered throughout Tehran, many Iranian civilians were as thoroughly amused by the agents' incompetence as SAVAK superiors were aghast. How could the anti-Shah underground be defeated when the Shah's security agents were in such disarray?

At one point, a similar question might have been posed in Taiwan, where the Taiwan Garrison Command and the Bureau of Investigation grapple with political dissenters and opponents of the regime —and not always as a unified team.

The Command and the Bureau are hierarchically above the Police Bureau, which has a Security Department of its own but which, exiles say, takes its cues from the Command or the Bureau. On big cases, the Command and the Bureau sometimes work together. But they are also known to work at cross-purposes.

Approximately a half dozen years ago, competition between the two organizations got out of hand, and the Bureau arrested high-ranking officers of the Taiwan Garrison Command on charges of drug smuggling. The case involved a boat going from Taiwan to Hong Kong.

The Bureau arrested two officers on the ship and then claimed to have found that they had connections with higher-ups in the Command.

When the Bureau took the matter to higher-ups in the Command, the Command denied any involvement in the case and refused to relinquish any names or files on the officers allegedly involved.

Then the Bureau of Investigation, apparently acting with the approval of the government, arrested the two department chiefs of the Command involved. A trial was held, and the two Command officers were both sentenced to death by the martial-law court.

During the trial, however, one of the Command chiefs said that he would take revenge on the Bureau of Investigation for its treachery. But the Bureau, it seems, acted first. Somehow, the entire family of the Command officer who threatened the Bureau was murdered. Exiles believe the murders were perpetrated by the Bureau.

But, whoever the murderers were, this series of sordid incidents did nothing to smooth over relations between the Bureau and the Command, and before long, the government was forced to move in. A major shake-up was ordered. But, one year later, the state of the Taiwanese security apparatus remained, it seemed, in considerable disarray. Like the Iranian Government during the mid-seventies, the Taiwanese Government at about the same time was encountering almost as much trouble with its internal security police as with its political critics.

But were the Iranian and Taiwanese security-police problems unique? Consider those faced by President Assad, of Syria. According to State Department sources, it is not uncommon that at the scene of a political crime or a politically related incident, three or four agents from the several security services will appear, arguing and shouting over the jurisdiction of the case. Sometimes an agent will be shot—not by a dissident terrorist or a revolutionary—but by another agent. Says one man with extensive on-scene experience in Syria, "This happens all the time."

3

It would not be exactly correct to suggest that recruits go into political police work for the money. There are few fortunes to be made in tracking down political activists, terrorists, and other enemies of the regime—unless the targets are also major narcotics traffickers. But security work is steady, and for many agents around the world, it *is* relatively well paid, especially when the alternative forms of employment are considered.

In Chile, which for most of the decade of the seventies maintained one of the most extensive secret police systems in the world, agents had security, even tenure, and pay scales were related to seniority. According to a former DINA agent, ". . . pay for individuals was calculated by length of time of duty." Salaries came out of the military's budget but were administered by the secret police bureaucracy itself. "All DINA men got paid through the Army payroll, but they would receive their pay at DINA offices," said the ex-agent. Salary scales were well graduated, but the longer an agent stayed in the service, the more it was worth to him. The salary structure helped to give DINA (later CNI) stability by reducing the degree of personnel turnover.

Security work is better rewarded than conventional police work where states are insecure. A black Security Branch policeman in South Africa earns about twice as much as the uniformed black policeman. He also gets a state car and substantial overtime pay, whereas the uniformed policeman rarely does.

Similarly, the Marcos regime takes relatively good care of its agents, financially speaking. The public schoolteacher in the Philippines starts at roughly three hundred pesos per month and may work up to roughly five hundred a month. The salary range of the political-police agent, however, ranges roughly from five-fifty to seven hundred pesos per month. With jobs relatively scarce and low-paying throughout the country, it is perhaps not surprising that there is no shortage of recruits.

Romanian agents of the Securitate are paid far more than army officers (and for that matter, far more than even a university historian, according to one such professional intellectual). The army officers resent this economic disparity as much as the professors. The animosity is so strong that at soccer games between army teams and police teams,‡ the hatred is visibly intense. And in addition to the salary advantages maintained by Securitate agents, they also enjoy important fringe benefits. Their rent is subsidized and they are permitted access by the Party to special restaurants and shops that stock goods ordinarily unavailable to most citizens. As one exile from Romania puts it, to work for the Securitate puts the agent in a "privileged category."

Similar courtesies are extended to security agents of other Eastern European countries. In Poland, military and security police officers have access to their own special shops, which sell the highest-quality domestic and imported goods. It was precisely this special system of rewards for security personnel that helped contribute to the Polish "meat price" workers' strikes of July and August of 1980.

Similarly, while the salary per se of a KGB agent is not smashing, there are other rewards: free cottages in which to vacation near a lake or some sort of resort town, and access to special stores around the country that sell Western-made goods ordinarily unavailable elsewhere, including Western liquors at cut rates.

The secret police agent who is truly secret (operating for an organization that is not officially recognized) is as well paid as his more visible counterparts. Mexico's Brigada Blanca agent, for example, is well rewarded for his efforts. The agent, says a Mexican journalist now living in the United States, is paid via a bureaucratic "blind," out of the accounts of four or five separate ministries, ranging from the Labor Department to the Public Education Department. The blind is a complex payment system designed to hide the expenditures.

SAVAK agents enjoyed modest salaries but had excellent "perks." They had no trouble getting visas, and they didn't have to concern themselves with paying for their airline tickets. Unfettered travel (with visa privileges) to London was the customary gift of this sort.

‡ Soccer is a national sport in Romania.

Free (or easy) admission to special events, plus easier access to housing (which is always in short supply in Iran), were also inducements to join SAVAK.

In addition to what is given to them by authorities, secret police agents in many countries tend to help themselves to whatever they can get their hands on—especially when there is no one around to tell them to stop.

In Uganda, agents were practically issued invitations by the government to take whatever they wanted from a suspect under arrest. The 1971 Armed Forces Power of Arrest Decree not only gave all armed forces members full authority to search any person or premises, but it also provided them with the right to seize victims' property. Almost predictably, there were a good number of persons arrested by Uganda's State Research Bureau allegedly for political crimes, but in reality they were arrested because they possessed some things that State Research Bureau agents wanted for themselves. The agents' take might have been a house, or car, or cattle, or coffee—or even a wife. Accordingly, the wealthy person, as well as the poor peasant, was apt to be designated a "security problem" by State Research Bureau agents during Amin's rule.

In Argentina, Triple A death squad agents exercise their right of *"botín"* (attributed to some Chilean DINA agents as well): the right to steal from the "security risks" within their custody. The wife of an Argentinian medical doctor testified on this subject, describing an incident that occurred in 1976:

". . . I looked through a peephole and saw four men crouching against the wall. When they realized I was at the door, they told me to open up or they would shoot. My son, Alfredo, was watching television in their line of fire, so I opened the door. . . . They then began to search the house, going through everything. They turned the living room upside down, dismantling the stove and the blinds and tearing down pictures from the walls. They took all the money we had in our pockets and all the jewelry they could find. . . . We were then taken to different cars. . . ." The kidnapping agents have been known to confiscate so much, in fact, that according to a report issued by the Inter-American Commission on Human Rights of the Organization of American States, "In some cases they are accompanied by additional support forces in vans, in which, after the mission is completed, they transport the household goods that are taken from the homes of the victims."

In Brazil, OBAN agents (OBAN was created by a group of about eighty right-wing individuals from the Army, Navy, Air Force and the police force to establish a team of specialized police capable of crushing the guerrilla groups and "working over" any suspects) had free rein in the early seventies. A Brazilian woman testified: "I am a painter, and when I was arrested the police took eighteen paintings, an easel, and cases full of clothes. . . . All of these possessions were taken by OBAN and none have yet been returned to me. What words can one use to describe such actions?"

With their considerable powers of arrest, detention and interrogation, often accompanied by torture, the possibilities for graft and blackmail on the part of the secret police are enormous. "While I was trying to hide [with relatives in the countryside]," testified one Haitian exile in a written deposition for U.S. federal court in Miami, "I was arrested in January 1978. . . . The Tonton Macoutes went to my father's house and asked him to pay eight hundred dollars for my release, or else I would be sent to prison in Port-au-Prince. They told my father that if he told of the bribe to anybody else they would come and shoot him. My father is a farmer and he had the eight hundred dollars. He gave it to the Tonton Macoutes. I was released from jail, and my father came to pick me up at night."

In Haiti, the system of rewards and promotions for secret police agents practically encourages corrupt practices—not just graft-taking but also a kind of rumor-mongering that leads to the implication of innocent citizens in antigovernment activities. As one former Tonton Macoute agent has testified in court, ". . . each time . . . you denounce a person, either coming from the United States or some conspiracy against the government—not only are you given money but they also increase you in rank. For example, if I see two young men speaking, I go and tell [my superiors] that they were speaking against the government, and they said to me, 'You did your job.' They give you money."

"Bribes are a common practice," says a man now living in the United States who once served in a municipal police department in the Philippines, a unit whose name has surfaced time and again amid allegations of torture of political as well as narcotics violators: "I knew it was rotten and riddled with graft then, and even more so now." The graft system appears to be institutionalized. ". . . Relatives are forced to try to track down the papers of the prisoner from office to office, shedding tears on the carpeted floors of generals', majors', colonels' offices," explains one Philippine citizen who spent a lengthy period of time detained by the military in a secret camp, "cajoling lieutenants, sergeants, and whoever happens to be around into doing their assigned task by buying them lunch, snacks, or gifts. This system renders the relatives particularly vulnerable to demands for bribes—anywhere from two hundred thousand pesos [about ten to fifteen thousand dollars] for higher-ranking officers. This system of bribes is rampant and exempts no one; bribes go to the highest officials of the Department of National Defense and the Armed Forces, down to the lowest constable, private or policeman. Others take their bribes in the form of sexual accommodations, of the wives and/or sisters of the detained ones."

Nearly absolute power does not engender an atmosphere of reserve. Sources who are well versed in Latin American politics, history, and police affairs say that narcotics are almost totally controlled in Paraguay by the police in charge of the torture centers and President Stroessner's spy network. Who is going to argue with the secret police on this subject? Take the Brigada Blanca, which operates in as high a style in Mexico as the occasion warrants. On a mission to a remote area such as Oaxaca, Brigada Blanca agents do not travel via buses or oxcarts. Their usual form of transportation is air force planes. But when official equipment of this sort is not available, Brigada Blanca agents will literally commandeer a private plane from a private airport. Their style in doing so is to identify themselves as "federal agents," wearing plain clothes and carrying pistols. They explain that they need to "borrow" your plane. Only commercial aircraft seem to be exempt from the practice. Hardly anyone ever says no.

Corruption is a problem with any police agency, whether it is clandestine in kind or not. The causes of corruption are (1) the tremendous discretion that a police officer inherently has, (2) the laxity of supervision by superior officers, who may in fact even regard extortion and bribe-taking as just compensation for inadequate pay or as a way of maintaining high morale, and (3) the general moral climate of the political system and the moral tenor of the government itself; if the sovereign himself is corrupt or family and relatives are corrupt, there can be a trickle-down effect into the ranks, which does not tend to produce agents of sterling integrity.

This general problem is of course exacerbated with secret police, due to the degree of discretion they have (so much broader than that of conventional police), the climate of tolerance by the government, and widespread intimidation of the general public.

Corruption in the ranks of security personnel is not confined to capitalist societies; it occurs in communist ones as well—corruption is the logical consequence of the inevitable abuse of unchecked police powers, whatever the ideological nature of the regime. No secret police force can escape the problem of corruption, no matter how moralistic the regime within which it operates. Even Fidel Castro, while proclaiming the moral and ideological purity of his revolution, has had corruption problems with his G-2.* The enormous power he has given G-2 agents—not to mention the economic poverty that Cuba has not overcome—inevitably corrupts some agents. All immigration officers of both separate immigration services (there is one for political offenders and another one for the rest of the civilian public) are G-2 agents. In 1980, four separate groups of G-2 officers assigned to Immigration were arrested and imprisoned for bribe-taking. Apparently, with no scarcity of potential emigrants from Cuba, the possibilities for bribe-taking are considerable. The Castro regime, stung by revelations of corruption in its security service, has sought to correct the situation—to the point where Cuban G-2 agents now feel the need to protect themselves from accusations of corruption. One Cuban exile told us that, while G-2 agents searched her home, the supervising agent said to her, "Watch us [conduct the search] so that you cannot say we are thieves."

4

Secret police agents around the world are recruited from widely varying sectors of the population, depending upon any number of factors.

At entry levels of secret police work, agents are likely to come from the lower economic classes. In South Africa, a white Security Branch agent will most likely be lower-class, an Afrikaaner, and a member of the Dutch Reformed Church; few middle- or upper-class

---

* G-2 is the branch of the internal security service responsible for controlling the domestic Cuban population. Although G-2 is a generic term derived from World War II (to refer to the second division of the general staff), Cubans both inside and outside of Cuba refer to this branch of internal security as G-2.

English-speaking whites (who are as much the enemies to the ruling Afrikaaners as are the blacks) are recruited. In Poland, the lowest operators of UB (Security Bureau) are sometimes even recruited from among the ranks of convicts and criminals.

Mexico's Brigada Blanca agents may arrive laterally from more legitimate or established sectors of police society: the standard police agencies (including the Dirección Federal de Seguridad, the Policia Judicial Federal, the División de Investigaciones para la Prevención de la Delinquencia, and the División de Investigaciones Políticas y Sociales of the Interior Ministry), various state and municipal police forces, and the federal armed forces.

In communist societies, the Party screens security recruits rigorously. In Czechoslovakia (and in other Eastern European states) recruits are selected along clear ideological lines. All StB (Státní Bezpečnost, for State Security) agents must be personally referred by a Communist Party official—"Not a single one" is not a member of the Party, a former high adviser in the cabinet of Alexander Dubček insists. And there are other proofs required, also along ideological lines, he says: whether by witnesses, references, or simply by virtue of having a clean record, the prospective agent must be able to show that he was not a Dubček supporter or sympathizer.

In Yugoslavia, the problem of deep-seated ethnic pluralism raises questions other than party loyalty to be considered in the recruitment process. The Croatian community, for example, strives for an independent state of its own. Accordingly, it is not considered proper for the decent young Croat to look for a job within the political police network in Yugoslavia. Even in the republic of Croatia, where Serbs account for only a small fraction of the population, most security agents are Serbs, who, coming mainly from poor mountain areas, generally regard the work as prestigious. It is only at the upper levels of the secret police system that one finds Croats. "There must be some ethnic distribution, at least at the top," says one Yugoslavian professor now living in the United States, "as if only for show."

Ethnic representation makes for some interesting secret police hiring techniques in Syria as well. President Assad was the first Alawite (a Muslim sect of Shi'i derivation) head of state and leader of the ruling minority party (the Alawites constitute only 10 percent of the population). Accordingly, it was vital to Assad that Alawites hold major positions within all the security services. Considering the small part of the population they represent, Assad has succeeded in drastically overrepresenting the Alawites in those services. While Sunni Moslems or other ethnic varieties may actually work in high positions in the security and intelligence services, Assad has seen to it that there are enough Alawites just within hearing range to watch out for his interests. Where there is a Sunni Moslem in a key position in the General Intelligence Directorate of Syria (the internal security unit oriented toward keeping an eye on the civilian population), there is also an Alawite within earshot.

5

The establishment of a strong police state is not always best achieved by relying on the personnel and the general mentality characterizing the military sector of society. In a wide variety of countries, military ranks have proved not to provide the best recruits for secret police work.

When the attack on the Allende regime was launched, in Chile in the early seventies, it didn't take long to realize that the standard air force officer wasn't going to be of much help for the kind of "dirty work" that DINA agents would later be called on to perform. The strict military tradition teaches not so much the need to torture political dissidents at home but to defend against potential and actual enemies from outside. The secret police tradition and the military tradition, despite some overlaps, do not always coincide.

Some Chilean soldiers were evidently very reluctant DINA recruits. "I was a member of DINA," begins the testimony of a young ex-DINA agent in Chile who describes in some detail the way in which he was made to work, reluctantly and unknowingly, for DINA: "At the beginning of 1973, I was drafted [into the Army]. After the revolution in September of 1973, I was ordered . . . to the Calama Regiment. They told me that due to [my having done a good job], I had earned a vacation. . . . I had to sign a paper, a document . . . whose contents I did not understand. On November 11, 1973, I was transferred to Tejas Verdes [a prison camp]. We were welcomed by Colonel Manuel Contreras [the head of the newly founded organization DINA], . . . then we were . . . briefed that we were with DINA. When we were originally drafted, we were drafted to be detailed to DINA. What we had signed was false. . . . Then we were transferred to Santiago. . . . I had been transferred from the Army to DINA as a private first class of the reserve. We were told we were to care for the security of the state and to be alert to all sorts of movements against the state. This training lasted three months. . . . In Santiago, we were put under oath. . . ." When asked why he joined DINA, the former agent simply stated, "That was a military order which I was unable to resist." In the spring of 1975, he left the service, he says, on his own wish, although not without consenting to perform some spy services for DINA on the side.

Many secret police organizations were founded on the basis of this principle of resistance, if not pure inadequacy, of the military to "handle" internal security problems. Uruguay's Department Six of the Dirección Nacional de Información e Inteligencia (DNII) was created when Congress was dissolved in 1973, because the hard-line civilian government decided that the military was not capable of managing the growing, post-Tupamaro opposition (the Tupamaros were an urban guerrilla movement otherwise known as the Movement of National Liberation). Similarly, Argentina's Triple A, a parapolice group that has allegedly entered the political field in earnest, kidnapping and killing on a large scale and concentrating in particular on trade unionists and left-wing activists, was created to do what the military intelligence services couldn't—or wouldn't—do. So too with the Brigada Blanca, as many of Mexico's military officers would inevitably resist indulging in some of the banditlike activities—kidnapping, hijacking private planes, etc.—practiced by the Brigada.

Iran's SAVAK was compelled to discover a way to circumvent the disapproval of well-trained military professionals who refrained from meeting SAVAK's special demands. At SAVAK's point of origin, Air Force officers resisted recruitment; but, among the ranks of the less sophisticated, more plebeian officers of the Army, where it was possible to become an officer without graduating from military school, SAVAK recruiters fared better. This pattern of resistance made even the Army, not to mention the Air Force and the Navy, suspects of SAVAK—and vice versa. "Army men were very afraid of SAVAK," confirms Ali Agha, the first Iranian chargé d'affaires of the Washington, D.C., Iranian embassy under the Khomeini regime.

It is the rawness, so to speak, of some recruits to secret police forces that makes them desirable to some state leaders. Papa Doc Duvalier, Haiti's former President, who died and left the throne to his son in 1971, found the military more a suspicious than a loyal ally. He took an immediate distrust to the Army, because he had seen armies overthrow numerous leaders before. So he relied on a motley and sometimes ridiculous collection of goons, thugs, and largely untrained men who were, however, immensely loyal to him. And so were born the Macoutes, the malleable and thoroughly trustworthy secret police force. As one native Haitian source put it, "The Tonton Macoutes† were a force created in order to do whatever the government asked them to do, as they were not trained officers."

In Israel especially, the value system as it might be applied to military and nonmilitary intelligence is clearly and appropriately identified. AMAN, for Agaf Modiin, the Information Bureau of the Military, offers its officers prestige and social status beyond all the rest of its benefits. It publishes a great deal of public information; is associated with technical, sophisticated computer work; and generally projects a professional and sophisticated public image. Lowest on the totem pole (lower than MOSSAD, the Central Institute for Intelligence and Special Missions—the espionage service of Israel) is the Shin Bet (a shortened version of Sherut Habitachon, the Security Department), a highly secretive and more or less unofficial organization. After all, if the work were desirable and honorable, why would there be such secrecy surrounding it?

6

The nun's work with the Catholic Commission in downtown Salisbury required considerable circumspection. With the Criminal Investigation Division of the Rhodesian internal security network situated in an office building nearby, the American missionary lived both an odd and a lonely life. The Catholic Commission for Justice and Peace, by the fall of 1977, was just about the only above-ground group of its kind in the country. If it was looking for opposition to the regime, and that, after all, was its job, the CID did not have to look very far. The opposition was catty-corner across the street.

Just months earlier, the Commission had published a report on the torture of black civilians by white Rhodesian troops. A few

---

† There is no agreement among scholars of Haiti about what "Tonton Macoutes" means. Some claim the name refers to a primitive bad figure in Haitian voodoo culture who takes you away when you misbehave—sort of the opposite of a Santa Claus.

weeks after publication, CID agents confiscated copies of the book. And just recently, CID supervisors cabled London about a secret meeting of a number of Commission backers to take place in London, making sure that a copy of the cable fell into the hands of a Commission member. The message was obvious: CID now had an informant inside the Commission.

With regard to CID agents harassing her personally, the nun had every reason to believe that it was only a matter of time. And so it came as little surprise when six CID agents stormed into the Commission building one morning in search of "subversive material." But the only document that the American nun genuinely worried about falling into CID's hands was her diary. It had everything: every name and every address that the CID could possibly need in order to understand the opposition network with which she was very much involved. But the diary was at home; the agents had so far invaded only the office.

The CID agents announced, in a somewhat self-conscious way, that they were searching for papers that might cause "alarm and despondency." The sister thought this phrase rather absurd: imagine banning everything that would tend to develop alarm and despondency in an alarmed and despondent country like Rhodesia.

Junior agents, under the watchful gaze of the clearly senior supervisor, scurried through the office file cabinets like mice through food shelves. "Take it," the supervisor said when shown one sheaf of documents. "Leave it," he said when shown another. Though the supervisor seemed to know what he wanted, the junior agents seemed not to know what he wanted.

And then the nun was given the jolt she didn't want. The supervisor announced, placidly but firmly, that the search would continue at the "good sister's home."

At her home, she did all she could to steer them away from the diary, but she wasn't lucky. They found it, and when they did, they promptly left. They knew they had found what they most wanted. "With that diary," she recalls thinking to herself at the time, "they will learn everything." She berated herself for keeping the diary at all, but habits of a lifetime were not easily broken, and the convenience of the diary had made her incautious.

The nun walked back to the Commission office, deeply worried now. So, apparently, were her co-workers, who had heard of the search and were just convening an emergency meeting of all members when she arrived. She joined the meeting, and they hashed over the options they thought they had. But their options were soon to narrow. There was a heavy knock at the door. It was the CID.

"Where is your warrant?" the nun demanded of the agents on the doorstep.

"We don't need one," a CID agent answered, now formally placing her under arrest. "We are protected by the Law and Order Maintenance Act. You should know that. After all, you know our laws well enough to break them."

At her house, she kept her lips sealed, but the two agents, almost mockingly, read excerpts from her diary.

"You're a supporter of terrorism," one of them said.

"You came here from the U.S. to stir up trouble," said another.

The nun kept silent, trying to suppress the angry emotions that were raging within her.

"The longer you're silent," one agent told her sternly, "the longer you're going to be detained."

The word "detained" hit her like a shock of electricity. Maybe she had miscalculated. Her work against the white-dominated regime of Ian Smith was, she had known all along, very risky. But she figured all along that although she was risking arrest and maybe deportation, she was not risking prison. She did not know how she would cope with prison. What if she found that she really had no tolerance for the privation and isolation it entailed? Trying to mask her fears, she asked the agents coolly, "What do I take to prison? This is my first time."

"Just simple things," one agent advised. "Pajamas, toothpaste, a toothbrush."

Her hands were shaking as she traipsed through her bedroom and living room, loading these things into a little overnight case. Still in something of a daze, she put as few things as possible in it, as if in the belief that the more she packed, the longer they would make her stay, as if when she ran out of toothpaste, they would have to let her go.

The next hours and days rushed by her in a blur. Only some deep-seated faith and hope kept her spirits alive when her lawyer broke the news that she might be jailed for a long time, although he added the observation that her case had attracted a considerable amount of international attention and that international observers were planning to attend her trial. He reminded her of what she already knew: that U. S. Ambassador Andrew Young and British Foreign Secretary David Owen were on a swing tour through Africa —and that they might be persuaded to intervene in her case.

If nothing else, their presence in Africa did alter the climate of the country somewhat, so that Rhodesian officials conducted an astonishingly snappy trial and levied a surprisingly lenient sentence.

The sentence was immediate deportation, and thinking back years later on how she felt as she waited to board the plane, she recalls only two impressions: She recalls seeing some foreign reporters at the departure gate whom she later spoke to on the plane, and she remembers, in particular, an odd exchange that took place between herself and two of the CID agents who had first arrested her at the Commission building. "Now, Sister, I hope you'll write us," she remembers one of them saying just before she left. She recalls the remark being odd enough. What was odder, she says in retrospect, was the way she answered the agents: "I don't even know your address," she said to them.

The sister left more in Rhodesia than just her diary, but about a year later, now back in the United States, she had the desire to at least retrieve that. She didn't know how to go about it, but a lawyer tried a frontal approach. He made a telephone call to CID headquarters in Salisbury and then gave the sister this report: the CID still had the diary. In fact, it appeared to have become some sort of training manual for them.

"Oh, that's funny," said the CID officer in Salisbury over the telephone to her lawyer in the United States. "I was just rereading it the other day. I was instructed to reread it."

7

The training of the secret police agent often proceeds from such real-life cases. There are no particular political-police textbooks from which the rudimentary lessons of political suppression might be gleaned, as if the political police were medical doctors and opposition leaders were foreign agents whom the normal antibodies of the body politic or the conventional chemicals of the pharmacist could arrest. The lessons of secret police work often proceed as extensions of regular police work, or as hand-me-down homilies from the word-of-mouth experiences of other agents with whom they have contact.

The communist states are the most open and formalistic about the training of their political police. The Czechs send many of their bright young men to the Academy of Security Forces (rough translation from the Czech), situated in Prague. Fittingly enough, since secret police work is essentially an extension of regular police work, both the regular and the secret police are trained there. Recruits are taught (besides the usual police courses in surveillance, interrogation, and so on) Marxist philosophy and other programs designed to orient the recruit to proper ideological positions. The school consists of two main programs. One, lasting two years, is designed for graduates who go off to fill the lower ranks of the Interior Ministry. The other program lasts four years—and these graduates fill the upper-echelon positions in the political police as well as the Interior Ministry.

Similarly well-developed schooling works throughout the Communist states of Eastern Europe. In Yugoslavia, the cream of the crop attend the Faculty for Security and Social Self-protection (again, rough translation). This course of studies lasts for a full four years, with studies in the fields of social sciences, criminology, and law. After graduation, an immediate job in the security network is assured, except for those who are sent on to further study. The Yugoslavian Communist Party puts such a high priority on secret police work that it is not unknown for high-ranking UDBA agents to polish off their training at Oxford, Cambridge, or Harvard Law School.

Or in Moscow. Students from Eastern European countries as well as KGB-bound graduates of the Soviet university system receive expert training at the so-called "KGB School"—formally known as the Dzerzhinsky Academy. Known in Yugoslavia and Czechoslovakia as the "highest school," its students study specialized courses in law, economics, and engineering (despite the civilian-style course, the highest school is a military school and its enrollees are required to wear uniforms).

The KGB's course of study, ranging from courses in languages, operations, specialization in engineering, new equipment for defense, and of course, criminalistic courses, is designed, says a former Soviet procurator‡ trained in a similar fashion, to "improve your skills."

The school is also designed to confer prestige on satellite agents—

‡ In the Soviet system, a criminal investigator, with vast experience, involved in the prosecution of criminal cases.

thereby helping the KGB keep controls on the leadership of foreign security police. The agent from an Eastern European country who is admitted to the KGB school in Moscow is well on his way to a satisfactory career. A sour Czech defector named Josef Frolik, who for seventeen years served in the security police, put the KGB-controlled upward-mobility system in his own bitter, anti-Communist terms:

"The system of the Czechoslovak intelligence apparatus did not favor the advancement of persons who were capable, experienced and devoted to the Republic (not just devoted to the regime—there's a big difference), but favored spineless careerists, who called attention to themselves through subservience and flattery in dealing with [Soviet KGB] advisers. Whether they actually had a taste for such things or not, they went on fishing and hunting expeditions arranged for the [Soviet] advisers, usually in territory out of bounds for ordinary mortals (the Staňkov pond, upper reaches of the Moldau, hunting preserves around Zelezná Ruda, forbidden border sections along the German and Austrian frontiers), and they persisted until they reached their goal, i.e., being sent to Soviet Russia for training and thus becoming part of the elite cadre with career possibilities in intelligence and counterintelligence. At headquarters, amusing stories were told how these eager-beavers, in their zeal to please, were ready to beat the bushes to flush out animals, to stalk the bush with rattles and to do many of the chores performed by hunting dogs. [And the ambitious careerists saw to it that smuggled into Czechoslovakia in diplomatic pouches] were crates of whiskey, French perfumes, cognac, American cigarettes, razor blades, razors, cigarette lighters, automobile parts, fishing rods, reels, and other merchandise requested by their principal employers—the KGB advisers. The pomaded and scented advisers, who were so fond of cologne and perfume, smelled like retired barmaids. That was the best way of detecting the presence of a KGB adviser. And the corridor or office of the particular careerist smelled all day like a perfume factory!"

Cuban G-2 agents may also be treated to special training abroad. And selection for such training is a sure sign to the agent that bigger and better things lie ahead. A certain well-known official of the Cuban G-2 was sighted at security schools in Moscow and Prague in 1960. By 1962, he was promoted to vice-minister of the Interior—where he was second in command to Interior Minister Valdés. Other

G-2 officials and agents may, however, receive their training solely in Cuba. As of 1966, the main school for secret police training in Cuba was in a building situated in the Sierra Maestra—the mountains where Fidel Castro and his band of revolutionaries got their start.

There is surely no exact analogue in the West to the principal KGB school, but if there ever was anything remotely comparable, it may have been the International Police Academy, in Washington. Summarily closed down in 1975 after a tidal wave of negative publicity, the IPA was set up and funded by the U. S. Agency for International Development (AID) under the overall aegis of the U. S. State Department. In the early seventies, the list of graduates of the IPA read like a who's who in the international police world. Chile, Nicaragua, Panama, Guatemaia, and surprisingly, Mexico, had the most alumni from this school, followed by Brazil, the Philippines, Hong Kong, British Honduras, Korea, Paraguay, Peru, Iran, and Uruguay. The program of studies that the agent sought to attend was called the Technical Investigation Course, conducted in two phases of four weeks each. The first phase was held at the academy in Washington. The second, with the more elaborate fieldwork, was held at the Border Patrol Academy, in Los Fresnos, Texas. Courses varied in their applicability to the work of political police in various foreign countries. No doubt the two-hour lecture on the U.S. police systems must have seemed perfunctory to the students, but there were courses to satisfy almost any appetite. One was "Police Intelligence" (defined as "the need to organize intelligence into a useful form available for storage and retrieval." Another was "Basic Electricity" ("including concepts of simple electricity, basic terminology, and Ohm's law"). Then there was the well-attended "Surveillance Course" ("a discussion of various weapons which may be used by the assassin . . . a demonstration of the possibilities of carrying hidden or disguised weapons"). Perhaps some of the students in these courses had more than purely preventive policing of the conventional sort in mind. And the same observation might well apply to students attending the six-hour course on "Bombs and Explosives." ("An all-day presentation by an outstanding authority in the handling of bombs and explosives. Slides, movies and models are used in this presentation.")

The optional fieldwork in Los Fresnos, since it was first offered in

1969, graduated at least 165 policemen, almost all of them from countries in Asia, Latin America, and Africa. The lectures were given by instructors from the Central Intelligence Agency. Field trips to other U.S. police departments were taken. One IPA contingent visited the Boston Police Department. These visits were conducted in the fraternal style of fellow professionals exchanging information, gossip, and advice.

As one Mauritian graduate of the U.S. school put it, the most important thing he learned from his colleagues was "the necessity for all the police forces of the free world to work together and establish a climate of mutual understanding between their organizations and the public they serve. This is because the most important aspect of our responsibilities is our endeavor to make this world a better place . . . to live in." In other words, like the KGB school, the IPA served to reinforce ideological attitudes that could last a long time— and might ultimately redound to the short- and long-term advantage of the superpower.

The IPA may also have reinforced attitudes that did *not* redound to the United States' credit. The left-wing press in places such as Greece, which printed accusations about the IPA in the mid-seventies, was probably the first to refer to it as the "U. S. Academy of Torturers." Such political rhetoric certainly blurred a few distinctions, but the fact of the matter is that the IPA blurred a few distinctions itself. Unless CIA intelligence about the domestic activities of foreign police institutions was terribly flawed, it would have been impossible *not* to suspect that IPA programs could have been ultimately used to serve purposes not explicitly described in the course catalogue, despite the official denials. "Torture is contrary to our beliefs," said the commanding officer of the U. S. Army Institute for Military Assistance, at Fort Bragg, North Carolina, another school that trained foreign police. "We do not in any way instruct, mention, condone, or even encourage it. . . . As you know, foreign cultures are different from ours, and, in many respects, they don't have the same values that we do What they do when they get home depends on how they view the issues."

This statement may have been somewhat accurate, but it ignores the essential sense of fraternity with which all police officers, whether political or criminal, approach common problems. While it is perhaps true to say that torture was not a formal elective at any United States schools that trained soldiers and officers who allegedly engaged in torture after they graduated,* the commanding officer's statement ignores the issue of what these officers talk about when class is out.

The results speak for themselves. U.S. investigators in the Philippines found an officer commanding a compound of tortured political prisoners who had received military training at Fort Bragg and at Fort Benning, Georgia. Several dozen Argentine military personnel were trained at the Army Command and General Staff College, at Fort Leavenworth, Kansas, including (as of the late seventies) the head of the Secretaria de Informaciones del Estado (a branch of the Argentine secret police). Brazil's Department of Political and Social Order (DOPS) maintained a special prison and torture center on the Isle of Flowers, across Guanabara Bay. The island's commander was a graduate of the School of the Americas at Fort Gulick, in the (Panama) Canal Zone. And back in the late fifties, when SAVAK was just getting started, twenty key officers who had retired from the Iranian military received special training at the Marine base in Quantico, Virginia, and attended lectures at CIA headquarters, in Langley, Virginia. Other SAVAK agents were trained under the very same AID Office of Public Safety program that produced the International Police Academy.

Is it possible, therefore, to pin the *responsibility* for SAVAK torture on United States training? Such a conclusion would simply go beyond the evidence. A retired Iranian Army general, now living in the United States and well aware of SAVAK's notoriously brutal practices, admits that SAVAK agents were in part trained by the intelligence services of Britain, Israel, and the United States. "They were, however, trained by those countries *not* for torture," he insists, "but to learn how to spy, to do research—that sort of thing."

In the absence of more conclusive evidence, it is perhaps best to stick close to what facts have become available. In truth, like the other superpower, the United States did help train secret police agents for service in their home countries. But as the negative publicity about these training schools rose in volume (a problem the Soviets have not had to contend with, given their control of the press), the United States has had to rely on surrogates to serve this purpose. One type of surrogate of this sort is a national police academy situated within the foreign country itself. In Brazil, for instance, the

* For more discussion of U.S. training schools of foreign police officers, see chapter notes.

Federal Police Academy, established with U.S. aid in 1968, served this purpose. A number of police agents from other Latin American countries have attended the school, including DINA agents from Chile, who in turn helped train anti-Castro Cubans harbored in such countries as Costa Rica, Guatemala, and Nicaragua. Bolivian officers involved in the 1980 coup led by General Luis García Meza reportedly received training at this Brazilian school. The officers went there instead of to the United States for their training, as U.S. military assistance programs to Bolivia had been cut back.

There are still other loopholes, despite the closing down of the most obvious foreign police training centers such as the IPA. Federal law still allows the CIA to train foreign police, for example, in narcotics control (not surprisingly, therefore, a number of former CIA officials may now be found in the U. S. Drug Enforcement Administration).

Between 1971 and 1975, for instance, the Philippines received U.S. aid and training under the auspices of the International Narcotics Control Program. Over those years, some $1.3 million was spent on (1) training Filipino drug-law enforcement officers, (2) providing equipment, and (3) organizing police narcotics units. The program opened Pandora's box. As the U. S. General Accounting Office, in a critical review of the program, put it, it is difficult "to monitor the use of the commodities and training supplied and prevent the use of these units for other police functions." On the contrary, according to some knowledgeable persons, the whole point of these international "narcotics" programs is to disguise continued U.S. training of foreign secret police from a theoretically critical Congress, which closed both AID's Office of Public Safety and the International Police Academy. "Through our investigations," claims Nancy Stein, of the North American Congress on Latin America, a human-rights organization, "we know that the U. S. Drug Enforcement Administration has a similar setup to OPS, with advisers stationed around the world. This provides a cover for aid to continue, under the guise of drug control operations." In the Philippines, AID's own mission director admitted that he had severe doubts about the "narcotics" control program "because of its connection with police support activities." The AID official may have had in mind one horrible 1973 incident in which agents from the Constabulary Anti-Narcotics Unit (CANU) invaded the home of a suspected anti-Marcos radical and tortured her to death.

Nor is there any stipulation in federal or state law to prevent private corporations or private schools from picking up where the CIA has had to leave off. Especially in an age of persistent terrorist activity, there is a continued demand for technical training in courses of study that could be applied just as readily to political dissidents as to violent terrorists. These schools conduct their business in the utter secrecy their nongovernmental status entitles them to, though many of them are supported in part by taxpayer funds.

We visited one school in the United States offering a special course designed to train officers (chiefly Americans but a small percentage of foreign students from "Free World" countries as well, according to the school's director) in the techniques of combatting terrorism, and chatted for a considerable length of time with the school's director, a graduate of the U. S. Army War College. He showed us a series of slides, which he felt answered our request to attend a few of the school's courses. He showed a slide that quoted the definition of terrorism of the Socialist Workers Party. "The problem with this slide," he said defensively, "is that it only addresses left-wing terrorism." Another slide contained Congressman Richard Ichord's definition of terrorism ("a wide variety of activities orchestrated by the Communist bloc"). A third slide presented the CIA definition of terrorism; it stressed terrorism by transnational organizations across international borders. Finally, the fourth slide developed a classification of war into two categories: one by "regular" army forces and the other by "irregular forces," of a paramilitary nature.

"We must find an American solution to political terrorism," the director insisted. "We must find a solution that is (1) effective, and (2) acceptable." But perhaps these goals are, from a practical standpoint, mutually exclusive? "Well, maybe," he conceded.

"We can't have it both ways," he went on. "We can't have freedom and control. The only way to diminish illegitimate violence is to raise the level of legitimate violence." But what price should a society pay for this? "Once society becomes impotent," he warns, "it will be impossible to prevent terrorists and vigilante groups from spreading. . . . What if they kidnap the governor? Or what if suddenly terrorists demand the release of prisoners from the state penitentiary? What do we do if we suddenly become informed that bombs will go off in such and such a place in such and such amount of time in two different places? Are we prepared?"

The terrorism course, he explains, teaches students the intricacies of "crisis/resolution role playing," using an in-house dial telephone system and closed-circuit television. He then put another slide into the projector. "To combat terrorism," it said, we need: "1. central and effective intelligence gathering, and 2. specially trained police task forces." But terrorists and narcotics violators are not the only targets such training can be used to control. The techniques would work equally well against political offenders.

8

"I have gone on foreign assignment only twice," said the late Bahman Naderipour, better known as the SAVAK agent Tehrani, in the course of a six-hundred-page confession delivered to an Islamic Court in Iran prior to his execution in 1979. "Once to Israel for a short term training and once to America for a month and a half training period. It was at the end of 1754 [1976, American translation] that six of us officials, without knowing why we were selected, went to Israel. The group included myself, [two other SAVAK officials], one translator, and two officials of the Eighth Department, whom I introduced over there. I went under the assumed name of Bahman Tehrani. . . .

"We went to Israel aboard an El-Al jet, and we were welcomed in Tel Aviv by the intelligence officials of Mossad. They took us to a hotel over there—I think it was the Plaza Hotel. After an introductory ceremony they said we have provided for a five-day course. . . .

"They used to take us to a building on the outskirts of Tel Aviv. It was on a hill. In the building we sat at a table for a seminar, in a four by five meter room. They would talk about the organizations they were confronting, like the Palestinians Liberation Organization and other groups existing within [Israel]. . . .

"Then they would talk about a method for gathering intelligence. In the same way that they had implemented a new intelligence gathering system in the Gaza strip and regions by the Jordanian river. They wanted to familiarize us with this new project. They said: 'For a population of two thousand we assign two persons for the leadership of activities. We place the center of these activities in the police station or military bases, so they will be protected.'

"Of course, their intelligence organization worked overtly. However, their method of contact with the spies [i.e., informants' network] is secret. Their intelligence official is known by all the people and he is known to work for MOSSAD.

"They continued saying that when the area under supervision was determined, its characteristics are determined on a map. For instance, how many avenues are found in the locality? How many families live in our area? And these families, what kind of connections they have with the outside, based on their dependency. Then we select spies from among these people, by considering which ones have outside connections, or have connection with the Palestine Liberation Organization. Then they talk to them about cooperation. Cooperation is achieved by either threats, force, or money. In any case, they persuaded them to cooperate."

With these words, Tehrani described a typical bit of cooperative training of agents across international boundaries. And so, in the seventies, just as Israel's MOSSAD helped train Iran's SAVAK, similarly Brazil's DOPS helped Chile's DINA and Uruguay's DNII, while Chile's DINA, Argentina's SIDE (among other Argentine internal security mechanisms), and Paraguay's Investigaciones shared resources, returned one another's prisoners, and generally cooperated with one another. The Malaysians offered intelligence training to some of the most sophisticated intelligence officers of the Philippines and Thailand, and the East Germans helped the Angolans, Yemenis, and Ethiopians in establishing their security services. The KGB helped Czechoslovakia and all other Eastern European countries with the exception of nonaligned Yugoslavia and Albania. Until the Shah of Iran fell, the Egyptian security police and SAVAK passed information. (And at the height of Palestinian terrorist activity, other intelligence services joined this network in order to help—including the internal security services of Morocco, France, and Turkey.) The U.S. CIA helped out the Canadian RCMP security section—once even loaning a black informer to the Canadians so that he could help the Mounties infiltrate militant black groups in Canada. And the CIA played a strong role in the operations of the Italian internal security police—helping the Italians out in coping with the plague of terrorists. The growth of international terrorism brought together the French secret service, DST (for Direction de la Surveillance du Territoire), with the West German BND (Bundesnachrichtendienst, for Federal Information Service); the British MI5 and SIS worked closely with the Spanish security services; and terrorist activity helped spawn a new sort of

Europolice network in 1977 that involved the police forces of the nine European Economic Community countries in a new network known as TREVI, for Terrorism, Radicalism, and International Violence.

Secret policing is therefore both an international profession and a nationalistic venture. Secret police agents may operate according to their own laws applicable to their own countries, but they also operate according to no strict laws *outside* of their own countries. In 1976, the former Chilean ambassador to the United States (under Salvador Allende) was assassinated on Embassy Row in Washington, by agents of DINA. People were shocked, but the fact of the matter is that exile groups throughout the United States, Great Britain, and other relatively open societies remain prey to secret police agents from foreign countries (see Chapter Seven). At least part of the reason for this is that clandestine internal-security organizations from different countries cooperate at least as often as they compete.

Cooperation between various countries' internal-security police is not usually haphazard; it often takes the form of joint teams of agents from various secret police units that have been brought together for specific missions. To illustrate, in November of 1978, a brave magazine editor in Brazil uncovered a secret act of cooperation between Uruguayan and Brazilian secret police. It all started one morning when the editor was sitting at his desk in his editorial offices in Brazil. The phone rang; the caller was from São Paulo, Brazil, but he refused to give his name. "I have an anonymous bit of information for you. . . . Some Uruguayan citizens are about to be kidnapped in Pôrto Alegre [Brazil] by Uruguayan secret police. Please go there with witnesses and stop it. If they are taken by the police, they will never be seen again." The caller gave the address of the apartment and then hung up.

The editor tried to ignore the call. This was obviously a police matter, he thought, not his business. He had almost managed to forget about the call when, a few hours later, the phone rang again. This time the anonymous caller was more insistent.

Reluctant but now admittedly intrigued, the editor took one of the magazine's photographers with him and drove over to the apartment address that he had been given on the telephone. As he parked the car, he noticed another car parked in front of the apartment with the driver sitting behind the wheel, but at the time he thought little of it.

The apartment was on the first floor. The editor, with the photographer standing slightly behind him, rang the doorbell. A few minutes passed. He rang the doorbell again. Then a young woman opened the door slightly. She said nothing, but her eyes, the journalist recalls, radiated danger and worry. Suddenly someone dragged the woman back in the apartment and pushed the door open. Out stepped a man with a gun in his hand. He ordered the editor and his photographer to move inside the apartment.

In the living room, the two journalists saw five men dressed in casual civilian clothing—wearing T-shirts—and carrying revolvers. The one who seemed in command spoke with a distinct Pôrto Alegre accent. Two agents aimed a revolver at the temples of the photographer and the editor, forcing them against a wall with their hands in the air.

The two journalists quickly explained why they were there, and they gave their identities. They got the impression that the police agents had been waiting for someone else to call at the apartment when, instead, they made their surprise appearance at the front door. The commander of the group left the room for a moment to huddle with another agent. The journalists remained against the wall with their hands in the air.

The leader of the group of five then returned from the other room and asked the journalists to sit down on the sofa.

"You have fallen into a bad situation," he explained softly but firmly. "It has to do with foreigners in our country. Don't get mixed up in it. If someone brings up this matter, say you've seen nothing in this apartment. We will take care of that. We are the police."

They then showed their Brazilian security police identification to the journalists, after which they commanded them to leave.

Returning to his office—shaken but now even more curious—the editor decided to make a few calls.

He phoned the local São Paulo police department to check the story out, but it was impossible to trace down anyone with any knowledge of these events. The journalists let the weekend pass, and then on Monday they went to a local security office in São Paulo. They told their strange story, but no one, again, seemed to know anything about it. It was suggested to them that they make contact with Brazil's federal police. Which they did, but once again they got nowhere.

In frustration, the magazine editor went to a local newspaper with his story. The newspaper published the testimonies of the two journalists—together with that of a Pôrto Alegre lawyer who had also been contacted by the same anonymous individual from São Paulo who had called the magazine editor.

The lawyer testified that one night he had gone by the apartment to see whether the people inside needed legal representation. The front door was open, and upon entering, he saw that the apartment had been left in a state of total chaos. Everything was turned over, bottles were lying everywhere, there wasn't an ashtray that wasn't filled with cigarettes. The lawyer then checked with the apartment manager, who told the lawyer a strange story: that, several days before, a note had been left in the apartment, signed ostensibly by the tenant, apologizing for having to leave the apartment under such haste and with no notice.

What did this all mean? At this point, we rely on a report from the International Secretariat of Jurists for Amnesty in Uruguay to fill in the gaps:

"Remember that as in Argentina and Paraguay . . . Uruguayan police don't hesitate to work in foreign territories with the consent of the local police. In general, this story shows how it is done, this is how cooperation is achieved: a mixed command of policemen conduct a kidnapping at a home, then there is an illegal transfer by plane, ship or car, depending on the place involved; then finally they are taken across the border and said to have documents of a subversive nature on them (and to want to be crossing the border on their own). This procedure is done to try to justify the presence of exiles. This particular . . . case, however, was interrupted by the presence of independent witnesses and the rapid reaction of the press and lawyers in Brazil. The 'classical process' of cooperation found itself contradicted. . . . Later, one of the Brazilian policemen from Pôrto Alegre involved in the kidnapping was formally recognized by both journalists as a former soccer player of Brazil . . . and a member of DOPS (Brazil's Department of Political and Social Order). . . ."

In a formal complaint filed with the Inter-American Commission on Human Rights of the Organization of American States by a prominent American academic on behalf of the International Secretariat of Jurists and the International Federation for the Rights of Man, both headquartered in Paris, it was charged that the kidnapping team consisted both of agents of the Pôrto Alegre branch of Brazil's DOPS and members of the OCOA, an important branch of the Uruguayan secret police network (OCOA stands for the Uruguayan

Armed Forces' Organismo Coordinador de Operaciones Antisubversivas). The complaint alleged that two Uruguayan citizens were handed over to OCOA agents by DOPS agents and that, accompanied by Brazilian and Uruguayan agents, they were driven across the Uruguayan frontier, where they were handed over to OCOA agents. The two citizens have not been seen or heard from since.

While we do not know precisely how these citizens were transferred to Uruguay, other reports confirm that secret police transfers are often made in the utmost secrecy, taking all precautions deemed necessary and risking no chance of discovery.

Here is a good illustration: at the height of its power, DINA dealt simply and brutally with the political Left in Chile by liquidating significant portions of it. Leftists who were arrested and imprisoned often disappeared without a trace. In many instances, the families of these detainees had neither the economic clout nor social status to raise much of a fuss about the disappearances. But every once in a while a ruckus was made, forcing DINA to produce some explanation or other.

One common official reply was that the suspect in question had not been arrested by DINA at all but had in fact fled the country. And to make the story seem credible, DINA would occasionally call on its Argentinian comrades in the Triple A death squad for help. A deal would be struck, in a neat if grisly way.

After some leftists were executed, their ID papers were collected and stored in DINA's files.

Remember: DINA was an official government agency with all the accouterments of a bureaucracy, including a vast, computerized (as well as a non-computerized) filing system. Now, if the matter had to be made to "look good," DINA would announce that the political figure had left Chile some time ago and had fled to Argentina.

This is where the cooperation would come in: for its part, the Triple A would provide the body—any body. The Triple A, which was secretly involved in the assassination of Argentinian leftists, would produce a corpse, preferably charred or mutilated so that it was beyond recognition. The corpse would be dumped on some street corner, with ID papers for some Chilean, forwarded, of course, by DINA agents via diplomatic pouch. And so would a bogus note informing the public that the execution had been committed by the MIR (the Chilean Movement of the Revolutionary Left), to give the impression (1) that the deceased had been caught by his colleagues and executed because he was believed to have worked as an informant for the secret police or (2) that the victim had perished as a result of some heated internal power struggle with fellow revolutionaries.

In this way, DINA washed its hands of the inquiry—with a good cover story documented by an ID and an unidentifiable body in another country. Of course, this sort of scheme didn't always work. If the family of the deceased visited the body to make an identification, and if the mutilation was not thorough enough, family members would swiftly realize that they had been duped—the body was not that of their missing loved one. But, often enough, the trick worked exceedingly well: after all, DINA had more ID papers than bodies (having buried them in clandestine graves in Chile while bureaucratically keeping the papers on file; or forging them on its own printing presses when required); and the Triple A had plenty of bodies but was not about to collect IDs, since the Triple A was in theory not an official governmental institution and therefore had no business collecting either IDs—or bodies.

This is one way that cooperation has worked between two secret police organizations.

The Paraguayan police also helped DINA agents with various schemes. A prominent Chilean leftist who once fled Chile was picked up by Paraguayan security police in Asunción, Paraguay, and secretly flown back to Chile, then taken by DINA agents to a secret camp. When pressed about the leftist's whereabouts, the DINA authorities were able to produce documentation that the suspect had indeed passed through an emigration checkpoint. Thanks to secret police cooperation, however, there was no documentation to prove that he had returned.

Cooperation among secret police forces also takes the usual mundane forms that are typical of traditional police organizations. Some organizations simply create a reciprocity of files. Files of the Seventh Central Office of SAVAK were always open to the CIA and other Western intelligence agencies, and to Israel's MOSSAD, as well.

Similarly, British and United States intelligence officials have long shared a series of broadcasts known as FBIS, for Foreign Broadcast Information Service. The service provides tapes of important foreign broadcasts, translations of speeches, and news items, and reports to other agencies about the political situation in key countries. Though clearly pedestrian compared to more cloak-and-dagger operations, over the long run FBIS has proved rather valuable. Indeed, it soon became indispensable to Foreign Service officers and ambassadors, and even to the American press. Described somewhat bureaucratically as a "service of common concern," it was managed by the CIA, which established a liaison with a similar monitoring service for Europe that operated under the British Broadcasting Corporation for the benefit of the government in London. For the next three decades, this information service, copying and translating hundreds of thousands of words daily, transmitted the product electronically for prompt availability wherever needed in Great Britain, the United States, and their posts overseas.

On the operational level, fraternal secret police cooperation is helpful in tracking down criminal fugitives and political exiles on the run; for this, Interpol, a private organization of ex-policemen from a number of countries, with headquarters at St. Cloud, France, is occasionally helpful. As a nongovernmental agency, it can move across international borders comparatively easily, and with its extensive files, serves as an information pool for police agencies around the world.

Interpol (for International Criminal Police Organization) is a sort of international clearinghouse, with methods of identifying offenders, assembling comprehensive information about them, and making the information available to law-enforcement officials throughout the world.

The organization itself is responsible to no national government but is at the disposal of all. National governments pay annual fees for its budget. The concept behind Interpol originated among the police of Paris during Napoleonic times, when the city was struck by a major crime wave and local police suspected that many criminals were aliens known to the police of other countries. Says Secretary-General Jean Nepote: "The real Interpol is simply a machine for permanent and organized cooperation between the police forces of more than one hundred nations."

Interpol has more than one hundred members. In the United States, Interpol works directly with local police throughout the United States. By electronic means and through the exchange of personnel, federal, state, and local law-enforcement agencies freely and regularly exchange confidential information with Interpol. Interpol also works closely with Communist countries such as Hungary, Czechoslovakia, and Bulgaria—which, ostensibly, are nonmembers.

Interpol claims to have no powers of arrest, but since Interpol's national center bureaus are directed and staffed by experienced police officers, the question arises as to whether or not a bureau itself ever takes direct police action. Interpol policy specifies that in normal situations the national central bureaus should "refrain from action while the national police carry out the actual investigation, arrest and related activities." However, there is evidence that Interpol agents are more than librarians or keypunch operators. As one authoritative analysis put it, agents "are empowered . . . to request assistance from the police of other countries . . . conversely, they can initiate within their own country, in accordance with their national laws, any police operation on behalf of another."

Interpol prides itself on being an organization that does *not* concern itself with political crimes. But this is a line that is easily crossed. In 1972, Interpol members agreed that Interpol would involve itself in antiterrorist and antihijacking activities. Precisely because skyjackers and terrorists tend to have clear political motives for their criminal offenses, Interpol's actions necessarily have political consequences.

Louis Sims, the U.S. chief of Interpol, admitted once that some governments "could use it [Interpol] for political purposes, but say it's for criminal purposes—anything's possible—but I haven't seen it happen. . . . We check each request. . . . We get as much information from the requesting agency as is possible." But there are no formal guidelines—and sometimes Interpol chooses not to ask too many questions.

The U. S. Central Intelligence Agency and Interpol have a close working relationship. As one official U. S. Government response to a Freedom of Information Act request for CIA files on Interpol put it: "Disclosure of the documents would reveal that the government had cooperated with Interpol in the collection of intelligence, and the possibility of maintaining that relationship or others like it vital to the national security would be impaired. This document contains information concerning deliberations regarding the means by which Interpol collects intelligence abroad and describes intelligence sources and methods. It contains the name of a CIA employee."

Today, Interpol is practically a symbol of international cooperation among police agencies of widely varying types. But Interpol is not all that selective: it is hooked up to computer terminals in many countries of the world. Despite its Nazi taint—a number of former

Interpol heads were Nazis—today it is almost ideology-blind, taking in members of, and cooperating with, left-wing as well as right-wing governments. Interpol does have something to offer: for instance, a vast storehouse of cards, fingerprints, and photos of suspects from around the world. Persons at Interpol headquarters are trained to pull a dossier in hours—in minutes if the situation is urgent. Interpol maintains three special filing systems that are unique: the *portrait parle,*† the analytic index, and the punch-card index. Says the chief of the section containing the specially designed cards, "Starting with only a few characteristics, or even one, it is possible to come up with a name and a dossier."

Computer technology is as important a contribution to be made by one secret police organization for the benefit of the other as is riot gear. When the Argentinian security police helped General García Meza plan his 1980 coup in La Paz, Bolivia, computer experts in Buenos Aires, Argentina, prepared an intelligence analysis to determine potential leaders of an anti-Meza government. Within hours after the coup took place, some persons on the computer's printout were imprisoned, exiled, or killed. Argentinian wiretappers —some intelligence sources say there were as many as two hundred of them—were sent to Bolivia within days of the July coup to begin wiring the capital for Bolivian security units. Following a somewhat similar pattern, a Cuban "aid" team arrived in Nicaragua in 1980 that included an all-Cuban panel of telephone and communications experts and technicians (all trained by the East Germans). Within days, a member of the new Nicaraguan Government was astonished to find that the Cuban communications team had called at the offices and homes of all civilian members of the government in order to have them "checked" to "see if they were bugged."

Advanced technology makes the bigger internal security operations more valuable to the operations of the smaller secret police —as well as more threatening to the terrorist, or to the nonviolent dissident. A good example of this important technology is the computerized files of West Germany's criminal police. These files, kept near Wiesbaden, are said to contain thousands of records collected in the past few years on terrorist suspects. The major terrorist groups that the West German security police worry about are the Red Brigades and affiliates in Italy, the Baader-Meinhof gang and its suc-

† The file that categorizes the identifying and distinguishing features of subjects' faces.

cessors in West Germany, Provisional I.R.A. in Northern Ireland and Britain, and a French group called Direct Action. Not surprisingly, then, the credo of a terrorist organization known as Clodo—Comité Liquidant et Détournant les Ordinateurs, or Computer Liquidation and Hijacking Committee—includes passages such as: "The computer is the favorite tool of the dominant. It is used to exploit, to compile files of information, to control and to repress."

9

The East German secret police—described by one former U.S. CIA agent as "drill masters with advanced technology"—is the A team of the Communist bloc security services, and Communist-bloc cooperation is at least as carefully thought out as Free World cooperation among internal security organizations. While secret police cooperation does not proceed in as quiet and perhaps unofficial a manner as in the case of some Latin American examples, the Communist style is far more studious and thorough and is all the while under the steely overall guidance of the U.S.S.R.'s KGB. With the exception of Albania and Yugoslavia, the KGB coordinates the intelligence activities of every country in Communist Europe. "Task people," as the American CIA agents prefer to call them, accept their work assignments from the Moscow KGB center as though they were students at a KGB school taking on homework. The 11th Department of the First Chief Directorate, formerly known as the Advisers Department, runs day-to-day operations with the clandestine services of Cuba and the East European satellites. Officers are posted at service headquarters in Havana, East Berlin, Warsaw, Prague, Budapest, Bucharest, and Sofia. The Russians inform the center of all significant actions of the satellite organizations, forward copies of all reports of interest, and secretly direct agents recruited by the KGB in the satellite services.

A former high CIA official puts the matter this way: "When the Russians gained control of Eastern Europe, they gained control of the two things that they considered the most important: (1), communications systems, and (2), intelligence services." Not fully appreciating this truth more than twenty years ago, the former CIA official recalls admiringly the response of George Kennan, the historian and former ambassador to Russia, to his terribly confident assertion that of course the Russians wanted to gain control of Western Germany by force. The two experts were debating the nature of Soviet intentions along these lines. Kennan's attitude, the ex-CIA official recalls, was, " 'They will not [do that] . . . they have not yet fully consolidated East Germany. . . . What the Russians think of as control is not military occupation . . . it is control of the internal *security systems* so that if someone opposes the regime . . . they have the power to go to his house at night . . . [and the] prestige . . . so that no one can do anything about it.' "

The control of the secret police systems of totalitarian regimes is the key to those societies. How, exactly, has the Soviet Union managed to keep such tight controls on the other East European security systems—a goal of the utmost importance to Moscow? They start by assigning to the foreign intelligence service *one* deputy to the chief of that service. They follow up by sending in a "deputy assistant" or a "special assistant" to each and every single department under the chief.‡ These departments of course vary in size, so that any num-

‡ The KGB is broadly organized into four chief directorates, seven independent directorates and six independent departments, according to John Barron's definitive study *Inside the KGB*. For the purposes of understanding the relationship of the KGB to other security police, we might mention here that the First Chief Directorate conducts all Soviet clandestine activities abroad. The Second Chief Directorate, among other duties, supervises foreigners inside the Soviet Union. Operational divisions of the Fifth Chief Directorate include a special Jewish Department, and religion, ethnic minorities, etc. The Technical Operations Directorate develops and produces most of the technical devices used in KGB operations, with the exception of communications gear. The Administration Directorate performs the routine housekeeping chores of the KGB. The Personnel Directorate tries to anticipate and fulfill all manpower needs, through recruitment of new officers and transfers among divisions. It must approve all hirings wherever they are initiated, and it also administers and plans the curricula of KGB schools. The Surveillance Directorate does what its name suggests. The Communications Directorate tries to monitor and decipher foreign communications.

The Special Investigations Department makes sensitive investigations in cases involving suspected treason or espionage, penetrations of the KGB or GRU (Chief Administration for Intelligence, a division of the general staff of the Soviet Army) by foreign intelligence services, and criminality or gross derelictions by important Party members of government officials. It also investigates the circumstances, fixes the responsibility, and assesses the damages of each defection. The Department for Collation of Operational Experience has analysts who study intelligence operations of the U.S.S.R. and foreign nations for useful lessons. The Registry and Archives Department maintains a master index that summarizes the contents of each file and gives its physical location. The archives contain records of investigations and operations dating back to the days of the Cheka.

ber of special assistants—from five to twelve, generally speaking—
will be placed in each department of the foreign security service; but
the KGB is able to make personnel plans well in advance of any assignment, for the subdivisions of the foreign secret police correspond
precisely to the internal subdivisions of the Soviet Union's KGB.
This is because the KGB set them up.

This is merely the start of a properly conducted penetration by a
large security apparatus into a smaller one. "Cooperation" can filter
right down to the level of the control agent, a level at which the
KGB feels it is crucial to have its own appointees involved in foreign operations. These appointees could very well be foreign nationals who passed through the pearly gates of the KGB school. In
this way, argues the ex-CIA official, orders from Moscow go "from
Soviet hand to Soviet hand until they decide to tell the Cubans," i.e.,
until they decide to let the Cubans in on the operation. At this point,
"cooperation" has really come to mean "infiltration."

This is the classic Soviet pattern: cooperation a/k/a/ infiltration.
Take the case of Cuba again. The Moscow KGB, in any major operation, will draft a coded message to the chief of the KGB at the embassy in Havana. "Now, it is important to understand the nature of
these coded messages," the ex-CIA official says. "They are coded so
that only the Russians can read them; the Cubans remain in the
dark, under the orders, then, of the KGB, which inevitably 'knows
more.' In short, it's a one-way street." This coded message will then
be passed on by the KGB chief of the embassy (in whatever laundered form he deems appropriate) to the top security official of
Cuba's DGI (rough translation, General Directorate of Intelligence
—Cuba's overall intelligence service).*

In a minor operation, the "cooperation" occurs at a slightly lower
level (at least lower than the top-ranking men).

Say it is a question of arms shipments to El Salvador, for example. The Havana Soviet Embassy will deliver Moscow's instructions
to a smaller section (and a lower-down section head) such as the
paramilitary section or the Caribbean section of the Cuban DGI.
There, in one of these smaller sections, cooperation is literally

---

* The translation for DGI is Directorate of General Intelligence, the
main intelligence service of Cuba. According to some sources, DSE (for
Department of State Security) is the "new" DGI. Whichever, G-2 is the branch
of the overall intelligence service that is responsible for controlling internal
subversion.

achieved "over a desk," as the KGB representative delivers instructions to the Cuban DGI section chief involved.

But no deal is too trivial. Whatever the level of the deal going down, the KGB tries to monitor the entire range of intelligence activities of the system it is working with, through KGB personnel working out of military establishments or embassies, so there will be no possibility of intelligence going through and outside of the system without the Russians knowing.

The "cooperating" secret police are not insensitive to this classic pattern of cooperation. They may not like it, but their hands are tied. "They [the Poles, Czechs, whatever the country being controlled by the KGB may be] bitch about it all the time," says the ex-intelligence official, "but there is nothing they can do about it once the arrangement is entered into." Besides, he argues, the KGB advisers tend to deliver their messages and pitch their control with a "deft touch"—or at least defter than many Westerners suspect. The bear can growl, but it can also make believe it is asleep. The Soviet Union advisers, for example, create a "polite understanding" that the Soviet Union has superior equipment and can save the other intelligence service from a lot of trouble by offering its resources, more aid, or even its decision-making powers.

Part of the Soviet technique is knowing when and how to stay hidden. In some cases, the Russians rely not on themselves but on the East Germans to help them develop the intelligence system within a country with which the Soviets are just beginning to cooperate. For example, they have used the East Germans to set up internal security systems in Ethiopia, Yemen, and Angola.

The Russians hold the Germans in high regard—as models of efficiency, especially in the use of bugs and communications gear. The Russians also, generally speaking, have a great deal of respect, almost awe, for their preferred subcontractors, who perform a consultative managerial job for the benefit of new clients.

The East Germans are exceedingly useful to Russian security officials, who have yet one other motive for using the Germans to help them out in Third World countries: only the Russians, says the former intelligence official, terrify the Africans, not the East Germans.

Perhaps one African the former CIA official may have had in mind—and perhaps a good example of the multiteam style of Communist "cooperation"—was President Nguema Biyogo Macie, of

Equatorial Guinea. As correspondent David Lamb, of the Los Angeles *Times,* once wrote, the 1979 overthrow of his regime ended "a despotic rule as bizarre and brutal as independent Africa has ever known. During his eleven years in power, Macie, 57, turned his prosperous, peaceful West African nation into a concentration camp where torture, murder and forced labor became national policy." International human rights organizations hold him responsible for fifty thousand deaths.

But Macie did not accomplish this feat on his own. He had a lot of help. East German advisers ran his intelligence network; Cuban soldiers worked the internal-security beat; the North Koreans, who had an embassy in the capital city, Malabo, chipped in with some technical assistance; and the Soviet Union helped out with some rudimentary paramilitary equipment for Macie's band of strong-armed thugs and loyal servicemen who, like Papa Doc's Tonton Macoutes, were recruited to the cause—known as "Youth Marching for Macie." But the Soviet presence was far overshadowed by the presence of the Cuban and East German surrogates—with the East Germans calling the shots as if the Russians simply weren't there.

Thus was the "deft touch" of the Communist cooperative model on display. The Cubans supply the troops or policemen, the East Germans supply the staff security advisers.

The number of East German advisers will tend to be small. The usual range is from five to twenty, but if the cooperation involves sabotage and training, more advisers will have to be sent. In 1968, when Macie was elected President, Equatorial Guinea was one of the most prosperous nations in Africa. By the mid-seventies—in part, thanks to KGB and Eastern European "cooperation"—many African heads of state were privately referring to Equatorial Guinea as the "Auschwitz of Africa."

Such cooperation is inevitably manipulated by the superpower through its surrogates, ultimately to serve the superpower's best benefit. The KGB system of cooperation is well designed.

"We tell our allies the same things," admits a former intelligence official, with commendable honesty, when referring to the United States system of cooperation. He suggests an example: "We may say, 'We have another agent in Poland already . . . and we may save them [an ally] from sending another man to work on that particular thing in Poland. In this way, by 'task-giving,' the United States cooperates with the security services of other countries."

The former intelligence official argues that the CIA approach is neither as thorough nor as refined as the KGB's. "But where the United States uses 'persuasion' [the let's-compare-notes approach], the attitude is 'official but not enforceable.' Unlike the Soviets' KGB officers, the United States does not penetrate and infiltrate each and every division and department of the intelligence services it is cooperating with."

The Russians, he says, would be wholly uncomfortable with the CIA approach. The Russians would argue that the cooperation rests at too high a level; lower levels, they would emphasize, count too. On a major issue requiring cooperation between United States and British intelligence services, for instance, the initial message goes out at a very high level—from CIA chief to station chief, for example— largely because the level of penetration and infiltration achieved is superficial.

10

Up to a point, the procedures of the security-police arrest tend to be more or less standard. But variations occur, with differences regarding such factors as the aim of the regime within which the police operate, the status of the person arrested, and even the time of day of the arrest.

The procedures are clearly related to the goals. As Czechoslovakia sought to chill the Charter 77 human-rights movement during the late seventies without unduly alarming the entire nation, not to mention international opinion, the arrest was likely to occur at four or five in the morning. Says former Czech security officer Frolik, "People are sleeping, so the arrest can remain more secretive from the bulk of the people. And since those being arrested are sleeping, it is the time of their least resistance. And there is another reason. At this hour, police are in poor moods, and are feeling fierce and less controlled because they don't want to be out doing what they are doing; and so it is easier for them to perform undesirable acts at this hour." For less serious, or potentially difficult, arrests, agents of the Czechoslovakian security service tend to come at seven o'clock or so in the morning, "at a civil hour, generally, after you've had breakfast," to use the words of one exile.

Polish UB agents also seek to give the impression that nothing un-

usual is going on when they conduct arrests.† According to our
sources, much like the Czechs, they most often arrive early in the
morning, during the postbreakfast period of the day. Romanian Securitate procedures have also begun to conform to this "polite" style
of arrest. Like the Russians with their "neutral-persons" rule (see
Chapter Six), the Romanian agents have felt compelled to observe
certain amenities, whether out of concern regarding public pressure,
a sincere desire within the agents' ranks to reform, or an unswerving
sense of duty in terms of following orders from the Moscow KGB.
Until several years ago, in Romania, you were liable to be arrested
any time of the day or night by the Securitate. But the practice has
been refined, so that now agents are required to search and/or arrest
you at your home between the hours of six in the morning and eight
at night. "The law is sometimes violated," says one exile, "but not
very often." And similarly, Yugoslavian agents still show up at their
targets' homes oftentimes without prior warnings and without arrest
warrants; but UDBA agents often appear to be under strict orders to
present themselves in a polite and seemingly friendly mood.

If one were searching for an overall trend in the style of the political-police arrest of the past decade, one might say that many secret
police styles of arrest proved to be less secretive and more polished
than one might have expected. But "light touch" arrest procedures
may have more to do with successful repression than with sincere
ambitions on the part of various secret police forces to reform. A secret police organization that has been in control of a society,
repressing and sharply curtailing the activities of many of its
members, has all but eliminated any organized opposition and can
therefore afford to go easy on its targets. Chile's DINA, for example,
was such a thorough and brutal tool used to control the population
in the years immediately following the coup that its successor—CNI
—indulges in far more selective, rather than massive, repression in
Chile today. DINA did the job well. Conversely, the secret police
force that acts no more sophisticatedly than the semitrained goon
squad probably has a long way to go before achieving DINA's goal.

The felicitous improvements in secret police procedures of arrest,
surveillance, etc., do not always indicate that the secret police are
weakening in the face of markedly growing opposition and have

† Although the name of the Polish secret police has been changed (see
Chapter Three), it is still commonly referred to as UB, for Security Bureau.

been forced to tone down their activities, so to speak (as in the case of SAVAK, which in its final days was forced to curb the extent of torture administered to political prisoners), but that they have succeeded in their long-range goals and so can afford to maintain a quieter, less menacing style. Accordingly, the KGB does not apply systematic physical torture to political dissidents (this observation is not meant to detract from the inherent brutality of a system of special psychiatric hospitals for dissidents). It doesn't have to. The public has been sufficiently intimidated to respond, in the way that the regime desires, to a more courteous KGB style of arrest and interrogation. Following this logic, in Cuba during the sixties—times of deep turmoil, when the revolution had not yet settled down—G-2 arrests were customarily conducted late at night. But Cuba's G-2 agents today tend to be quite open and considerably cooler in style. Recent exiles report that when agents approach a house to surround it, they keep their revolvers hidden unless they feel absolutely compelled to display them. Indeed, it is not uncommon for a group of agents to stand in front of the house as if they were doing nothing more than talking to one another, planning an evening out on the town. (The technique is a quite common plainclothes-police technique, as the incident recounted about the South African Security Branch in Chapter One suggests—and for the obvious reason: the goal is to present an appearance of normalcy to neighbors and passersby.) Once the house is surrounded, explained one Cuban exile who was arrested by G-2 in the late seventies, a pair of agents will knock on the door—and only then will they draw their guns. Once inside, she told us, "they act as if it is their house." Or, perhaps more accurately, according to a second Cuban exile, who corrected her friend: "Once they enter your house, it *is* their house."

Despite the general tendency to observe some amenities, certain aspects of the secret police arrest remain contingent on a wide variety of features peculiar to each particular country. In Israel, the style of arrest may depend on where it is made. That is, different procedures apply for the West Bank and the Occupied Territories than for Israel proper. Plainclothes officers from Shin Bet (in the company of LATAM agents) in Israel proper will only *observe* an arrest being made by a LATAM officer (LATAM, for Emergency Service and Special Duties, is a unit of the Israeli police); the Shin Bet agent won't get involved publicly, so to speak, unless the arrest occurs in an area of the West Bank or the Occupied Territories, where the agents' need to maintain a low profile is less acute.

Generally speaking, the more professional the secret police operation may be throughout its entire organizational structure, the smoother the arrest it tends to conduct. Perhaps as an aid to comprehending the admiration of the former CIA deputy director (and that of the KGB as well) for the East German "deft touch," we recount an arrest that took place in Afghanistan in the late seventies.

By the time of this arrest, the Afghan security police had been trained, if not staffed, by East German security officials. The story involves a Kabul political figure whom authorities believed needed to be removed as quickly and quietly as possible. And so the Afghan official was picked up at his home by a courtesy limousine provided by his boss. The boss had called ahead and told this middle-level official that an emergency meeting had been called. The limo drove up, the official stepped in, the doors of the limousine were locked, and the chauffeur drove him directly to the Pule Charkhi political prison.

11

An arrest will be highly visible and obvious if the regime wishes to make an example of the arrest as a method of suppressing and intimidating the populace (the same may be said for surveillance procedures, as discussed in Chapter Six).

In Argentina, one branch of the secret police conducts arrests in full daylight and in full view of the neighbors. And Argentine security authorities are not always discriminating with regard to whom they arrest. As a lawyer who investigated the human-rights situation in Argentina as part of a 1979 U.S. fact-finding commission put it, "The Argentine authorities figure if they arrest ten and one gives information, the odds are good enough."

In Uruguay during the early seventies, some agents seem to have gone out of their way to conduct their arrests in frightening and obviously intimidating ways. The young Juan Ferreira, son of the well-known presidential candidate of the liberal opposition Partido Nacional‡ was forced to walk out of a late-night meeting with other officials of his father's party, with their arms held up over their

‡ Partido Nacional is the formal name of this political party also known popularly as "Partido Blanco."

heads, after being commanded to do so by a voice over a loud-speaker. It was two-thirty in the morning, and the jeeps and un-marked cars of the agents had blocked all the exits. The agents wore sweaters that stretched up over their shoulders and clear across their faces, with only their eyes showing. And with that eerie sight before them, Ferreira and numerous associates were interrogated by teams of agents throughout what remained of the night and through the next day—a full twenty-four hour ordeal. For almost the entire du-ration of the interrogation period, they were kept standing in the street with their hands over their heads. At one point, an agent searched Ferreira's car and pulled out a sweater. The sweater was only half knitted, but it was a gift that his mother was working on for him. The agents questioned him about the sweater. It seemed a ludicrous and irrelevant question at the time, but he told them whom it was for and who was knitting it. "So, this is what your mother did," one agent said. "Well, this is what we do," and he pro-ceeded to disassemble the sweater yarn by yarn before Ferreira's eyes.

Matters went farther downhill after that. The agents grew increas-ingly angry and violent as the night progressed, kicking the head-lights out of Ferreira's car and indulging in emotional tirades of ac-cusation: the car was stolen, he was a violent revolutionary, his father did not speak out against violence. . . . No one who hap-pened to live nearby could *not* have understood what was happen-ing; the agents did nothing to hide it. But nobody in the area did anything to intervene. After twenty-four hours of intense interro-gation in the middle of the street, the agents got into their fleet of cars and jeeps and drove off, leaving behind them a demoralized Partido Blanco and possibly a terrorized neighborhood as well.

In one rural province of the Philippines, one police agent alone managed to terrorize whole villages. He had the style of a character actor in a horror show. His arrests occurred at three or four in the morning, and he arrived at the scene by announcing his name proudly in a booming, ominous voice. He was known throughout the province as a torturer, and he carried sidearms, wore a mask, and had a large, bulky build.

One night the voice boomed: "We want to borrow the girl." This 1978 arrest occurred on a hot summer night in the province of Ne-gros Occidental. "But I am warning you not to report this to the au-thorities, the people or the priests," he told the girl and her family.

"Because I know you are close to the priests. We shall take her and within two days you will know where she is. Do not tell anyone."

But the agent did not live up to his word. After trying unsuccessfully for days to learn the girl's whereabouts, her sister worked up the courage to appear at the police station at which the notorious agent was stationed. But he played it cool and simply told her that he didn't know anything about the case. She persisted: "But I recognize you. I know you have her because the one who picked her up looks so much like you."

"No," he responded. "You can't depend on faces, because many people have the same appearance."

The girl, an active catechist in the parish, devoted to "building people's awareness within the context of the basic Christian Communities program of the Church," as one exile group describes the organization, was held for several weeks. When she was discharged from a provincial hospital (she was transferred there because, as one colonel put it, "the girl is in the care of our psychiatrist, [who] needs at least two days to complete the tests to determine the girl's sanity"), her discharge record contained a diagnosis of an "acute psychotic reaction."

Such flamboyant behavior is often the luxury of being away from the cities; in most close-quartered urban environments, agents necessarily prefer anonymity over notoriety. In Mexico, most security agents from the Brigada Blanca and from other federal and state police agencies wear plain clothes, drive cars without license plates or other identification, and produce no official documentation, despite the requirements of Article 16 of the Mexican Constitution.*

Chilean DINA agents conducted their arrests wearing plain clothes, without producing identification, and without official Interior Ministry confirmation of the arrests they made. Suspects were taken away in unmarked DINA cars while hooded, blindfolded, or with Scotch tape covering their eyes. The DINA agents' passion for anonymity was complete, as well as thoroughly institutionalized. Most DINA agents were not known by their real names. Most, if not all, officers in the command at "Terranova"—the code name for the DINA operations and torture center otherwise known as Villa

---

* Article 16 of the Mexican Constitution states that "No one shall be molested in his person, family, domicile, papers or possessions, except by virtue of a written order of the competent authority setting forth and justifying the legal cause of the proceeding."

Grimaldi—addressed one another only with first names, never using last names. And victims of interrogations conducted at Terranova were never convinced that these first names were the agents' real names. They probably weren't. Upon admission to the secret police force, the new DINA recruit was provided with a new (and false) identity card as well as false identification papers; and he was instructed to break all previous social ties—except for those with his immediate family. He was further instructed to move the family to a new neighborhood after enlistment, and if, within a family, there was someone whom DINA officials believed that they could not trust, the agent was forbidden contact with that person. Finally, male agents were required to inform their supervisors of new contacts they had with any female, who was instantly suspect as an enemy agent. This remaking of the DINA agent's identity was so complete that the information on the new identification papers was transferred onto all personal documents—and put into government files. Except for DINA itself, no government agency knew the agent's *real* identity.

The passion for anonymity on the part of DINA extended to the formation of arrest teams. According to the testimony of one ex-DINA employee, the DINA agent was not always informed of the exact identity of the arrestee. "It is true," he said in a deposition published by the United Nations Economic and Social Council in 1980, "that I belonged to CNI [the new name of the Chilean secret police] and was previously on the force of the former Directorate of National Intelligence and Information DINA. . . . I remember having taken part in an operation which occurred in the city of Viña del Mar on 21 January 1975. I remember that on the morning of that day I received at headquarters an order to proceed in a unit vehicle to Viña del Mar, in order to effect the arrest of certain persons, members of a cell of the proscribed MIR [Movement of the Revolutionary Left] which was active at that time. . . . I received that order at headquarters and was given a photograph of the individual concerned. . . . When this person was arrested, I did not know his name; I knew only that he was a member of MIR. I should mention that all members of those MIR groups used three or four aliases, so it is difficult to know their true identity.

"I travelled in a van and I remember that it was a white Chevrolet C-10 with a canvas top. Three other officers accompanied me and I think their names were José, Mario and Juan. The leader of the group and the person who gave us our instructions and was in charge of the operation was Mario. . . . I must say that I do not know the full names of these people, nor can I say [that] the Christian names by which I knew them were in fact their real names. I had not seen these people beforehand and I think that this group worked together only on this operation. Nor have I seen them since. I should point out that, because of the nature of security work, the members of the groups formed to carry out a specific operation are selected at random among the people available and assumed names are given for each mission. In this case, I think that the agents who were assigned came from other DINA divisions since, as I said, I do not know their true identities and ranks."

This ad hoc arrest team found its target down the street near the central market of the town.

"Mario knew that the MIR person had to make contact with another member of his cell at that time and in that place; I think that this fact was known as a result of a confession by another of the members of the MIR cell who must have been arrested before this . . . [but] I was not given any particulars."

The arrest went smoothly; they took the leftist into custody.

"Later, after lunch, we went to the home of the wife of the detainee . . . and we took her also, without any problem. . . . I do not know what happened to the detainees subsequently. . . . When we got back to Santiago, the group broke up and I have not seen any of them since, and so I suppose that each returned to the division he came from. . . ."

12

Like many transactions in life, the nature of the secret police encounter depends to no small extent on who you are.

The absolute nobodies of the world tend to receive the worst of everything: arrest by the crudest agents, with little or no observance of amenities of any kind. By comparison, the *somebodies* of the world—even the most vocal and ardent opponents of a regime, whether they be lawyers, doctors, historians, professors, etc.—tend to benefit from what many exiles refer to as the "kid-gloves" treatment (analogous to the kid-gloves search; see Chapter Six) even during an arrest that will lead to detention.

The lawyer in charge of the defense department of the Chilean

Peace Committee in the seventies was a definite somebody. Educated, urbane, and highly professional, he helped shepherd the committee from a small organization of only eight members when he joined, in 1973, to an organization with a staff of 180 in the Santiago office alone, with another hundred or so members scattered throughout twenty-two provincial offices.

On the night of November 15, 1975, this Chief Legal Counsel to the Peace Committee, which worked to assist the tens of thousands whom DINA had imprisoned by that time, was reading in his home study in downtown Santiago when there was a knock at the door. He remembers that he knew at the time it had to be DINA, that it couldn't be anyone else calling after the curfew hour.

Nevertheless, the lawyer asked who was calling, from behind the still-closed door.

"The Dirección Nacional de Inteligencia," an agent answered in a clear, formal voice.

He opened the door. Five agents stood in the doorway with their hands poised on their guns, which, however, hung at their sides.

"Well, I'm sorry," one DINA agent began, "but it is your time."

The lawyer nodded, accepting the inevitable, hoping that at the very least this would be, as many Chileans would put it, a "Class-A [kid-glove] type arrest."

His mind raced through a series of semiconsoling thoughts: that they knew he was a person of prominence in the community, a well-known lawyer, a leader of the people; that they probably didn't want much from him; that they most likely just wanted to hold him, in order to keep the Peace Committee from accelerating its activities any more; and finally, that DINA was not really a business of sadism, pure and simple.

He remembers thinking: no one represses beyond the extent to which the agent or the secret police system feels it needs to go. He—lawyer, activist, leader—was quite open about what he was doing, and there was little that they could actually learn from him. They most likely wanted only to neutralize him as one of a vanguard of the opposition. Or so he hoped.

The DINA agents moved swiftly and quietly throughout the house, combing through files, shelves, books. The commanding officer, letting his subordinates do the work, was casual, even friendly. Looking around the house, he remarked, "What a nice place! You people at the Peace Committee sure earn a lot of money." The lawyer, trying not to cough on his words, explained that he had earned the money for the house as a defense attorney, and that his work on the Peace Committee was practically charity work.

When the search was completed, the officer in charge told the lawyer that it was time to go. "Can I bring a blanket?" he asked. The agent in charge said yes. "Could I go to the bathroom?" he also asked, to which the agent again said yes.

The lawyer then went into the bathroom, quickly opened the medicine cabinet and swallowed two tranquilizers. In case they interrogated him, he wanted to be as calmed down as he hoped these Valiums would make him.

It was when they were all inside the unmarked DINA car that he became aware that he wasn't going to be subjected to torture. He sat in the back seat, between two agents. Three other agents sat up front. As they all settled in, the lawyer took his glasses off. Surely they were going to hood him, as he knew was customary, and he didn't want the discomfort of the hood pressing against his glasses. Besides, with the hood, there wouldn't be a whole lot he'd be able to see. But when he took the glasses off and placed them in his lap, one of the young agents asked him just what he thought he was doing.

"Aren't you going to hood me?" he asked.

The agents seemed stunned, disturbed by his ready familiarity with the DINA routine.

"No, we are taking you to *Tres* Álamos," one of them snapped.

Tres Álamos was a lower-level scare: in the center of the complex was a separate detention center—the notorious *Cuatro* Álamos—administered solely by DINA agents and torturers—but the surrounding buildings of Tres Álamos constituted a common prison. The lawyer could assume that the agents did not hood him because this was intended to be a class-A arrest; he probably wouldn't be tortured, he probably wouldn't disappear into the hell of Cuatro Álamos, he probably would, sometime soon, be released, shoved on a plane going out of the country, and deported.

In the end, this was precisely the sequence of events. He was released on January 30, 1976, having spent the first eighteen days in the isolated misery of solitary confinement. But afterward he was allowed visits from friends and family twice a week, and although subjected to some treatments that were humiliating, he was not tortured.

On March 26, still out of prison, he learned of the existence of an official deportation order against him. He petitioned authorities for the right to prepare his own defense for his trial, and the deportation order was temporarily suspended. But the request only angered the government, which ordered his rearrest pursuant to the provisions of the state of siege. But he was not kept in jail long. On April 12, 1976, the prison gates opened up, and he was handed over to DINA agents at the front of the prison and whisked off to the airport.

Rough as this treatment may seem according to U.S. standards, it is quite common in a number of countries run by type-A secret police.

In the Philippines, Charito Planas was one of the more prominent leaders of LABAN (the opposition political party to which Romy Capulong also belonged). An avowed rival of Imelda Marcos, she once ran against the First Lady for a seat in the Interim National Assembly.

It was therefore only a matter of time when they came for her, but her arrest was handled well. She was, after all, from a very wealthy and prominent Philippine family. The sister of Carmen Planas, a Filipino pioneer for woman's suffrage as far back as 1937, she was a well-known community leader with plenty of contacts. The director of thirty or forty varied human-rights organizations, she was involved in everything from the Red Cross to the Girl Scouts. And she was a prominent, well-educated attorney.

The Philippine security network seems to keep things of this order in mind when planning their arrests. And so, Charito's first arrest began almost politely.

It occurred one day in 1972, just after martial law was declared. She had gone to a meeting of the National Press Club, hoping to run into an activist priest whom she had been told was likely to attend. Suddenly, a man dressed in civilian clothing whom she vaguely thought she recognized made his way toward her through the crowd. As he slowly approached her, he addressed her in a polite, almost deferential, tone of voice.

"Sister," he began, "when I saw your name as one of those to be arrested, I volunteered to do it."

The reason he had done so, he told her, was because he considered her arrest inevitable. He liked her, he said, and hoped that by conducting the arrest himself he would save her from any rough handling that overzealous agents who didn't know her would be inclined to use. It was then, when he informed her that he was a major in ISAFP, the Intelligence Service of the Armed Forces, that she realized why he looked so familiar (after all, she was by profession a lawyer and by dedication a human-rights activist who made it a practice to keep abreast of who's who among the security and military leaders of the Philippines).

The ISAFP major then escorted Charito Planas to a car and drove her to several places—the Immigration Office, the airport, among others—where he picked up other dissidents and put them in the car with her. As they rode around in search of his various targets, she took the opportunity to discuss martial law with him. "As an army man, I can only follow orders," he answered. "I would not arrest you if I had the discretion."

He did, apparently, have discretion—for Charito Planas was not tortured during the entire arrest process. But, she says emphatically today, she was one of the lucky ones. Not everyone benefited from this type of first-class treatment.

THREE

From SAVAK to SAVAMA:
The Universality of the Secret Police

1

Two seemingly contradictory propositions about internal security organizations (a/k/a secret police) tend to be true. One is that no two secret police organizations are exactly alike. The other is that no one secret police organization is altogether unique.

In this chapter, we examine aspects of secret police behavior in the following countries: Argentina, Brazil, Chile, Cuba, Czechoslovakia, Egypt, Haiti, Iran, Italy, Jordan, Mexico, the Philippines, Poland, Romania, South Africa, South Korea, Syria, the U.S.S.R., and Yugoslavia.

Unquestionably, each one of these secret police forces has its own unique features, reflecting (1) its particular political mission, (2) its time and place in the society's history, and (3) unique or distinctive cultural features of the society within which it operates.

Despite all these differences, secret police organizations do not vary from society to society so greatly as to make them individually incomparable. On the contrary, to examine the secret police of recent times is to be struck not by the differences among these internal security organizations but by their similarities.

They tend to look alike, operate in surprisingly similar ways, cooperate with each other to a great degree, and cause the regime (whether communist or capitalist, Third World or heavily industrialized) strikingly similar problems.

In order to gain a clearer understanding of the contemporary secret police phenomenon, we have distilled some observations about the secret police organizations of several dozen countries, selecting, in essence, the better known and in many instances more infamous organizations.

It is clear that internal security organizations tend to be more alike—even across vast expanses of geography and cultural variation—than different. To illustrate the point, we offer a series of propositions about the secret police—some more important than others, but all underlining their universality, and their universal features.

2

Whatever the formal system of law or set of governmental guidelines under which they are asked to operate, secret police inevitably arrogate to themselves astonishing powers and almost unchecked discretion to investigate, arrest and detain.

In a recent case involving the plight of Haitian refugees in the United States, the presiding judge offered the following succinct appraisal of the mightiness of the security forces operating within Haiti: "The system of justice in Haiti allows the Duvalier security forces to be all-powerful. It is their decision who should be punished, for what offense, and how the punishment should be carried out. They may act on orders, or on arbitrary whim. But their actions are conclusive. There is no law in Haiti, there is only the forces of Duvalier."

While in its stages of formation the Tonton Macoutes were little more than a rough, unofficial band of thugs known as *cagoulards,**

* *Cagoulards* were hooded men who sometimes presented themselves as nothing more than private ruffians, rather than as functionaries of the government; they were alleged to have beaten and killed many Haitians at night and to have destroyed many shops and homes as well.

the Macoutes soon evolved into something far more pervasive than that. The evolutionary process of a secret police organization can be swift and sudden.

The parent of the famous and pervasive Chilean secret police known as DINA also had fairly meager, if not modest, beginnings. In the early seventies, when Allende was still in power, SIFA—Air Force Intelligence—was originally made up of a staff of only seven or eight persons outfitted with poor, limited equipment. But SIFA expanded almost overnight; while for some time SIFA customarily made use of some air bases for purposes of detaining, questioning, and torturing suspects, it eventually came to possess a whole network of rented and purchased safe houses (private homes, mostly, that were used for the same torture/interrogation purposes—part of a system that DINA was later to emulate). Furthermore, SIFA's entire ambition seemed to expand with its facilities. In the early seventies, SIFA at its outset focused its attentions largely on determining the loyalties of its own employees by measuring their opposition to the Allende regime. But, by late 1974—with Allende dead, replaced by President Pinochet—SIFA had gone wild, focusing its energies on anyone and everyone who could possibly be conceived of as connected with the revolutionary left-wing group called the Movement of the Revolutionary Left (MIR)—indeed, leftists and even liberals of all persuasions were pursued, though the emphasis remained upon vigilance toward its own Air Force personnel; SIFA's paranoia became so pervasive that even spouses and children of Air Force officers who announced themselves opposed to the coup against Allende in 1973 were not spared persecution.

After the junta settled into power, SIFA's counterintelligence capabilities, which in the ordinary definition of "counterintelligence" should have been focused on foreign spies, was unleashed on any friend (past or present), ally, or even mild sympathizer of the ousted Allende regime. And the rationale for this change of focus was simple enough: those who had sympathized with Allende were simply reclassified from "citizens" to "spies." By way of changing the definition of what constituted a spy, SIFA changed and expanded its franchise. "The officers of the Air Force Academy who made up SIFA," said one former SIFA officer who bolted SIFA after the coup, "had to observe only one rule—their own. Congress had been destroyed, the Justice Department had lost its power, to the point where it was handling at this time only such issues as alimonies and separations. The aggressive attitude among officers developed: 'Let's go out and get them [the MIR].' Everyone was after the MIR," as the former SIFA officer put it.

It is instructive to compare the almost unnoticed growth of SIFA to the way in which SAVAK grew to possess its extensive powers in Iran. To simplify matters somewhat, the articles of Iran's government that put SAVAK into motion simply had the effect of permitting SAVAK to define that which was illegal and then to proceed more or less at will—and with considerable room for maneuver. In essence, this secret police force was from the outset enfranchised with both judicial and executive powers.†

SAVAK's considerable powers were virtually predetermined—not simply by the characteristic proclivity of secret police agents to bend the rules as necessary but by the very rules that at the outset established the franchise of the secret police.

But SAVAK might have been able to develop its comprehensive powers even without the formality of this astonishingly broad incorporating charter. A secret police force, as much as any other government bureaucracy, will tend to reach and extend its grasp, even

† Excerpted, the articles that incorporated SAVAK in 1957 read as follows:

Article 1. For the purpose of the security of the country and prevention of any kind of conspiracy detrimental to the public interest, an organization under the name and style of "National Information and Security Organization," affiliated with the Prime Minister's office, shall be established. The Chief of the Organization shall hold the rank of Assistant to the Prime Minister and shall be appointed by a Decree of his Imperial Majesty the Shahanshah.

Article 2. The functions of the National Information and Security Organization are as follows:

a. Obtaining and collecting items of information required for the maintenance of national security.

b. Pursuing the activities which constitute a portion of espionage and the acts of such elements conducted against the independence or integrity of the country or those who act in favor of an alien;

c. Repressing the activities of those groups whose establishment or management has been or will be declared as illegal; likewise, preventing the formation of the groups whose aim or policy is against the Constitution.

d. Foiling conspiracies and plots against national security. . . . Security Organization shall, from the standpoint of prosecuting the crimes mentioned in this Act as well as discharging their functions, be considered as the *military magistrates* and in this respect shall enjoy all the authorities extended to the military magistrates and assume the responsibilities of such office [authors' emphasis] . . .

in as controlled a political environment as that of a Communist country. We interviewed a high adviser to the Cabinet of former Czechoslovakian President Alexander Dubček on this point. The former adviser holds the view that even an all-powerful Communist Party can do only so much to keep the secret police on a tight leash.

Commenting on the Czechoslovakian secret police of both the pre- and the post-Dubček eras (known prior to Dubček's time as StB)‡ (Státní Bezpečnost, meaning State Security), the former adviser said, "The main principles of the StB are formulated by the Party and the government." But while agreeing that the Communist Party sets the overall ideology of the secret police, perhaps even guiding the police as regards philosophy and policy formation, he argues that even the Party, the omnipotent authority of any genuine Communist state, cannot possibly know all that much about how secret police agents go about their business on a day-to-day basis. True, he agrees, the Internal Security Division of the Central Committee of the Communist Party does exert its influence upon the secret police by (1) holding weekly briefings with the heads of various sections of the StB, (2) giving instructions on individual cases of major import, and (3) reviewing prospective personnel and new recruits of the secret police. But in their more routine, daily functionings, secret police agents go largely unsupervised. "In Czechoslovakia as in other socialist states," the former adviser explains, "the StB is a state within a state."

A bitter observation made by Frolik buttresses the former adviser's point: "State security is the most powerful and most influential in the land. . . . It is the power which is ready and able to remove anyone inconvenient, and for the sake of its own narrow interests and its firm ties with the KGB, it is ready to betray the interests of its own country, which it has the duty to protect." This defector may be carrying his analysis a bit too far, but it is obvious that if a government is not careful, it may have a genuine secret police monster on its hands.

The exact powers of a secret police force—and its place in society —are not usually discussed in front of the public, but in South Africa, which for all its authoritarianism retains a parliamentary sys-

‡ According to Frolik, the name of the internal security unit has been changed to FSZS (see page 115), although it is still popularly referred to as StB.

tem that occasionally affords freewheeling discussion, precisely such a discussion once took place.

The occasion for the exchange was the culmination of a great deal of very worried debate in Parliament and in the press, in the early seventies, with regard to the Bureau for State Security (BOSS), the new South African superagency of the entire intelligence structure. What exactly was it? Who really controlled it?

In response to a nascent apprehension in influential liberal circles of South Africa, the government appointed a special commission of inquiry headed by a Supreme Court judge named Potgieter. The commission's task was to study BOSS and to recommend any changes in its structure, organization, and supervision.

The hastily arranged formation of the commission came on the heels of violent, widespread raids by security police in the fall of 1971. In addition, a great deal of publicity surrounded the circumstances of the death of an Indian schoolteacher who, said security police, had "committed suicide" by jumping from the tenth floor of police headquarters at John Vorster Square, in Johannesburg.

Mr. Michael Mitchell, a member of the South African Parliament, questioned publicly how such a "suicide" could have happened while security officers were present in the very room. At the time, Mr. Mitchell was the opposition United Party's "shadow" Minister of Justice.

Harsh questions were also raised by Mr. Colin Eglin, the leader of the Progressive Party, who voiced the growing worry in South Africa that the security police, in the words of a report that appeared in the London *Observer,* had become "a law unto themselves," answerable not even to the Cabinet for their actions.

When the blue-ribbon Potgieter Commission finally issued its report, there was considerable doubt as to exactly what the commission's recommendation would do. The commission recommended both new powers for the security forces—and new curbs, calling for a new State Security Council to sit over both the Bureau for State Security and the Security Police, as if to make the point that this new reorganization would ensure civilian control over the country's massive secret police network.

The initial reaction in South Africa to the recommendations was surely what the authorities had hoped for. A professor of law at the University of Witwatersrand was on board. "It indicates a degree of open-mindedness on the government's part," he said. "It also shows that protest can bear fruit. The announcement must be very heartening for those who have spoken out against the BOSS Act, particularly the branches of the legal fraternity." Another law professor confined his criticism to the point that the commission was appointed "so late in the day [that] irreparable harm had been done to the image of the administration of justice in South Africa."

But soon doubts began to emerge. How could BOSS and the security police be prevented from "becoming too powerful" by the mere establishment of an overseer: a State Security Council consisting of the Ministers of Defense, Police, Foreign Affairs, Justice, and others?

Some said it couldn't be done this way. "It seems ironic," commented the liberal *Rand Daily Mail,* "that a commission that was appointed to allay public anxieties that the powers of BOSS were too sweeping should in the end recommend that those powers be extended."

But Prime Minister Vorster couldn't have been more pleased by the Commission's work. In a 1971 debate in Parliament, he explained that, contrary to the view of some alarmist critics, the Security Council made sure that BOSS "is not a super government department which had been instituted over other government departments. . . ." General Van den Bergh, the new head of the security system, certainly had no difficulty accepting the recommendations of the report, which "recommends that I do much more than I am doing at the present time." As he put it, "I think it is an excellent report."

General Van den Bergh sought to defuse alarums by describing the division of powers between BOSS and the security police, as recommended by the Commission. But it is important to read the words of his explanation carefully, as he seeks to elucidate what certainly seems like a labored distinction without a difference: "I want to make it very clear that the Bureau for State Security and the South African police are two completely independent State departments. Although—in the nature of things—they cooperate with each other, the one does not have any say in the affairs of the other. The police are an executive body, and one of their functions is to maintain internal security—in other words, they act against people and organizations which threaten the security of the State. To enable them to carry out this task effectively, the police are equipped with the necessary executive powers; they can carry out searches—and so on. On the other hand, the Bureau for State Security is by no means an executive department and members of the Bureau have no executive powers whatsoever. They cannot arrest people, detain them or question them. It's the Bureau's responsibility to investigate all matters affecting the security of the State, and this information is then correlated and assessed with a view to informing and advising the government, interested State departments, and other bodies, when this is necessary."

But, in fact, the considerable achievement of the Potgieter Report (of the Commission of Inquiry into Matters Relating to the Security of the State, 1971) was not to trim the security police down to size, but to lay legal and philosophical foundations for the transformation of the BOSS / security-police network into one of the most powerful secret police organizations in the world. To be sure, BOSS itself was established formally in 1969 by a parliamentary bill introduced by the Minister of the Interior. But the careful bifurcation of the South African secret police network—into the BOSS brain and the security-police body—was not completed until the triumph of the Potgieter Commission.

"I am saying that 'coordination' is the key word on which the greatest emphasis must be placed," said the South African Minister of the Interior defensively in 1969. Thus, on the pretext of allaying public fears that the secret police were becoming too powerful, the Potgieter Commission created a newly coordinated secret police network that could not help but become even more powerful than it had been.

From today's perspective, in fact, the State Security Council appears to have developed into a kind of super "inner cabinet," notwithstanding the Council's relative disuse under the previous Vorster government. Created by the Security Intelligence and State Security Act of 1972, the Council met fewer than half a dozen times during Prime Minister Vorster's tenure. But, under Prime Minister Botha, the Security Council has met an average of once a fortnight. It has become the senior of five cabinet committees; it includes the chairmen of the four other committees; and other officials on the Security Council include the head of the national intelligence service (formerly BOSS—a name change discussed later in this chapter) and the Minister of Police. It is reliably believed that the Security Council now usurps the authority of the full Cabinet. Ministers and deputy ministers who are *not* members of the Security Council can attend sessions of any cabinet committee that they want—with the exception of the Security Council. In conclusion, it would appear that the Security Council under Vorster was designed to give the appearance of control of, and limitations imposed on, the secret police network; but it met so infrequently as to raise profound questions about its effectiveness. Now, under Vorster's successor, the secret police network enjoys even more unfettered power, as the Security Council outranks all other committees representing those constituencies which otherwise might have been able to trim the sails of the secret police network. What was originally advertised as a method of limitation evolved, under this "security management system," into a method of expansion.

Few debates on the nature of police power could have had so ironic (if not unexpected) a result. Indeed, in few societies are such issues even remotely debated; in many, such matters are not considered a proper subject for public discussion. In South Africa, the structure and operating rules, which were thoroughly discussed in public as well as official circles, helped create a clear and well-thought-out system. Consequently, it is not a particularly covert one.

To a considerable extent, clarity and secrecy are probably incompatible. In Mexico, for example, in return for a lack of clarity, the government benefits from a great deal of secrecy (perhaps more than it actually wants).

Mexico is not normally thought to maintain an extensive secret police structure, but it appears that Mexico has an overall intelligence organization somewhat like BOSS—even if it is not nearly as well organized. A central directorate gathers information on political dissidents, union organizers, potential strikes and strikers, and so on.

But probably no internal security system is quite so confused as Mexico's. Today in Mexico, as traditionally in the past, small private armies flourish in the countryside and even in some big cities. And then there are varieties of federal police in Mexico: political police organized and trained to do political surveillance and interrogation (dependent upon and answerable to the Ministry of the Interior); federal police, which coordinate with the Interior Ministry and which have been accused of systematically torturing drug traffickers; the Mexican Secret Service, which is concerned with both political and common criminal cases; and perhaps even political police, who some sources say work for the ruling Mexican political party, although the party of course denies this. Add to this fifty-seven or more police forces throughout the states of Mexico (every governor has two or three state police forces under his control) and the pattern is one of tremendous confusion.

But "there is no sense of a DINA in Mexico," says one United States law professor who has studied the situation carefully—that is, there is no single, all-powerful police structure known to both the public and the government as the antisubversive secret police. Instead, in an incoherent but thoroughly clandestine manner, the Ministry of the Interior appears to exert some measure of control over a number of secret-police-style units that do precisely the sort of "dirty work" formally assigned to the security police in South Africa. While the Interior Ministry directorate is active to some extent in this area, there is another organization which the government of Mexico does not even admit exists—and which may enjoy a near monopoly of control over political dissidents.

This organization is a death squad known as the Brigada Blanca (White Brigade; a death squad, in the usual definition of the term, is a unit of police, military, and/or security personnel acting in a highly clandestine, anonymous, and unofficial manner—although sometimes with express approval of the government—which disposes of political and sometimes criminal targets by assassination). But the government adopts a sort of "ostrich policy" toward the Brigada Blanca, therefore escaping direct responsibility for the hundreds of dead bodies of political leftists found every year in Mexico—all with notes pinned to the bodies claiming that the deaths were in fact the handiwork of the Brigada Blanca.

The secret police in Mexico operate on a totally unofficial basis. It is therefore possible to determine which police organization is doing what at any one time in Mexico only by the very nature of the action itself. To illustrate: if the government has no formal, legal basis by which to proceed against a target, illegal acts of repression may be used. This is the extralegal option: the involvement of one of the small, private armies (often called death squads) such as the Brigada Blanca.

The Brigada Blanca is an unofficial organization whose members are in fact recruited from the high levels of the traditional, official police organizations within the country. The co-optation of informers, and the administration of the political informants network, are also primarily left to the Brigada Blanca, since the existence of an informant network as a tool of political repression is, again, not officially recognized by the government.

It is a peculiar paradox in Mexico that while practically everyone knows that the Brigada Blanca exists, the government insists that it is ignorant of the organization. While everyone knows what is in fact going on, the government keeps up a pretext of concern for legality. "It is a sort of yes-and-no maneuvering of the Mexican people which this subtle approach represents," says a well-informed source. "To scare them into knowing it exists, but not taking the responsibility for its actions. It is a clever maneuvering of the public consciousness."

The great plus, from the government's perspective, is its lack of accountability for the system. But every system has its costs as well. If in South Africa the system is not subtle but is in fact well organized and relatively coherent, in Mexico the price of subtlety is that the government cannot always control the system it permits to exist. Although the general direction to all political activity is given by the Ministry of the Interior, by the very nature of the government's denial of reality, the system has the built-in tendency to go off on its own, like an unguided missile. Add to this the presence of so many overlapping police groups in Mexico (in the context of Mexico's complicated political structure) and its long history of private armies, which is exactly what today's Brigada Blanca resembles, and you have a formula, if not for chaos, then surely for a great deal of uncertainty.

It is possible, then, that having created this remarkable system, the federal government could not bring it to heel except after a major crackdown campaign. But that campaign would have to be predicated on a resolve to eliminate all illegal police action against political dissidents. The government apparently has no such resolve, and the system, loose as it is, continues to function in its rambling, terrifying way.

In an important respect, the AAA (otherwise known as Triple A, for Argentine Anticommunist Alliance)* in Argentina, is similar to the Brigada Blanca.

Although even respected groups such as Amnesty International agree that there is no conclusive evidence to suggest that there is a

* Some sources contend that AAA is a blanket name to apply to a variety of rightist terror squads operating in Argentina. Whether or not this is so, we do know that the AAA operated under the aegis of the Isabel Perón regime (the regime overthrown by the military coup of General Videla) and was actually organized under the direction of José López Rega, Isabel Perón's closest military adviser.

direct connection between Triple A and the regular police and military, several circumstances suggest at least official tolerance of its activities. Operating at times in broad daylight with no interference by public authorities, the Triple A conducts arrests and brutal interrogations. The disappearances and arrests are not investigated, the crimes are never solved, and everyone agrees that it is a sheer "coincidence" that the vehicles used by the Triple A just happen to match up exactly with vehicles of the same make and type used by the official police and military. And so, for example, when the Federal Police, tipped off by an eyewitness neighbor, once arrived at the scene of an abduction of a man and his wife by a small private army like the Triple A—a group of men who identified themselves to the Federal Police as members of the Combined Forces of the Army, Navy, and Air Force—the police offered no resistance and let them take the couple away. Unlike DINA or BOSS and the South African security police (secret police organizations that were created into official agencies by government statute), the Triple A and other small Argentinian private forces are—according to the government—totally unofficial, illegal, and illustrative of at most the "fanatical" tendencies of a few "scattered" policemen.

Brazil's death squads have also attracted growing attention. After Rio Police Chief Aladir Braga announced the formation of a military police team to help "track down" the so-called death squads allegedly permeating his country, he offered this analysis of the situation: "If White Hand [the self-nicknamed telephone caller who identified himself to police as the public-relations agent of all of the country's death squads] really exists, I appeal to him not to kill these people but to turn them over to us. . . . If this continues there will be chaos and the killed are just the same as the bandits. . . ." But, Police Chief Braga added, he believed that "this supposed White Hand does not really exist." We believe it does.†

† The death squads, while most prevalent in Latin America, can be found in other areas of the world also. In South Africa, an underground white vigilante group that calls itself Die Wit Kommando (for The White Commando) has become involved in a number of activities resembling those of the Brigada Blanca, the Triple A, and the White Hand. For example, the White Commando claimed responsibility for the recent bombing of the office of Jan Lombard, a University of Pretoria professor. The reason for the bombing? Lombard proposed using Natal, the predominantly English-speaking province of the country, as an "integration model" for the rest of the country. The proposal was well received by black and white moderates but was vetoed by the government.

The classic pattern of the growth of a secret police organization, however, is perhaps best illustrated by the South Korean example. In 1961, the KCIA was formed in order to combat subversion and infiltration by agents of the North Korean secret police. The threat was *real,* not imagined. But over time the original franchise of the KCIA was expanded by President Park. Instead of confining itself to detecting subversion from the North, the KCIA, with Park's approval, began hunting down South Koreans: opponents of the regime, even street protestors were marked for surveillance, intimidation, arrest, detention—and even torture.

A watershed incident occurred in the late sixties, when KCIA agents kidnapped almost two dozen students and professors in West Germany who allegedly were in contact with North Korean secret police agents working out of East Germany. With this kind of expansion of its franchise, the KCIA grew into a bureaucratic monster, expanding into eight major subdivisions (Internal Affairs, Overseas, the North, etc.). Before long, the KCIA was spying on South Korean embassies abroad, Koreans abroad, Seoul officials abroad—and funneling U.S. aid money back to U.S. politicians and journalists so that no one asked very many questions.

3

Secret police throughout the world arrogate to themselves such enormous power that the government must inevitably struggle to maintain the upper hand.

It is no easy task to threaten the control of the Communist Party. In ideological theory, the Party is supposed to operate from unchallenged hegemony. From cradle to grave, every Communist is taught to worship the Party. Only a secret police force would dare challenge the Party.

In Poland during the late sixties, a power struggle broke out between the Party and the Minister of Internal Affairs (in 1956, the name of the Polish secret police was changed from UB, meaning Security Bureau, to Ministry of Internal Affairs, although most

---

The White Commando has allegedly also made a habit of delivering threats to leading black South African churchmen over the telephone. As of this writing, there is no clear evidence linking the South African Government to the White Commando.

sources still refer to the Polish secret police as UB and consider it a separate entity from the Ministry).

It would appear as if the Minister of Internal Affairs embarked on a course of action that was destined to bring him into head-on conflict with high Party officials. Organizing a movement to gain support from the Party outside the Central Committee, in areas around the country and outside of the capital, he gained control of institutions like the Polish War Veterans and a number of newspapers that were ordinarily in the hands of the Party.‡

It became known as the campaign of General Moczar, the Minister of Internal Affairs and head of the secret police of Lódź, to achieve control of Poland. The struggle lasted several years, climaxing in 1968 with Moczar's dismissal from the Politburo. The Party was slow to respond, but when it reached the consensus that the secret police apparatus Moczar had built was more loyal to Moczar than to the Party, Moczar was purged. In the showdown, the First Secretary of the Communist Party won out over the Minister of Internal Affairs.

One would expect, of course, that in a truly communistic society, the Party should inevitably win in such a showdown. Communist society is simply more conditioned to venerate the Party than the secret police. What was astonishing was not that the Party won—but that the Party was even challenged.

Even after that decisive showdown, in the late sixties, while the conflict between the secret police and the Party has remained on the back burner, every so often it boiled up again.

In 1975, a member of the opposition movement in Poland was collecting signatures on a petition that was critical of the government. Just as he was leaving an apartment building in Warsaw, UB agents, with guns drawn, jumped out of two unmarked cars and arrested him. (This incident occurred before the Charter 77 movement,* when the Party was trying to maintain a diplomatic peace

‡ Sources say that a secondary issue in the struggle was a purge of Jews from the secret police system, in defiance of a number of high Party officials who themselves were Russian Jews; although the head of the secret police ultimately lost the struggle for supremacy, as the result of this conflict there are few, if any, Jews in the Polish secret police force today. Indeed, sources say this campaign caused most of the nation's thirty thousand Jews to emigrate.

* The proclamation of the charter that came to be known as the human-rights movement, Chapter 77 was released in January of 1977. It was a movement of Czechs, chiefly intellectuals, artists, and professionals, who demanded

with the opposition movement and hence to avoid unfavorable international publicity.)

The man the secret police had arrested was well known in literary and scholarly circles. On the morning following the arrest, a respected Polish poet went to the Central Committee of the Party to demand the dissident's release.

Within two hours, he was released: the Party instructed the secret police to release him. The Party's compelling argument, at the time, was that it was a mistake to arrest literary and university higher-ups, because such activities only induce a chain reaction in these circles, which have good access to international news media. For its part, the secret police argued that such activity is patently antistate and therefore ought to be treated like any other form of antistate activity. On this particular issue, the Party argument won out.†

A similar power struggle is played out in the U.S.S.R., whose KGB maintains such wide latitude that it inevitably creates friction with competing organs of government. In theory, the KGB reports to the Moscow Procuracy, an investigative-judicial arm that decides how, when, and if cases are to proceed through the investigatory and prosecutorial process. But theory and reality do not always coincide, for the KGB usually has ideas of its own.

Time magazine reported in 1980 that among the primary objectives of Yuri Andropov, chief of the KGB and member of the ruling Politburo, is to keep the KGB under firm Party control so that the secret police can never again wield the power it possessed under Stalin, when it arrested, tortured, and killed thousands of loyal Party officials.

That sort of extreme heavy-handedness would only make it more difficult for the state to control the secret police and to maintain po-

---

that their country observe and adhere to international and domestic law (with regard to human rights). Although only Czechs signed the charter, it of course had an impressive impact on other East European countries. The movement, headed by shifting spokespersons, is still going on.

† Some sources carry this analysis farther, arguing that when the Party and the police come into conflict, what you have is a conflict but no real contest, for the ultimate victor is necessarily the Party when major issues and policy decisions are involved. They say that the police contest the power of the Party successfully only when the matter involves an isolated and relatively unimportant case. In other words, you can determine the gravity of any dispute in the minds of Party officials simply by observing the outcome of that dispute. It seems doubtful that the matter is this simple.

litical control of the ethnic provinces, where resentment of Moscow's control is greatest. "The Party tries to run the KGB through centralized bureaucratic planning," John Barron, author of *Inside the KGB,* has written, "just as it does other Soviet institutions. Every spring, the KGB leadership, known as the Collegium, must prepare and present to the Politburo an overall operational plan for the forthcoming work year that begins July 1. This plan is based in part on proposals from foreign residents and chiefs of domestic divisions, who are required to stipulate their objectives for the coming year and to specify in detail exactly what the officers in their commands should do to help fulfill them. Once the master plan is ⁃ pproved in Moscow, it becomes binding and in effect saddles individual officers in the field with production quotas or norms."

And the KGB is now saddled with one other encumbrance. If the Politburo wishes to take one of its own out of the running for consideration for higher office, it will appoint the ambitious Politburo member to run the KGB. "No KGB head can become President or Chairman of the Party," explained one recent political defector (a well-situated member of the Moscow foreign-policy establishment). "Being made KGB head is the kiss of death for your political career. The Russian people just would never accept the head of the KGB becoming head of the Soviet Union."

One incident that took place in the mid-seventies amounts to an exception that proves this rule of Party supremacy over the secret police on all major concerns. According to a former procurator in the Leningrad office of the Soviet Procuracy, he was assigned to the strange case of a Frenchwoman studying at Moscow University who fell in love with a Moscow man devoted to his mathematical studies. The KGB knew of the affair, of course: agents had all foreigners at the university under constant surveillance.

But, at one point in this affair, events took a strange turn. The woman, surprisingly, reported to university police that the young mathematician had raped her. Not much later, the procurator was handed the rape case by the KGB.

His investigation was no more than a few days underway when a colonel and the Chief of the Foreign Department of the KGB came to his office to offer new information.

"This girl is an agent of the Israeli intelligence service," they told the procurator.

They also stated that the young man was involved in some sort of undetermined clandestine activities and that the Frenchwoman was trying to recruit him for the Israeli secret service. They showed the procurator their file, which included a report from an informer who was a neighbor of the young mathematician.

The report alleged that the mathematician had passed on to the young Frenchwoman secret security information. The KGB agents also gave the procurator a transcript of bugged conversations between the couple. "You must find something," the KGB agents told him.

But the procurator was suspicious of the KGB, and he felt the evidence was inadequate (not to mention illegal). He interviewed the mathematician. The young man denied that he had passed any information to the woman. And he also insisted that he had not raped her. The procurator was convinced that the young man had not raped her, that the couple were in love, and that the rape allegation stemmed from some sort of lovers' quarrel and nothing more.

The procurator was also worried. He felt that, for whatever reason, the young man was being set up. So he forwarded an official letter to the KGB telling them that there was simply no basis on which to proceed.

To say that the KGB was angered by the procurator's obstinance would be an understatement, because, within days, several officials appealed their case to the offices of the Moscow Procuracy—which is almost as high as one can go in the Soviet internal security system.

But the procurator had the complainants beat, even to the last turn. When the KGB agents arrived at the office of the headquarters with their stormy appeal, a letter from the procurator had already reached the Moscow office from the Leningrad office. The letter was thorough and unflinching. It stated clearly and incontestably that the KGB's case was flawed. Thus armed, the Moscow Procuracy told the KGB to forget it, that they were entitled to do nothing more. The mathematician was cleared of formal charges, but the Frenchwoman was asked to leave the country.

The procurator says today that it is possible to take on the KGB, but you have to be very sure of your ground, you have to have a lot of determination, and you have to have a case that either the KGB is not terribly concerned about or upon which the KGB has not staked a substantial amount of its prestige.

4

A secret police force tends to become so powerful that the government or sovereign usually feels it necessary to create a second, smaller, and utterly loyal secret police organization to watch over the larger one.

This maxim is not so much an ironclad rule, as the almost predictable consequence of the fact that an immensely powerful secret police force tends to make everybody nervous, including the sovereign or government elite that has created that organization.

In Haiti, when Papa Doc Duvalier came to power, in the late nineteen fifties, he created the Tonton Macoutes, and with a prescience that might belie the notion that Duvalier was anything other than a dictator who knew exactly what he was doing, he created at around the same time the SD—initials for Service Detectives. Though camouflaged within the overall security structure as part of a security-guard detail at the Presidential Palace, the SD is not to be confused, as some have done, with the Palace Guards, the army officers who protect the President's well-being.

Though the exact size of the SD is not known, it is believed to be an elite unit headed by two army colonels who report directly to President Duvalier. "It is a special body for the government to detect all political causes," testified one former Haitian army officer, but one of the SD's chief responsibilities—and probably its most important one—is to watch over all the other security forces operating within Haiti, including the Tonton Macoutes. The perspective opponents that this elite unit is concerned with, then, are often those potential dissidents *within the secret police network itself*.

Within the frequently overlapping security-police structures of the Philippines, the task of watching over the secret police falls to the National Intelligence Security Authority (NISA), an intelligence-gathering organization that is autonomous and independent of the military. (It has been accused of torturing suspected assassins and very high-up political opponents of Marcos.) While a number of clandestine and semiclandestine agencies work on political investigation and suppression, NISA, staffed by only the most loyal of the pro-Marcos loyalists, is the superunit that watches over the other intelligence and secret police services. For instance, NISA agents are planted within the many military intelligence units (called S-2s in the Philippines, G-2s in other countries), the second sections of the army battalions present in every town.

A long time after Egypt's President Nasser greatly expanded and strengthened his GI (for General Intelligence, the security service that under Nasser's rule maintained a very pervasive system of civilian intelligence), a few documented cases appeared that proved that some General Intelligence agents had infiltrated the military intelligence service of the country. According to some well-informed U. S. State Department officials, it is highly possible that many more cases of this type of infiltration occurred. As one source put it, for the GI to infiltrate the military was no more bizarre than for the German Gestapo to have infiltrated the German Army—a practice that was known at the time that it took place, although few people knew, of course, who those agents actually were.

It has been something of a pattern, then, for rulers to make use of personnel within a particular branch of an intelligence service (which has as its *chief* mission the surveillance of discrete elements of the population aside from the other security services) to spy on their colleagues working within the other intelligence services of the country, as is the case with Haiti and, at one time, Egypt. But it has also happened that leaders have established a special unit, branch, or separate office that devotes itself *solely* to spying on the secret police network.

In Iran during the seventies, possibly the most secret police unit of all the many secret police units operating within the country was the Special Bureau, which was given the unenviable task of watching SAVAK agents. Similarly, Czechoslovakia's Third Administration of the FSZS, which does have responsibility over criminal activity in the armed forces, is not permitted to conduct counterintelligence among members of the secret police / Interior Ministry network; this assignment is reserved for the Inspector's Office of the Ministry of the Interior.

G-2 is the name most commonly used to refer to the Cuban secret police, which for two decades has been one of the most dominant police powers of Cuba. As are all security forces present in Cuba (or in any Communist society patterned after the Soviet model), G-2 is a subdivision of the Ministry of the Interior. While most civilians are well aware that G-2 agents roam the country more or less freely, they often do not know precisely who some of those agents are. They will be surprised, then, when a plainclothes officer on the street stops them, demanding to check the contents of a woman's purse or demanding to have handed over to him a letter of liberty (a letter that releases the prisoner yet requires that individual to report to security authorities regularly). But there is one group of agents that know who and where the G-2 agents are—and that group is known as G-5, an organization consisting of very select individuals —most likely high staff members of the Central Committee of the Communist Party. G-5 works over G-2 and worries about what G-2 agents are up to, not only inside Cuba but in foreign countries as well.

No one, it seems, trusts a secret police force—not even the ruler who rules by it.

5

Despite the insurance policy of a separate secret police force to keep an eye on the secret police designed to watch over the general public, a sovereign leader often feels the need to develop within his secret police personnel a loyalty not so much to the abstraction of the state but to the person and personality of the leader; to effect this identification, the secret police system is usually structured to report directly to the sovereign.

While the Central Committee of the Romanian Communist Party has divisions in charge of all walks of life, such as foreign affairs, cultural affairs, youth affairs, etc., there is no Party division over the Securitate, which is the name for the Romanian internal security police. There is, then, no bureaucratic overseer lording it over the Securitate, because the Romanian secret police report directly to President Ceausescu. Like President Duvalier, of Haiti, Ceausescu apparently believes that one safe way for the President to check up on his secret police is to require that they report directly and personally to him.

Ceausescu adds his own personal touches, to further ensure the loyalty and immediacy of the Securitate in terms of their answering directly to him: the Minister of the Interior—under whom the Securitate, like all Eastern European internal security services, nominally operates—is usually changed every two years; the top men of the Securitate also rotate jobs with clockwork regularity. The point of these changes—to make sure that the monster doesn't devour its creator—is thereby assured.

When Duvalier came to power, in 1957, he worried about the Army. At that time, there were no well-entrenched secret police, except, possibly, for the ragged band of goons called *cagoulards,* who scared the living daylights out of the voting populace of Port-au-Prince in 1957 with their stockinged faces and thuggish behavior.

Duvalier soon turned to the *cagoulards* to become the core of the Tonton Macoutes.

"Duvalier decided that he had to have a military force that would be completely loyal to him because in the past . . . whenever the President would be forcing the army to take very repressive measures," one source reports, "the army would hesitate. . . . And so he decided he could not trust the army. . . ."

Commenting along these lines at a trial involving Haitian refugees and their plight in the United States, a U.S. federal judge concluded: "Much as Haiti's military helped bring Duvalier to power, it presented his greatest threat. The only consistent center of power in Haiti was the military; Duvalier was now subject to the actions which had unseated his predecessors. . . . Duvalier's solution was simple: Weaken the military. He disposed of the very army military commander who had helped him obtain office, and set about creating a force loyal to him which could counterbalance the military . . . by dividing the military, by shifting military officers around, sending them off, by setting up his own private (army) militia."

Duvalier, proceeding to undermine the Army, created the Tonton Macoutes to be blindly loyal to him. But he carefully sought to avoid putting together a secret police force that might prove to be capable of devouring him. For this reason, avoiding establishing a streamlined organization, he put together a force so decentralized that, for instance, Macoutes chiefs are forbidden to communicate with one another—they take their questions and answers directly to Duvalier himself.

In view of this staggered yet simple structure, the Tonton Macoutes could not be described as the most complex of secret police

organizations.‡ The head of the state and the head of government
—in Haiti's case, the same person—sits at the top of the secret
police structure. At the head of each region is a Tonton Macoutes
commander; under the commander, a joint commander, then a first
sergeant; the layer underneath consists of the Macoutes themselves,
without further hierarchical distinctions.

There is a simple elegance as well as a primitivism to this organization. There is no joint committee of commanders. Each commander reports directly to President Duvalier. From each of the regions of the country, the lines of authority shoot upward like
bamboo sticks directly to the office of the President.

Before Ferdinand Marcos came to power in the Philippines, in
1967, NISA was a far less prominent, less pervasive feature of the
Philippine security system. It was, in fact, a comparatively weak
Presidential Guard Battalion, consisting of highly trained professional soldiers who bore no particular political loyalty and had no
particular political intelligence skills. But Marcos reorganized NISA
during his early days in office, splitting it in two. One division was
concerned with the security of the First Family, the other with the
stability of the regime.

"The key to the supremacy of NISA," says one source, "is in the
degree of loyalty of its men to Marcos compared to that of other
servicemen in the security structure." While the leaders of both
ISAFP (Intelligence Service of the Armed Forces) and the constabulary are loyal to Marcos, the rank and file are more professional
careerists than Marcos devotees.

But *all* ranks within NISA are loyal to Marcos. Many, if not most,
NISA personnel come from the same province as Marcos (this in itself is considered a sign and near guarantee of absolute loyalty to
Marcos). And finally, to put the finishing touches on the idea of the
preeminence of NISA, the Philippine President went out of his way
to promote the head of his favored security unit from colonel to
major general. This was a higher rank than any NISA official had
ever previously held—a reward for loyalty and services rendered.

‡ And perhaps they can't even properly be described as the Tonton
Macoutes anymore. In 1971, the government changed the name of its chief
internal security force to Volunteers for National Security. The U.S. ambassador to Haiti was elated. No more Macoutes. No more secret police. But
what are the VSN? "They are volunteers who love their country," explains
one Haitian official. "They are Macoutes," explains a Haitian exile.

President Assad, of Syria, found other, more obvious ways to ensure the loyalty of his security services to him. To head the Defense Units, or Defense Companies, which are the Praetorian Guard, concerned with protecting the regime against coups, Assad chose none other than his very own brother, Rifa'at Assad.

Loyal as Assad's men may be, the President has taken yet one more step to strengthen his position. Within each of the several intelligence services operating in Syria, there can be found individual personalities who are particularly loyal to Assad and who answer solely and directly to him. This is particularly true of the General Intelligence Directorate, the largest internal security apparatus in the country, which is concerned with surveillance of the civilian population. Those who are particularly close to President Assad usually can lay claim to several qualifications: they are long-term associates of his, they are Alawites, and they may have helped him in the 1970 coup that brought him to power. Otherwise, those in the old-boy network of the intelligence circles have no doubt recommended those men to Assad.

President Hussein, of Jordan, unlike President Assad, relies not on his brother but more on an unofficial, elite group of individuals within the intelligence services of Jordan (as just discussed, Assad has both). For example, the current head of the Jordanian Army is an old boyhood friend of Hussein's. It would be safe to assume, contends a State Department official, that within all of the security services of Jordan, there are a few very loyal individuals who are particularly close to the King in an unofficial but no less fraternal way.

President Nasser, Anwar Sadat's predecessor as head of state of Egypt, set out to make GI, or General Intelligence, the pervasive civilian intelligence force, an instrument of his tight control. Accordingly, "GI became like our CIA," explains a U. S. State Department official. Nasser built GI into a body that acted directly and unquestioningly on his instincts. GI also had offices in foreign embassies, so that if Nasser didn't care for the head of a particular country or faction, as in Lebanon, let's say, he would turn to GI agents to help put that leader or faction out of business. GI launched terror campaigns so that people would learn not to cross him. The beginning of 1959 was marked by brutal repression, for Nasser placed the intellectual ranks of the Egyptian Marxists (to whom Nasser, as an Arab socialist, was staunchly opposed) in horrifying conditions of internment. And Nasser launched a veritable witch-hunt against not only Communists but all sorts of individuals of leftist persuasions.

Perhaps some of the intelligence services of Egypt were too close to be effective. DGSSI, also concerned with keeping an eye on subversives, was not nearly as powerful as GI, which Nasser used to keep himself in power. But even some of the smaller intelligence structures served particularly friendly purposes. For instance, the Office of Presidential Intelligence, which sources say may have been permanently dismantled from Sadat's security structure, was a small unit that once performed a highly important function for Nasser. This office processed and conveyed written reports to the President, making it into a sort of media service which, although it couldn't initiate policies or actions, nonetheless had power and influence under Nasser's rule. The office operated under the aegis of the Ministry of the Interior and was also part of the presidential cabinet structure. The office was said to be so "close" to President Nasser that it was not unusual for it to convey what sources call "jaundiced" information to the President. The Office of Presidential Intelligence was a close ally of Nasser, and as such, it didn't want to be the bearer of bad—or negative—news.

When Chile's DINA first came into being, it was a commission with no legal status; it was not even publicly known for the first few months after the coup, until General Pinochet laid down Decree Law 521, empowering DINA to carry out his directions according to the State of Siege laws.

Pinochet devised a structure for DINA that consisted of five chief sections: Government Service, Internal, Economics, Psychological Warfare, and External (foreign operations). The Government Service and Internal sections, the largest and most secret divisions, concentrated on control of opposition forces within the government bureaucracy and the population as a whole. The Psychological Warfare section operated in close liaison with the Directorate of Social Communications, the office in charge of press censorship, supervision of foreign correspondents, and pro-junta campaigns inside and outside of Chile. The Economics division guided the junta's fiscal policies, and the External section of course handled foreign operations.

These branches were bound together by DINA's Information and Processing Center, in Santiago, a sophisticated communications center equipped with computers and surveillance equipment—the full panoply of modern intelligence activity, provided courtesy of the U. S. Central Intelligence Agency. But one of the first pieces of equipment that General Pinochet had installed, however, was a simple, basic piece of technology: a private, secure phone link between this main communications center, DINA centers around the country, and the area where the junta was housed and where Pinochet spent a great deal of his time. Command—and control—over the intelligence system for Pinochet was thus facilitated.

There was also within DINA an inner circle known as the General Command, which comprised between thirty and forty men trusted by then-DINA boss Manuel Contreras Sepúlveda for their loyalty to him and their dedication to a common cause. Only this General Command knew the whole of Contreras' plans and the details of daily activity in the five sections. All else remained compartmentalized.

Similarly, just as DINA answered directly to President Pinochet and BOSS answered only to the Prime Minister of South Africa, the head of SAVAK, with the title of Assistant to the Prime Minister, answered directly to the Shah. Arguments that the Shah knew little of SAVAK's actual doings are thus not credible, unless SAVAK deliberately insulated the sovereign from the reality of what it was doing—but, due to the various safeguards that so many rulers find it necessary to maintain, total insulation would be nearly impossible to achieve.

In conclusion, there are few very strong, aggressive, and deeply entrenched secret police organizations that are structured so that their men do not report either directly or marginally directly to the sovereign leader. What sovereign would ever take the risk of deliberately insulating himself to a significant degree from a force perfectly capable of destroying even the sovereign himself? "In an authoritarian police state, nobody trusts anyone," said the former director of the Office of Korean Affairs in the State Department and former political counselor in the American embassy in Seoul when describing the steep competitiveness characterizing the various overlapping internal security organizations of South Korea up until October of 1979.

Accordingly, the protestations of a sovereign leader that he has no idea what his secret police are up to and that he finds allegations of "atrocities" and "torture" simply incredible—that sort of protestation itself seems incredible. Everything that we have learned from this study of secret police tells us that the sovereign knows exactly what his secret police are up to. He has to—if only to survive, himself.

6

A very aggressive secret police force will almost inevitably draw such bad notices in the international press that even the uncaring sovereign may find it necessary to put the secret police system through a name change and perhaps even a reorganization, if for cosmetic purposes only.

Sometimes a secret police organization will find itself faced with an image problem. While part of the leverage with which a secret police force intimidates a public derives from the ruthless image it upholds, sometimes that ruthless appearance poses as many *disad*vantages as advantages for the secret police.

In the total orchestration of a society, the sovereign needs to manipulate hope as well as to stimulate fear. The secret police are thought of as secret police not so much because of their operational secrecy but because of the unacceptable reality of what they do; if it is not possible to modify that reality in any substantive way, it may be useful to moderate the image just enough to engender hope that the reality has also been modified. And an adjustment in a secret police organization's image may also serve to buffer hostile international criticism of its activities.

As if putting old wine in a new bottle—backed by a lavish media manipulation campaign—name changes are part of that image adjustment. A secret police organization can benefit from a face-lift. For example, the Tonton Macoutes, of Haiti, had become an embarrassment, more to the U. S. Government, which helped support them, than to the Duvalier regime itself in the early seventies; but since the Duvalier regime was a U.S. ally, this meant that the Macoutes suddenly had become a problem for the Duvalier government as well. But to change the nature of what the Macoutes actually did would have required a change in the essential character of the regime. That was not possible.

What was possible was to change the face and the name of the Macoutes. And so, on "Face the Nation," in 1971, the U.S. ambassador to Haiti was able to claim that the Macoutes had been disbanded and that a new organization had taken its place. The name of the new organization was the Volunteers for National Security— quite a different sort of thing, the ambassador cheerfully explained, from the Macoutes. Not explained by the U.S. ambassador, however, was the instant ability of the new organization to recruit "volunteers" practically overnight. Who were the new VSNs?

The answer was to be found in the timing. The year 1971 was when Jean Claude Duvalier—Baby Doc—took over for the late Papa Doc. The change in administration provided all concerned with an excellent opportunity to make some changes, if only for cosmetic purposes. As a Haitian refugee has put it, the U. S. Government (and other Western allies) "made him [Baby Doc] understand that the Tonton Macoutes had to become less obvious."

In fact, the Macoutes promptly and quickly became hidden from view. They were moved out of the few urban areas of Haiti (coincidentally, where most of the tourists roam) and relocated in the countryside. In the capital area, under the new organization, the Macoutes ceded authority to a more visible, less clandestine force known as the Leopards.

The Leopards are a specially trained, highly organized, and well-equipped force now numbering close to one thousand officers and men. Unlike the Macoutes (VSN), which is a civilian organization whose officers and agents may or may not wear their characteristic blue uniforms, depending upon the nature of their missions, the Leopards are a thoroughly military organization whose uniforms are colorfully designed to reflect the name of their organization. They are under the tight command of an army officer (rather than a designedly nonintegrated collection of rural warlords), and their very visibility was calculated to detract from the odorous reputation of the more secretive Macoutes.

The Leopards (a smart-looking, well-drilled organization) were designed to fill the void left by the withdrawal of the Macoutes to the more remote countryside. "The Leopards are a crack group," says a former consul officer in Haiti. "Generally, they are provincial men who are especially good in athletics or especially strong, who have proven themselves at brute force. And they are taken and trained to be this crack military force. They're not known to have the wide-ranging freedom of action that the Duvalier government permits the Macoutes (VSN)."

But changes in the Haitian security forces in the past decade may be more attributable to adjustments in the perception of international opinion, with the consequent diplomatic and public-opinion pressures on Haiti, than to changes in the basic political outlook of the Duvalier father and son. "Repression in Haiti, with the familiar image of the Tonton Macoutes with dark glasses who shocked the tourists and the businessmen, was not in conformity with the ethical standards of the institutional, hierarchical and disciplinary organization of the forces of repression American-style, and was changed. But it is only a surface change at the level of the appearances, mostly restricted to the big cities where Macoutes were replaced by the Army," testified one former Haitian prisoner.

"Moreover, in the countryside," he testified, "where 80 percent of the population lives, the repression has not lost one inch of the striking character of the previous dark years of the Papa Doc dictatorship. And the Tonton Macoutes continue to implement their indiscriminately savage, repressive acts." A former Haitian journalist says that "Every small village has its VSN station," adding that they "seem to be a *slightly* milder version of the Tonton Macoutes." (our emphasis)

Many Haitian refugees insist that the rural VSN are every bit as vicious as the Macoutes. When asked, on trial, whether the Tonton Macoutes and the VSN were the same thing, a refugee replied: "It would be like saying God and saying Jesus Christ."

And some would carry the analysis one step farther, arguing that the Leopards were established the same year the disbanding of the Macoutes was announced so as to persuade concerned observers, both within the country and abroad, into thinking that significant policy changes, in the way of substituting a supposedly substantially milder Leopards for the supposedly fiercer Tonton Macoutes, were taking place.

In his final opinion on the famous 1980 case of the Haitian refugees in the United States referred to previously in this chapter, U. S. District Court Judge James L. King offered a succinct appraisal of the current security forces in Haiti and the changes in those forces that have or have not taken place: "His [a Macoute who testified at the trial] identification of himself as a Tonton Macoute rather than a VSN was echoed by every Haitian witness at trial; they all referred to the Macoutes. . . . The evidence indicated that they are present in every township of Haiti, and that their method of operation touches nearly everyone." And, the judge added, "The State Department country report for 1980 stated bluntly that 'the influence of the relatively undisciplined militia increased in Haiti in 1979.'"

Even more thoroughly reported than the name change of the Haitian secret police was the name change of the Chilean secret police. In August of 1978, two years after the shocking assassination by DINA agents operating freely in Washington, D.C., of former Chilean ambassador Orlando Letelier—and one year after the trial, in Washington, D.C., of some of those implicated in the murder—Chilean President Augusto Pinochet announced a reorganization of the nation's security forces, the "elimination" of DINA, and the establishment of a new internal security organization to be called the Center for National Intelligence, or Centro Nacional de Informaciones, to be known thereafter as CNI.

And so, according to President Pinochet, there would be no more DINA-like terror, because there would be no more DINA. Is that an accurate presentation of fact? The answer is both yes and no. Consider the factors that contributed to the changing of DINA into CNI.

One was increasing pressure from the Carter administration, which in its early years in office was still publicizing its "human rights" approach to foreign policy. The Letelier assassination only exacerbated relations between the two countries.

A second factor was the Chilean Army, which complained to Pinochet that its own international and domestic image—not to mention Chile's own image—was being besmirched by DINA's notorious reputation.

And a third factor, not so thoroughly understood beyond the borders of Chile, was a pragmatic one: DINA had been so effective in achieving its goal (which was the elimination of all organized opposition to the regime), that it had in essence abolished the need for a DINA-style terror, or a level of terror equivalent to what DINA, at its height during the mid-seventies, was able to accomplish.

Still, CNI remained more like DINA than anything else. For one thing, a substantial number of DINA agents, theoretically out of jobs when DINA was abolished, effected a smooth lateral transfer over to CNI. In the words of a United Nations report that put the matter rather delicately, "With respect to the staff of CNI, article 3 of Decree Law no. 521 [creating DINA] referred only to staff from institutions of national defense. It might be supposed that the established [CNI] staff consists of the twenty percent taken over from DINA. . . ." Indeed, the United Nations' suspicion seems increasingly perceptive in view of that fact that, on July 23, 1980, President Pinochet accepted the resignation of General Odlanier Mena, chief of CNI, at the height of a power struggle between General Contreras (former head of DINA, who left DINA at about the same time as DINA's role in the Letelier assassination was made public) and some *friends of Contreras' remaining within CNI,* and General Mena. The conflict (Contreras insists that General Mena was involved in a personal vendetta against him) peaked only eight days after the assassination, on July 15, 1980, of Lieutenant Colonel Roger Vergara, head of the army intelligence school. The official version attributed the killing to the MIR (Movement of the Revolutionary Left), but General Mena, after his dismissal, rejected that view, commenting, "This operation did not have the earmarks of MIR." And while President Pinochet has denied that two people who died apparently after being tortured at secret detention centers were in the hands of any official security service, suspicions have long existed among various sectors of Chilean society that agents of the disbanded DINA have formed a clandestine organization, working parallel to the legal security forces operating in Chile today, that is responsible for the arrests of hundreds of people since the July 15 assassination.

Besides the fact that there were, no doubt, many of the same faces in DINA as in CNI, there was something else about the new CNI that reminded a lot of Chileans of the old DINA. Chilean lawyers examining the articles of incorporation of DINA and CNI, the junta's decree laws, noticed a remarkable structural parallelism.

When DINA was officially established, in 1974, an unusual feature of Decree Law 521 caught the attention of Chilean attorneys. The law's last three articles (9, 10, and 11) were not published in the official journal of the government; the government announced flatly and unapologetically that they were of a "reserved," or "secret," nature.

The decree law that established CNI, four years later, relies on more or less the same clandestine formula, except that there is a slightly different twist. Whereas DINA had three secret articles, CNI has only one.

But the CNI secret clause is suspiciously broad. It states that the "organic regulations" of the new agency shall have a "reserved nature."

What does this mean? The lawyers turned back to Article 3 of the CNI charter, which states clearly that the structure and the duties of CNI would be established by the director—by orders that he himself promulgates (*"Reglamento Orgánico dictado a propuesta de su director"*).

In essence, then, Pinochet had provided CNI with a DINA-like open provision, 1978 style. It permits the CNI director, rather than the charter law, to define CNI. More to the point: a transitional article in the CNI charter provided for a reserve (or secret) article(s) to be established as necessary farther on down the road.

As one prominent Chilean attorney now in exile put it, "The only difference between DINA and CNI is that in the DINA case they told you something was secret and you couldn't find out about it; and in the CNI case, they tell you that they don't know yet what will be secret, but that when they do know, you—the citizen—won't be able to find out."

In Communist countries, too, a number of similar name changes and secret police face-lifts, so to speak, have occurred, for the Interior Ministries of these countries have proved themselves capable of comparable bureaucratic virtuosity.

The Czechoslovakian secret police underwent a number of reorganizations during the sixties. But bureaucratic gamesmanship, more than anything else, was involved in the shuffles. In one move, according to the defector Frolik, "The Third, Fourth and Fifth departments were abolished and placed under the Second Department. These changes, however, did not mean changes in the responsibilities assigned; only the numbers and titles became different."

Then came the 1968 invasion of the country by the Soviet Army, after which point more changes of a cosmetic nature were made. The name of the secret police had been StB. After the invasion, however, the secret police organization was folded into a bureau of the Federal Ministry of the Interior and renamed FSZS (for Federální správa zpravodajských služeb), meaning Federal Administration of News Services (occasionally referred to as Federal Division of Information Service). If the reports of defectors and of exiles (who still refer to the secret police of their country as StB) are to be believed, FSZS and StB are virtually the same thing.

In Poland, when the secret police force was put together by the Communist Party, with, of course, a strong assist by the Soviet KGB, it was named UB (for Security Bureau). But in 1956, UB was theoretically abolished and the secret police was folded into the Ministry of Internal Affairs—again, more in response to public opinion than anything else. By the mid-fifties, UB had made itself too visible and unpopular as far as the Party was concerned. But, again, just about everyone *outside* of the organization of the secret police, living either within Poland or elsewhere, still refers to it as UB (or more simply, the secret police).

Image and reality: in Yugoslavia, the name of the domestic secret police was UDBA until, in 1966, after the ouster of long-time Tito crony and UDBA head Aleksandar Ranković, UDBA underwent a name change, and in fact, thousands of UDBA agents were expelled from the security service. The government had created support for the purge by making public the fact that the files of UDBA's Zagreb office alone contained dossiers on at least 1,700,000 citizens. The government also helped circulate the rumor that UDBA chief Ranković had bugged Tito's bedroom, although in view of Ranković's total dependence upon Tito in the past, most Yugoslavians found this assertion a bit much. In any event, the scapegoat Ranković was gone, and at least to all appearances, so was UDBA. A positive, upbeat, cleaner image of the secret police was put out by the government as the new Party line. Even a new name was trotted out: the security service would now be known as SDB. SDB would be a different sort of organization. But the suspicion that the changes made in the organization were more cosmetic than real is enhanced by the fact that Yugoslavian citizens still tend to refer to their secret police as UDBA, not as SDB. Every Yugoslavian exile we interviewed—even recent exiles—still call it UDBA. And why not? they argue. The actions of SDB, in the manner of arresting and spying on all critics of the regime, are no different from UDBA's. "How do you give people hope and faith again—in their country and in their regime?" argued one exile. "You change the name of the secret police, and maybe you also conduct a few public trials of a few high-ranking officials."

By the time Leonid Brezhnev came to power in the U.S.S.R., the KGB had enjoyed a monopoly over the policing of dissidents for some time. But, in the words of a former Leningrad procurator, the KGB had gotten to look "too much like the Gulag." The Soviets therefore were compelled to design a way to divert attention from the now renowned practices of the KGB, as well as from the too huge number of political offenses that had accumulated under the KGB's jurisdiction.

The Politburo's solution was clever indeed. To diminish the number of political crimes, the KGB was instructed simply to pass them off as common crimes and to shuffle them over to the MVD—the Ministry of Internal Affairs. In this way, the MVD was able to take some of the heat off of the KGB. And so, a great number of political crimes in the U.S.S.R. are simply reclassified as conventional criminal violations. Although preliminary investigations still generally begin with the KGB, cases are subsequently transferred to the procuracy and the MVD. Take, for example, the worker who destroys a portrait of Brezhnev. The KGB will initiate the investigation. Soon thereafter, the MVD will step into the picture, classifying the crime as common "hooliganism." Political crime? What political crime? "This is a well-tried method of the KGB," says Alexander Podrabinek, author of *Punitive Medicine* (an indictment of Soviet psychiatric hospitals, smuggled into the United States and published by Amnesty International). "The authorities are afraid of dissenters and present them as supposedly criminal offenders." And so the KGB is superseded by the MVD almost as though a Communist CNI were taking over for a Communist DINA.

In the competition between the KGB and the MVD, the KGB has been limited to "especially dangerous crimes against the state." But, practically speaking, the KGB's sails have hardly been trimmed. The KGB is inevitably involved in the preparation of cases against "prisoners of conscience" charged even under conventional criminal law, for it is usually KGB surveillance—electronic and otherwise—that precedes prosecution.

Still, there is no question that the Party has sought to downplay the KGB. The "investigation/isolation" prisons of the MVD, at this writing, are chronically overcrowded, whereas the KGB's "investigation" prisons are not. This state of affairs did not come about by accident.

Communist societies have no monopoly on such maneuvers. The change from BOSS (Bureau for State Security) to DONS (Department of National Security), in South Africa, as alluded to earlier, occurred in the wake of a corruption scandal. High officials of the government were caught with their hands in a slush fund, made possible by the secret appropriations for the secret police and informational system, that was used for questionable trips and expenses. Attendant on the scandal were revelations that the Department of Information sought to co-opt and even purchase certain newspapers, both at home and abroad, in an effort to refurbish the regime's image and to sell the government's apartheid policies. The attempt to co-opt

South Africa's media was not as scandalous in South African ruling circles, however, as the misuse of funds. There is, in the strict Afrikaaner tradition, a morality that extends to questions of personal corruption if not to those of personal freedom. The information scandal, which resulted in the dismissal of General Van den Bergh (former head of the secret police), led, quite predictably, to the changing of the name of the secret police from BOSS to DONS. (In 1980, yet another name change: from DONS to NIS, National Intelligence Service.)

In Italy, the Defense Information Service (SID) was the title of the secret intelligence service until, in the mid-seventies, it was renamed the Security Information Service (SIS). From the time of its inception, in 1965, SID gained quite a reputation for itself, having been variously accused of complicity in right-wing bombings, helping fugitives and right-wing plotters, and neglecting to inform the government about impending terrorist activities when it suited SID's purposes to withhold such information. And investigations by Italy's judiciary into the workings of SID had been severely hindered by several key features of the complicated organizational system characterizing SID: there was no clear chain of command within the organization, and in addition, the proliferation of semi-independent police and right-wing terrorist groups—acting with or without official tolerance by the secret police or the government (it was impossible to clarify the incidents in terms of this point)—further obscured the exact role and actions of SID. According to the reorganization of the intelligence service accomplished in the seventies, that service must now report directly to the Prime Minister, rather than to the chief of the defense staff—a move that in theory ends Italy's tradition of an autonomous intelligence service responsible solely to the Army.

Or was the "transformation" of SID into SIS really nothing more than a cosmetic name change? Whether or not any name change of a secret police organization signifies a substantive change in its character as an institution is always a difficult question to answer. The Korean Government, for example, was well aware of the fact that the KCIA had made quite a name for itself (negatively speaking) in the world press and that, accordingly, some changes had to be made. And so, in January 1981, the KCIA was renamed the Agency for National Security Planning. "Despite the change in name," reported the *Korea Herald,* "the NSP will continue to carry out such jobs undertaken hitherto by the KCIA."

To be sure, some real changes in the structure and personnel of the KCIA, not the NSP, appear to have been made. For instance, before the name change to NSP, many officials of the secret police had been shunted aside (three hundred were purged from the KCIA by President Chun Doo Hwan, who, at the time of the purging, was a lieutenant general *and* acting intelligence director of the KCIA, responsible for "purifying" the powerful agency). There was no question that the KCIA had passed through a rather ignominious period after Park's assassination, but did South Korean authorities really intend to diminish the far-reaching powers of the organization? According to those authorities, the answer is yes. Then-Lieutenant General Chun Doo Hwan boasted that he would reform and streamline the organization, adding that it was so corrupt and had become so alienated from the people that it was coming to resemble Iran's SAVAK. But, according to some U. S. State Department officials, whether or not the KCIA was intended to become less powerful or even somehow reformed was not terribly significant, since the Army Security Command (a military counterintelligence unit), designed to monitor the loyalty of generals and key officers as well as to balance the excessive powers of the KCIA, in effect became empowered to do the very same things according to the dictates of martial law that the KCIA did without the authorization of martial law. Furthermore, although then-Lieutenant General Chun Doo Hwan (now President) resigned from his post as head of the KCIA because of widespread student protests in May of 1980, some four months later he appointed a classmate of his at the Korean military academy as the deputy director of the KCIA (not to mention the fact that the Army Security Command is also headed by another classmate of his at the Korean military academy who is considered by some to be the brains of the junta). "He just didn't need to be its [KCIA's] head anymore," says the former director of the Office of Korean Affairs in the State Department.

On the whole, our general conclusion is that name changes conceal more than they reveal. Once a secret police system becomes the very basis for domestic stability in a society, a real structural change is not so blithely accomplished. Names can change, but little else can. In 1968, Fidel Castro removed his long-time Minister of the Interior, Ramiro Valdés, who in that position had strong control over the security and intelligence forces of the country, and shuffled him off to another government position.* The problem with Valdés was that during his administration, homosexuals and others whom he chose to define as social deviants, including some priests and ballet dancers, were made to do hard labor for periods of up to two years. This practice, protested by the National Union of Writers and Artists, was stopped in 1968, when Mr. Valdés was replaced by Sergio del Valle, a physician who tried in the next ten years to professionalize the police. Was Del Valle successful, and did the shift from a more notorious Minister of the Interior to one with a lower profile truly signify changes within the police and security forces? The answer may perhaps be suggested by the fact that, when in January of 1980 Del Valle became Minister of Public Health, thereby creating a vacancy at the post of Minister of the Interior, Castro reappointed none other than Ramiro Valdés to that post.

We would like to take one step farther our assertion that a secret police force does not easily fade away—sometimes not even after a coup that involves a severe ideological shift in a different direction. The secret police network tends to survive often by emulating the underground tactics of the political opposition that it had heretofore been persecuting. When Castro's army took power, in 1959, the first intelligence unit, prior to G-2, was called DIER—for Directorate of Intelligence of the Revolutionary Army. Its head was René de Los Santos, a major in Castro's army. But, before long, Castro realized that Major de Los Santos had no more idea of how to run a secret police force than he did, and that someone with real technical expertise was required to do the job. And so, after a considerable talent search, Castro brought in an outside expert to backstop Major de Los Santos, who had been a captain in the secret police of the Batista regime, which Castro had of course overthrown. The expert reportedly secretly aided the underground rebel movement while he was still serving in Batista's intelligence body.

The story of the return of Moczar, Poland's once-powerful Minister of the Interior and former head of the secret police in Łódź, may have an ending somewhat along the lines of the Valdés story. Remember that, in the late sixties, Moczar was dismissed from his ministerial post at the climax of a major struggle between himself

---

* Some sources say that Valdés was shuffled off to the Ministry of Construction, which constituted a lateral move, rather than a demotion.

and the Party. Moczar attempted to topple Gomulka by trying to gain control outside of the Party, with private institutions (a campaign that also led to the widespread purge of Jews from the secret police and other public institutions). After the dismissal, Moczar held a position as chairman of the Supreme Control Chamber (which is involved in investigating officials' wrongdoings), where he remained in obscurity. But, powerless or not, the job got Moczar involved in accumulating information on corruption and other negative actions on the part of Party officials, and the information served him well, enabling him to play a role in the drive against corruption that the new leadership is aiming at restoring to the Party's authority. The dividend was significant: Moczar himself was reappointed Minister of the Interior in 1980—not unlike Fouché's return to power under Napoleon.

Left to right, right to left, CNI to DINA, BOSS to DONS, Tonton Macoutes to VSN, StB to FSZS, KGB and MVD, KCIA to Agency for National Security Planning—what's in a name? There is a universality in the secret police tendency to undergo somewhat superficial name changes and/or reorganizations so as to effect better public relations both internationally and within their own borders. A final example concerns the late, unlamented SAVAK.

Hilariously, a short time after Khomeini's takeover in Iran, minor SAVAK employees (file clerks and low-level agents) demonstrated publicly in front of the Prime Minister's office in Iran. Their complaint? That, given their past employment, they were unable to find jobs. As the *Kayhan International,* the international edition of one of the two major newspapers in Tehran, put it, "What surprised Prime Ministry officials was not the fact that SAVAK had so many staff members, but that most of them had gone into hiding, yet managed to contact one another and organize the gathering. The gathering of so many SAVAK agents is seen as proof that not only is their number quite large, but that they are also in constant contact with each other." A former SAVAK agent, reached by correspondent David Jackson of *Time* magazine, complained about the plight of the unemployed secret police agent: "Many of us will have problems making ends meet, and that includes me."

But, before tears come to your eyes, consider the fact that the Shah's SAVAK agents may no longer be so unemployable. There is a new intelligence organization in Iran, and of course, it has a new name: it is no longer SAVAK, but instead it is SAVAMA (K in

SAVAK standing for Country, M in SAVAMA standing for Nation). Already, a number of the lower-level employees, according to a retired general in the Iranian Army now living in the United States —the "real information gatherers," to quote the general, "who once served in SAVAK—now work for SAVAMA."

7

Perhaps the most closely guarded secret about any secret police force is its genuine magnitude. . . .

A central job of many secret police organizations is the intimidation of the total society within the context of the clandestine tradition. On the one hand, the less that is known about a secret police force, the more people will tend to fear it—the unknown having its own deterrent power. On the other hand, if the secret police remain entirely sub rosa, there may seem to be less to fear, precisely because so little is known.

The public must be slightly informed—whether by a scrawled note on the corpse of a prominent political activist inscribed in the name of a secret police that the government insists does not exist; or by more arrogant, public demonstrations of raw secret police power; or by a simple government proclamation of a "state of siege" and the establishment of a new secret police organization.

Whatever the approach, the authorizing government will tend to talk about its secret police in general, rather than specific, terms. The advantages of full disclosure are outweighed by the advantages of establishing a certain degree of uncertainty. No harm, after all, in feeding the paranoia; people might behave better if they think they have more to fear than in fact they do.

And so the authorizing governments establish something of a numbers game: for instance, how many agents were in SAVAK, the famous and infamous secret police of the Shah of Iran?

To critics of his regime, the Shah admitted to fewer than four thousand. A major U.S. newsmagazine in 1974 put is estimate of the number of SAVAK agents at thirty to sixty thousand. But while there is great uncertainty about the number of SAVAK full-time employees, a variety of sources agree that SAVAK had a much larger number of informers spread throughout Iran.

In fact, the SAVAK informant network was so widespread and

well developed that it is conceivable that, by the mid-seventies, one out of every ten Iranians in one way or the other worked for SAVAK in some informant capacity.

But the line between the full-time agent and the fully involved informant is rather fine; an informant network can be set up so that a full-time control agent (a salaried employee) can run an information network involving dozens of regular informants at a time. If, then, we are talking about a SAVAK organization that had, by the mid-seventies, even as few as thirty thousand full-time agents of varying ranks, then with the multiplier effect of dozens of informants per agent, the net numerical impact of the organization could have easily numbered into the hundreds of thousands.

Let us pursue the calculations a bit farther. By the mid-seventies, the population of Iran was about 30 million; by this rough calculation, therefore, it may have been that one in every sixty Iranians was in some sense working for SAVAK. Factoring out children, the figure looms even higher. Factoring out the sprawling rural areas of Iran, over which the regular uniformed military presided, and therefore leaving SAVAK to concern itself solely with the tinderbox cities, the SAVAK concentration estimate may be increased dramatically.

The size of a secret police organization, therefore, may be better gauged by the extensiveness of the informant structure than by raw numbers of agents per se. Some Iranian exiles who struggled against the Shah insist that in Tehran one out of every three or four Iranians was in the employ of SAVAK. This claim may be a wild exaggeration, but, given the structure and extensiveness of the informant system and the possibilities of uneven deployment, the impossible becomes conceivable.

Similarly, the full-time agent and informant figure often associated with NISA (the most notorious secret police unit in the Philippines) is about ten thousand. But this figure does not take into account, in addition to the factors developed with regard to SAVAK, the existence of other secret police and intelligence units in the Philippines.

Defectors from Eastern Europe tend to report rather high figures for their secret police organizations, but their estimates very probably include enrolled informants, both full- and part-time. A major American newsmagazine recently said that for every KGB spy abroad there are five working within the Soviet Union. The KGB's Second and Fifth chief directorates, responsible for domestic security, employ an estimated fifty to one hundred thousand agents. Western intelligence experts estimate the KGB's present strength at five hundred thousand, and of these, ninety thousand are believed to be directly involved in intelligence and counterintelligence work. (An estimated three hundred thousand are uniformed troops responsible for the safety of the country's leaders and the protection of its borders.) Other KGB employees perform administrative duties and help run prisons, concentration camps, and psychiatric institutions in which dissidents are held.

The figures of most secret police organizations are valid if you consider that the term "part-time" agent is something of a misnomer. The informer is observing all the time, even if there is not always something to report. It is the multiplier effect of the informant system that magnifies the secret police presence.

The Czechoslovakian secret police system is huge and made up of so many overlapping divisions and subdivisions that it sometimes seems to collapse as a result of its own weight.

In a rather caustic way, the Czech defector and former StB agent Josef Frolik once described how Czech secret police and military intelligence organizations practically tripped over one another when information was once received that a certain army officer was suspected of espionage on behalf of British intelligence. Writes Frolik, in a translation of his memoirs (*Spión vypovídá,* 1979) (*A Spy Testifies,* published by Index in Cologne in 1979), about an incident that he insists was typical.

"The plant in Vodochody was under the aegis of the Fourth Section of the Second Department [of StB]—defense industry. However, since the matter concerned an army officer, who had simultaneously been listed as a member of a certain air force unit, the Sixth Department wanted to perform the work-up." (The Sixth Department was detailed to military counterintelligence.)

"Ultimately the Second Department was heard from; this Department, which had been assigned surveillance over British intelligence operations in general, showed that it had deep experience in the methods of the British secret service and that it should handle the case.

"The situation might have been even more complicated than this example. The officer might have been in touch with someone who was of interest to the Third Department [the actual political police of the StB, involved in hard-core political counterintelligence]; or he might have been in contact with a Czechoslovak airline pilot who regularly flew to the West and was therefore an object of investigation by the Fifth Department (transportation counterintelligence) of the StB.

"The case was taken over by the Second Department (counterintelligence against foreigners on Czech territory), but this did not end the conflict. It had to be decided whether the case would be handled by "Section SIS" or the "Section British Embassy," because the officer in question had been allegedly lured into espionage by an agent of [the British secret service], who had been working under the cover of a diplomat.

"Now, a whole file existed on this diplomat, and on his activity during his sojourn in Prague. But it was not easy to determine who the 'referent' [case officer] in the case was. One thing was certain, however: while no suspect need have any doubts that a referent for his case would first have to be found, he could be sure that such a person was already waiting in the wings.

"Every citizen of the Republic had a referent assigned to him or her in advance; in fact, under some circumstances there may have been more than one. There was nobody who would not fit into some pigeonhole of the StB."

It is the very size of the secret police system, Frolik suggests, that necessarily creates the sorts of problems that could be solved only by reducing the size of the system, a step that the Party was unwilling (or unable) to take.

"At the time when I was leaving the country [1968], the intelligence service had a staff of approximately 3,000 people . . . ," recalls Frolik. "Approximately 2,000 people are probably members of the legal component of the intelligence service, and the remainder are engaged in illegal activity. If we compare the estimated number of people working for West German intelligence [Frolik is writing now about the period of the late sixties], which is 5,500, it is evident that, with the corresponding staff of Czechoslovakia—a nation many times smaller—the Czechoslovak intelligence operation represents a mammoth undertaking." As Frolik puts it, "Thus, on the basis of the Soviet model, the Czechoslovak Republic was completely staked out, and indeed, nothing was omitted."

Numbers are therefore both suggestive and misleading. As of this writing, South Korean analysts in the United States estimated, prior to the name change to NSP, that the KCIA has a permanent staff of about thirty thousand agents—plus what they refer to as "outside agents." In the South African security structure, which today involves three major groupings—(1) the Defense Department, the traditional military structure; (2) the Police Ministry, including the uniformed and nonuniformed (Security Branch being the nonuniformed) police; and (3) DONS, the Department of National Security, the more recent name for BOSS†—the best estimate is that the Police Ministry employs fifty to sixty thousand full-time officers, of whom roughly half work in the nonuniformed Special Branch. This is the unit that does the dirty work for BOSS (a/k/a DONS, a/k/a National Intelligence Service).

But how big is BOSS? Again, a numbers game; probably at least five thousand agents, but does one count the informants?

Perhaps the most honest, if pointedly imprecise, answer to the question of numbers was given by Prime Minister Vorster himself in a freewheeling exchange that took place in the South African Parliament. How big was the new BOSS to be? he was asked in the debate over the enabling legislation.

Said Vorster, BOSS would contain "a large number of people."

† Figures for the newly named (June 1981) National Intelligence Service have not been made available.

FOUR

Putting the Human Factor in Its Place: The Role of the Interrogator

1

One might almost feel sorry for the secret police interrogator. Interrogation is not light work. It is certainly not the sort of work to appeal to all tastes. But it must be done, and somebody must do it. Confessions must be collected before the supervisor wonders why none of the detainees are talking; leads must be fed to fellow agents out in the field before their trails grow cold and their investigations stop dead in the water. No wonder everyone gets very impatient when no answers are forthcoming.

Even when no answers are forthcoming, it is important to show opponents who has the upper hand. Even when the interrogation is conducted thoroughly, surely, efficiently, it does not always produce the desired informational results. But there must be a payoff. No interrogation should be entirely wasted. Those who do *not* talk (or who know *little*) can still prove useful, if not as useful as those who do talk—and know what they are talking about. Lessons can be *taught* by the interrogator, as well as *learned*. The interrogation can pay off in *intimidation* of the detainee's colleagues, if not in *information* about them.

To the functioning of the secret police, the interrogator is as essential as the informer. The informer provides such detail as may be available about *potential* detainees; the interrogator finds out from the captured target about those who are still left to be discovered. But the interrogation can send a message as well as elicit information. In a secret police organization in which torture is a systematic, administrative method of interrogation, the message is one of fear. Under the circumstances, the interrogator's work is a study not in understatement but in excess. Where the goal of the system of interrogations is intimidatory, understatement is counterproductive.

Accordingly, the grilling must be done so that no feelings are spared along the way. Everyone, including the interrogators and their supervisors, will be under a great deal of pressure. The interrogation will last as long as it has to, or according to the custom of the secret police applying the pressure; but such sessions are seldom short.

Even the most resistant soul will find it almost impossible to endure the unbearable indefinitely. And the harder the subject under interrogation the harder the interrogation. The job of the interrogator, who oftentimes may not be as skilled as the circumstances warrant, is difficult, arduous, and exhausting.

2

There are substantial differences in the demands that secret police organizations place on their interrogators.

The typical interrogator in Paraguay works only a one-hour session at a stretch, but his breaks are short, certainly shorter than those of his counterpart in South Africa, who generally works a four-to-eight-hour shift but then will be relieved for the day. The Paraguayan interrogator works to exhaustion, often dealing with his fatigue by taking amphetamines, which get him through the long day.

But sometimes even the amphetamines are not enough to get him through it, and unplanned relief teams, often at a higher level in the organization, have to be called in. The pattern is similar in Argentina, where agents have been known to interrogate prisoners for twelve hours at a stretch. But, here again, the twelve-hour shift is followed by a full day off.

Most supervisors understand just how draining these sessions can be. In South Africa, interrogators are permitted to take coffee breaks. An astonished black former prisoner recalled being subjected to an intensive session at the hands of four Security Branch officers when suddenly everything stopped.

Everyone had had it. "We're going for a break," one of the officers said. The four agents stalked out of the interrogation room, leaving their subject where he was—exhausted, confused, worn down. It seemed as though an hour or so had passed before they returned. But when the four interrogators walked in, they acted as though they had never left. "Are you ready to talk yet?" one officer asked, now that he had renewed vigor.

As routine as it is, interrogation by torture is hardly relaxing work. In order to keep in shape and to benefit from a psychological break in the routine, Security Branch officers at John Vorster Square, in Johannesburg, avail themselves of the district and divisional police headquarters' recreational facilities. A black activist now living in London who was held there several times remembers that he would often overhear officers talking to one another about their exercise schedules, so that "Have you been to the gym yet?" was a typical exchange in the casual conversation among ingoing and outgoing teams of interrogators around his cell.

The work of interrogation is understood to be so difficult, psychologically as well as physically, that it is not solely for reasons of physical relief that the interrogation sessions tend to be conducted by teams. The team structure of interrogations is at least partly prompted by supervisors who are understandably leery of the consequences of leaving interrogators alone with their subjects.

Secret police supervisors need to control the behavior of their interrogators as much as the behavior of those being interrogated. There are a number of ways to accomplish this level of dual control.

The South African security police seem to prefer a sort of buddy system. Interrogators often conduct their sessions in minimum teams of two. The pattern seems broken only in the event of celebrity interrogations. A team of five, for example, was appointed to interrogate most high-level black-power detainees, including Steve Biko. The South African system may be more patterned than most because it has had more time to develop. By contrast, any given interrogation session conducted upon Arab political prisoners on the West Bank is likely to be at least slightly improvisational: from one to seven Israeli interrogators and soldiers generally participate.

There are maximal—as well as minimal—limits to the size of the team. Too many cooks, so to speak, can overdo the heat. British interrogators work within the Crime Squad, the Criminal Investigation Department, and the Special Branch. Where torture has been reported in Northern Ireland, the total number of officers interrogating one suspect has sometimes grown to be so large that organizational problems have undermined the interrogations. Questioning has sometimes become irrelevant or repetitive. One solution to this problem in Northern Ireland was for each interrogation unit to provide a number of pairs of officers, who in turn interrogate a single suspect. To minimize the possibility of redundant or fruitless questioning, if one pair fails to make progress with a suspect, another pair will be put to work in its place (sometimes even furnished by their predecessors with the notes they compiled from the previous interrogation they conducted).

But interrogation teams cannot always be left entirely on their own. In Chile during the DINA era, interrogation teams were kept separate from the prison guards. The latter, the detention team, maintained overall control, even to the point of organizing and scheduling the interrogation sessions for the torturers. But the sessions themselves were conducted by a separate team of agents—special interrogation teams. Prisoners who experienced this system in Chile believe that the supervisors were trying to organize a system that minimized the possibility of leniency and sympathy on the part of the interrogators. Those who were required to spend the most time with the prisoners (the detention teams) were not those who were required to conduct the grueling interrogations. It was important to conduct the operations on as objective and risk-free a basis as possible.

To ensure objectivity on the part of the torturers and to establish roadblocks so as to prevent the development of sympathetic ties between torturer and victim, guards at the military unit Fusileros Navales, in the harbor of Montevideo, Uruguay, take care to maintain impersonal, unemotional façades while performing their work. And so they wear cloth hoods—outfitted only with slits for the eyes. Hoods are even worn by the armed soldiers watching the recreation yard—and by agents standing behind the prisoners while they talk to their visiting families through mesh-covered holes in the wall.

The team system is now widely used by other secret police forces as well. In addition to removing the interrogators from the captors, the team approach to interrogation removes the individual conscience from the momentary exercise of self-doubt. "Even the worst torturer showed some human instincts when he was alone," said one Greek prisoner arrested and tortured by ESA (Greek military police) in Greece during the early seventies. "It was when he was with others that he became like a wild beast." Said another Greek torturer to a prisoner he was trying to coax into confessing: "Do you know why we have been in power for six years? It is because we relegate the human factor to second place. . . ."

3

The training of the torturer sometimes seems as cruel and bizarre as the interrogation sessions the interrogators conduct.

In Portugal in the early seventies, at the DGS security police headquarters, instructors relied on films and photographs to school interrogators in the fine art of inflicting pain. While some films showed Portuguese security police demonstrating torture techniques on political prisoners, other photographs of victims at various stages of their interrogations were made available to prison doctors who wanted to study the scientific effects of torture. The doctors examined prisoners before, during, and after the torture sessions and evaluated their ability to undergo further torture.

At an Uruguayan torture center in a military barracks, a kind of lab work is preferred. Interrogators are instructed by practicing techniques on human guinea pigs, much like anatomy students hunched over a cadaver. But the guinea pig (whom the training officers would call *"el flaco"*—meaning, literally, weak one) tends not to be a dead human being, but a live one; or at least, one who is technically alive. With *el flaco* lying on a table, the training officers, surrounded by rookie interrogators, demonstrate the possibilities of electric shock treatment on the various sensitive parts of the body. After the opening lecture, the trainees are then instructed to duplicate the interrogation technique. At the end of the lab session, *el flaco,* his day done, is returned to his storage cell, barely alive, to await the next day's training session.

As grisly as the *el flaco* system is, it is not unique. The design of some interrogations seems to tell as much about the interrogators as the interrogated. In Greece in the early seventies, raw recruits into the secret police *themselves* served as guinea pigs.

"The moment we arrived at KESA [the training center of ESA, the military police] from the Basic Training Centre," confessed one ESA interrogator, "the torture began. They snatched us from the army lorries and threw us down like sacks. The beating began, and they made us eat the straps from our berets. . . . They beat us with belts and clubs. . . . I thought of asking to be transferred from ESA, but I realized it was as much as my life was worth." The desensitivity training apparently worked. The interrogators began to think as little of the detainees as they did of themselves. "It's nothing, Mr. Chairman," one officer confessed at the torturers' trial in Athens in 1975,* "to give someone five blows when you've had sixty from your comrades. . . . We were made to forget what we had learned in school and from our parents. They tried to awaken the beast in us."

A certain perversion of ethics was achieved. "They [the ESA torturers] justified themselves," said one former Greek political prisoner, "by saying that they had been beaten severely during their training without having done anything, and therefore we—who had done something—must be beaten too."

4

"I had really prepared myself for this statement but I am rather nervous because I know what it means to me. I shall be killed by one side or the other. That is quite clear. . . . I am threatened with death and I know that I am going to die sooner or later. I shall not be killed by a bullet, because they are not so stupid, but I shall have a heart attack or I shall slip away while I am waiting for a bus or fall from somewhere—a bullet is not the only way to die."

This melodramatic but nonetheless convincing confession was made in 1977 by Juan Muñoz Alarcón, a torturer and DINA agent. Muñoz had originally made his mark, however, not as a DINA agent but as a member of the hunted left-wing revolutionary group MIR (Movement of the Revolutionary Left). But when he was

---

* In July of 1974, the Gizikis government turned over power to a civilian government headed by Karamanlis. In August and September of 1975, the military police (ESA) were tried for torture.

caught by DINA, he was imprisoned, "reeducated" ideologically, and before long, converted into a full-fledged DINA agent. Muñoz was too well informed (with regard to his knowledge of the revolutionary movements in Chile) to kill, and too well informed (with regard to his knowledge of the workings of DINA) to release. The only alternative was to place him in DINA. Before Muñoz died, in the late seventies, he issued a virtually complete confession. He explained what he used to do for DINA, and how he felt about it.

"I was trained in interrogation and counterintelligence work," he said. "I was then given the job of hunting people down and interrogating, torturing and killing them. Because . . . of the situation in which I was living and what I had to do, I reacted and tried repeatedly to leave, but this was impossible, because once you are in you cannot get out.

"The purpose of this statement is not to seek pardon or reconciliation with myself. What I have done is truly unspeakable; I do not recognize myself and cannot understand how I have been able to do such unbelievable things. In my defense, however, I will say that it is very difficult, when you have no support and when the intelligence services grab you, to escape from them."

Former DINA agent Muñoz revealed that the prime target of DINA's extensive network of agents, informers, and torturers was the labor unions—to intimidate them and impede their growth by detaining and torturing their leaders and activists, as needed. As he put it, "This labor apparatus comprises a veritable army of informers who enable the intelligence service to detain, interrogate, torture and . . . kill people for showing dissatisfaction or acting against the government.

"I believe that the time is right to face up to the DINA monster. I also wish to place on record, and to swear if necessary, that some of the prisoners are alive, in poor physical condition, but many of them on the border of insanity because of the very harsh treatment they have suffered." Those who did confess to DINA, he said, only did so because they were "terribly and barbarously tortured."

5

Interrogator, or torturer, is not a rank; it is a role. Various secret police forces differ on the rank at which severe interrogations are conducted, but very few such organizations conduct their business without harsh interrogations, and many use torture. Some organizations prefer that virtually all ambitious young officers engage in torture to demonstrate their loyalty to the organization and their ideological commitment to the cause, while others prefer that the officer corps refrain from such degrading and tarnishing involvement, leaving the arduous work to lower-ranking agents, or even outside civilian employees.

In Paraguay, the secret police prefer to leave the work of severe interrogation to about two dozen full-time torturers. These are men who either could not make it up the ranks to supervisorial levels, or who demonstrated early in their careers particularly brutal or sadistic tendencies that earmarked them for this sort of work.

In Uruguay, Department Six often recruits outsiders to conduct the severest interrogations. They look for marginal men, preferably with a criminal background. "He is a lowly character in a desperate situation," one source told us. "He is what some Uruguayans would say would be 'lumpen'—that is, someone who just doesn't look right in a shirt and tie. You could spot the torturer most of the times you saw him—because of the hard, coarse look on his face, the toughness of his expression, and the strikingly incongruous youthfulness." There is no question that they are young. One woman who was tortured at Uruguay's famous detention center nicknamed by prisoners "El Infierno" caught a glimpse of her torturers by peering down below a small opening where her hood fell over her chin. "They wore jeans and Oxford sneakers," she recalls. "You could tell from their voices that they were very young."

In Iran, SAVAK appears to have spotted its most successful and notorious torturers at quite a young age. Our sources remember the infamous torturer Naseri when he was a student at Tehran University, in the early sixties. They recall him as a thoroughly unhappy soul who was profoundly humiliated by his family, from whom he severed all relations at an early age. They also remember him as a terrifyingly aggressive personality who liked to carry a knife with him and who usually made a big show about carrying it. SAVAK began to cultivate him when he was still a law student at Tehran University. Years later, when he became head of the famed torture Joint Committee for SAVAK, no one who knew him from the past was surprised by his career advancement. When, in 1973 or 1974, Naseri was made secretary to the top SAVAK general, Nematollah Nassiri, it seemed almost predictable. Almost the same story characterized the career of Naji, another famed SAVAK torturer. An aggressive and violent man, he attracted the attention of the secret police at an early age. His former schoolmates recalled him as the little boy whose mother even had to admit that he enjoyed killing cats.

There have, however, been torturers who were more subdued and refined than these. "His head was never out of a book," the mother of the Cambodian Kain Kech Ieu, sometimes known as Brother Deuch, has testified. The son of a fisherman, Brother Deuch was a lonely young man, with few friends and surrounded by books. He appeared to get his politics right out of his books, and in the early seventies he joined up with the Khmer Rouge in its struggle against the regime of General Lon Nol. By 1973 he was involved in hand-to-hand combat against Vietnamese-trained cadres fighting the Khmer Rouge, before long gaining a reputation as a quietly efficient and vicious killer. "I always knew he would go far," his mother once told *Newsweek* correspondent James Pringle.

He went too far. When the Pol Pot regime came to power, in 1975, the ruling elite enlisted Brother Deuch to set up its secret police system, the notorious Nokorbal. Moving quickly, he established the main torture center in Phnom Penh and staffed the center with a torture and interrogation team numbering some two hundred agents. One member of the team was a former teacher who suffered from a terrible disease akin to leprosy. Another was a brutal sadist who sharpened his knife every day until the blade was sharp enough so that he could shave the hair off his leg. Then the former pig-buyer would use the knife to cut out various organs of political prisoners, usually while they were still alive. A heavyset woman nicknamed "The Monster" was in charge of torturing and killing women. With colleagues like these in Nokorbal, Brother Deuch stood out like a refined intellectual. "He was deceptive," said one former political prisoner of Nokorbal. "He was polite to me. . . . But when he said someone made an error and had to be reeducated, that meant he could be 'crushed to bits' after torture."

Survivors of brutal interrogation sessions conducted in Argentina recall their torturers as rough young men, many of them under the age of twenty. "They are very young men who have come straight from training school," one prisoner told us. "Their attitude was one of complete obedience to orders from above." Another survivor seems to have recalled that "they were fed books like *Papillon*," but it was not clear that they were intelligent enough to have the conviction of ideology. Sometimes, in fact, they seemed quite cowardly. "They often only beat prisoners who are blindfolded," said one survivor.

The best—or rather, the most sadistic—torturers tend to have experienced prison on more than just the level of the secret police employee. The best recruits may be former inmates—not political prisoners (too suspect) but hard-core criminals, whose antagonism toward the "subversives" can be taken out richly in the punishment they levy. In Indonesia, at blocks G1 and E of two prisons in Malang, interrogators are recruited largely from the ranks of ex-convicts.

In the Philippines, according to a former security officer, authorities in a local police department accused of torturing sometimes use "goon syndicates." Recidivists under the protection of powerful politicians receive special treatment. They can go out at will and have special food brought in. In exchange, they perform contracts for their patrons. The head of the goons may be designated head of the torture squad. He may be called in at any time to torture prisoners so that the police can say that they are not responsible for any acts of torture.

Certainly on any employees list pertaining to any variety of occupational roles, mundane job characteristics outnumber the eccentric ones. Accordingly, in the so-called Third World countries, where jobs are scarce and the torture of prisoners is more than a sporadic occurrence, one could make the axiomatic assumption that torturing, for many torturers, is just a job. Such an assumption does not reduce the horror of comprehension, but increases it. It is the banality of evil, as the historian Hannah Arendt (borrowing from Joseph Conrad) has suggested, that is disturbing, not its eccentricity. The occupational role of the torturer is so central to the conduct of the operations of so many secret police forces as to make the job, and the work, commonplace.

But these are only reasonable assumptions, based on the fragmentary evidence available. The theory that the torturer views his work as a means of subsistence, more than as a patriotic endeavor, was not altogether refuted, but was certainly challenged, by a document obtained from a left-wing Chilean exile organization. More prominent and more respected than most, Chile Democrático in 1974 compiled a list of alleged torturers in the employ of the internal-security network of Chile. The list made the rounds of the international Chilean exile underground, and it no doubt fortified the anti-

Pinochet movement in its belief in the essential fascistic evil of the regime.

Ninety-eight alleged torturers made the list, which taken as a whole made the point that there was nothing ordinary about any list of torturers. Let us include a few examples. One alleged torturer, a high official of the Army, was noted for his admiration of the military of Hitler's Germany and for his proud belief that the Chilean Army observed the spirit of the German Army even today. The leftists who prepared this list of alleged torturers reported that the army official was the sort of torturer who felt it important to make sure that the screams of his victims in the torture center under his command were audible in the streets outside.

Another alleged torturer, a member of Chile's military intelligence network, reportedly participated in sex-torture sessions inflicted upon a leftist who was stretched out naked on a table while water was injected into his nostrils, electric currents applied to the soles of his feet, and cigarettes snuffed out on his body. After he was sadistically whipped on his genitals, the leftist was shot.

Another high army official headed a torture team that suspended prisoners from the ceiling and applied electrical currents: ". . . the prisoners are suspended and receive blows from fists, feet and truncheons; they undergo simulated executions and are given pentothal injections."

The report cited a physician as torturer, who also helped compile a list of leftist physicians of whom more than thirty were murdered. Others listed in the report: An Air Force officer who specialized in the torture of young children in front of their parents in order to obtain confessions or denunciations. An Air Force official who "boasts that all those who have fallen into his hands have confessed, have become insane or have died." The army officer who had attacks of laughter and hysteria during torture sessions. The "attending" physician to a torture session who told a female prisoner who had been repeatedly raped by interrogators that "she should be proud of her pregnancy which would give her country the son of a soldier." The Air Force officer who became known for inviting his girlfriend to witness torture.

The point of this list seemed to be that ordinary people do not make torturers; contrary to the belief that the occupation of the torturer is nothing more than a job, this respected though left-wing organization insists that there are people who obviously enjoy themselves in this line of work.

6

What of the relationship between torturer and victim? Little is known about this subject, because few who endure the severest levels of torture emerge from the experience to talk about it.

In Paraguay during the mid-seventies, the interrogator was, typically, a young man who worked for the Investigaciones (police) on a part-time basis. One such interrogator attended night classes at the university. He was well liked by his Investigaciones supervisors, because he did his work well, did not complain, and was very reliable.

Besides being quite sadistic, he was also capable of inhuman detachment. One day his supervisors came to him with a new prisoner. He was a university professor, and the Investigaciones were seeking information about leftist activity at the university.

The young man went into action with considerable determination, working the man over thoroughly and himself into a state of total exhaustion, then finally dumping his detainee into a prison cell. There, responding to his torturer's question, the man began to describe, in a greatly weakened voice, his job at the university. With that, the young interrogator came once again to life. He wanted to know what course of studies the professor taught. Barely able to speak, the professor awkwardly outlined his academic background: he was an expert on the Middle Ages and the Enlightenment. The young interrogator warmly told the professor that he needed his help, that he faced a grueling university examination about the history of the Enlightenment.

Possibly ecstatic at being asked questions he had no problem answering, the professor gushed forth an incredible stream of talk. Everything he knew about the Enlightenment seemed to pour forth. The interrogator, sitting next to him on the floor of the jail cell, responded by bombarding the professor with question after question. The Investigaciones, for the next hour or so, would gain no new information about left-wing activity at the university, but one of its torturers—and part-time students—would learn a great deal about the Enlightenment.

After about an hour of this, even the interrogator, tired of the subject, satisfied himself that the professor had no more energy to talk about the Enlightenment that afternoon. And so, as if to make up for lost time, the interrogator went back to questioning the professor about more contemporary matters. But where his questions about history had been put politely, in the manner of a respectful student at the feet of his professor, his questions about contemporary politics were put quite differently. He beat the professor unmercifully again, using fists and a club, in the end learning as much about university politics as he had about the Enlightenment.

A couple of months later, after the professor had been released from prison, the torturer/student was walking in downtown Asunción when he caught sight of his former charge.

As if striking up a conversation with an old friend, the young man became quite friendly and asked the professor to buy him a beer. The professor—stunned, taken aback, and perhaps afraid of being sent back to jail—felt compelled to respond favorably. The two went to a café and talked for a while. The intimidation continuing even outside the torturers' chamber, the two talked about . . . the Enlightenment.

Not many prisoners are rewarded with such postoperative tête-à-têtes. Colonel Zamani, the notorious head of the political unit of Qasr prison, in Iran, during the mid-seventies, left few prisoners in any shape to talk once he was through with them. Zamani made a practice of toying with his prisoners. His policy was to break their hearts as well as their bodies. They were permitted no solace either during interrogation sessions or after them. Prisoners who were transferred to him had to know that they were near the end of the line. Zamani's personal preference was for whipping detainees with a whip made of horsetail hair, then depositing them for the human refuse he had convinced himself they were, stuffing them into cells that already held insane prisoners who had been found guilty of particularly gruesome crimes of conventionally criminal nature. Zamani, like a zoo keeper feeding his pet exhibits, fed the political prisoners to the psychotics, like raw meat to caged lions. And inside those cells, the psychotics were free to do as they wished, for Zamani enforced no prison code of behavior.

Zamani believed in the power of cruelty as an article of faith. One day, nine political dissidents had been shot in the streets of Tehran by SAVAK agents. Word of the slayings soon spread throughout Zamani's prison. In protest, the political prisoners passed the word for everyone to observe a moment of silence. The silence was scheduled for a certain hour, but Zamani's staff got word of the silent protest and passed that word on to Zamani. Furious, Zamani yanked about thirty prisoners out of their cells and dragged them to the entrance of the prison. There, at the precise moment that the moment of silence was scheduled to begin, Zamani personally whipped them with that weapon he most favored: the terrifying instrument made of horsetail hairs. With the rest of the prisoners observing their own moment of silence in protest against the murders, Zamani staged his own moment of mayhem in protest against the protest. The shrieks and sobbings of the thirty victims filled the prison air. Zamani had, no doubt, concocted one of the noisiest moments of silence in any prison's history.

Not surprisingly, the prevalence of torturers at almost all levels of many secret police organizations can make those who do not torture as famous as those who do. In the Philippines, where the interrogator may be a corporal, a sergeant, or even a major, the only rank that seems exempt from this grueling service is that of general. At that level, it would seem, one no longer has anything to prove.

One of the most famous generals in the Philippines heads the Philippine Constabulary. The reputation he enjoys among those who inevitably tend to attract the attention of the Philippine secret police is that he has never been linked to any particular case of torture or bribery. Accordingly, those who are arrested by the Philippine Constabulary pray and hope to find themselves in the custody of his unit—as against other possibilities. Under his command, their chances of relatively early release without torture are considered good. To say that humanitarian behavior by the security services of the Philippines is an exception may be an overstatement—but a good many exiles lead us to believe that it is not an overstatement to any large degree.

7

Lieutenant Julio César Cooper, who had defected from the Uruguayan Army, had been assigned to internal security tasks. His defection was regarded as genuine; few individuals in human-rights circles believe him to be a double agent planted in the exile circles to which he defected, though in the secret police world anything is possible, including a reconversion to the old faith.

Cooper said in an interview:

"Ninety percent of the Uruguayan officer corps, and I mean all ranks . . . are involved directly or indirectly in torture." It all started in 1971, when intelligence units of the Army began to be involved in repression. The choice of different personnel to operate in intelligence missions was not very clear, and it seemed as if everyone was required to pass through a testing phase. Before long, supervisors seemed to favor those "who had displayed the most care and zeal in the accomplishment of their duties," he said, explaining the relationship between torturing and career advancement.

"I think advancement was linked to the efficiency and general performance of the officer in different branches and details of his military career. However, this capacity and efficiency in repressive methods, among which I include torture, definitely demonstrates his military capacity, and it is just this capacity which is rewarded by the authorities either in promotion or in assignment. . . ." Revealingly, when Lieutenant Cooper himself refused an order to conduct an intensive interrogation, he was promptly arrested and then tried by a military court.

"I was given the order to take part in a torture session against a detainee with the surname of Sutil. That person was going to be submitted to what is known as the submarine torture, but even before its application he showed signs of the ill treatment he had already received."

An incident a few months prior to the Sutil incident had begun to work on Cooper's conscience. A well-known revolutionary leader had finally been captured, and he was brought to Cooper's supervisor for the initial interrogation. His supervisor was a major, the second in command of Cooper's unit. Cooper sensed that in order to prepare himself for the session, the major seemed to require an intense inner psychological preparation. And so, when the major first looked upon the revolutionary leader, he seemed, according to Cooper, to "suffer a nervous attack, and he ran up to the detainee, shouting loudly at him." The detainee, for his part, had his hands tied behind his back. He was also hooded. And though he obviously could not see the major, he could sense the coming confrontation. "Responding to the action of the major, the detainee began to hasten his steps [away] and eventually began to run. But when he got to full speed, the major steered him toward a pillar in the building, which was approximately forty centimeters thick. The result was that the detainee ran and dashed himself violently against that pillar." The impact of the pillar on the detainee's body was so vividly described in Cooper's interview that one cannot doubt its impact on Cooper himself.

The incident was still fresh in Lieutenant Cooper's mind when, several months later, he was given orders to conduct his own interrogation session with the detainee whose surname was Sutil.

The prisoner was hooded—and carried in by officers in a semiconscious state, then thrown onto the floor. And the detainee would have remained just another anonymous interrogation subject had it not been for a telling physical characteristic. Cooper noticed in the man symptoms of a peculiar type of rickets, a disease contracted during infancy. Cooper was struck by a vague memory. He recalled that a friend from childhood with whom he had grown up and who had suffered from that same type of rickets had recently been arrested. But Cooper had not expected his luck to be such that this former friend of his would be brought to his own regiment. Now his childhood friend was lying semiconscious on the floor before him. When the order to proceed with the interrogation was given by a superior, Cooper could not obey.

Lieutenant Cooper was immediately removed from interrogation work, arrested, and tried. But the Uruguayan military court was surprisingly lenient. Ordinarily, Cooper said, an officer who refuses to torture arouses the deep wrath of authorities, who will customarily "inflict a very severe punishment" in retribution.

Perhaps the circumstances of the incident weighed heavily in the court's judgment. Perhaps, too, the fact that many Uruguayan officers are required to conduct interrogation sessions, and that such work is not the exclusive province, as it were, of specialists, contributed to the military court's compassion toward a fellow officer. For everyone knows that torture is not easy work.

Whatever the reasons, Cooper was put back into the secret service. His commitment from then on, though, was not to the status quo, he says, but to change: "harboring an illusion that some sector of the Armed Forces would react, putting an end to this situation; that some sector would seek an opening to create a new perspective in which the nation's problems could be seen. This was my constant hope and belief during all those years."

Even after his defection from the Army, Cooper believed that the change in his society could only come from within. "I am totally repentant, and within that rejection of torture can be found the most traumatic and important factor marking my evolution in connection with the whole series of problems I have experienced in my country." Lieutenant Cooper's emphasis on torture as a very key element in the history of his country—as well as his own personal development—was a very conscious and telling assessment, even if made in the cool perspective of retrospection.

"There are officers whom I have actually seen who are fairly discreet as regards displaying any reaction in applying torture. In other words, their conduct is confined to carrying out the torture without displaying any kind of feeling about it. But I have also witnessed commanders and officers who in their reactions showed pleasure in applying torture and satisfaction, even in tragic cases such as those resulting in death. I was able to witness and sense the pleasure of certain commanders and officers, verging on mockery, in the presence of the dead person or [even] in the presence of . . . his or her family."

8

It might be difficult to imagine what attractions the job of interrogator would have for those not disposed, for reasons either of heredity or conditioning, to sadism. For many interrogators, apparently, it *is* just a job.

An Iranian torturer described to an Islamic revolutionary court in 1979 his feelings toward the victims he beat with wire cables until their flesh peeled: "I never expressed any personal hatred toward these people. I was just doing my job." And another Iranian torturer on trial at the same time who also took his work quite seriously gave the court the impression that he carried out his work as unemotionally as any technician. When he found the screams unsettling, he would stuff a slipper in his victim's mouth so he could work in silence.

At the 1975 trial of the Greek torturers, there was evidence that economic necessity would have driven the officers to anything, which in fact it apparently did. Pressed as to why he tortured prisoners, one confessed ESA torturer invoked the humble origins of his family, the uprooting from Turkey in the exchange of the populations following the 1922 rout of the Greek invasionary forces, the pension of six hundred drachmas that his mother was forced to subsist on, and the low salary of five thousand drachmas for which his brother worked. It was just a job, he pleaded.

His words have the ring of a familiar story. "Their only concern," said a prisoner who managed to survive a brutal period of internment in an Argentine prison, "was for promotion at the end of the year and the salary they will collect at the end of the month." At La Coronda prison, one of the most notorious torturers matter-of-factly told a prisoner, "I don't mind who wins the war in Argentina. I don't mind if it's this lot or your lot. I'll be retiring in four years and I just want a good rest." A *comandante* also at La Coronda prison used to say, "I am a professional. I obey orders like a good soldier. If they order me to kill someone, I will do it without hesitation. But of course, I will allow the condemned man spiritual or religious comfort before his death, because I am a deeply Christian man."

But this mentality of professionalism has got to be less prevalent among Argentinian torturers than, say, among Argentinian postal clerks. Torturers in some Argentinian prisons apparently received as much ideological training as their detainees, though from the opposite side of the fence. "They were made to hate the prisoners, whom they were taught to consider as enemies of the country," reports one political prisoner who, with her husband, spent time in a secret camp for political prisoners. Another victim of the special treatment reserved for political prisoners in Argentina recalls, "Every Tuesday or Thursday there were meetings of 'Formación' or 'Consolidación Ideological' [for the guards]. We called the meetings brainwashings. During the meetings, slides are shown of shoot-ups between the forces of order and the guerrillas. The aim of this is to toughen up the guards and win them over to the idea that political prisoners had to be destroyed. Usually the guards do not fully understand the real problems of the country and their intellectual ability is very low. . . ."

The torturer, even if he has doubts about the validity or ethics of what he is doing, finds his morality under constant assault within the environment of the secret police. But the peer system and ritual reinforcement instruction seem to help to remove the doubt. "I hated you," said one prison torturer in Uruguay to a political prisoner who was ultimately released. Saying this, the torturer then pulled out of his back pocket a photograph of a nineteen-year-old member of the local Communist Party, saying, "I was after him. I hated him because I knew I had to." A colleague of his, glowering at a line of political prisoners at "El Infierno," viciously punched a detainee in the ribs, saying, "That's to make you walk properly, you Communist."

The hatred of torturer for victim could in many instances stem as much from class hatred as from ideological conviction. "You, the upper-middle classes, are wrecking society," said one ESA torturer as he taunted his victim. "You earn in a month what we earn in a year." The ESA officer was also candid about whom he and his colleagues wanted in the secret police, at least at their level of misery. "We don't want clever people," he said. "We want mediocrities."

When a detail of DINA agents descended upon the home of a lawyer working for the Chilean Cooperative Committee for Peace, an antigovernment organization sponsored by Catholics and Jews but considered by the Pinochet government a threat to national security, the agents were burning with obvious hatred. Whether they had psyched themselves up to be able to make the arrest and later to conduct the necessary interrogations, or whether the envy and resentment developed naturally out of feelings of class inferiority—we do not know. But the behavior of the agents was antagonistic and taunting. They ransacked the home, and when they discovered some personal correspondence of the lawyer's, they made it seem more intimate and personal than it was. Expressions like "my love" and "my dear" (some even from male correspondents) were interpreted in their mocking, extemporaneous oral readings with sex-maniacal connotations: but the agents—young, low-level DINA employees—were not just sarcastic, but also uninformed with regard to proper literary address.

Such untrained and unsophisticated agents are no fun to supervise, much less be interrogated by. As General ben Eliezer, of the Israeli Army, put it in response to allegations of torture performed by army soldiers: "Am I happy with all our men? Well, I'm not. Some don't have standards of education, of intellectual and moral values. I'd wish they had. . . ."

There is no question that the task of the torturer is less difficult if he is able to convince himself that he is acting out of patriotism. This should be especially true of a torturer of humble origin and education. It was clear from the testimony taken at the ESA torturers' trial, for example, that many torturers identified themselves as "the greater Greeks," through whose ministrations against political evil the nation would purify itself and, once thoroughly cleansed, rise to majestic heights of destiny and greatness. "It is we who will create the greater Greece," said one major to his captive.

And there can be no doubt that patriotic sentiment is high among torturers in those secret police organizations where sufficient attention is given to ideological and reinforcement training. But it would be naïve to underestimate the degree of cynicism that exists at the torturer's level, for the job that such a functionary is asked to perform is neither ennobling nor elevating, no matter how high the level of morale may be. In Yugoslavia, where political prisoners used to be tortured by teams of interrogators (and where the secret police system is as finely thought out as any that we know of), the UDBA torturers seemed to have an objectively focused sense of self and role. "The UDBA man with the scar on his forehead was especially cruel," a political prisoner, since released, recalled. "He walked and danced on my legs, and boasted of his having killed Ivo Masina. He asked me if I wanted to be famous like Masina, if I wanted to be a martyr to the Croatian people. He told me that in a free Croatia, they might name ships and squares after me. 'If it will give you satisfaction to believe,' he continued calmly, 'that your rude and violent death at our hands will cause you to occupy a high station in the remembrance of your countrymen, then, please, believe it.'"

9

The use of brutal methods of interrogation is not to be understood as the exotic behavior of the atypical secret police torturer. Such methods are of the essence of what a secret police force can do if its powers are unchecked or if its franchise is too widely drawn. These interrogations are often, but as we have seen not always, left to the lower-level employees. There can be no doubt that in a number of secret police forces, service as a torturer is helpful to career development, because—among other reasons—the perfection of these methods and the effective application and execution of the interrogation is clearly regarded by the institution as an aid to information-gathering and intimidation. While the ethics of these methods can certainly be questioned, their effectiveness, at least on a short-term basis, cannot.

But their effectiveness is certainly related to the ways these interrogations are structured and designed. A poorly conceived and executed interrogation can be as harmful to the secret police as one not conducted at all. Political prisoners report instances of tortures, and torturers, who went too far. The dead political prisoner who went to the grave with information still intact is of course of considerably less value to the secret police than the live one who might still talk. Said Major Harold Snyman, the South African security officer in charge of the now deceased Steve Biko, on the subject of Biko's death, "I was sorry, because he was worth more alive to me than dead."

But the annals of the secret police are replete with bungled interrogations. In Paraguay, for instance, where torturers are as unskilled as they are hard-working, the accidental deaths of prisoners is common—knowing when, in the process of submarine torture, to bring the victim's head up above the putrid water before submerging it again calls for patience in measuring the victim's pulse after each dunking—a virtue not always characteristic of the Paraguayan torturer. In the management of a secret police force, the techniques of interrogation are in constant need of refinement and improvement. With the secret police under tremendous pressure to produce, the number of human casualties stemming from that pressure are oftentimes higher than even the police desire.

Secret police, then, feeling the need to professionalize their interrogation techniques, are turning increasingly to the advice, counsel, and even supervisorial input of physicians and psychiatrists. In some instances, these medical professionals have been asked to design interrogation procedures; in others, they have been asked to administer them. A number of motives are at work here. Police institutions throughout the world have felt compelled by the increasingly complex nature of their franchise to expand their expertise—by availing themselves of professional consultation, especially in the areas of modern management techniques and behavioral-sciences systems. Secret police institutions, since they are probably as well understood as a *continuum* of ordinary police activity as they are understood to be representative of aberrational behavior, have also been affected by this trend, their institutionalized arrogance notwithstanding. Another factor, probably, is a certain sense of professional inferiority, which that arrogance tends to hide. Except in those societies where the heads of the secret police institutions derive from first-class military or police academies, a supervisor of a secret police organization does not ordinarily have confidence in his educational or intellectual background. This affects his ability to suppress the activities of a well-educated political opposition, precisely because he worries that the men in his organization may not understand the people they are being asked to control. For these reasons and many others, a number of secret police institutions have sought to enlist, or co-opt, or require by force and/or intimidation the involvement of trained medical and behavioral-science personnel in the administration of secret police work. Sophisticated secret police officials know better than to place their entire professional fate, as it were, in the hands of relatively unskilled interrogators using methods that are at best rather crude, even if on the average they have proved effective enough.

Kopkamtib, the secret police organization of Indonesia, was accused in the late seventies of enlisting accredited Dutch psychologists on the faculty of the University of Jakarta, as well as one or more Dutch psychologists at Oxford University, in England. Surprisingly, perhaps, Kopkamtib did not deny these charges but instead come forth with a slightly different version of its relationship with Indonesia's mental-health professionals.

The charges are fascinating, with important implications for the future of both secret police interrogations and the mental-health professions. They include:

• That academic groups at Indonesian universities may have helped design incarceration environments for Kopkamtib.

• That their designs may have been based at least in part on fieldwork conducted on political prisoners at the Buru Island prison camp.

• That the research design was theoretically conceived by the secret police in the identification of the type of student more likely than not to oppose the government.

• That computers with such design programs may have in fact been used to identify such students.

• That type-testing procedures were refined to segregate political prisoners into categories, rated according to their likely continued commitment or likely noncommitment to leftist ideology.

• That extensive "transmigration" studies were conducted, involving social-psychology designs to make political prisoners more accepting of relocation (i.e., social banishment). In public-relations terms, Kopkamtib sought to sell transmigration of political prisoners to world public opinion as altruistic "prisoner releases." In this category, the research designs have also focused, it is charged, on "village development," under which the transmigration and resettlement of large numbers of ex-prisoners is facilitated.

One high official of Kopkamtib has openly discussed this matter. Kopkamtib is the Indonesian secret police unit that empowers Indonesian Army men to carry out arrests and interrogations of subversives in the secret police mode. Kopkamtib was set up on October 10, 1965, by the government of General Suharto, to cope with a large, well-equipped, and energetic left-wing movement. In an astonishing interview with a Dutch journalist, one Kopkamtib official admitted that social-science tests of the sort described in the preceding section had been given to political detainees and probably would continue to be administered. He had ordered the psychological testing, he explained, after he had inquired from the Central Intelligence Agency whether it had "some equipment to detect Communists and was told it had none."

The official's only quarrel with the Dutch journalist interviewing him was over the degree to which the psychologists were involved in actually designing the tests. Almost as if resenting the notion that Kopkamtib was not itself capable of designing such sophisticated testing strategies without requiring the consultation of professional psychologists, the official insisted that the secret police simply had a few "conversations" with these professionals.

While being either coy or defensive on this point, he was less reserved on others. It was not until this interview, in 1979, for instance, that it was learned that Kopkamtib consulted with a wide variety of international experts, not confining itself to home-grown Dutch expertise:

Q: (Dutch journalist): "Is that psychology test for political prisoners, to which Dutch psychologists contributed, still in use?"

A: (Kopkamtib official): "Yes, it is still used. But I want to correct this. . . . We only talked to them [Dutch psychologists] about a system to find out what a person's ideology is like."

Q: "But they helped design the test?"

A: "No, that is not true. I myself was present at the designing of the test. They had nothing to do with that. It was an ordinary discussion. The team of Indonesian psychologists have also been in England and America, where they spoke with a couple of professors. Well, with the results of these talks, a test was designed to be 80 percent reliable. . . .

"The Indonesian psychologists talked with other psychologists, in the Netherlands, England and America, and returned after that. The questionnaire was composed later, and by Kopkamtib, really, not by Indonesian psychologists.

"The problem is, what measures can we take to find out someone's ideology? I have said to the Americans, 'Don't you have a computer that we can put to someone's head so that we can know exactly what his ideology is?' "

Q: "How are the results of the test used?"

A: "The test is carried out every six months. For instance, you may have result A, and after six months, result B. Then we compare: has he changed, or not, et cetera. . . . In addition, we use the declaration that the suspected person signs after interrogation. You have to compare the test with that. We get to know if someone is lying or not, and so we know the state of ideology of that person."

Q: "People whose psychology tests have indicated that they cannot be trusted ideologically will be monitored carefully once they have been released?"

A: "Well, not exactly. In general, these people will always be monitored. For us, it is only a kind of documentation for all prisoners. You should remember that we have had some bitter experiences. In 1948, we had the first communist coup. In 1965, the second. I don't think we can afford a third one. Therefore, we have taken measures so that it won't happen again."

Q: "How is the ideology of a detainee determined?"

A: "We cannot read people's thoughts. By means of psycho-tests, we can measure their knowledge of ideological matters, and then check this with the report of their interrogation. From this, we know and determine their classification.

"There are two categories.

"K [keras, or hard], which is further divided into four groups; and "L [lunak, or soft], which is further divided into L-0, L-1, and L-2.

"Observations are taken every six months. . . ."

Q: "You have said that about 30 percent are classified as 'diehards.' What age group are these?"

A: "It doesn't only depend on age, but also on the position in the party. The diehards are the ones classified as K."

General Sumitro, the major general who administered the battery of psychological tests to twenty-nine thousand political prisoners in

1976, studied psychology at the Universities of Leyden, in the Netherlands, and Freiburg, in West Germany. He was a bit defensive about his work. "We already knew that they all are Communists," said the major general. "The tests were only to determine the degree of their Communist inclination."

General Sumitro was quite specific about the tests. He explained that five tests had been administered by a specially trained group of two hundred assistants. First came a basic intelligence test. Two other tests *not* especially devised for Indonesia included an American test, the Edwards Personal Preference Schedule. Its application to Indonesia's political prisoners, the general said, was to test the firmness of their convictions and motivation and their capacity to influence others.

"It shows us if they are good fighters," explained the general. "If their score is high, that's bad for us."

The other test on political attitudes was designed by a British psychologist. The degree of intensity with which Communist sentiments were held was scored on a scale ranging from "tough-minded" to "tenderness." And the two final tests were "thematic differentiation" tests especially devised for Indonesian conditions. Cleverly, General Sumitro declined to disclose what questions were asked. Sumitro then added that the test scores were fed into a computer and supplemented with interrogation files and observations recorded about prisoners during their detentions. The results of the tests, he said, were 80 percent accurate.

1

In Chile, whole sectors of the medical profession were co-opted by the secret police. Political prisoners in Chile were subjected to sodium pentothal and other drug injections by physicians attending interrogation sessions. According to a United Nations report, with the aid of doctors, psychological pressure was exerted upon victims to increase by measurable amounts the level of fear and anxiety in them. Furthermore, attempts at hypnosis were also reported. A doctor at Cuatro Álamos prison known as *"el Brujo"* (the sorcerer) allegedly used hypnosis, pentothal, and/or other chemical drugs to try to make prisoners talk, or to make them forget the period when they were subjected to torture or held incommunicado. A 1980 United Nations report described what happened to one woman activist who was arrested by CNI (DINA's successor) in 1979: "She was taken to a CNI clinic. . . . The doctors behaved professionally, but did not help her. She heard them saying, 'none of her vital organs are affected' and they handed her over to CNI, although she had a temperature, was bleeding and had low blood pressure. She was taken to an unknown place, a basement . . . they began to torture her. . . . She was given medical examinations before being tortured, and while torture was being administered the doctors said: 'Stop, otherwise this bag of bones is going to give out on you.' The doctors collaborated fully with the torturers. A drop in blood pressure resulted in the torture being stopped. . . ."

While Chile during the mid-seventies seemed to be far ahead of some countries in its sophisticated use of scientific and medical experts, Chile was by no means alone in making use of such consultants. In Greece, army doctors for ESA attended to the medical needs of political prisoners with steady doses of inattentiveness. One prisoner recalled being visited by a physician after he had been forced to stand upright in his cell corner for four consecutive days. The physician took the prisoner's pulse, then asked him how long he had been left standing in that position. When the prisoner told him, "Four days," the physician said, "All right," and left. Among the inmates of the political prison, the doctor soon achieved the popular recognition of a nickname, based on the most common prescription he would tend to write out whenever anyone complained of illness resulting from torture. He became known as the "orange juice doctor."

Doctors in the service of the secret police tend not to kill political "patients" with kindness. One physician—nicknamed Dr. Mengele (after the famed Nazi torturer) by inmates of Rakowiecka Street Prison, in Warsaw—worked in the Twelfth Pavilion of that prison, which former prisoners say was devoted entirely to prisoners of UB, the Polish secret police. One day, the physician was asked to sign a health certificate verifying that the prisoner was well enough to be admitted to a punishment (isolation) cell. Without even looking up at the prisoner, the doctor signed the form. Within twenty-four hours, the patient—too weak to stand the rigors of isolation and the special, reduced diet—expired. Still, the UB authorities had their "certificate of health" in response to all inquiries.

In addition to writing prescriptions or signing the necessary forms, physicians have been attentive to the extreme difficulties of keeping prisoners alive while not reducing the rigors of the interrogations. The testimony of a former political prisoner in Argentina, regarding the travails of her husband who was incarcerated with her simultaneously, illustrates the point all too vividly:

"Once, while I was hearing the screams of Alberto [her husband] the loudspeakers called for a doctor. Then I heard the doctor say, 'That is all, if you still want him alive.' "

Testimony from a Uruguayan political prisoner is strikingly similar: "To begin with, the prison had only one doctor. He supervised the torture, and, during interrogation, I heard him advising the torturers on which part of the body to hit a person who had got some illness. The doctor dealt with such details."

Doctors collaborating with secret police torturers advise not only on where to hit—but for how long as well. The torturers at the central police station in Bilbao (Spain) employed the services of a doctor. He examined torture victims, patched them up, bandaged their ribs, or recommended hospitalization. His chief role was to advise the police on how long it would take for the torture victims' bruises to disappear. "After the first week they left me alone," said one Basque separatist-activist. "On [date omitted] and again on [date omitted] I was examined by a man dressed like a doctor. The police asked him how long it would take for the bruises and marks to go away, so they could tell how long to keep me at the police station. In my case, the 'doctor' said ten days."

A Brazilian imprisoned in 1974 was left semiconscious and dangling by handcuffs on a prison wall when he sensed someone coming up to him again, and he braced himself for the pain—but instead, he felt only a piece of cold metal being placed on his chest. "The cold metal moved to another spot," he recalled, "and I perceived that it was a doctor's stethoscope. Apparently they wanted to check my heart to see how I was bearing up."

Upon his release, a former political prisoner held at a camp in Manila attempted to describe, for the benefit of those on the outside, the behavior of the doctors on the inside. "Doctors and nurses share the common military attitude that prisoners should not be viewed as human beings," he wrote in 1974.

In the Soviet Union, the physician tends to monitor the physical health of prisoners with an equally uncaring hand. During one hunger strike in 1974 at a camp in Perm Colony VS393135, nonstriking prisoners demanded that striking prisoners be force-fed. "Force-

feeding will be resumed on the basis of medical symptoms," declared the doctor, an army major, "as soon as they begin to smell of
acetone." (The body begins to smell of acetone when in an acute
stage of starvation.)†

11

The use of "mental hospitals" to incarcerate political dissidents is
common in Eastern Europe, especially in Romania and the U.S.S.R.
A political dissident is admitted to a mental hospital on the grounds
that anyone in opposition to a regime that has created near-utopian
social and economic conditions must necessarily be deranged. With
the use of drugs, electroshock treatment, insulin shock, and the like,
physicians, in the context of the mental hospital, seek not only to
destroy the patient's will but to reorder his mind as well. Interrogations are conducted in the presence of the psychiatrist, with questions regarding the patient's attitude toward socialism, the political
leaders of the government, and the system itself. In essence, a political history as well as a physical history is taken down by the admitting physician. The Romanian psychiatrist works alongside of the
Securitate agent.

In the U.S.S.R., the KGB has in numerous cases played a major
role at various stages between confinement and release, although the
only agency outside the psychiatric service that is given a formal
role under these procedures is the police, that role being administered by the MVD.

The Serbsky Institute (the Moscow Central Research Institute for
Forensic Psychiatry) collaborated closely with state security organs
in providing false diagnoses of offenders' mental conditions. In a
brilliantly titled book, *Punitive Medicine* (not published, of course,
in the U.S.S.R.), a young emergency medical technician by the
name of Alexander Podrabinek laughingly described the way the
Moscow emergency ambulance service often was the vehicle by
which dissidents were forcibly hospitalized. Instead of being picked
up by a squad car or an unmarked vehicle, the political criminal is
taken away by ambulance. Instead of filling out an arrest report, the
authorities complete a medical report. If the incident occurred in a
Western country like the United States, one would imagine that in-

† The current practice in the U.S.S.R., laid down in an unpublished MVD
directive, is to resume feeding only when the body smells of acetone.

stead of requiring a bail bondsman, the "patient" would only require evidence of medical insurance before release.

Once committed, the political prisoner (a/k/a mental-hospital inmate) spends most of his time in the custody of the Serbsky Institute's lesser-tier psychiatrists. The renowned psychiatrists bother with them only for a quick, ten-to-fifteen-minute interview. The final diagnosis is done by the lower-level staff, while the director of the Serbsky Institute arranges for the way the diagnosis is done.

Some of the chiefs of staff of the special psychiatric hospitals, which are designed for "treatment" of the especially provocative or dangerous dissidents, are MVD (Ministry of the Interior)‡ officials. There is no question about that. Each special psychiatric hospital is headed by two chiefs: the director (an MVD commandant) and the chief doctor. All doctors who are heads of departments, as well as many of the treating doctors, are commissioned officers in the MVD. And some senior nurses and medical assistants are also MVD personnel. There is no question, then, that to achieve prominence as a psychiatrist it is quite helpful to be a member of the MVD. Since the definition of mental health is directly related to political attitude, it makes sense that state security organs should have some say in the structure and leadership of the mental-health industry. When a Leningrad engineer was confined to a psychiatric hospital for the fourth time, in 1974, for his *samizdat* writings and his open protests on human-rights violations to authorities, another well-known dissenter went to see the deputy chief doctor of the psychiatric clinic where his friend and colleague had been diagnosed and ordered committed. "We possess the information and an evaluation from the competent authorities," the doctor told him, ". . . officials of the KGB. . . . They make a political judgement and phone us, advising us to intern Ponomaryov [the engineer]. For us to make a medical diagnosis it's enough simply to know of the existence of anti-government letters. There's no need to read them."

According to one political prisoner who defected from the U.S.S.R., release from a mental hospital, which is decided by a semi-annual review of an official hospital commission, is dependent upon the admission of a "corrective statement." Without it, the patient is

‡ There is some question as to whether or not there are more MVD or KGB officials in charge of the U.S.S.R. psychiatric institutions. Certainly the KGB has delegated much of its authority to the MVD (see Chapter Three, Section Six).

still deemed mentally ill. A doctor in a Leningrad special psychiatric hospital told one of his patients: "Your discharge depends on your conduct. By conduct, we mean your opinions precisely on political questions. Your disease is dissent."

12

The political pressures on the medical profession to aid the state in maintaining the level of security the regime requires are often severe. In Chile, Argentina, Indonesia, and South Africa, to mention just a few countries, the penalties for noncompliance range from slowed progress within the profession to banishment and even liquidation. Chile's DINA purged many leftist doctors from the ranks of the profession and murdered many others. Doctors who catered to the medical needs of the poor, especially in places like the Barros Lucos Hospital, in Santiago, were targeted by DINA. In this effort, the secret police was ably assisted by the leaders of the Chilean medical profession. "We will not gain anything by letting antisocial elements back into the hospital," said the head of the Chilean Medical Association after the 1973 coup. "We have to settle accounts with these doctors who played politics." In South Africa, physicians are clearly conditioned to ignore surges of conscience in sticky political situations. During the postmortem proceedings that followed the death of Steve Biko, the black-consciousness leader who expired while in the custody of the famed South African Security Branch, one physician who examined Biko while he was languishing in detention was asked whether he had inquired of the police, or of Biko, as to the origins of the bruises on his head. "I didn't think I was required to do so," said one examining physician. "I didn't think of it," said another examining physician.

In Iran, SAVAK intruded upon the course of legitimate medical procedures by nurturing a close relationship to the coroner's office. The former deputy director of the Tehran coroner's office alleged that several doctors in the coroner's office "were themselves handpicked by SAVAK and their boss was also a SAVAK agent." These doctors, he says, when visiting SAVAK prisons to issue death certificates for those executed by SAVAK, were not permitted to mention in their visiting reports that the nails of the prisoners were inhumanly removed, or that they had been tortured or burnt. "Often we would torture them to death," said one torturer. "We would stick hot iron bars in their noses and eyes. And we would tell the coroner to write suicide as the cause of death." When SAVAK once executed nine revolutionaries, despite the fact that there was clear evidence of physical torture having been performed on the deceased, doctors were not allowed to report that the bullets had been fired from the front. "Surely, if they were shot while trying to escape, the bullets would have hit them in the back," commented the deputy director of a provincial coroner's office after the Shah's fall.

The most sympathetic analysis of this process of involvement and co-optation on the part of doctors with regard to the application of torture suggests, according to Drs. Leonard Sagan and Albert Jonsen, in the *New England Journal of Medicine* (1976), "Physicians who are employed to examine or treat prisoners may slowly realize that they are being accomplices to torture, if only by providing the appearance of legitimacy to the process, or by providing information to the torturers that allows them to proceed. Caught in this situation, the physician may find forces of economics, career or loyalty to the organization stronger than the moral compulsion to protest, especially when protest may put him and his family in jeopardy." How could this come about? In Canada, for example, doctors register the prescriptions they issue on secret lists maintained in order to prevent "doctor shopping" by patients seeking second or third prescriptions and to aid them in cases where unfamiliar patients may have adverse reactions to a prescribed drug. These otherwise secret lists they have compiled have been put to other ends. As required by law, the lists are sent to federal health authorities in confidence. But the RCMP obtained Edmonton lists and was using them as late as the spring of 1978 to check with doctors regarding their patients as to reasons why the prescription was issued. That is, RCMP agents were perusing these prescription lists in search of anything that might later be used to blackmail or intimidate targets. In April of 1978, the federal government introduced legislation designed to bring police and RCMP activities in this area under tighter control, so that police must now obtain warrants from judges in order to obtain such lists. In addition, for many years the gathering and cataloging of information from medical records concerning the treatment of sexual or mental problems was used by the RCMP to disrupt radical groups— under the code name of Operation Featherbed.

In essence, if we are to believe Drs. Sagan and Jonsen in their theory of innocent co-optation of the medical profession, much the same factors that compel some poor, indigent, hopeless soul from some decrepit ghetto to enter the secret police profession and engage in torture, compel professional physicians and psychiatrists to perform more or less the same services for the secret police, albeit in a more controlled and sophisticated fashion. But surely there is more to it than this. Surely the educated professional would feel restricted by certain constraints that the less developed mentality might not?

Perhaps there is more to the problem than simple equations or economics. Perhaps the intermingling of politics and medicine creates certain new problems that have not been fully explored. One wonders at the dilemma of the physician, for instance, faced with the request to examine a detainee awaiting an intensive interrogation session. To wash one's hands of such involvement may be noble in the abstract, but what does such noble philosophical detachment do for the detainee? If the physician is called in by the secret police to determine the degree to which the detainee can withstand further interrogation, is it in the interest of the detainee for the physician to refuse to render judgment? It is the old question: at what point does the refusal to serve within the system, in however limited a capacity, equal impotence?

The questions are apparently trickier than they might at first appear. A royal commission in Great Britain studying the problem in fact came to the conclusion that it is important for the interrogation to proceed only if the interrogator has the professional input of the physician or psychiatrist. Does such input make the doctor a torturer? Or would such input reduce the long-term negative effects of the interrogation, and therefore constitute a positive, if limited, contribution? The royal commission had less trouble with this question than we do, but its reasoning is worth thinking about. According to the Parker Committee Report, of 1972, which was considering (it believed) interrogations that are severe only in their degree of oral combativeness (no electric-shock or submarine torture here), the degree of interrogation must be correlated with the medical condition of the detainee. "A doctor with some psychiatric training should be present at all times at the interrogation center, and should be in a position to observe the course of oral interrogation. It is not suggested that he should be himself responsible for stopping the interrogation—rather that he should warn the controller if he felt that the interrogation was being pressed too far . . . leaving the decision to the controller." The formulation of the Parker Committee is both instructive and troubling. Operating on the optimistic and idealistic assumption that the interrogation never strays beyond the intensity of oral pressure, it may be possible for the medical profession to live within these guidelines. But what should be the doctor's position if the detainee was subjected to excessively stressful environments of the sophisticated sensory-deprivation sort prior to the interrogation? And what should be the medical profession's position, knowing that the detainee is likely to have to resume existing in a stressful environment if he fails to perform adequately for the security service during the interrogation? Should the physician permit the interrogation to proceed a bit longer, despite his best judgment, in the belief that this is the lesser evil for the detainee; that what he faces outside the interrogation room will be far more harmful to his mental and physical health than what he has to endure inside of the interrogation room in the presence of the observer-physician? And what if the doctor suspects, but is not sure, that the postinterrogation environment contains at least a little, if not a lot, of torture? Should he remove himself entirely from the process of advising the secret police, on the grounds that the adviser is necessarily a supporter of the system? Or would the decision to withdraw entirely, assuming that it could be made without serious consequences to the decision maker, in effect produce an interrogation system without any safeguards whatsoever for the detainee? How partial must the conscience be? Or how absolute?

In a stark analysis of the relationship between the growth of state power and the ethical problems of this nature by Dr. Earl Cooperman, published in the *Canadian Medical Association Journal,* Dr. Cooperman is so exceedingly distrustful of any state involvement in the practice of medicine that one would not be astonished if he were less surprised by the prospect of physicians serving as torturers or torturers' accomplices than most of us. Pointing to the dissolution of the intimate and private doctor-patient relationship, and the growing obligation of the physician to the state under any number of political systems involving state-subsidized or socialized medicine, he argues that abuses in medical care are entirely related to the unchecked growth of the power of the state.

"Chile and Russia are at diametrically opposite poles," he points out, "yet in both countries the medical profession has become merely another state agency." He further believes that serious problems for the profession will occur in less polarized instances, too.

Even in such democratic countries as Canada, which are experiencing seemingly inevitable movements toward socialized medicine, state power could expand to the point where, for instance, once-privileged medical information would be handed over to the state on demand. It is, of course, possible to view Dr. Cooperman's analysis as nothing more than narrow-minded pleading against socialized medicine. But, in view of the fact of growing involvement of physicians and psychiatrists in the interrogation procedures and practices of nation-states, that assessment might tend to dismiss what in fact is an important point.

What should the medical profession do? "Besides the individual responsibility of every doctor who as a result of circumstances has become involved in torture procedures," write Professor Alfred Heidjer, of Amsterdam University, and Dr. Herman van .Geuns, formerly of Amnesty International's Executive Committee, "a much wider responsibility rests upon the medical profession." But their solution to what has only recently been understood as an increasingly serious problem is less compelling than their idealism. They call for a professional code of ethics to help physicians resolve these sorts of conflicts. Good luck; as the 1946 Declaration of Geneva, formulated by the World Medical Association the same year, puts the ethic of the medical professional: "I will maintain the utmost respect for human life from the time of conception; even under threat, I will not use my medical knowledge contrary to the laws of humanity." What precisely does that tell the physician or the psychiatrist practicing under the twilight-zone circumstances of the contemporary world of the secret police? At the inquest into the death of Steve Biko, Sidney Kentridge, the attorney for the Biko family, put this question to one of those who examined Biko just before he died: "In terms of the Hippocratic oath, are not the interests of your patients paramount?" To which the doctor answered, "Yes." "But," Kentridge continued, "in this instance they were subordinated to the interests of security?" To which the doctor again replied, "Yes."

13

The prevalence of torture today, whether at the hands of some uneducated, low-life character clothed in the garb of a secret police organization and bolstered by the sense of authority associated with such work, or at the hands of a trained medical scientist, may be attributable to factors beyond those examined thus far.

"The situation in which one agent commands another to hurt a third turns up time and again as a significant theme in human relations," concluded Dr. Stanley Milgram, of Yale University.

Dr. Milgram's conclusion may have been the understatement of the past few decades (he was writing in the sixties), but his pioneering experiments designed to test the conditions under which the torture of one human being by another might be performed were hardly understated. Those experiments may bring us closer to a profound understanding of the mind of the torturer.

The Milgram experiments were simply structured. Under what condition will Y carry out the command of X to inflict pain on Z? And under what conditions will Y refuse the command of X to hurt Z?

Put the secret police torturer, or physician, into the role of Y, and the relevance of Milgram's study to these issues becomes clear.

Milgram conducted his experiments at Yale. Hiring volunteers at a mere pittance, the Milgram team told the volunteers that he was trying to establish the effects of punishment on memory, that what they were doing was very important to the advancement of science, and that they must follow X's instructions.

And so the Milgram team put the volunteers into situations in which they believed that they would be inflicting pain on their Zs for every failure of those Zs to answer questions correctly. Of course, the situations were setups: no electric shock pain was actually being transmitted. When any one Y (the volunteer) pressed the lever to deliver the "punishment" on any one Z, the Y did not understand that the Z was acting. No real pain was transmitted, but the Y did not know this. The Y thought his lever was punishing his Z.

Through this experimental design, the Milgram team sought to establish a crucial question: In this authoritarian structure, how far would the volunteer (Y) go? How much pain would the Y inflict on the Z? Even after hearing howls or seeing the apparent effects of the punishment, would the Y go even higher in the level of pain administered?

To be sure, many of those Ys inflicting the "electric shocks" were markedly distressed. One subject, in fact, screamed (with regard to the Z upon whom he was "inflicting pain"): "He can't stand it! I'm not going to kill that man in there! Who is going to take responsibility if anything happens to that gentleman?" Yet, oddly, terrifyingly, despite such distress, the subject unfailingly obeyed the experimenter's demands to proceed to administer shock at the higher level on the "generator."

The Milgram team was astonished at the high level of obedience of the Ys to the commands of the Xs (the Milgram team) to really "lay the pain" onto the Zs. The psychiatrists had predicted that most subjects (Ys) wouldn't go beyond the tenth shock level of the electric generator (which was, of course, a dummy machine). But, in fact, fully 62 percent of the volunteers went *beyond* that level.

Milgram speculated about what he and his team had observed, coming to this tentative conclusion: "Somehow, the subject becomes implicated in a situation from which he cannot disengage himself . . . . In certain circumstances, it is not so much the *kind of man* as the *kind of situation* in which he is placed, that determines his action."

Milgram speculated: "Human nature . . . or . . . the kind of character produced in American democratic society—cannot be counted on to insulate its citizens from brutality and inhumane treatment at the direction of malevolent authority. A substantial proportion of people do what they are told to do, irrespective of the contents of the act and without limitations of conscience, so long as they perceive that the command comes from a legitimate authority. If in this study an anonymous experimenter could successfully command adults to subdue a fifty-year-old man, and force on him painful electric shocks against his protests, one can only wonder what government, with its vastly greater authority, and prestige, can command of its subjects."

FIVE

Safe Houses, Background Music, and Athletic Clubs: Interrogation by Torture

1

The author of the lesson plan was remarkably clear on the point.

The professional interrogator, according to the outline, "avoids so-called third-degree tactics and never deviates from the fundamentals that a prisoner must be treated according to legal and humanitarian principles:

"A. It lowers his own self-respect.
"B. It impairs police efficiency.
"C. It lowers the esteem of the police in the public eye.
"D. It leads to false confessions and miscarriges [sic] of justice."

Sound advice? To be sure—and it was taken from the lesson plan for the course "Interviews and Interrogations," taught at the International Police Academy. But before the academy was closed down by the United States Government, in 1975, it had a reputation in some parts of the world as the "School for Torturers." The fact of the matter was that the International Police Academy, in downtown Washington, D.C., was widely suspected, if not of training agents how to torture in formal fashion, then at least of preparing police agents in some generalized sense for this line of work.

As the lesson plan aptly put it, "An interrogation is a questioning of a person suspected of an offense or a person who is reluctant to make a full disclosure of information in his possession which is pertinent to the investigation."

In the seventies, it seems, there were many such reluctant persons around the world, and accordingly, secret police in many countries —Communist as well as non-Communist, Third World countries and others—employed interrogation techniques designed to overwhelm their subjects' reticence with fear. According to the documentation gathered by Amnesty International, the respected human-rights organization, the use of torture as an arbitrary administrative practice occurred during the seventies in the internal-security organizations of nearly three dozen nations.

Of course, all police institutions interrogate. The more notorious secret police organizations, however, become notorious precisely because they employ physical and psychological torture as a routine technique of interrogation. The interrogation by torture is as central to the operations of the notorious secret police as are peremptory arrest and indefinite detention. Torture, to many secret policemen, is not an appendage of their operations; it is of the essence of many secret police institutions.

The plausible aim of any interrogation is to obtain information. But the aim of the interrogation in which torture is used may go considerably beyond this. It may include the element of administrative revenge and the element of an intimidatory message to resound throughout the populace. "DINA was not in the business of sadism," insisted a Chilean defense attorney once arrested by DINA (but not tortured). "No one repressed beyond what one needed to repress. Torture is only a means to an end, a political tool. You repressed an amount proportional to the model operation you had before you."

In theory, perhaps, a correct formulation . . . but torture is not an unemotional science. In reality, the use of torture as a routine practice tends to develop an administrative—and human (or inhuman)—momentum of its own. Despite efforts to streamline procedures and to innovate for more efficiency, torture is not an exact science. It is, rather, a monstrous art, designed in a moral vacuum.*

2

The momentum at which torture is carried out in various countries accelerates according to the resources of the secret police and the time frame they are working within.

In Singapore, political prisoners have been forced to do repeated and strenuous exercises during round-the-clock interrogations, resulting in severe fatigue. In Haiti, prisoners received beatings that were rough but routine. "I was beaten twice daily," said one former political prisoner. "Mornings and evenings, each day by a different guard. I regularly lost consciousness."

In Iran, according to one source, at least a half million people were "beaten, whipped or tortured by the SAVAK." Recalled the Iranian poet Reza Baraheni, "Most of the horrible instruments were located on the second floor [of the SAVAK building]. I was not taken there, but the office of my interrogator . . . was next to his chamber, and one day when he was called to another office for some sort of consultation, I walked into the room, glanced around and then went back. It resembled an ancient Egyptian tomb and is reserved for those suspected of being terrorist or accused of having made attempts on the life of the Shah or a member of the Royal Family. Not every prisoner goes through the same process, but generally, this is what happens to a prisoner of the first importance. First, he is beaten by several torturers at once, with sticks and clubs. If he doesn't confess, he is hanged upside down and beaten; if this doesn't work, he is raped; and if he still shows signs of resistance, he is given electric shock which turns him into a howling dog; and if he is still obstinate, his nails and sometimes all his teeth are pulled out, and in certain exceptional cases, a hot iron rod is put into one side of the face to force its way to the other side."

In South Africa, as in many other countries (see the "A Torture Glossary"), electric shock treatment was the preferred technique. "There are of course other methods," explained U. S. Congressman

---

* Please refer to "A Torture Glossary," in the Appendixes, for details on the standard torture techniques.

Andrew Maguire after an investigation of conditions of detention and allegations of torture in South Africa. "Simple physical assaults are common. [But] the one that is most commonly identified is electricity. Electrodes are placed on the head, neck or wrists."

Some white South African exiles say that electric shock torture is used with far more caution and far less frequency today in their native country, explaining that the treatment, having resulted in some deaths of detainees, caused enough scandals to induce the police to use it more sparingly. The South African Government of course altogether denies allegations of applying electric shock torture and other physical tortures. In a government reply to allegations of torture levied by Amnesty International, officials attributed those allegations to "some Communist plot to undermine morale in South Africa."

So, too, the Philippine Government denies that torture is a customary practice of its security services. But the denials lack credibility in the face of overwhelming evidence to the contrary. As one former member of the Quezon City Police Department put it: "It [torture] is standard operating procedure. It's part and parcel of the arrest procedure. . . . The police are trained to do it."

"With regard to torture," said one Chilean lawyer testifying before the U. S. House of Representatives on the issue of DINA, "I can say that I agree with the more publicized reports on the subject. They unanimously point out that torture is a systematic practice, especially during the first period of the arrest, [while the arrested person] is kept incommunicado. . . . The main impact of torture is psychologic or moral. . . . More than broken bones, they are broken personalities. . . ."

Interrogation procedures in the Communist-bloc countries—like those in so many other countries—take on the form of established routine. One Zionist activist in Moscow was interrogated [though never tortured] every day for two weeks in one particular run-in with the KGB. "It is like a job," he recalled. "A nine-to-five day, with a one-hour break in between." The KGB even provided his employer with a form, much like a sick excuse from school. "These are standard forms," he said. "So-and-so has been called to the KGB from the hours of nine to five."

The KGB does not, however, favor physical forms of torture. Nine-to-five interrogation may contain subtle hints of physical intimidation, but the KGB is no SAVAK. To the extent that political targets are incarcerated at all (leaving aside the forced-labor camps), the KGB seems to favor isolation cells (to cool subjects off and give them a chance to consider their predicament) and psychiatric hospitals (to alter the personalities of the subjects).

And since the early fifties, the KGB has especially preferred the application of medicines over and above physical torture.† Powerful tranquilizers are commonly used on dissenters—haloperidol, for instance, which produces at the same time an excruciating rigidity and a restlessness within the victim. Inmates given the drug complained of "unimaginable anxiety, groundless fear, sleeplessness." (The use of haloperidol has even inspired a song among inmates of special psychiatric hospitals, which begins with the words, "You can't sit, you can't lie, you can't walk.")

Repeated ingestion of haloperidol caused this type of reaction in a Ukrainian cyberneticist who was punished for "anti-Soviet agitation and propaganda" by confinement to the Dnepropetrovsk Special Hospital for two and a half years:

"When they brought Leonid Ivanovich into the visiting room," recalled his wife, "it was impossible to recognize him. His eyes were full of pain and misery, he spoke with difficulty and brokenly, frequently leaning on the back of the chair in search of support. His effort at self-control was evident as from time to time he closed his eyes, trying to carry on a conversation and answer questions. But his inner strength was exhausted. Leonid Ivanovich began to gasp, to awkwardly unbutton his clothing. . . . His face was convulsed and he got a cramp in his hands and legs. . . . It was evident from time to time that he lost his hearing. . . . Leonid Ivanovich could not control himself, and it was he who asked that the meeting be ended ten minutes ahead of time." The object of the KGB pharmaceutical torture is not to obtain information, obviously, but to remove a dissident personality from the scene without killing him. Another purpose is to reform his political views. Certainly the drug tortures serve a third purpose, similar to the desired object of interrogation coupled with physical torture in other countries: to send a message of warning to the population at large.

† Allegations of torture treatments involving the application of drugs have surfaced in numerous other countries as well. In South Africa, for example, black mental patients have allegedly been given large amounts of psychotropic drugs. The facilities used to administer these drug treatments have supposedly been provided to security police by some psychiatrists.

3

A black South African activist said he wasn't terribly bothered by the taunts ("How can you black monkeys run a country? Look at what Amin did.") coming from white Security Branch officers holding him at John Vorster Square. "When you really get frightened," he went on, "is when you realize that someone has broken and has spilled out a lot of information incriminating you. You know by the specific questions they ask. And this is when the beating begins."

A magistrate visited his cell every two weeks during his imprisonment, asking him if he had any complaints. But when the magistrate showed up at the cell, he was always in the company of the interrogation team that had been doing the beatings. The team was dumbstruck when the activist decided to complain. "Yes, I was beaten," he told the magistrate. Even today, five years later, he recalls the menacing expressions on the team members' faces. "They will never beat you again," the magistrate replied. But two white Security Branch officers, who began to beat him in the last of several series of beatings that *followed* the complaint to the magistrate, told him, "So you told the magistrate we beat you up. Well, now you will get worse. There is nothing he can do." With that, a huge, 250-pound man nicknamed by inmates "Struwg"—the Beast—began pounding him on the back of the head like a jackhammer.

It is rare for the political detainee to complain about torture. The complaint seldom does any good, and it often makes matters worse. On the West Bank of the Jordan, an Arab who claimed to have been tortured by Israeli secret police ultimately decided against making a formal statement, despite the fact that his injuries (damages to the testicles) had been witnessed by an official of the International Red Cross. "He changed his mind . . . ," said one source, "because his interrogators had threatened to return him to torture if he persisted."

Israeli State Attorney General Bach has argued that a suspect is protected against a confession extracted under duress by the procedure known as the "trial within a trial," or the "little trial." Here, as he explained, whenever the suspect alleges that his confession was taken under duress, the court holds a special hearing to examine whether or not the confession has been given freely. Bach even cited three cases in which the courts had ruled a suspect's confession inadmissible. But, according to some lawyers who claim to have advised their clients to dispute the nature of their confessions only when there is an absolutely compelling reason to do so, to enter a "little trial" and lose the case often results in a higher sentence. And for the alleged victim to lose is not an unlikely occurrence, partly because evidence in support of an allegation of maltreatment is difficult to produce, since the detainee may well have been denied access to his family and his lawyer throughout that period.

A South Korean opponent of the Park government remembered how, during his first encounter with KCIA interrogators, he was warned not to look to other people to get out of his predicament. "I was taken to an interrogation room at the KCIA, where two agents and two or three policemen administered the water torture. First, I was forced to kneel on the cement floor, where I was beaten with the side slat of an army cot all over my body. I was being threatened; one of the agents said to me, 'You know, Professor (name deleted) died at KCIA headquarters? Not a rat or a bird told a soul. Nobody said a word. You know you could die, we could dispose of your body and that would be the end of it. You didn't know the KCIA was such a frightening place, did you? . . ."

On the surface, the main aim of the interrogation is, first and foremost, to obtain information—usually about others; if they have you, they tend to already know a great deal about you.

An analysis of the famous SAVAK Joint Committee interrogation system appeared in a left-wing newspaper published in Iran. In this analysis, SAVAK's method of tracing antigovernment networks was outlined with precision—and with a keen eye to the need for coordination, of both agents and suspects. Ignore, if you can, the anti-Shah rhetoric, and observe the clarity of the guerrilla spokesman's understanding of the operations of the enemy:

"Due to the tremendous fear of the growing power of the guerrillas—expressed by SAVAK, the Information Bureau of the police and the Second Branch of the Army—the regime arranged that these three groups would combat the revolutionaries side by side and hence control one another's actions.

"The building in which the committee interrogates its [important] political prisoners is itself of great value in achieving this objective. It is a three-story building around a circular court which has all its rooms facing out upon a court. These rooms are for interrogation and torture.

"On each floor there is also a balcony which looks out onto the court and provides for a means to connect all the rooms to one another. In addition to this physical setting, which permits the members of the Committee to control one another, when some of the agents of the Committee torture a revolutionary, all the other agents compete with one another to show their allegiance to the regime by joining in the action and physically abusing [their own] tortured person.

"Another reason for the formation of the Committee is that the regime seeks to have a centralized program to combat the revolutionaries. . . . The regime wants to discover the connections between different people more efficiently. In the past, [prior to 1975], when SAVAK arrested someone, they would take that person to their own place of interrogation . . . and the city police would do likewise. . . . Consequently, the connection between different groups was not discovered. Now, in the Committee, there is a centralized structure. . . ."

A second aim of interrogation (after information) is to obtain a confession, which may or may not contain accurate information. Often, getting the results—i.e., a lengthy confession—is more important than the need to obtain an absolutely accurate report. A Taiwanese dissident described an experience that took place in 1979:

"In the security division, six people, divided into three groups of two, took turns questioning me for forty days. Among the six men, one was responsible for beating me. These six people took on different roles. Some were fierce, others were refined. But there was one common denominator among them all. It had already been fixed in their minds that (I was a member of) a seditious organization. . . .

"For at least three solid days and nights without sleep, I was asked the same questions over and over again. If the investigators weren't satisfied with an answer, they would hit me. Hit me until I couldn't bear it any longer. . . . Everything was done to extract that perfect and convincing record. . . .

"Over and over again the same questions. I couldn't take this kind of situation. I asked them if I could spin a long yarn. They replied, 'Just the facts.' They didn't want me to say too much, and too little wouldn't do. 'If you don't cooperate, we'll beat you into a communist.'

"I . . . couldn't see any friends or relatives. . . . I felt removed from the world. Cut off from newspapers, news and radio, I experienced total despair and dejection. Under these circumstances, I wrote the confession with complete compliance to their demands. . . . I yielded to end the torment and suffering. In my record I know there are a few points that are complete fabrications."

Under the Pol Pot regime of Cambodia, thousands of prisoners were tortured into making whatever confessions the agents desired of them, whether this meant saying that they were agents for the CIA, the KGB and/or the Vietnamese, sometimes even at the same time. The head of Nokorbal, the Cambodian secret police, would peruse the confessions, marking with a red pen what he did or did not like about the confessions. And prisoners knew that what he did not like, if not altered to suit his tastes, would lead to further torture.

The Uruguayan defector from the Army (Lieutenant Cooper) described the point of many interrogations:

Q: "What was and is the object of torture?"

A: "Well, in the beginning I consider, because I was involved personally and could observe it in the general run of officers, that the purpose of torture was purely and exclusively to obtain a statement from the detainees."

Q: "In other words, to extort confessions?"

A: "To extort confessions. Although owing to a degeneration in the application of the method and also in the attitude of the different men who worked in applying it, I consider and can even prove that there were cases of officers who frequently left aside this aim, objective or its achievement and tortured just for the sake of torturing. . . ."

Q: "And if the detainee were completely innocent, had no knowledge and had nothing to confess . . . what happened?"

A: "Well, I have always considered, and still consider, that in Uruguay there are a large number of people (who were) detained who are completely innocent, since, taking into account the way in which torture is applied, practically no margin is left to the detainee to demonstrate his innocence in any way. From the first moment of the detainee's arrival at the detention center, torture was applied; the form of the application was something impossible for him to avoid, nor could he demonstrate himself innocent of what he was charged with. I also consider that because of the human condition of the individual, principally, in many cases, the detainee preferred to invent and attribute to himself responsibilities which were not real, pro-

vided he could be free of torture. . . . A great distinction was made
between the methods of torture and interrogation applied on those
detained for political reasons and those detained for common law
reasons. . . . Very few of those detained for common law reasons
were tortured."

A South African interrogator revealed at the inquest into the
death of black-consciousness leader Steve Biko that getting the
"truth"—whether in the form of simple information or a lengthy
confession—was his goal, although in the pursuit of that goal he
might have absolutely no idea how to recognize the truth if he was
told it. And the interrogator seemed not to care about this potential
for misrepresentation of fact. "It is general practice that if you come
to a detainee, then you tell him to tell the truth," he said, adding,
however, "You sometimes don't even know what the case is about."

Intimidation usually begins before the prisoner has a chance to
assess his situation. A Greek ex-prisoner testified in 1975: "On arrival at headquarters, the detainee would usually be taken to the
commanding officer and verbally threatened with imminent and severe violence. In order to intimidate him, he might be shut up into a
guardroom where there were clubs, whips and canes hanging on the
wall. He would soon be locked in a cell and told to write a statement of confession. . . ."

One reason for the rush to get the confession, it seems, is the need
to justify, bureaucratically, the time and expense of the arrest, interrogation, and detention. A Taiwanese dissident laughingly described
how desperately interrogators wanted to feel that they had performed adequately (although in his particular case they failed abys-
mally):

"After the forty days in the security area, an official investigator
came to ask me how my life was, how the investigators were treating
me, and if the record was freely given. After asking me these questions, he even praised my honesty. Despite the conditions, I had to
laugh at that one. The record and the confession were only a couple
of pages. If the inspector had asked me himself, it wouldn't need
more than one or two days to complete. And I was in here over
forty days, and now they come to put on this act. How could I not
laugh . . . ?"

But the interrogator is not laughing; he is responding to pressure
from above to *produce*. The secret police agent will sometimes have
his detainee sign a confession in the wake of the torture ordeal, and

sometimes that document will be enough to satisfy. But, on other occasions, the detainee signs two confessions. One, under torture, before the actual interrogators; and another, a duplicate of the first, before an ordinary, uniformed policeman who did not use force and was not involved in the interrogation. With this technique—used only in states where judicial review remains a viable force—the state can then appear in court and testify that in fact the accused had signed freely, that no untoward compulsion had been used to obtain the signature.

In the People's Republic of China, by comparison, the interrogation is not rushed; a wholly different approach to obtaining confessions is practiced by the Public Security Agency. Political offenders, during the interrogation period, are required not to write down *something* but to write down *everything*. Under this clever system, the political police require that the prisoner reveal all that is on his mind. While many secret police forces require suspects to supply just names, dates, and places, the Chinese security forces require the exposition of attitudes, philosophies, and criticisms. And there is no hurry: the pretrial detention period is limited to four years in China. With as much time as is needed, the accused is led to write what amounts to a political autobiography—amounting, perhaps, to hundreds of pages—in the course of which, inevitably, incriminating evidence of some sort can come to light.

And where an important political defendant is involved, the investigation does not stop with just the intensive interrogation of the accused. If a detainee writes about past friendships, relationships, and activities extensively in his autobiography, what he writes is checked step by step with possible witnesses or against the reports already on file of people who may already have been investigated in connection with the case.

In China, there are generally three main phases in the full interrogation of a suspect and the investigation of a case before it is brought to trial.

The first is the preliminary search for criminal evidence by the internal-security group making the arrest. Evidence at this stage includes witnesses' and accused's testimonies.

The second stage is the examination of evidence at a higher level, including interrogation of witnesses and of the accused.

The third phase is the interrogation of the offender by the authorities in charge of preparing the trial.

At various stages, when Public Security authorities are checking the accused's confession with witnesses' testimonies, it is of the greatest importance that the accused "confess"—that is, recognize that what he has done or said is a crime for which he must be "reformed." Otherwise, the interrogation and investigation process will continue indefinitely.

One case, involving an intercepted letter on the subject of members of a political study group, illustrates the elaborate investigation/interrogation line of action taken by the Public Security authorities in prosecuting those whom it deems political enemies.

The intercepted letter was hot stuff. The young author, referring to the studies of Marxist books that he and his colleague were engaging in, mentioned the need to remain "quiet" now that the situation was very tense. Somehow, a copy of the letter was passed on through channels to the Public Security authorities in the county where a young man named Zhang (the recipient of the letter) lived.

The Public Security personnel of the production brigade‡ where Zhang worked convened a meeting and decided upon the following masterfully indirect course of action in response to the letter: they organized a "study class of Mao Zedong Thought" in the brigade's school for all the young people in the brigade, including Zhang. At the end of the study session, Zhang and two other young men were locked up separately in different classrooms for interrogation; Zhang was interrogated by members of the brigade's Security Defense group and militia.

In the course of the interrogation, a member of the militia discreetly slipped a piece of paper under Zhang's cigarette pack, advising him to confess immediately about the "spy ring" that he and his friends had formed.

But Zhang would not admit to any crime; further questioning continued for a week in the brigade headquarters.

After a week, the head of the brigade's Security Defense group accused Zhang of not being frank. With the full approval of the county Public Security authorities, the security official transferred him to a "reception station," where he was supposed to confess.

At the reception station, his case was, in effect, bucked upstairs to the county Public Security authorities, who proceeded to ask him questions about his friends and their ideologies.

‡ A production brigade is virtually the same thing as a village.

But Zhang was stubborn, and again would not confess. And so, after one week, he was again transferred to "reflect on his crimes," in the words of the county Public Security authorities.

At this point, a detention warrant was issued, and Zhang was held in solitary confinement for one month. During this month in isolation he was interrogated, like clockwork, every day from 8:30 A.M. to 12 noon—and from the middle of the afternoon till 6:30 P.M.

Zhang had now become a hard case. He was interrogated by Public Security officials from other counties, as well as his own, and was forced to place his thumbprint on all written records, which were taken after every session.

Finally, after four months, when Zhang broke down, he told his interrogators what they wanted to hear: that his thinking was "reactionary."

And that was no little political crime: Zhang spent the next eighteen months of his time in daily "study, criticism and self-criticism sessions." These draining, enervating sessions were held in cells with other prisoners, to make them "reflect on their crimes," to raise their consciousness, and to confess.

Though no arrest warrant or indictment was ever issued against Zhang, it was two years before he was released. Upon his release, no explanation or official statement was issued or provided.

4

When it is the policy of a secret police organization *not* to let it be widely known that it is in fact an institution of torture, certain precautionary measures must be taken. Marks of torture must not be left on victims' bodies.

For all its notoriety, the Chilean regime, for one, acted as if it preferred not to be discovered. Decree 187 of 1974* seems to reflect, at first glance, a genuine concern on the part of the secret police to demonstrate humanitarian behavior, for that decree provided that any arrested person must be subjected to medical examination not only before entering a place of detention but also at the time of release.

However, there was madness to this method. "This decree was to be applied only to three places of detention that are publicly admit-

---

* Decree 187 is still on the books.

ted," a former DINA prisoner testified, "but is not applicable to the secret torture houses that DINA manages. The medical doctors are designated by the authorities and are not of the choosing or in the trust of the arrested person or his family. In addition, DINA will not permit an arrested person to leave a place of detention if he still bears marks of torture."

Certain precautions seem to be worth the effort. Agents of the Mexican Federal Judicial Police have a reputation for not leaving marks. When Mexican security authorities are on joint operations with U. S. Drug Enforcement Administration agents, the Americans get their answers from the Mexicans, who question detainees on the basis of a list of questions submitted by the U.S. narcotics agents. The questions are put to the detainees at the same time that authorities administer torture techniques that tend not to leave identifying marks. The United States agents, according to former DEA administrator Peter Bensinger, "leave immediately when the torture begins." Accordingly, there are no Mexican witnesses, no direct U.S. implication—and no body bruises or scars which, when photographed, could be submitted to a court, or to some international body such as Amnesty International or the International Commission of Jurists.

Conversely, marks will be left on the victim and no effort will be made to cover up the fact that torture is being practiced by secret police agents if the purpose of the exercise is to intimidate the population. As the 1975 Greek torturers' trial vividly showed, ESA's torture program was divided into two distinct phases, based upon the desired secretiveness or openness of ESA practices in terms of their willingness and/or unwillingness to leave marks upon their victims.

The first phase, from 1967 to 1971, was designed to extract information about resistance activities. The interrogations were accordingly conducted by highly specialized officers. The policy was to avoid leaving marks, or at least not to permit the detainee to be released until the marks had disappeared.

But, between 1971 and 1974, the main purpose of the exercise was intimidation: in particular, to demoralize the student movement. In this context, the torture sessions were conducted by simple police conscripts with no particular expertise. These conscripts were in fact encouraged by superior officers to leave torture marks on their victims, then release them after a relatively short time in captivity.

The danger of noise, as well as marks, is another factor to be considered by secret police torturers attempting to perform in a truly clandestine fashion.

Sometimes the victims' screams must be muffled. A prisoner described the way in which South African agents silenced him during their administration of electric shock in 1976:

"They took me to an interrogation room. They told me to take my clothes off. I took them off and then they told me to sit on a chair behind the door. . . . Then they came with a wet cloth and put it inside my mouth. . . ."

Similarly, a Chilean woman testified to the United Nations investigators in 1980 about her experience of the previous year: "I kept telling my captors that I was two months pregnant, but it did not make any difference to the awful treatment I received. . . . I was taken to a basement room and there they gave me electric shocks on my pelvis and my breasts. . . . Every time they did it they covered my mouth with a piece of sacking to muffle my cries and make it difficult for me to breathe. . . ."

But the victims' moans tend to persist even after the torture has ended. The playing of loud music at torture centers, or detention centers where torture is being carried out, is yet another way in which torturers attempt to drown out their victims' screams.

"We entered a building with a very large door," testified a woman imprisoned in Argentina in 1976 to an investigating commission of the Organization of American States. "They took me down a spiral staircase to a basement. There they told me to close my eyes and they put on a very tight blindfold with elastic. . . . They handcuffed me and shackled my feet together by a chain with padlocks on both shackles. . . . Then they took me to a kind of cell. . . . A record player was constantly playing all kinds of music very loudly. . . . During the entire time I was there, I heard the same sounds. The loud record player. Screams of pain. . . ."

In testimony before a United States House of Representatives subcommittee investigating allegations regarding human-rights violations in Indonesia, a former political prisoner said, "The dreadful screams of the people under interrogation could be heard morning, afternoon and night. To prevent these screams from being heard outside, songs were played over a tape recorder very loudly. . . ."

In downtown Asunción, Paraguay, the secret police conduct most of their interrogations within the large Investigaciones (police) building. While in many countries the use of music to muffle the cries of the tortured represents the interest of the secret police in shielding both the general populace and other prisoners from the fact of torture, the loud radio that is played continuously throughout the night at the Investigaciones building seems calculatedly designed to keep the populace in line. The point is not to drown out the cries of those inside the prison, but to send a message to all within hearing distance outside the prison.

Music used to this end in the torture process can also compound the torture. A Uruguayan political prisoner held at Infantry Battalion ⚔13 from 1975 to 1976 offered the following observation: "There was constant screaming and that music was driving me insane. . . . There was an indescribable noise from the loudspeakers, which were installed on both sides of the room and tuned in to different stations. It went on all through the night. . . ."

These grisly interrogation procedures have developed their own black-humor vocabulary.

A Philippine Constabulary detention center had its own torture room, known among captives and captors alike as the Production Room.

The Interior Ministry in Kabul, Afghanistan, had a special basement torture chamber known as the Operation Room.

In Argentina, "Club Atlético" (Athletic Club), operating as a sort of "prisoner depot," was an underground, unventilated secret-detention center in which prisoners were held in shackles, with tight cloth blindfolds over their eyes. Ironically, then, prisoners could not move more than forty centimeters in their Club Atlético holding cells. Prisoners referred to the place (at Club Atlético) that was used to "tame" new arrivals as the "lion's den." The "operating theater" was the torture room.

In Chile, one torture center was named the House of Bells by ex-prisoners held there who could recall hearing the chimes of a nearby church. SIFA (Air Force intelligence) agents conducted their interrogations at the Air Force Academy itself, in what was dubbed the "Scream Room."

And DINA's largest torture center, holding from one hundred twenty to one hundred fifty political prisoners at a time, became known as the Palace of Laughter. The Palace of Laughter included a prisoner detention area, workroom, accommodation staff, a *parilla* area (the *parilla* is an electric grill—see "A Torture Glossary" in the Appendixes), guardhouses, bathrooms, tiny cubicles smaller than telephone booths, where prisoners were locked up with hands and feet bound, the special tower for special tortures and punishment, and the pool, which was used for the submarine torture (consult "A Torture Glossary").

Uganda's former President Idi Amin himself gave his torture chambers "nicknames" that for him held a special, personal significance. One such chamber was known as the "Singapore Room," after the fact that his predecessor, President Obote, had been overthrown while attending a conference in Singapore. The other torture chamber was known as the "Dar es Salaam" Room, after the fact that President Obote, once ousted, took asylum in that Tanzanian city. Amin evidently thought it all terribly funny.

Techniques, as well as facilities, acquired distinguishing names. Some Paraguayan interrogators had some contemptuous fun with President Carter's human-rights campaign. The metal rods the agents used to administer beatings were named, according to size, "Human Rights," "Liberty," "Democracy," and "Constitution." And so, as they administered beatings, the interrogators would shout: "Here is your Human Rights. Here is your Liberty. . . ."

Even electric-shock torture has a few names of its own. In Brazil, the apparatus whereby the torture has been administered is described by prisoners as the "dragon chair"; in Malawi, it is referred to as "electric hat" torture.

5

While the activities of the secret police in many countries are not kept all that secret, sometimes interrogation procedures will be conducted under circumstances of absolute secrecy.

The safe house is a favored secret police site for interrogation when the operation being conducted is fairly clandestine. "Aside from the detention center proper," testified a man who was held under custody by the Philippine military, "the military also maintains a number of private houses, called 'safe houses,' paid for with unaudited intelligence funds. These houses are plush and they are intended primarily for housing those intelligence agents of the military working in a definite district or area. However, these houses also serve as effective hiding places for arrested persons whenever the military does not wish such persons traced by their relatives or

friends. Because these 'safe houses' are never officially acknowledged, no rules obtain within these premises as to the manner of
treatment dealt out to arrested persons." And two leading United
States religious figures testifying before a House of Representatives
commission investigating human rights in the Philippines added that
these safe houses, almost entirely reserved for the interrogation of
political activists, are oftentimes soundproofed.

Mexican safe houses are under the control of the Brigada Blanca.
The safe houses are the scene of most secret police torture that takes
place in the country. Some targets are taken to safe houses after
their formal arrests. The safe-house experience, then, often constitutes a kind of twilight-zone experience that occurs between the time
of arrest and the beginning of the formal, state-authorized detention.
But some targets are taken to Brigada Blanca safe houses without
the formality of official arrest and detention sequences. "You can be
taken to a safe house just for two or three hours," said one well-
informed source. "Or five days. Or two days—just to be tortured,
and after that, you may be let go."

Some Indonesian citizens arrested for political reasons claim that
they have been taken for questioning by military arrest teams to
buildings near Jakarta that look like private dwellings or shops.
They are not officially designated detention or interrogation centers,
and most people (nonprisoners) do not know of their existence.

But safe houses are only part of the picture, as far as torture sites
are concerned. In Chile, one very clandestine secret police torture
center used by DINA was a private farm most likely donated by
wealthy supporters of the regime (i.e., opponents of Allende). This
extremely remote torture center, situated in the Chilean countryside, was both a place for conducting interrogation and for experi-
mentation designed to develop the most effective torture techniques
that could be used during interrogation sessions. Prisoners there
have allegedly been subjected to a wide range of bizarre experiments: "to dogs trained to commit sexual aggressions and destroy
organs of both sexes," according to one United Nations Report, "to
'tests' on the limits of resistance to different methods of torture (resistance to beatings, electricity, hanging, etc.); to experiments designed to drive detainees insane through administration of drugs;
to prolonged periods of isolation and other sub-human conditions. . . . There appears to be a torture (place) there of a particu-

lar kind in a specially equipped place underground. There are small, completely soundproofed, hermetically sealed cells for prisoners. Leather hoods are placed over the prisoners' heads and stuck to their faces with chemical adhesives. In these cells, torturers allegedly carry out interrogation over a closed-circuit radio system, with the detainees naked and tied to their berths while electric shocks are applied."

In Zaire, the clandestine torture facility to which political suspects arrested after demonstrations or for suspected complicity in antigovernment plots are taken is a CND (for Centre National de Documentation, or National Documentation Center, which is actually the name for the national security service) interrogation center in the President's guards' barracks in the Cité de l'OUA, near the Presidency, on Mount Ngaliema, in Tshatshi military camp. The interrogation center consists of several approximately two-by-three-meter underground cells as well as five ground-floor cells. And the CND headquarters in Gombe-Kinshasa contains a number of large cells measuring about six by two meters, as well as some smaller ones, in which some prisoners have allegedly been subjected to electric-shock torture.

The interest of secrecy is often well served by a rural environment. "I was arrested on the 25th of March, 1976," testified one South African black activist. "I was taken to a remote camp in the forest. . . . During all my thirteen days I was blindfolded while the interrogations and physical tortures took place. . . . During this torture-operation, I screamed out loudly, but was told by my torturers that my screaming is of no use because we are in a forest and at a very isolated spot where no one will hear my screams."

6

It was April 1979. Agents of the Brigada Blanca had surrounded the house in the city of Torreón, Coahuila. At four o'clock in the morning, they announced their presence with a volley of gun fire. In minutes, the entire family was in custody: the husband, wife, husband's sister and brother-in-law, . . . and the family's fourteen-month-old daughter and two-and-a-half-year-old son.

The entire family was then taken to clandestine detention quarters. "They threw me to the floor with my baby. . . . My husband

and his brother-in-law were tortured. . . . They told me later that they were going to kill my daughter, my sister-in-law, her son, and me. Shortly after, they added, "We have already gotten your son-of-a-bitch husband, so talk or the next one to get it will be your daughter. . . ."

The woman was then transferred to a prison in Mexico City. On the ride from the airport to the prison, she shared a car with three or four agents.

"A man blindfolded me and checked to see that my hands were securely tied behind my back. The car began to move and I heard the voices of three or four men. One of them said to me:

" 'Do you have any children?'

" 'Yes, a one-year-old daughter,' I answered.

"Another agent said, 'Well, now we're about to let this bitch know what we can do.'

"Yet another agent said, 'Do you know that we're going to kill you?'

"I asked why.

" 'For being a guerrilla, don't be stupid.'

" 'I'm not a guerrilla.'

" 'In a while,' said one agent, 'you're going to swear by your own mother that you are.'

"Then another agent said, 'Do you know what we do to bitches like you? We kill them, but slowly . . . and they die when we decide they are going to die. You're going to beg us to kill you.' "

The woman was then incarcerated in a special military camp in Mexico City.

"They took me out of the car and put me into a cold place with a wet floor (I didn't have any shoes on). The first thing that I heard was a radio at full volume. . . ."

Then, through the blaring radio music, she picked out the muffled screams and cries of her nephew and sister-in-law.

"Then they took me to the basement. I recall that I counted approximately sixteen steps and then they placed me in a cell. My sister-in-law and nephew were placed in another one. We went that entire day with no food or water.

"They didn't physically torture us anymore, but the psychological torture was incessant, as they would repeatedly say things to me like the following: 'We are going to kill you.' 'We already killed your husband.' 'Your daughter was taken to the United States.' 'We have your daughter here in a place where we have many others.' So I was very worried about what condition my daughter was in. . . .

"I quite intentionally left until last what I am now going to state, as it is the most abominable and terrible thing that they did to me: My fourteen-month-old baby daughter, Tania, was tortured in my presence. They mistreated her and gave her electric shocks all over her little body, after having tortured her psychologically by forcing her to watch her parents being beaten. I recall, and shudder at the very thought, how she cried and called out, 'Papa,' and my suffering faced with an inability to be able to defend her and console her. They are terrible moments that I would like to be able to describe in hopes that it won't happen to others.

"When I was set free, my life was threatened and I was told my family and my daughter would suffer the consequences if I talked."

The torture of the victim's children and family is a common—and effective—torture technique of the secret police. In Chile, according to a United Nations report, children were often tortured in the presence of other prisoners. Their screams could break detainees who could not be broken by their own sufferings or by the screams of other inmates. In fact, according to this United Nations report, which is thoroughly documented, there came a time when there were enough children made parentless by DINA's savage interrogation techniques that it became necessary to establish state-run orphanages.

In a secret police state, where arbitrary detentions and disappearances are not uncommon, detainees' family members, as well as detainees themselves, are not immune to the secret police experience, so that they become nonpersons in the eyes of their captors. Whether justifiably or not, the family of the detainee becomes implicated in his alleged "crime." In one famous Paraguayan case, authorities arrested four whole generations in one fell swoop: a great-grandmother, her two sons, their grown children, and infants.

For the parent of the detainee, the search to locate one's children can prove heartbreakingly frustrating, because the internal security authorities—in the effort to remake all those in their net into nonpersons—will move detainees around from prison to prison like peas in the shell game. As *The Christian Science Monitor* described the routine existing in the eastern Cape area of South Africa: "Another practice among security police . . . has been to move detainees to prisons all over the area, that is, to prisons remote from their homes. It has often been impossible for parents to trace their children, who can be held without being charged under any one of a vast array of laws."

But perhaps stubborn mothers produce stubborn revolutionaries. The Iranian Mrs. Ozra Araghi had several sons. (Mrs. Araghi is the same woman you met in Chapter One.) Her son Ahmad was in the military service in the early seventies, when, on leave, he and an associate committed a politically motivated bank robbery. When caught by SAVAK authorities, the young Ahmad refused to confess. "My friend and I needed money," was all that he would say. SAVAK was unable to get more out of him than that, and sentenced him to ten years in jail.

Not to one jail, however: while he had been arrested in Isfahan, he was some time later moved to a jail in Tehran, then later moved on to a prison somewhere in Shiraz, a southern town.

Mrs. Araghi described her furious attempts to locate her son:

"I would go and beg them [SAVAK authorities] to tell me, where is he? But they wouldn't give me an answer."

Eventually, Ahmad was able to slip word to his mother through a fellow prisoner, who had been transferred to another jail. The prisoner, who was finally allowed a visit with his family at his new place of detention, told his family about Ahmad's location, so that they could pass the word on to Mrs. Araghi.

But even with this tip, Mrs. Araghi was not halfway there. She knew where her son was, but she didn't know how to get to him. She still had to go through SAVAK.

It was a long, dusty, grueling bus ride that took her, along with three other mothers who were also trying to locate their sons, to Shiraz. The local SAVAK officials they met with there granted the three mothers permission to visit with their sons, but Mrs. Araghi's request was denied.

She cried before the SAVAK official and made a terrible scene.

"I came all the way from Tehran," she pleaded.

But the SAVAK official seemed unmoved, and Mrs. Araghi left the SAVAK office in tears, while being consoled by her three companions.

Outside, the three women stoutly offered to forfeit their rights to see their sons if she was being denied the right to see hers.

Mrs. Araghi, refusing their kind, sympathetic offer, explained that, somehow, the SAVAK authorities must consider her son some kind of ringleader—perhaps because he was the brother of an executed revolutionary.

The three mothers promptly took leave of Mrs. Araghi and hustled over to the local prison to see their sons.

Some fifteen minutes later, Mrs. Araghi returned resolutely to the very same SAVAK office where the authorities had refused her request.

Overwhelmed with tears, distraught with emotion, and ready to fight for all she was worth, Mrs. Araghi stalked into the reception area and began to plead uncontrollably with the desk officer.

"I talked to your boss," she began, barely looking up at the person whom she was speaking to, "and he said I could not see my son. But can't *you* please help me?"

It was only after her eyes began to clear, after the officer seemed to be taking pity on her, after he had said, "All right, Mother, I will help you," that Mrs. Araghi realized that by sheer accident she was pleading her case before the very same officer to whom she had spoken only fifteen minutes earlier.

Mrs. Araghi, who loved her sons, was on the outside of the Iranian security system, looking in.

But Father Hagad, a priest who sympathized with the Moslems and who loved his spiritual sons, found himself on the inside looking out. Father Hagad had been active in the Philippines for years in politically organizing against the Marcos regime. So, although they had blindfolded him when they arrested him, he knew exactly where he was when they arrived at the prison in Jolo, a very small town in the southern Philippines. He had visited people held in detention there on more occasions then he cared to remember. There was only one jail in Jolo. And besides, he would always recognize it by its unmistakably foul smell.

The agents of ISAFP (Intelligence Service of the Armed Forces) kept the blindfold on Father Hagad for two days. When they removed it, Father Hagad recalled years later, "They [the agents] acted as if *only then* I knew where I was."

One week later, the ISAFP agents again blindfolded Father Hagad and moved him out of the jail. During the jeep ride, he asked his captors where they were taking him, but their response was stony silence.

But the priest was about to get a second laugh. For, when they arrived at their destination, Father Hagad again knew, despite the blindfold, exactly where he was.

"I have walked these steps every day," he told the ISAFP agents as they led him up a long spiral staircase.

The agents had taken him to the religious school in town that Father Hagad himself was in charge of. It seemed that the one and only jail in Jolo was filled up. The religious school was the only other building in town that would do, especially since the school, like the entire town, had been practically leveled in the wake of fighting between Muslim secessionist rebels and government forces.

The agents took Father Hagad up to a room on the fifth floor. A lieutenant, obviously in charge, then said to him, "Father, I hope you don't mind the blindfold. . . . I was just under orders."

The priest listened not to the words but to the voice. It sounded very familiar.

"I know you," said the priest, "even if I can't see you."

The lieutenant said nothing.

The priest broke the awkward silence: "Didn't I perform your wedding ceremony?"

"Yes, Father," said the lieutenant. "You were the one. I hope you will forgive me."

Most Filipinos in the southern Philippines who aren't Moslems are Catholics. The traditional church wedding is a social necessity in the Philippines. The town is small, and local priests are not all that plentiful. It was, thinking back years later, not as coincidental as it at first seemed. Nor was the lieutenant's peculiar brand of mercy surprising. He, like many in the security services, was born and raised a Catholic. He had enough guilt to feel bad about what he was doing to the priest that had married him, but enough of a sense of responsibility to the security service to carry out his orders. The guilt, then, attended—but did not prevent—the lieutenant's participation in the interrogation sessions, during which the priest was kicked and beaten for a period of two weeks.

After a few beatings supervised by the lieutenant, the young officer would try to apologize.

"I hope, again, that you will forgive me, Father," said the lieutenant.

"I understand," Father Hagad would answer. "You are under orders."

7

The former security officer from Chile was telling us that DINA and SIFA (Air Force Intelligence) employed, like most political police, the two well-known systems of interrogation. One interrogation system uses the device of the officers pretending to know everything about you. They insist you have no choice but to confess.

The other system involves the familiar technique in which two people interrogate the victim at once. They alternate, taking turns interrogating. One officer acts like a madman, while the other agent plays the role of the friendly next-door neighbor. One tortures, while the other one will say, "Oh, how terrible! Look what he did to you. Would you like some wine?"

Prisoners in many countries have described to us this "good-cop bad-cop" system of interrogation in vivid terms. In Uruguay, the superior officer sometimes puts on a show of kindness, to compare favorably with the brutality of his underlings. One supervising officer, in fact, brought tortured detainees cups of tea. A congressman from a liberal opposition party was once given a bottle of scotch to help him weather the storm of the interrogation. Furthermore, in prison, said another Uruguayan, the "good torturer" might even help smuggle messages outside to the family. It is these types, he says, who will tell you, "I hear that you're going to be released soon," all the while knowing that that is untrue.

There are variations on this theme. One SIFA torturer became known as the "gentleman of torture." He embodied within himself both the "good guy" and the "bad guy," a sort of Jekyll and Hyde personality. He would interrupt a savage session of electric-shock interrogation, for example, to take his victims to a nearby downtown pizzeria. He would tell them how lucky they were to have fallen into the hands of SIFA, rather than DINA, where agents are "much more cruel."

The proffered cigarette is a sure sign of the good-guy technique. One Arab detainee alleges that, after torture by Israeli agents, he realized that he would have to come up with some story or else endure the pain forever. On realizing this, he told his interrogators that he would confess. "'Now we are friends,' said one of the agents. He pulled out a cigarette and handed it to me," the Arab claims. "I took the cigarette and started smoking and he said, 'Now talk.' So I had to start lying."

In the secret police world, a cigarette has become a virtual symbol of friendship under odd circumstances. At the Greek torturers' trial in 1975, a lawyer who was arrested recalled the following: "The previous evening a soldier came, very scared, and gave me a piece of cake . . . another time . . . a soldier brought me a packet of cigarettes and a box of matches." A government prosecutor evaluated such kindnesses in these words: "What have we come to? A light for a cigarette is regarded as a benefaction."

At the inquest into the death of Steve Biko, a colonel in the security service at first vigorously denied that torture took place in South Africa. "We have a lot of time," he said, explaining that a detainee remained detained until all questions were answered fully. No assault charges had ever been laid "against my assaulting team," he said, correcting himself to "interrogation team" in the wake of gales of laughter in the courtroom. But he continued, "We are very disappointed by this criticism because we are aware of the politeness and concern with which we treat detainees. We buy them cigarettes, cold drinks and nice things to eat."

Amnesty International, in noting that 70 percent of the prisoners its people interviewed on its 1975 mission to the Philippines claimed to have been tortured, put the matter of special treatment this way: "In virtually every case of prisoners who were not tortured, there tended to be a particular factor which appeared to explain why the person had been spared: the detainee interrogated was a woman, or was well known, or had highly placed friends, or had some personal connection with martial law officers, or was a foreigner. . . ."

Benigno Aquino was a well-known politician in the Philippines, a leader of the Liberal Party. He was arrested in 1972 only a few hours after martial law was proclaimed. While members of his staff allegedly were tortured, he was not; in fact, the authorities provided him with an air-conditioned detention room in a Manila military camp. (President Marcos even permitted him to conduct a press conference at his detention center.)

When class-A treatment is provided the prisoner, it means that the detention and/or interrogation is preventive, rather than punitive. In the early seventies, for example, Philippine student leaders were arrested. The point of the arrest was to quell disturbances that had occurred shortly after martial law was declared, in September of 1972. The students were placed in a prison at Camp Crame, headquarters of the Philippine Constabulary, with an elite group of detainees, including delegates to the constitutional convention, labor leaders, and so on. They had a "decent commander," one student leader recalls—i.e., no torture was performed. The commander's name was Colonel Alejo, and before long opponents of the Marcos regime, who were well treated enough to maintain a sense of humor while in prison, nicknamed the Camp Crame prison the "Alejo Hilton," since they did, actually, benefit from relatively royal treatment.

In 1978, a former Dubček cabinet adviser was summoned for an interrogation session to an StB security office in downtown Prague, for what proved to be a mild interrogation session. The official had been active in the Charter 77 movement, the human-rights movement that had been gaining force since 1977 in Czechoslovakia and was having an impact throughout the rest of Eastern Europe as well.

The interrogation session was intense, but the former official was never physically mistreated. Two officers, in teams of two, asked questions throughout the day. The officers were, he recalls, "friendly and mild." They began each session by introducing themselves as agents of state security and then would begin their line of questioning with the statement "You probably know why we are here." They would then proceed to ask him about his relationships with various personalities in the human-rights movement: "What do you think of so-and-so?" "What subjects did you discuss with them?" The first session lasted three hours, and the agents eventually became exasperated with the paucity of information that they were receiving. At the end of the day, the two agents sternly warned him to cease his human-right activities. And then they let him go—a class-A interrogation, for sure.

"An associate of mine—a Haitian," testified a U.S. consular official in federal court in Miami, "was put in jail six months while I was there. And after he was released, we chatted a bit about the conditions. He was from a somewhat powerful family and the conditions, according to him, were quite nice. He was in a private room. He was well fed. He was allowed visitors. . . ."

Recall the case of José Zalaquett (see Chapter Two, Section 12), chief legal counsel of the Cooperative Committee for Peace in Chile, another beneficiary of the class-A treatment. "I was not tortured," he testified, "but on one occasion . . . [in 1975] I was subjected to a humiliating treatment: I was sent for twenty-four hours to a damp basement filled with rats, because I had planned to send Christmas cards to the cardinal and other bishops, in the names of the prisoners."

And this, he insists, was class-A treatment.

A liberal lawyer and civil rights leader imprisoned in Indonesia in 1974 recalled, "I was not interrogated for long. . . . I listened [to the interrogators] at first because I wanted to understand the scenario these officers were trying to fit me into." Although he was imprisoned for thirteen months (on charges of plotting to overthrow the government), he once testified before a committee of the United States House of Representatives, "I was a relatively privileged prisoner. . . . I was never physically maltreated. I had food coming in from outside, and drugs when I was ill, and I felt fairly sure I would be released. . . . The value of the experience for me was that I could now see the situation first hand, when I met the detainees who have been in prison for seven, eight, ten years and still have no prospect of release. Before, I knew about their suffering intellectually; now, I know about it in my stomach. . . . The real torture is to keep people for many years with no term to set to their imprisonment. That is the torture of the spirit."

While routine beatings were sometimes used on common criminals in Poland during the late seventies, the political detainee was usually given preferred treatment. Certainly, the standard heavy-handed interrogation methods, including torture, were not used on the famous dissidents, according to our sources. "An underground printer, maybe," said one source. "But not on a bigwig." The Polish secret police exercise caution and restraint. They are almost always gentle with the intellectuals and artists. They are gentle with known activists. Such restraints and caution surfaced with the Charter 77 movement. "Usually, they just arrest you, and when you don't talk, they let you alone," reported one politically active exile.

In 1977, Vladimir Georgescu, a dissident Romanian historian and author who had taught at UCLA and Columbia University was arrested and interrogated. His manuscript *Politics and History* had been smuggled out of Romania by a friend. The Romanian secret police had a score to settle.

"There was nothing to confess," Georgescu recalled. "They had the manuscript, I had signed it, they had no need to be tough." Besides, he points out, at the time that he taught at Columbia University, in New York, he had befriended then-Columbia University professor Zbigniew Brzezinski. When word of his arrest became known, all his friends wrote letters to the White House.

With connections like these, the professor was destined to receive relatively fine treatment on the part of the Securitate agents who had him in their custody. Nevertheless, he was interrogated thoroughly. But, like many prominent dissidents, historians, lawyers, and academics in other countries, he remained physically unharmed by the experience. "I can handle this kind of treatment," he says now, admitting, however, that he does not know how he would respond to physical torture.

The interrogations were not nearly as unpleasant as one might expect. First, the professor was able to laugh at the Securitate agents when they threatened him by telling him that he would remain in detention indefinitely. "I was in a country that needs U.S. support against the Soviets, and American economic help," he says, explaining his relative lightheartedness throughout those interrogations. "I was able to view my imprisonment in a different light." Second, several times the deputy minister of the Interior personally conducted Professor Georgescu's interrogations. The official was also a historian, and in the course of the interrogations, they realized that they had a lot to talk about. They even had coffee together.

Ultimately, however, Professor Georgescu was sent to Jilava Prison, forty miles south of Bucharest. There he was, again, neither beaten nor otherwise tortured. But when he got to Jilava Prison, he realized that the criminals received better treatment than the political prisoners. "They had televisions, parcels from home," he recalled. "They were allowed to work in the furniture factory, and we weren't." Still, the professor insists that because of his stature and connections he benefited from very privileged treatment at the hands of his interrogators. Some of the prison officials eventually warmed up to him—one of them even told him, "You are a reactionary of a different type."

When the time for his official release came, he was taken back to the Criminal Department, where he had been originally held, in Bucharest. In an interrogation session conducted back there, the deputy director of the department grew almost friendly toward him.

He offered the professor books to read. "I knew then," he says, "that the cards were in my hand."

Although, before being released, he did promise the Securitate official the one thing that he wanted: He promised that from then on he would remain quiet.

8

The secret police eventually must dispose of their charges. If the prisoner does not die in prison, then he must either be released or disposed of in some other way. Some very competent secret police forces, such as Chile's DINA, set up a number of clinics in which the tortured political prisoner can cool out and recover. The care included the administration of antibiotics, analgesics, and tranquilizers. In Greece, prisoners were transferred to a military hospital, where they were admitted under pseudonyms. They were then remanded to the custody of the neurological clinic until certified as acceptable to release.

The Chilean secret police also set up a high-security recovery center known as Cuatro Álamos (Four Poplars). Cuatro Álamos was a clandestine detention facility within the physical confines of Tres Álamos (Three Poplars), a public detention center, but only DINA personnel had access to Cuatro Álamos. After the initial torture experience, a prisoner would be given time to recover at Cuatro Álamos before being transferred to Tres Álamos, where he would be allowed to receive visits from family and friends.

These facilities represent one way out of the secret police experience: through the front door. The other way out is through the back door, a route that ends in one's disappearance from the face of the earth. Tehrani, the famed SAVAK torturer who confessed that he tortured on orders from the deputy director of SAVAK, explained how and why he forced his victims to swallow poisonous capsules as part of a virtual ritual: "From 1976, when the Human Rights issue was first raised in Iran and the Shah was talking of an open political air in the country, SAVAK techniques and methods underwent an abrupt change. All anti-Shah activists, after arrest, would be made and forced to swallow a cyanide capsule, or would be killed with a revolver fitted with a silencer, and the deaths arranged to look like suicides." Tehrani said that he would take a prisoner for a walk, speaking kindly and telling him that soon he would be released.

Then he would grab the neck of the detainee, force his mouth open, and push the capsule in.

Another SAVAK agent described a different way in which deaths or disappearances of prisoners could be explained away. SAVAK agent Jazani told a nationally televised revolutionary court that he was part of a four-man firing squad that shot nine prisoners point-blank outside of Evin prison. Later, SAVAK concocted the tale that the nine had been trying to escape and were subsequently shot. Again, the torturer Tehrani described in detail the way in which the mission was accomplished:

"Over lunch, Atarpour [a SAVAK superior] said that today is the date that the secret mission is to be carried out and no one is allowed to refuse to take part. He then explained in detail what had to be done and added that Sabeti [another SAVAK superior] has given explicit instructions that the mission should be carried out most efficiently and immediately. . . . After lunch, we went to Evin prison. Shabani and Nozari [other SAVAK employees] went to collect the prisoners, and the rest of us went and waited for them in the teahouse of Akbar Evini. After some time, a mini-bus, containing the prisoners, arrived at the teahouse. . . . We went with the prisoners to the hills overlooking the Evin prison. There Colonel Vaziri sent away the soldier who was patrolling the hills. We brought the prisoners out of the mini-bus, and with their eyes blindfolded and hands tied behind their backs with ropes, made them sit down in a row on the ground.

"Atarpour then gave them a short speech and said: 'Your friends and colleagues—and you are their leaders and theoreticians and are in contact with them from the prison—condemn our friends and colleagues to death and kill them. We too have now decided to condemn you to the death.' At this point . . . Colonel Vaziri or Atarpour—I cannot remember which—opened fire at them with an Ouzi submachine gun. After the first burst, the machine gun was passed to all of us in turn and I was either the fourth or fifth to open fire on them. Of course, by the time I was firing, they were all dead. . . .

"The next day, Atarpour provided a text to be released to the press, stating that these nine prisoners, who were being transferred from one prison to another, had attempted to escape, and in doing so were shot at and killed by their guards.

"This text was amateurish for two reasons. Firstly, because they were all killed whilst shot from the front, and could not, therefore, be trying to escape. Secondly, the method of transfer between prisons was such that any escape attempt was physically impossible."

According to the testimony of a former DINA agent, prisoners who couldn't be released because DINA was afraid that they would talk too much were designated for execution. The agent said that in DINA files, the detainee would be marked for a specific form of execution. "Puerto Montt"† marked on the prisoner's file meant that he was to be liquidated on land. For instance, the detainee might be transferred to one of DINA's experimental torture centers, from which few emerged alive. "Moneda"‡ marked on the detainee's file meant that the detainee was to be liquidated by air or by sea. For instance, he might be thrown out of an airplane or thrown into the ocean, bound to a sack of rocks. It was all very organized.

With no excuses and justifications offered, the outright disappearance of political prisoners has become increasingly common during the past decade. In Argentina, Chile, East Timor, El Salvador, Ethiopia, Mozambique, Nicaragua, Paraguay, the Philippines, Uganda, Uruguay, and Mexico, for example, large numbers of political opponents of the regimes simply vanished. In the Philippines, leading figures of the religious opposition coined a new term for the disappearances that happen at the hands of the secret police. "Salvaging," explained Sister Mariani C. Dimaranan, chairperson of the Task Force Detainees of the Philippines, which has been ministering to the needs of political prisoners and their families since the imposition of martial law, in September 1972, is a euphemism for execution that "occurs when a person is arrested on suspicion of subversion and is taken by the military (usually constabulary, Army soldiers, and police). The suspect then disappears without a trace, until his bullet-riddled body turns up in a forest, field, creek or river." While in the urban areas salvaging may be on the decline, the sister insists that in the rural areas it is still practiced. "Many sources we talked to said that the practice of 'salvaging,' or torture or murder, the same as the 'disappearances,' which have horrified observers of Argentina, are on the upswing in the Philippines," commented Representative James M. Jeffords (R-Vt.) before a U. S. Congress investigatory subcommittee.

† Puerto Montt is a port situated south of Santiago, Chile.
‡ "Moneda," literally translated, means "money."

The disappearance is a form of torture that presents obvious advantages to the secret police. "They [disappearances] are a main form of arrest in Mexico," says one academic and legal expert on the situation in Mexico. "It is a particularly intimidating technique of the secret police. I'd explain it this way: If someone is killed, then you may have a hero created. And the public may be mobilized. The public will have concrete grievances and direct targets for their hostilities. But disappearances, on the contrary, have a 'chilling effect' both on the families involved and on the population at large. They are much less obvious than killings. It is harder to investigate a disappearance. The chances of Amnesty International doing so are much more limited."

The practice of "disappearing" people does indeed put organizations such as Amnesty International in an even more difficult position. That organization itself once described its great frustration in trying to ask the government "for the release of these persons whom DINA is trying to make us believe do not exist." Or, as an Organization of American States investigatory commission put it, "It [the technique of disappearances] is, moreover, a true form of torture for the victim's family and friends, because of the uncertainty they experience as to the fate of the victim and because they feel powerless to provide legal, moral and material assistance."

The OAS report goes on to point out the very real advantages, from the point of view of the secret police, afforded by the technique of having people disappear, as opposed to torturing and detaining them. Says the OAS: "The status of 'missing' seems to be a comfortable expedient to avoid application of legal provisions established for the defense of personal freedom, physical security, dignity and human life itself. In practice, this procedure nullifies the legal standards established in recent years in some countries to avoid legal detentions and the use of physical and psychological duress against persons detained."

The OAS went on to describe in some detail the "normal" disappearance procedure that occurs in Argentina:

"The operations for the most part are effected by groups whose number varies from six to twenty persons, who arrive at the home or place of work of the victim in several unmarked cars without license plates, and equipped with radios that allow them to communicate with each other. In some cases, they are accompanied by additional support forces in vans, in which, after the mission is completed, they transport the household appliances that are taken from the homes of the victims.

"The people carrying out the operation would arrive in civilian clothing, with long and short firearms to intimidate the victims and the witnesses. If the operation is carried out at the place of employment or on the public thoroughfare, they would take a very short time; however, at a residence it would take several hours, especially when it was necessary to await the victim's arrival.

"It has also been reported that when relatives, witnesses or building supervisors reported the occurrences to the local police, the response usually was, after admitting knowledge of the fact, to say they were unable to intervene. In a few cases where police did arrive at the scene, they withdrew shortly after having spoken to the persons directly involved in the operation. . . ."

The OAS report adds that appliances aren't the only items sometimes removed by the security agents. "It is a generally held view throughout the country that some babies are removed both from their homes where confrontations have occurred and from the places where their parents 'disappear,' or from the prisons where they were born are given away. . . ."

And finally, the report said, "In none of the cases where the fathers asked to accompany their children were they allowed to do so. . . . In some cases, they were told that the minors were being taken away for an interrogation or investigation, and the forces indicated the police division or division of the army to which the family should address inquiries hours afterwards. This information always proved totally false."

9

Some secret police organizations do not even bother denying that torture is one of the tools of their trade. "Every country uses it," the Shah of Iran was alleged to have said. "Show me the country which does not." Defendants in the 1975 torturers' trial in Greece were members of ESA who had served in the Special Interrogation Section in Athens. In his closing speech at this 1975 torturers' trial, the government prosecutor sought to sum up the philosophical attitude of the defendants with regard to the work they did: "Some of the defendants," he said, "wanted to represent [the headquarters of their special unit] not as a place of torture but as a national reformatory.

Modestly reserving to themselves infallibility of judgment, they have tried to follow in the footsteps of the Holy Inquisition." Not quite so eloquently, a Colombian security officer said, "It is undeniable that in innumerable cases, the interrogator is forced to use moral or physical coercion to obtain the truth that the person knows." And an inspector in a security unit in Nepal once said, "As a last resort, torture is practical and necessary."

Few government spokesmen are so forthcoming, and some may honestly believe that their security forces do not regularly indulge in the practice of torture. "We do not discount the possibility that criminal acts can be perpetrated by Israeli officers . . . ," said Gabriel Bach, Israel's state attorney. "In 1977, a number of wardens in the Beersheba prison were put on trial before a disciplinary court for overreacting." (In fact, Israel is one of the few states that has disciplined overzealous security officers.) "As I said before, I will not vouch for this or that police officer. But as far as security officials are concerned, all accusations of brutal behavior during interrogations are patently false. The security people involved are highly trained men and I do not doubt their moral integrity." Said General Benjamin ben Eliezer, military commander of the West Bank, "Those security people are specialists. They do not need to become violent to get the truth out of the suspected terrorist. In addition, violence is not efficient and is usually counterproductive. In short, it is against our laws, against morals, and against proper results. So why would we use it? Furthermore, we are constantly under scrutiny of the Israeli Supreme Court and of the International Red Cross." (See our section on the relationship between the secret police of many nations, including Israel, and the International Red Cross, in Chapter Seven.)

The former chief of BOSS (now the National Intelligence Service), in South Africa, interviewed on television in March of 1977, was questioned as to why so many detainees allegedly commit suicide. The interviewer was, of course, implying that the victims were tortured to death. General Van den Bergh answered that he was of the opinion that police action had nothing whatsoever to do with a detainee's decision to commit suicide, adding that from a crime-investigation point of view it was most decidedly in the interrogator's interest that the detainee should remain alive and well in order to be used as a witness.

General Lee Hi Song, the martial-law commander of South Korea, staunchly denied that the imprisoned dissident leader Kim Dae Jung, the former opposition presidential candidate who collected 45 percent of the popular votes against President Park Chung Hee in the 1971 election, was in terrible physical condition after allegedly being tortured in prison. General Lee asked a group of foreign reporters, "Do you think military investigators are so reckless as to batter him out of shape knowing that they will have to put him on trial?"

Some secret policemen defend themselves and/or their organizations by claiming that torture marks on their detainees are self-inflicted so as to discredit the security forces. In a report, the chief constable of the Royal Ulster Constabulary, in Northern Ireland, claimed that "terrorist organizations had adopted a deliberate policy of manufacturing allegations or contriving incidents including self-inflicted injury. . . ." The RUC also claimed that individual terrorists inflicted wounds on themselves in an attempt to exculpate themselves in the eyes of other members of their organization, so as to suggest that information was forced out of them by intolerable physical pressure. Philippine Defense Secretary Juan Ponce Enrile has also joined in this accusation. "Self-inflicted torture is not a new technique by these people who are underground, who are members of the left." And in an interview conducted by *Time* magazine, the Number Two official of SAVAK alleged the same. "In January, demonstrators paraded a man who was blind and had lost his arms," he said. "They said SAVAK had done this to him, and they called him a hero. In fact, he was a terrorist who lost his sight and was maimed when a bomb he was making exploded. If SAVAK had been responsible for his injuries, we could easily have gotten rid of him. We would not have let him live as a document of torture."

10

The extent and degree of torture as an interrogation procedure and intimidatory device is an excellent measure of the character of a secret police force. The security service that confines itself to the torture of particular groups, or particular inhabitants of particular geographical areas, must be classified as of a different character from a security organization that uses torture less selectively.

In Israel, for instance, all the evidence that we have been able to obtain points to sporadic, isolated cases of alleged torture, and, at the same time, some degree of maltreatment of Arab detainees in the West Bank and Occupied Territories. But maltreatment (day-to-day brutal treatment of detainees, in the way of rough beatings, or intensive interrogations conducted under glaring lights) is one thing; torture as an administrative practice (using, for the most part, special equipment, such as instruments for electrical torture), as discussed in this chapter, is something else. In this area, more than in almost any other, subtle distinctions can be very important ones. In 1977, the *Sunday Times,* of London, after a five-month investigation, concluded that torture by Israeli security and intelligence services is systematic. Maybe "systematic" maltreatment, but not systematic torture, as compared to what we have seen in many other countries around the world—at the hands of Chile's DINA, or South Africa's Security Branch, or at the hands of any one of several security services in the Philippines, to cite just a few. We believe that interrogation by torture in the West Bank and Occupied Territories has occurred (although perhaps not elsewhere in Israel); what is in doubt is whether the practice can be described, by any stretch of the imagination or of terminological precision, as systematic. Probably not.

Fine distinctions on the subject of torture are terribly important to make. Allegations of torture of members of the provisional Irish Republican Army by the security forces of the Royal Ulster Constabulary surely have merit; but does the secret police system there systematically encourage torture? Here is the wisdom of a South African court commenting on the situation of its country: "The actual conditions of detention in Northern Ireland put us to shame," said the court, "since visits by relatives, friends, doctors, priests and lawyers are permitted, and detainees are permitted to associate with each other and to have reading matter." Again, a comparative understanding is necessary before reaching absolute judgments.

Sometimes the distinctions must be exceedingly fine—so fine that they seem to disappear under prolonged scrutiny. It would, for instance, be absolutely incorrect to say that the Cuban secret police engage in systematic physical torture. This statement is true as far as it goes; but does it go far enough? Critics of the Castro regime point out that the secret police administer such a high level of psychological terror (including, for instance, day-after-day incarceration in very cold, lightless rooms and simulated executions) that it is meaningless to say that torture is not an administrative practice of the Cuban secret police. But such a distinction is not meaningless; if the idea of progress is incremental, then the slightest improvement in conditions of detention for political prisoners is noteworthy.

The use of torture is, in effect, such a litmus test in the understanding of a secret police force that it may even be used to establish historical benchmarks. Take SAVAK, for instance, which in the early sixties applied torture only to Communists (members of the Tudeh Party). (The point is not to condone the practice but, rather, to establish distinctions in the evolutionary nature of the process of torture.) After 1963, however, with the rise of the guerrilla movement in northern Iran, SAVAK began applying torture less discriminately. When, for example, a general in the Iranian Army was killed and a number of top right-wing politicians were assassinated, SAVAK, which wanted revenge, adopted the practice of torturing political dissidents of wide-ranging persuasions as routine administrative policy. And the rest is history . . . until 1976, when torture at the hands of SAVAK began to subside almost as quickly as it had increased in 1963. While prisoners were still subjected to psychological torture such as cold and wet cells, random verbal abuse, and deprivation of sleep, the previous standard of systematic torture, by the well-developed catalogue of techniques, fell into disuse. This change did not make SAVAK any less powerful a secret police force; but it did change the face, if only the face, of SAVAK during the last few years of its existence. Did the change in the character of SAVAK contribute to the fall of the Shah? Any answer is necessarily speculative, but it is possible to make the argument that the change in SAVAK's character came not *too* soon, but not soon *enough*. It is not only *possible* to have a secret police force that does not practice torture routinely; it may ultimately prove quite *desirable*.

Finally, a measure of the approval with which torture and the secret police administering it may be regarded by the regime in power can be judged by the extent to which, if at all, torturers are prosecuted and torture charges are investigated. When the military junta fell in Greece, the new government in 1975 held a torturers' trial. Except for the trial of a few SAVAK torturers by the Islamic Revolutionary Government in 1978, which was a very fragmented effort, to say the least, this was the sole wholesale bringing to justice of torturers—and a torture system—in recent history. It should be noted that there have been several cases, in recent years, of police personnel being prosecuted and convicted by the Civil Guard courts of Peru following allegations of torture or brutality toward prisoners. In fact, the then President, Juan Velasco Alvarado, launched an investigation into allegations that resulted in his demand for the resignation of the current head of the Peruvian Investigative Police, whom a number of people alleged to have been involved in inflicting torture, whether directly or indirectly. Also, with the ouster of the military government in Portugal, a halfhearted attempt to bring some torturers to justice was conducted, but it was nothing on the scale of the Greek torturers' trial, in Athens. In 1977, the Portuguese military courts released twelve former PIDE (secret police) agents who had been convicted of assassinations and acts amounting to torture, because the sentences they received were shorter than the period they had spent in prison since the Portuguese Revolution, of April 1974. While there have been torture trials in Venezuela, Egypt, and the U.S.S.R., these have all dealt with specific cases of brutality, rather than with officials responsible for state systems of torture.

There is also among secret police (as among all police) a high degree of fraternity and loyalty. One of the most striking examples of this involves an Air Force colonel who did not immediately file charges against two lieutenants and constables of the Metropolitan Command Intelligence (Metrocom) Division of the Philippines Constabulary allegedly accused of torturing his pregnant daughter. His reason? He had been in the military service for twenty-eight years, and he did not like "to smear the good image of the armed forces of the Philippines."

On the whole, therefore, the torturer enjoys a relatively nonhazardous job.

SIX

Looking Glasses, Hearing Aids, Tails, and Tattlers: Informers and Surveillance

1

The memorandum from SAVAK "Center" was labeled confidential, and it was easy to see why. The author of the memorandum—a high-level functionary at SAVAK headquarters in Tehran—must have been just a bit piqued. For, judging by the tart wording of this confidential communication, it seemed as if a number of SAVAK field agents had become either lazy or sloppy.

While internal security work is not an exact science, certain operational rules are customarily observed. After all, no trained agent, for example, would run the risk of meeting with an informant in his home. Why take a chance on being observed? Why risk exposing ("burning") an informant?

And yet the SAVAK memorandum—sent to SAVAK field offices —complains that "one of the operations leaders outside of the country, contrary to security principles, regularly meets the sources in his/her residence."

Incredible! And would any self-respecting secret police organization permit rendezvous between agents and informants to take place at the same place—time after time? And at locations normally frequented by the informant? What, therefore, is one to make of this extraordinary SAVAK communication: "No meeting should be held in areas frequented by the subjects. . . . Meetings should be held in remote areas where there is no possibility of the source being discovered, and if meetings would compromise the security of the sources, then middle-men, mid-addresses, post-office boxes and telephones should be used."

The lesson recital continues, in what sounds very much like a classroom lecture on the first principles covering the operational relationship between a clandestine security agency and its informants:

• Telephone use should be minimized, but when it is used, all names should be in code, and all conversations should be as short as possible, to save "the source from being burned," in the language of the operational instruction (translated from the Farsi). If a lengthy conversation is absolutely necessary, several short phone calls are better than one long one.

• Agents should be exceedingly cautious about written correspondence with an informant: "If necessary, the number of addresses for the contact should be increased. Do not communicate with a source through the same single address." And to avoid forgery of correspondence, "see that the sources use pseudonyms and code signs."

To deal with emergencies, "an arrangement should be made so that the sources can inform the leader of operations of urgent news without compromising security."

• Don't dawdle, in contacting new informants brought to the attention of the field officers by SAVAK center in Tehran: i.e., field agents may not have been taking referrals from headquarters seriously enough:

"Sources introduced by the Center should be contacted immediately, their trust and confidence should be secured, and the material they produce, even though immaterial and insignificant at the beginning, should not be treated as insignificant. These sources should be thoroughly indoctrinated with regard to the objectives and methods of obtaining information, and their work, considering the interest of SAVAK, should be assigned importance."

• Field agents were advised to develop a personal relationship with informants: "Conduct of operations leader toward the sources should be at the same time friendly and kind. Expressions of personality of the operations leader should be of the kind that bring the source under his/her complete influence and dominance."

• Detailed knowledge of the informant's private life can always prove useful: "Through appropriate channels, operations leaders should be thoroughly familiar with the personal problems, financial situation and moral characteristics of the sources so that this knowledge, in case of need, can be exploited and perhaps used to strengthen the friendship and to create the moral dominance which is necessary for the work of operations leaders."

This remarkable communication, one of a number of confidential papers seized by Iranian revolutionary students when they raided the Geneva, Switzerland, headquarters of SAVAK in 1976, is noteworthy on several counts. For one thing, it demonstrates that late in the game against the Shah's opponents, SAVAK was apparently troubled by basic operational defects that raise some question about that secret police organization's fundamental competence. But fundamental operational problems of this nature are not in themselves remarkable. Every security organization faces difficulties of all sorts—especially with its young, inexperienced field agents. What is remarkable about this particular operational directive, however, is that instructions on such basic operational matters were dispatched as late as 1971—SAVAK, after all, was established in 1957. Fourteen years should have been more than enough time to iron out such basic wrinkles.

In addition, the memorandum inadvertently demonstrates the major, towering importance of an informant system to the operations of a secret police force. Without an informant system, a secret police organization would have eyes but no ears. It could see all of the storefronts, homes, university lecture halls, and churches, but it could not hear what was being said behind closed doors. It could perhaps install bugs and wiretaps inside every home and place of business of concern to the secret police, but that kind of investment would require as many agents to monitor the conversations as there were bugs and wiretaps in place.

Very few nations have the technology to overcome the manpower requirements to conduct extensive electronic surveillance. It is believed that the United States National Security Agency, a highly secret arm of the U.S. intelligence network, possesses the technology to monitor telephone and cable traffic in such a way as to reduce the manpower requirements required to "edit" the audited conversations. Under the law, the NSA is empowered to intercept international communications when national security matters are involved, but its technological capabilities exceed its legal franchise. "From the late forties continuously for three decades," wrote Frank J. Donner in *The Age of Surveillance,* "the National Security Agency (NSA)—the most secretive, lavishly funded, and largest of all agencies in the intelligence community—monitored international cable communications for intelligence data. . . . The targets were not confined to embassies and other foreign intelligence sources but included domestic political subjects without grounds for suspecting espionage." There is also reason to believe that the British Government has benefited from U.S. advances in electronic eavesdropping. According to officials of the 125,000-member Post Office Engineering Union, the U. S. National Security Agency, in conjunction with Britain's Post Office (which also operates the nation's telephone system), monitors an astonishing array of phone conversations, not limited to those conversations participated in by subversive groups, suspected spies, or major criminal organizations. A secret computer center in central London, the Union said, can monitor from one to five thousand phone lines at once—with the help of an NSA computer that is capable of monitoring 75 million calls a year. And the *New Statesman,* a respected British weekly, claimed that NSA operates a huge eavesdropping center in northern England that monitors telephone and telex communications throughout Europe. The NSA system is said to be particularly impressive because of a computerized data-storage-and-retrieval system that obviates the need for a one-eavesdropper/one-conversation relationship. Telephone conversations can simply be recorded and stored—and are subject to retrieval when needed. The NSA network in England is known as "System X." Only the U.S.S.R. is believed to have a system even remotely comparable to it.

Accordingly, in the absence of extensive electronic surveillance equipment, most secret police organizations require an extensive informant system to function as the centerpiece of their intelligence-gathering operations. Electronic surveillance can supplement this system to some extent, but it cannot replace it.

In some ways, a well-run informant system is more like a magnifying glass than a hearing aid. It not only magnifies the society under control, but it enhances the magnitude of the secret police presence itself. If every field agent handles only a dozen informants, the effective strength of the secret police is magnified a dozen-fold. This helps a secret police force to feel confident about its ability to intimidate and control, especially if the citizenry is aware of the existence of an extensive informant network.

Without an informant system, on the other hand, the secret police force can become isolated from the society it must police. But the extensive, well-run informant system permits the secret police organization to extract from that society such information as it requires to maintain control, while weaving into that society such levels of fear and doubt as to reduce the amount of information on which it will be required to act. The informant system can help maintain a chilling effect on the actions and movements of a population to such an extent that the amount of revolutionary activity may be significantly curtailed simply as a consequence of popular uncertainty and fear.

Like many other secret police forces, SAVAK relied heavily on an extensive informant system. Security sections of virtually all offices, organizations (whether government or private), businesses, and such were established in order to compile secret reports, and by 1976, those reports were being sent directly to the famed "Joint Committee to Combat the Destructive Elements," the superagency made up of combined forces that was designed to coordinate the work of SAVAK, the police, and the Gendarmerie.*

A retired general of the Iranian Army now living in the United States claims that there would customarily be one SAVAK informer per class at any university. The situation at Tabriz University was evidently typical: SAVAK informants and agents were embedded at every level of every department. Within the ranks of the student body, there were six informants in the field of medicine, one in nurs-

---

* According to the SAVAK torturer Tehrani, "Houses used for the activities of the 'Joint Committee' agents were always equipped with a central transmission system, and the cars used had shortwave radios. These houses were almost always in very close proximity of a garage, where the cars, motorcycles, bicycles and all other modes of transport used by the Committee members could be parked and kept.

"Our surveillance of individuals was generally done in either a triangular or parallel fashion. Using the radio system, the subject would be 'passed' from one agent to another in different cars. And when enough information was gathered on him, then with the permission of the central office [Third Central Office of SAVAK], he would be arrested for interrogation."

ing, two in the pharmacology department, five in agriculture, seven in science, two in social science, two in physics, and three in literature. On the Tabriz faculty itself, some of the most prominent professors were SAVAK informers, including two former presidents of the university, the chief of the imperial archives section, and the university adviser to the Ministry of Science. SAVAK's informers also included (1) the head of the student dormitory association, (2) the head of the university security office, (3) a paid employee of the Student Affairs Office, and (4) a student hospital employee.

And in terms of an extensive informant network, there was surely more than one SAVAK in the world.

In Chile, full-time DINA agents may have numbered between twenty and thirty thousand. The informant network was perhaps smaller than SAVAK's, but DINA still maintained a very widespread and efficient system. Penetration of secondary schools, high schools, factories, public offices, and universities was especially high. Penetration also increased at bus stations, at airports, and within taxi fleets: radio taxis routinely monitored the conversations of passengers, passing on whatever might be of interest to all-night DINA telephone operators who were in constant contact with operations and surveillance teams.

Informants are sometimes so highly prized by security organizations that those who perform satisfactorily inevitably become prime candidates for recruitment as regular agents. In Chile, according to a former SIFA officer, a standard system was used to screen potential agents. On some case in which peripheral information was needed (that is, where the consequences of the failure to obtain the information were not likely to prove too damaging), a new informer would be put to the test, authorities thereby creating an opportunity for the informer to prove himself. "If he shows himself to be loyal and comes up with accurate records and does the job well," according to our source, "he may get promoted."

In the event of such success, the recruit would be moved up a notch; the next step up the DINA ladder involved collating information collected by other informants. "For example, there will be a network of twelve informants in a particular area, and the graduated person is assigned to work them over," said the former Air Force intelligence agent.

Graduating to the next rung up the ladder, the cooperating individual is given a car.

"Once you have a car," he says, "you are working full-time, but as an informant. And you may be sitting in a car and receiving an envelope [of information], but you may not know what your crew is doing."

At this point, the former officer said, DINA would decide whether you are "safe enough" to be admitted as a full-time agent. But until this point, you are still an informant; that is, you are not officially a member of DINA.

2

Paraguayan informants—like DINA's and SAVAK's informants—were so numerous and notorious that they came to be called "pyragues."

Pyragueismo, as it was called, became practically a subindustry in the society, a source of minor remuneration for prostitutes, maids, newspaper vendors, and so on who, without the pittance received from the Paraguayan secret police, probably would not have had enough on which to subsist.

In Mozambique, as of 1978, more than twenty thousand amateur police informers in the Maputo area alone turned "professional"—operating under the close supervision of SNASP, the secret police. The twenty thousand were ordered to keep a watch on what people do and say, "at home, in restaurants, markets, cinemas, places of work or any other place," said Radio Mozambique. "They have been around a long time, but until now their work had been somewhat disorganized, without plans, well-defined tasks or the direct support of party and state structures."

The number twenty thousand also holds as an estimate for the number of informants in the early seventies belonging to PIDE, Portugal's now-defunct secret police force under the Caetano regime. If you were a tourist in Lisbon, for instance, where foreigners were prime suspects of the government, you could hardly even get inebriated at a nightclub without a PIDE informant notifying his or her control agent. One British tourist went to police headquarters to complain the morning after a seemingly very inconsequential barroom brawl. He was astonished, however, to discover that the authorities knew all about the details of the incident. Like SAVAK, DINA, or SNASP, PIDE had informants who, hoping for any and all remuneration, didn't bother to separate trivial from important information.

One of the most sophisticated informant networks (which relies heavily on the contributions of blacks) is maintained in South Africa. Both the expatriate and homegrown black nationalist movements are thoroughly infiltrated by the security services, which, through the dissemination of "disinformation"—planted rumors and stories designed to confuse and fragment the opposition—have succeeded in exacerbating the rivalries between them. "The protection of the police informer runs like a golden thread through South African law," former Prime Minister Vorster once said.

In East Germany, the term "mass vigilance" is a euphemism used by security officials when referring to their widespread informant system. As part of a campaign by the ministry of State Security to tighten controls, which was launched following the labor upheavals that swept through Poland in 1980, General Mielke, head of that ministry, announced: "We will increase our activities to intercept all attacks by the enemy and ward off dangers to the economy. We will heighten mass vigilance, enforce socialist legality, guarantee total secrecy and see to it that security, order, and discipline prevail in all branches of the economy and throughout the country."

But it may be in the Soviet Union that informant penetration of society at every level is most complete. Full-time employees of the personnel divisions (often referred to by citizens and government authorities alike as First Departments) of all government and private enterprises serve as the KGB's official informers on fellow employees.

Other East European informant networks are patterned after this KGB system. The former high adviser to the Dubček cabinet has said that pervading all levels of Czechoslovakian society there are informers working both part and full time. Josef Frolik, the defector from the Czechoslovakian security service, says that the Fifth Administration of FSZS (or Federal News and Information Service, the name, according to Frolik, given to the Czech service after Dubček's exit, in 1968) plays a major role in the analysis—and subsequent recruitment—of informers from "the ranks of gardeners, waiters, valets, house superintendents, cooks and other service personnel working at the residences of guarded persons, so as to ensure the security of premises during Party congresses and other mass meetings."

Besides the care and feeding of "regular" agents, the secret police force must worry about the care and feeding of its informants. While the cost of maintaining an informant is considerably less than employing a full-time agent, the consequences of *not* having a well-coordinated and loyal informant network can prove to be very costly indeed.

It is perhaps curious that an institution of government so much associated with fear should have so easy a time collecting informants in whatever numbers it requires.

Only in very few societies do the secret police appear to experience any real difficulty in recruiting informers. In closed, tightly knit communities such as some of those in areas of East Timor where strong bonds of trust exist among the village people, networks are not easily penetrated even by Kopkamtib, the secret police.

Similarly, language barriers can freeze out security police: since few Spanish security agents understand the Basque language, in order to gather information on the Basque separatist movement in Spain, they rely on a fairly ineffective and surely not very trustworthy network of local Basque informers.

Infiltrating the university circles is a tricky matter too. Student activists tend to be well schooled in police techniques. Accordingly, the student informer must be at least as well informed as those whom he is informing on. And so, only the sophisticated students will prove to be effective informers, but often, at universities, it is the antigovernment crowds who are the intellectual sophisticates. As Aldi Anwar, a twenty-nine-year-old physics student at Bandung Technical Institute, in Indonesia, testified before the U. S. House of Representatives: "They [the authorities] have hired a number of students as informers. But we know who they are and they do not have many friends."

Establishing an informant network is not usually so difficult. A good many secret police forces have more informants than they know what to do with. Not surprisingly, members of many societies are paranoid about who is probably working for whom. Informers in the U.S.S.R., for example, are so commonplace that one source said that when his mother entered the KGB headquarters in Riga to confront authorities for allegedly having denied her son, a Zionist activist, entrance into medical school, she feared that anyone on the street who saw her going in would peg her as an informer.

Working for the secret police as an informer may not necessarily be a sign of economic desperation on the part of the employee. Instead, in some societies, informing is a sign of patriotism. For many Taiwanese citizens, informing for the Taiwan Garrison Command,† the internal-security mechanism of the Taiwanese Government that was established in 1949, is evidence of loyal citizenship. The Taiwanese are taught to believe that information involving any person or activity potentially seditious in nature is the rightful property of the government—and that reporting it is a thoroughly patriotic, anti-Communistic act.

Every branch of government and every major business institution accordingly has security-police informers working within these various segments of Taiwanese life. Until several years ago, government and private institutions all maintained autonomous "departments" made up of personnel who were actually informers; but then these independent, self-sufficient departments were merged with the personnel departments of every factory and every place of business. The system, then, oddly enough, resembles the informant systems of those East European countries that are patterned after the KGB model (which established First Departments within all major institutions): any top executive of any personnel department of any major institution in Taiwan is probably the head of the informant chapter of the security services as well.

It is of course easier for a secret police force to recruit informants from a society such as Taiwan, where citizens, generally speaking, believe in the mission of the secret police. One true believer of this sort was a twenty-one-year-old student leader in South Africa. When he was not running the university student council, he was sending the security system information about the political activities of students. As a law student, member of the Methodist Church, and twice-elected head of the student council of a major South African university, the ideology of the South African security system was inculcated in him at an early age. He was also the son of a major in the South African civilian police. But he reached a point when he wanted to clear his conscience about informing.

"In my home, there has always been a heavy emphasis on law and order and at all times respect for the government of this country,"

---

† The Bureau of Investigation is also involved in internal security affairs, and it is said to be highly competitive with the Command, although most sources say that the Command is the predominant internal-security force at work in Taiwan today.

he explained. Pointing out that such patriotic emotions were ably reinforced during his high school education and during his period of national service with the South African Navy, he said that before enrolling as a student he had a "twisted" idea of what university life was like and admits that he thought students were nothing more than "a bunch of radicals intent on burning the country down." Armed with such beliefs and instincts, he had no resistance to the proposal that he inform for BOSS. "I sincerely believed that I was doing the right thing," he said. "You could call it misguided patriotism." But what changed his mind? Doubts about his involvement with BOSS grew as he began to make distinctions between patriotism and partisanship. "After my involvement with BOSS," he said, "I asked myself whether I was being patriotic to South Africa or to the National Party. . . . I was a fervent patriot—and I still am—although now I think in terms of an *all-embracing* South African patriotism."

This was the voice of a young ex-informer; but it is rare to ever hear such a voice, and it is to BOSS's credit, speaking from a strictly operational perspective, of course, that such defections from its informant ranks are so rare. But the rarity of such defections is no accident. The complete, professional secret police force must, as a matter of course, give considerable attention to the psychological reinforcement of its informants, as well as to the material rewards for such involvement.

Methods vary. In Iran, emphasis was placed on the material: payment for a student working as an informant might range from the equivalent of ten to twelve British pounds a month. While this was no colossal windfall, to be sure, it was a substantial subsidy for a student.

In Haiti, which throughout the seventies suffered the ravages of a terrible inflation, a maid could earn from three to ten dollars a month to inform. Again, not a windfall, but for a maid, a major boost on the road from bare subsistence.

In France, the police maintain a thoroughly extensive informant system. "Surveillance in France is so tight," says a former U.S. intelligence official, "that nobody moves without the local hotel clerk getting the numbers on everyone's passports. What an informer is paid is piddling, but the informer may be a maid who needs the money, so it won't cost them that much."

In the southern Philippines, there is a barter black market, entirely illegal, flourishing among Borneo, Malaysia, and southern Mindanao. Goods, ordinarily salable only at high prices, are exchanged for other goods. Informants who cooperate with the Philippine secret police network are permitted to participate. Other Philippine informants can find themselves elevated to Uncle Tom governmental stations (mayors without authority, councilors without influence), desirable for the steady remuneration they afford, if not for having to kowtow to commands from Manila. Some informants will get a prepaid weekend vacation trip to Manila (if, for example, they live in the more rural areas), where the tabs for the night life and the hotel room have already been picked up.

But, in some societies, particularly those of Eastern Europe, the rewards for informing are far more basic, less significant and less glamorous than a prepaid vacation at a ritzy hotel or a respectable government sinecure. Yugoslavian informants who do steady informing work for UDBA will find that their applications for a new job or for an apartment are processed more speedily. These are major subsistence inducements. The quality of the roof over your head may depend upon the quality of the information you give to the Romanian Securitate as well, or to the Soviet KGB, or to any of the other East European secret police bodies.

The reinforcement that comes from informing is negative as well as positive in many societies. You might, for example, lose your paycheck, your career, and your influence if you don't comply. "They forced me to do it," confessed the treasurer of the National University of Nicaragua after the Somoza regime had fallen and he had been exposed as an informer when state security files fell into the hands of the Sandinist guerrillas. "They said I would lose my job."

In all secret police struggles for control over their targets, leverage over personnel departments is a key to success. SAVAK in the seventies may have controlled virtually all government hiring. SAVAK also reviewed all government promotion lists.

SAVAK's control over *non*government personnel files was not as complete, yet almost as effective. When a young man was picked up at the Tehran airport in the mid-seventies by two SAVAK agents, they told him, "You have been under surveillance." He quickly understood that the left-wing group he had been involved with had been infiltrated by SAVAK informers. At the conclusion of a typical SAVAK interrogation (harsh questioning over a period of twenty-

four hours), he was released after signing the standard SAVAK
form stating that he would henceforth provide the secret police with
any information they requested. But, once released, the young man
refused to cooperate, and SAVAK promptly pulled the rug out from
under him. He found it impossible to land a job, in both the public
and private sectors. The young man did not know it at the time, but
the SAVAK informant system was so widespread that personnel
officers at private firms, as well as at government offices, were
often SAVAK informers. This young man learned the hard way. But
most others went the easier route: to get along, you had to go along;
and a great many did. To understand a secret police system is to understand why a populace will tend to go along—some even to the
extent of informing.

A high-ranking SAVAK official who was involved in torture
confessed after the Khomeini revolution that he originally joined
SAVAK as an informer; he was at the university and he needed
money. Iraj Jahangiri told the revolutionary court that he asked a
close friend for a job, and that friend "introduced me to several
SAVAK agents, who, after a short interview, decided to hire me as
an informer.

"I could not resist, because the agents said they would force the
university to expel me and they would beat me up. Once I joined,
they appointed me to the Ardebil branch, where I soon became deputy. By this time, I was so involved with the nefarious secret police
that I could not quit. My duty at Ardebil was to cooperate with CIA
agents and to identify SAVAK members betraying the organization.
I then became satisfied with my job, because I was receiving a high
salary plus continuous bonuses for revealing anti-Shah people."
(Jahangiri was eventually promoted to work at Evin prison as an interrogator of political prisoners.)

But the care and feeding of the informant network in Iran did not
stop at punitive or remunerative measures. SAVAK officials were
not so thickheaded as to believe that their employees could live by
bread alone. And so, SAVAK officials made the effort to develop a
psychological reinforcement system within both its informant network and its agent structure. For both, propaganda about atheists,
communists, socialists, and even liberals was provided. And the
message was constantly hammered home that the Shah was the ultimate patriot and anyone who opposed him was to be considered a

total subversive. Informers, once SAVAK had latched on to them, were not easily let go of.

Another surprising memorandum discovered among the confidential SAVAK files seized by students indicates just how seriously SAVAK took the job of propagandizing its informants. In a long memorandum titled "Guidance of the Sources," SAVAK headquarters in Tehran warned its Geneva regional headquarters (which bore responsibility for European operations) of the dangers of leaving its informers to their own devices even after paying out the usual retainer fee. We need to do more than that, said SAVAK.

"Since the sources who work within the target"—that is to say, SAVAK informers who remain in place (i.e., at universities) "are mainly exposed to the ideologies and thoughts of our opponents, as a result of propaganda and the study of harmful books and publications which are frequently made available to them through participation in lectures or discussion meetings; and since some of them have not as yet attained an awareness of the essence and truth of such ideologies, they are gradually influenced by elements of the opposition."

SAVAK, you see, was terrorized itself: terrorized by the possibility that its informants would become double agents.

"With this relative tendency for the sources to lean toward opponents," the memo continues, "a gap between the source and the leading apparatus [i.e., the SAVAK informant network] ultimately comes into existence. If awareness of the changed situation and the weakened morale of the source is not countered by measures aimed at neutralizing filthy and indecent issues that have contributed to his vacillating morale and possible change of attitude ultimately benefiting the adversaries—it is in case of this that the source, by losing his nationalistic spirit and faith in his work, becomes a security danger."‡

‡ SAVAK was by no means alone in its fear of agents evolving into major security risks. In an interview with *Time* magazine, Buck Revell, deputy assistant director of the FBI for criminal investigations, talked about the importance of a "control" man at the FBI serving as a monitor for agents who might otherwise become lonely or disoriented in strange, often criminal, roles, when they are separated from their families and fellow agents. One responsibility of the control man—the "lifeline to the organization"—must be to arrange periodic visits by the agents' families. he said, "and make sure the undercover operator realizes he's still an FBI agent."

The measures that SAVAK center proposed in the effort to counter the ideological drift of its informants away from the fold were remarkable for their operational specificity:

"Therefore, to prevent the occurrence of such problems, please see that the leaders of operations act according to the following procedures, effective March 21, 1972:

"1. Meet the source once every fifteen days.

"2. Half the time should be spent on enlightening him on current political issues and explaining the relationship of Iran to foreign countries.

"3. If the source has had, in the past, a special ideology [i.e., socialist tendencies], obviously the expulsion of that ideology will create a vacuum which must necessarily lead to his resorting to adopt positive nationalist [i.e., pro-Shah] ideas. Through analysis of, and attention to, the moral and family characteristics of the source, the morale of the source should be boosted.

"4. We must follow above procedures for sources who do cooperate out of nationalistic and patriotic sentiments—or even for material gain—since their thinking is also constantly subject to antinationalistic assaults and intrigues.

"5. Chiefs of agencies, too, to control and encourage the source, should meet with them every six months and communicate their ideas. . . ."

3

The secret police can be as rough-edged in recruiting informants as in interrogating detainees. Typically, "We won't do harm to them," the KGB agent says to his potential informer with regard to his associates. "We just want to know the spirit of the people."

But what if the potential informer politely declines the invitation to become a part of the KGB apparatus? In that event, the KGB agent is well armed: "We can still do anything we want to you," he will imply.

But the KGB is less often heavy-handed than its severest Western critics suggest. Only those caught in what the KGB considers to be patent antistate activity get the nonprivileged treatment. More typically, aside from cash, the KGB can offer the informant job promotion, and of course being moved up in the housing waiting line.

But what secret police agent is above blackmail (i.e., not being prosecuted for your crime)? A Czechoslovakian exile tells this story: After working at the United Nations, he returned to Czechoslovakia from New York in 1971, soon discovering that he was regularly "catching the attention" of the district office of the Státní Bezpečnost, or StB. In 1973, while he was working as a lawyer for a construction firm in Prague, he learned that the secret police were in fact regularly contacting his employer at his place of employment to find out more about him. Indeed, they came to his office in Prague once a month several times to ask about his activities. One day, after repeated inquiries on the part of the StB agents, the director of the firm made some suspiciously new arrangements, placing the technician who shared the lawyer's office with him in another office and replacing the technician with a young lady who, the lawyer recalls, was "very charming."

In fact, "we had a good relationship," he says, which is quite surprising, considering that he knew that the woman, an administrative assistant to the director of the firm, was approached by StB agents one day, who told her that they knew about her extramarital affair and strongly suggested that they would inform her husband about it if she did not agree to work with them. She agreed, and from that date on, she took up the task of informing on her friend and colleague.

Under that sort of pressure, it is understandable that human beings become something like political robots, in that friends, colleagues, and even lovers become actual and/or potential political targets. The pressures to inform can be enormous. In Taiwan, for example, a sentence of seven years for "failing to report a communist spy" or similarly severe punishment for "falsely reporting a communist spy" may be imposed. The Canadian Parliament was shocked when certain standard operating procedures of G-4 (a penetration unit of the Security Service which recruits informers within groups under investigation) were revealed. G-4 had apparently been doing some tricky, SAVAK-style business with some members of the Parti Québécois, which is dedicated to forming a separate, French-language nation. To turn the activists into G-4 informants, agents would pick them up (individually) after work or en route to work and take them for a chat to a motel twenty miles outside of Montreal. Held against their will for as long as fifteen hours at a time, they were offered both negative and positive inducements to inform. Passing before their very eyes arrest warrants made out in the names of those being held, the G-4 agents then sweetened their pitches by offering the prospective informants regular retainer fees. Years later, when word of this recruitment practice was made public by the McDonald Commission, G-4 agents defended their practice by pointing out that the detainees were under no obligation to continue the discourses they were engaged in at the motel. They "could have left the motel whenever they wished," said one agent. Or, alternatively, they "could have contacted the police for help," said another agent, entirely seriously.

What kind of person becomes an informer? In Cuba, they start them very young. Schoolchildren are inculcated with the patriotism of informing. When the schoolchild feels compelled to report "suspicious thinking" among his classmates, he will most likely turn to his teacher, who in turn will inform the principal, who then will report the matter to the Communist Youth Brigade representatives at the school.

This terrifying pattern of encouraging children to inform holds in the home as well as in school. "It is hard for many Cuban adults to believe that kids inform," says a political émigré who left Cuba in 1971, "but it has happened many times. For example, it has happened that a family is planning an escape from the country. They are holding a secret meeting. Now, how could the mothers and fathers sitting there with their children stop and think that their children could inform on them? But they have been known to do so."

Indeed, the organization of the high schools and colleges of Cuba is rigorously designed to facilitate the youthful informers network. A classroom of forty or forty-five students will be divided in half. Two members of the Communist Youth Brigade (one male, one female, as a demonstration of sexual equality) are placed in charge of each group. Before class, the groups line up in paramilitary configuration. "You were taught in school that if you see something strange (whatever that might be), you must report it to one of the two members of the Brigade," says the émigré. "The groups were so small and the whole school so carefully partitioned that the Brigade leaders would usually know right away whom you were referring to when you reported someone. And if you wanted to inform on someone not in your particular class, you could do that—by simply informing the

Brigade member representing that section of the school including the person whom you were reporting on."

The tightly organized classroom informant system is duplicated outside of the school system. The whole country is organized into block committees. Each block committee consists of ten families. Regular meetings are held, and patrol and intelligence assignments will be made. One family is designated to chair the committee and is required to attend periodic meetings of the chair families. The block-committee network rises on upward toward Havana.

These committees are known as "Comités de la defensa de la revolución," or "Committees for the Defense of the Revolution," and in the first spirited days of Castro's takeover, participation in the work of these informant committees was wholly cooperative. But as the bloom is now off Castro and his revolution, committee work is understood for what it really is: as auxiliary work for the Cuban secret police. As a recent Cuban exile put it, "The committees are tools to control all of the neighborhoods."

But the tool doesn't always work as well as it used to. In July of 1978, Cuba was the scene for the International Festival of the Communist Party. Accordingly, the Cuban secret police were told to put the best face on Cuba that was possible. But a woman who had served nine years in prison (for an aborted attempt to escape the country) crossed G-2 agents. She was placed under house arrest and ordered to sign a paper certifying that she would stay at home and would be there whenever the agents appeared. G-2 simply didn't want her, with her antipatriotic spirit, milling around in the crowds. But the woman repeatedly refused to sign the G-2 papers. She complained to them: "My sentence is over, you must leave me alone." G-2 agents then went to the president of the committee of her neighborhood to aid them in securing her signature. But the woman was a hard fighter, and even the neighborhood committee was unable to produce the desired result.

While in Cuba children are an essential part of the informant system, in Haiti the desired sociological traits for an informant are quite different. Haitian informers work in every stratum of the island's tightly controlled society, but the personal favorites of "Papa Doc" Duvalier, who died in April of 1971 before turning the island over to his son "Baby Doc," were voodoo priests. These witch doctors, feared and revered as they are in primitive Haitian subcultures, were ideal operatives for the government. A substantial portion of the Haitian people still believe in the power of voodoo.* By recruiting witch doctors as informers, the Duvaliers established a formidable informant system that was carefully woven into the cultural fabric of Haiti.

Children, voodoo priests, and ex-convicts, even, make reliable informers for societies with widely varying needs: the Chilean military junta trained criminals at the Pisagua and Chacabuco concentration camps to act as informers in slum neighborhoods. The first "graduating class," released at the end of April, 1978, became active in Santiago, Valparaiso, and Concepción, Chile's biggest cities. The group consisted of some three hundred underworld elements under the control of the civilian police force, now part of the Defense Ministry. Under the definition of "rehabilitated former delinquents," the military junta laid out its scheme with technical advice from DINA. After being caught in a wave of police raids, the gangsters were interned at a concentration camp, where they were placed under military discipline and given special instructions. They were worked over constantly with the notion that their failure to collaborate with the government and police authorities would lead to the sort of repressive treatment which they, traitors, deserved. The brainwashing worked well. The civilian police contracted close to eighty of those individuals (described as persons "who were ready for any kind of work"), while the remainder of the graduating class were assigned odd jobs in the municipalities of Santiago, Valparaiso, and Concepción.

Secret police systems tend to give their low-level informants a relatively free hand. The informer is able to wheel and deal at the street level without much supervision. Oftentimes, the secret police control agent would rather not know what his low-level informants are doing every minute of every day. In Iran, informers were more or less free-lancers—they were both opportunistic and entrepreneurial. "I have investigated the Shah's brother," confessed one Iranian informer, "and I have investigated lowly parking attendants on the street."

* Two historians, Robert Debs Heinl and Nancy Gordon Heinl, in *Written in Blood: The Story of the Haitian People,* remind that it is an old saying that Haiti is 80 percent Catholic and 100 percent voodoo. "This may not be a literal truth," they write, but . . . Voodoo has sunk its roots deep into Haitian soil . . ."

Sometimes, however, the informer is required to work according to specific guidelines. The Canadian security service typically places its informants under tight controls. Informants for the security service, it was disclosed during investigations into RCMP activities, were paid to infiltrate bookstores carrying left-wing or Third World publications, the offices of a black lawyer, and several universities. For such efforts, the informant was paid from one hundred to five hundred dollars a month. Another typical security-service assignment: a research director for a human-rights organization in Canada was paid to infiltrate a number of allegedly Communist-front organizations. A former employee of the Egyptian embassy in Ottawa, he translated wiretapped telephone conversations of Arab diplomats and attended Arab conventions, as well as filed confidential reports. Security-service informants also infiltrated labor unions and provided detailed information on the day-to-day routine of union leaders. The security branch of the Royal Canadian Mounted Police developed a network of informers that penetrated practically all branches of government departments. In 1977, a major Canadian newspaper said that informants held jobs that "run the gamut from janitors to secretaries to top-level civil servants," adding that "a top-notch informant will make as much as $10,000 a year from the police, on top of normal salary."

Security police will recruit journalists as informants when they are able to get away with it. Newspaper or magazine work provides a perfect cover for the work: after all, journalists are supposed to ask questions, even questions that the interviewee does not want to answer; the dogged persistence required to do the journalist's job, then, does not arouse much suspicion.

South Africa's BOSS has relied heavily on journalists. (The South African Government shelled out $11.5 million in 1978 in an apparent attempt to purchase the Washington *Star*.) Why did South African security police turn especially to journalists to work as informers? No one knows for sure, but one informer who worked for BOSS in the sixties and seventies claims that the South African Government of John Vorster became irritated that things were happening in South Africa that the secret police never knew about until the account showed up in the newspaper the following day. Accordingly, he says, Hendrik Van den Bergh, then head of BOSS, went to Prime Minister Vorster with an idea to recruit journalists for the security service. (The forerunner of BOSS was called Republican Intelligence, and it was for that organization that this informant went to work. In 1969, he claims he was automatically transferred to BOSS.)

The informant worked at first for two black journals in South Africa. Though he is a white man, he was able to befriend a number of leading South African black leaders. They trusted the informant because, he explains, he had "good friends in the black townships." Apparently, BOSS was prepared to pay a rather hefty price for this infiltration, in that it permitted the informer to continue with his slashing anti-apartheid journalism (which had resulted in his contact with black activists in the first place). What BOSS got in return, however, was terribly valuable: the names and addresses of black leaders, both inside of South Africa and abroad, especially in exile circles in London. "I knew they were addresses the police didn't know about," says the informant. "I submitted reports. In actual fact, I sent photostats of letters. . . ." The informant also befriended a British subject who was helping raise secret funds for various black nationalist parties. The British citizen became a close friend of the informant; this was how he became at the same time an unwitting fountain of information for BOSS. He was, recalls the informant, ". . . a human being who fell for it. Thousands of others have fallen for it as thousands of others will continue to fall for it. . . . They will still fall for deception."

The informant described his line of work in a fascinating way. "If you're a magician, you're geared to deception. If you're not a magician, you're in the public, you're in the audience. You know some of the tricks and how they're done. You guess how they're done but the tricks you don't know about, you start believing it's magic. It's the same with spying; it's the same, it's the double thing, it's deception, it's deceit. . . ."

The informant retained his credibility in antigovernment circles because he helped slip fleeing political figures over the border, even though he was still working for BOSS. Precisely because BOSS turned a blind eye to the proceedings, the informant gained even more stature in antigovernment circles. Then his career took an unexpected turn: he was implicated in a sensational murder case, but, by turning state's witness in another political case, he managed to get his sentence commuted. The next step was official deportation from South Africa by the government.

"But this was a fabulous opportunity," the informant claims, "to use my deportation, which was a total setup, so that I could spy in Britain."

In Britain, the informant stayed in touch with high-level BOSS handlers. He recalls one lunch with an intelligence agent just prior to his deportation. "We had lunch together . . . he gave me a Bible. . . . It's a leather Bible. On the front page he has written: 'Keep faith.'" (The informant claims that his handler's cover, when the agent was operating in London, was as First Secretary of the South African embassy in London.)

He claims that he joined the South African secret police as an informant out of love, rather than a need for money. "I love South Africa, I want to help South Africa," he says. "I will do anything, this country has been good to me." He claims that when he received his first official check for informing he was terribly moved. That first check, covering two or three months of work for BOSS, was for 120 rands. The check was laundered through a private firm, but even so, he worried about so open and traceable a method of payment. He questioned BOSS about the check, and the organization agreed that it would use a different method from then on. Future payments were made in cash. "I had quick wit," he recalls, thinking back over the experience, "I had tremendous knowledge of the underworld and criminal thinking" (he himself had been a street criminal earlier on in his life), which, he points out, not without accuracy, "is a great start for any man in journalism."

Or, he might have added, in working for the secret police.

4

At some point, the well-run secret police system will begin to act on the information at its disposal. A file may be opened. An agent may be detailed to the case. Informants may be pumped for more information or asked to nose around some more. The antennas of the secret police, now tuned to a new frequency, home in on the target.

At this stage of the operation, the secret police resources may prove impressive. Besides an informant system that permeates every level and sector of society, the well-run secret police organization will draw on a variety of surveillance techniques to determine how much farther it should go, and to what end.

Everything up to but not including arrest may be attempted by the secret police organization bent on working up a major case, but even the most sophisticated, well-equipped, and well-staffed secret police force will not very often pursue more than one approach at one time. A two- or three-track investigation (e.g., wiretapping while at the same time working up a dossier, or perhaps adding a tail team as a back-up surveillance technique) is expensive, complicated, and manpower-depleting. It will be used only when the secret police force has been ordered to go all out, no expenses or pains spared, or when the organization is exceptionally rich in resources, as is the KGB. Take the Seventh Directorate of the KGB. In addition to supervisors, case officers, analysts, and technicians, this directorate employs at least several thousand agents who spend their professional lives doing nothing but watching people. According to one source provided access to U.S. intelligence information, the directorate has twelve departments. One follows citizens of the United States and Latin America. Another follows selected foreign journalists, students, and businessmen. Two others share the task of spying on non-Americans. A fifth department supervises the militia guards posted at each foreign embassy to prevent unauthorized visits by Russians. Another investigates Soviet citizens being considered for KGB employment. A seventh maintains surveillance equipment, from cars and infrared cameras to television cameras and two-way mirrors. Yet another department patrols the streets that members of the Party oligarchy use in traveling to and from their offices. The largest department, covering Moscow locales that both foreigners and prominent Soviet citizens are likely to visit, employs many retired KGB personnel. It also operates a special taxi fleet and Intourist motor pool that enables the KGB to pick up anybody calling a cab or hiring a car. There is even a special department that designs and procures disguises, wigs, mustaches, clothes, and other paraphernalia employed in surveillance. Another department consists of a dozen expert and highly mobile surveillance teams for special operations (such as the entrapment of a foreign dignitary or the surveillance of a ranking member of the oligarchy).

Generally, however, the single-track approaches (for instance shadowing, to the exclusion of all other, more sophisticated surveillance techniques) are the most commonly used by secret police. They make more sense. They are more compact. They are subject to regular reevaluation. And costs can be controlled. Even for the lavishly funded secret police force, costs are always something to consider, as surveillances are invariably expensive. On the other hand, the government wants results, and the secret police organization that doesn't satisfy its government's demands along those lines will eventually be reorganized, shuffled off in a merger, or superseded by some new agency.

A surveillance program has four purposes. Properly conducted, it will: (1) provide new information; (2) confirm old information; (3) lead to a decision to make an arrest (and help determine the length of, not to mention the character and severity of, the detention); or (4) at the very least, contribute to the overall intimidatory goal of keeping those who are normally quiet deaf to the political pitch of those who refuse to be intimidated; it is as much to the quiescent as to the belligerent that the secret police force directs its activities.

After all, a surveillance program can enhance the effectiveness of the secret police by virtue of its mere existence, regardless of whatever its actual capabilities may be. "The enjoyment of privacy requires not only the reality but also the *feeling* of withdrawal from unwanted scrutiny," as A. Alan Borovoy, general counsel for the Canadian Civil Liberties Association, has pointed out. "To the extent that people feel they are being spied upon, they will have lost their privacy."

And when the populace feels that loss, a secret police force feels that gain. Its goal, after all, is not to enhance the feeling of personal privacy of the citizen, but to raise the level of social stability, even to the point of eliminating the sense of privacy. If the reality of omnipresence is impossible to achieve fully, the *impression* of omnipresence is not.

The carefully conceived surveillance program can go a long way toward achieving this impression. Part of the program may involve *not* being too careful. The secret police force that is almost invisible might also seem to be almost nonexistent. (This subtle approach might work for societies that have already learned their lesson, having been tightly controlled by an aggressive secret police force for a long time; but it will not work for societies still struggling for basic freedoms and still involved in the "learning process.")

Mexico is rarely thought of as a country that has problems requiring secret police attention to the same degree of urgency as the intense political battles faced by Chile's DINA, for example, just after the coup. But a surprising level of political surveillance is conducted by police agents, who, adopting a high profile, infiltrate political gatherings as if solely for the purpose of making their presence known. For instance, when a member of the Brigada Blanca is assigned to tail a political suspect, the tail might be flagrant: their black Fords with no license plates tend to be about as subtle as a Mexican hat dance.

It is not difficult, sources say, to know when you are being watched in Mexico. An outspoken Catholic bishop, holding a press conference to question government policies or alleged government complicity in an assassination or a disturbing political development, does not have to worry whether police agents are in the audience. They are. A few of the reporters in the press corps will undoubtedly be ringers, but the disguise does not fool. It is not supposed to.

Allowing the target of the surveillance to understand that the surveillance exists is a sort of preventive secret policing: the goal is to establish hegemony and to deter future political activity, even if, or especially if, past violations have occurred. "Even after their release," said a Taiwanese dissident, "my whole family was not free. Twice a day, they were required to report to the local security agency in person, and to make a detailed accounting on whom they met and what they did on that day. Besides, since their arrest on December 16, 1976, two plainclothesmen moved into my father's house to guard us around the clock. Anywhere we went, we would be followed by security agents. Our telephone was disconnected. People who visited us during that period were questioned."

The tactic of all South Korean law-enforcement agencies in the mid-seventies was to ensure that certain South Korean citizens were absolutely aware that the conduct of their daily lives was under surveillance. It was not unusual to wake up in the morning to find that plainclothes guards had been posted outside your house; or that when you opened your mail you were obviously not the first to do so, judging by the obvious paste-up job that had been done in resealing the envelope; or that when you went downtown to meet a friend, you were joined much earlier than you had planned by others, whom you had not invited. Sometimes agents would phone early in the morning to ask about your plans for the day, and phone often during the day and until late at night to keep checking on your whereabouts, especially if they had lost sight of you. The object of such obvious surveillance is not to gather information but to intimidate the population. Harassment is entirely open, not by mistake but by design.

Mihajlo Mihajlov, the famed Yugoslavian dissident author whose contacts with the American press brought him into special disfavor with Yugoslavian secret police authorities, maintains a bittersweet sense of humor about being watched so obviously and constantly by UDBA agents. He was followed, he claims, by agents in cars and on foot both behind and in front of him, most often when he would be out walking. How did it make him feel? "I knew I wouldn't be robbed," rejoined Mihajlov.

The Polish secret police force, UB, employs a similar fairly heavy-handed technique against many so-called revisionist critics of the state. When you are a target of the technique—called "blockading"—you are followed constantly and openly. The usual detail is three agents in two cars. The cars are often Fiats (a common car in Poland), and the agents make no particular effort to disguise their act. There may be, however, significance in certain seemingly minor aspects of the operation. If it is the common gray Fiat that is used in the surveillance, for example, then the object of the exercise is to discover the individual's patterns, his meeting places and who his associates are without his being aware that he is being followed. If, however, some more flamboyant car is used in the operation, then the object of the exercise is to make sure that the individual knows he is being followed.

The blockading technique can be as obvious as it is intimidating. You are walking, and at least one of the two tail cars follows you down the street at the same speed at which you are walking on the sidewalk. The shadows move along with you. It can be a most unsettling experience. Looking back on it today, however, one veteran of a Marxist-Leninist student movement in Warsaw found the experience of being blockaded almost comical. "I didn't have much to lose at the time," she explained, almost marveling at her ability to cope with the almost continuous secret police surveillance to which she was subjected. She and her husband had lost their jobs, and both of them faced trials for antistate activities.

"What did we have to lose?" she ponders. One morning, she glanced out her apartment window and said to her husband, "Look, we have a new fellow [spying on them from outside of their building]. Let's see how good he is." The couple left their apartment in downtown Warsaw and ducked into store after store in the area, as though they were on a shopping spree. The young police agent followed them frantically, trying desperately not to lose them. The couple turned into a crowded drugstore, then stood in a long line. The agent practically fell over them as, hot on their heels, he followed them into the drugstore. When the couple got up to the head of the purchasing line, the woman asked for a bottle of aspirin. The simple purchase was made, and the woman and her husband both stepped to the side of the line. The agent also purchased something quickly, then stepped out of the line, waiting for the couple to exit from the store. But, instead, she and her husband stayed put, which made the agent, now having no one to follow and no duty to do, a bit nervous. When he finally bolted from the store, the woman said to her husband, "Let's follow *him*," delighting in the idea of reversing their roles. The young agent, seeing that he was being tailed, appeared to be desperate and embarrassed. He didn't know where to go. Suddenly he ducked into an apartment building, but he stayed put inside the lobby. The couple stood across the street, glaring at him from the other side of the glass apartment door. Ten minutes of stalemate passed, neither side budging. Then two white Fiats drove up, and five men stepped out. The couple recognized the plainclothes agents immediately. Their faces were those of familiar UB agents who, they realized, had come to the rescue of the young agent. They whisked him away in their car, and the couple were never to see the young agent on their trail again.

But the Polish secret police enjoyed the final revenge against this couple. One day, an official from the state prosecutor's office asked the woman to appear for an interview. It was an official request, and this sort of thing was never ignored. "Why don't you get a job?" one prosecutor asked during her interview.

"How can I get work?" she complained. "Every place I go and give a résumé, 'they' come in a day later."

The experience of telling the state prosecutor what he already knew was quite unnerving. Surely he must have known that she had been fired as a proofreader after working only one day and fired as a librarian after working as one for only six weeks. He must have known that she had even tried working in a private café, selling beer, but plainclothes UB agents had disrupted even that attempt at a job. They would routinely harass her at the café, complaining about the service, alleging that they had been shortchanged, complaining to the manager about her. At wit's end, she wrote a letter to the state prosecutor's office complaining about this harassment. The letter was never answered. In 1970, she and her husband applied for visas, left Poland, and moved to the United States, which no doubt was just fine by UB.

5

Before they come to your home, the secret police are likely to come to your place of work. To cut a person off from his ability to make a living cuts as deeply at economic freedom as detention cuts off freedom of movement. G-2 agents, in Cuba, will suddenly appear at your place of work with questions for your employer, ultimately wrapping up their meeting with him or her with the command that "This worker must report on such and such day to the state security police." The G-2 technique was copied from that of its parent, the Soviet Union's KGB; its chilling effect works quite well. With the security police appearing at the place of work asking questions and giving commands, what employer is likely to advance the worker in question in terms of either pay or responsibility?

The technique is applied almost exclusively to former political prisoners. All Cubans over the age of sixteen must carry identification booklets, and those of political prisoners get stamped with special identification marks. This stamp, according to a confidential analysis of the employment situation for former political prisoners that was smuggled out of Cuba, "is the deciding factor in whether he gets work or not, the quality of the job he gets, and the salary." Most former political prisoners are lucky to find jobs in the construction business. "The exceptions," according to the smuggled document, "those who get jobs at other places, are few and are a result of someone using their influence." Children of parents with branded identification papers, says the report, "are denied scholarships in the vocational schools, and they are not allowed to attend the great majority of the schools [departments] within the University of Havana." The G-2 also maintains surveillance so that "members of the Communist Youth organizations and the Communist Party are forbidden to have any contact with former prisoners, even if they are relatives." As one former political prisoner in Cuba put it, "We have become robots, beings with our lives at half mast, men who have been transformed into something inhuman, terribly incomplete."

The pattern is similar in Indonesia, where measures taken by the government and implemented by the secret police force known as Kopkamtib probably affected the employability of some ten million people, plus their families.† Recently released prisoners are required to report to Kopkamtib on a weekly basis, and they are forbidden to travel from place to place without the permission of the secret police. An Indonesian newspaper advertisement demonstrates explicitly the degree of control that the secret police exercise over the job market. It was a want ad for jobs on the Holland-America Line (a steamship line) for carpenters, engineers, and so on. The ad listed the conditions of employment: One condition was a comprehension of English or Dutch. The second was the ability to work responsibly and without supervision. The third requirement was a letter certifying the applicant's lack of involvement in the attempted communist coup of 1965, together with a letter of good standing from the police. The secret police, therefore, help determine who gets hired and who does not.

The powers of the Federal Office for the Protection of the Constitution, in West Germany, are not nearly so sweeping as Kopkamtib's, but they are not markedly inferior in terms of their intended, if not in their real, effect. Under the so-called "Radicals Decree" adopted by the West German Government in 1972, individuals whom the Federal Office deems security risks can be denied even the most menial positions in the government. (The decree is enforced less severely in states where the left-of-center Social Democratic

---

† Kopkamtib (Command for the Restoration of Security and Order), the executive arm of the military government, was set up after the 1965 army coup in order to combat communist subversion. Kopkamtib involves itself in such matters as censoring the press, arresting those disturbing law and order, and curbing demonstrations. Kopkamtib, representing the political interests of the Department of Defense and Security, acts on the basis of formal military authority. Some of that authority is delegated to LAKSUS (Special Implementers) at each provincial army command.

Another important covert intelligence organization in Indonesia is OPSUS (Special Operations), which specializes in the manipulation of political groups. OPSUS' activities are conducted largely by its many civilian informers and are influenced by certain Chinese intellectuals and financiers. Unlike Kopkamtib, operating on the basis of military authority, OPSUS methods are said to be informal and covert.

Party holds power; though it was supported in 1972 by Willy Brandt, the former chancellor has since come to repudiate it on the grounds that it is more trouble than it is worth, that it is a blunt and therefore ineffective instrument for ferreting out subversives.) The law also serves to subject to security scrutiny those entering certain nongovernmental institutions such as the practice of law. The Federal Office's efforts are supposed to be directed against Communists and other Marxists, but in practice the scrutiny has been widened to cover wide-ranging political *thought* as well as political action and commitment. The Federal Office will, when authorized by the Ministry of the Interior, run wiretaps, buggings, and mail openings, but the Federal Office has its chilling effect, so much so that Hans Klose Ulric, the mayor of Bremen, once was compelled to remark that the employment of twenty communists in public-service jobs is a lesser evil than the alienation of two hundred thousand young people through a system of state surveillance of their political views.

But a technique that alienates some sectors of the population signifies to the secret police that they have established an effective vehicle of control. The whole point of surveillance is to maintain the appearance, if not the reality, of omnipresence. Just as visual surveillance techniques can be as purposely obvious as they can be clandestine, so telephone surveillance can work in obvious ways: for instance, the noisy tap is used when the secret police want you to know that your conversations are being monitored. And the secret police are even more direct than that. They may even interpose a comment or two in the middle of your conversation, turning a two-way conversation into a three-way argument.

A sector of the Uruguayan secret police used to telephone Juan Ferreira, son of a former presidential candidate of a liberal party and himself an active opponent of the regime during the years 1973–75, to question him about his friend living in exile in Buenos Aires. They would try to provoke him by accusing his friend of being a Tupamaro. Finally, on May 20, 1976, five months after the last harassing phone call to Ferreira had been made, his friend was assassinated in Buenos Aires.

Exiled South African author Donald Woods says the security police monitored all his phone calls as well as those of the famous deceased black-consciousness leader Steve Biko. "Often, after such calls," writes Woods (with regard to calls from one revolutionary to another, informing of a death of a political ally), "we would receive abusive calls from them anonymously, of course, or silent calls with heavy breathing—just to let us know they were listening at all times. . . . The security police were enjoying themselves while on midnight telephone surveillance duty."

Heavy breathing appears to be a nearly universal secret police affectation. The former director of the State Department Office of Korean Affairs (1970–74) asserts that when he testified before the House of Representatives in the late seventies with regard to the kidnapping of the famous opposition candidate to Park Chung Hee, Kim Dae Jung, for several months he would answer his telephone only to hear heavy breathing on the other end of the line.

But, no doubt, some victims of secret police telephone harassment would welcome something as simple as an annoying telephone call from time to time. The former adviser to the Dubček Cabinet and signatory of Charter 77 awakened to discover that his telephone was disconnected, one morning in 1978. He complained to the postal administration (which runs the phone system), but officials simply implied that there was some technical difficulty. Several months later, he inquired anew at the postal administration, again to no avail. Eventually he realized that his participation in the Charter 77 movement had literally cut him off from the rest of society.

The secret police usually work with whatever authority is in control of the phone service. In Egypt, for instance, the security police have all the advantages; the phones are owned and operated by the government. The same holds for France, where, accordingly, the security police practice extensive telephone surveillance.

According to the confessed SAVAK torturer Tehrani, SAVAK controlled between ninety and one hundred thousand telephones divided between two telephone centers, one on Aboreyhan Avenue and the other on Soraya Avenue, in Tehran.

The very comprehensive telephone surveillance system, said Tehrani, enabled SAVAK to hunt down and murder a long-sought revolutionary by the name of Mojaheed Seyed Ali Andarzgoo: "We were about to return to Tehran when a telegram was received from Tehran from Azghandi [a SAVAK superior], to the effect that Seyed Ali Andarzgoo is in Ghom and might live in the house of Mr. Eshraghi and Ayatollah Rabani Shirezzi. It also informed us that he rode a blue motorcycle and wore gray suits. We were ordered to try to find him with the aid of the tracing and surveillance team and the description in the telegram." (Tehrani describes making many such trips to various municipalities with the tracing and surveillance team, but the technique of traveling surveillance teams was not peculiar to SAVAK. For instance, within the Fourth Administration of the Czechoslovakian security police, there used to be a section called "flying squads"—*lítačky*—which were surveillance teams having no permanent, clearly defined goals.)

Continued Tehrani: ". . . I will first explain how it was discovered that Shekyah Abbas Tehrani, alias Seyed Ali Andarzgoo, was in Mashad. Some time ago, Azghandi gave me a telephone number of a dairy store in order to set up a phone eavesdropping system. This was done. Tapes of the telephone conversations arrived later to me. . . . During the three or four months that I listened to the tapes, as it gradually became necessary, the telephone numbers of well-known people, including the telephone number of Haj Ali Akbar, who was one of the partners in the dairy store, was surveilled with the decision of high officials. . . . The surveillance of telephones of houses and individuals indicated that these people had extensive involvements in the production and distribution of Imam Khomeini's leaflets. . . . It was also revealed that a person known as Sergeant Javadi was practically in charge of these operations. . . . In the process of listening to the tapes of the phone conversations and using the dialing telephone tape, it became clear that Javadi had contacts with a house in Mashad. And Azghandi [the SAVAK superior], after listening to the tape, confirmed that Javadi must be Seyed Ali Andarzgoo, and that the house in Mashad with which he was in contact must be his place of residence. The event was reported by Azghandi to Parviz Sabeti [known popularly as the "kingpin of SAVAK"], the chief of the Third Central Office [the chief SAVAK office that dealt with subversives and internal security], and consequently it was decided that the team would travel to Mashad, start doing surveillance and taking whatever measures were necessary to conduct an arrest and attack. The following day, therefore, members of the tracing and surveillance team and a few committee guards and I . . . drove to Mashad. . . . In Mashad we went to the local SAVAK, and measures were taken to 'watch' the house's telephone. Then the house was identified on one of the streets of Mashad community. . . . One day . . . around 6 P.M., Saidi suddenly called to say that Seyed Ali Andarzgoo was in Tehran. As a result, Azghandi reported the event to Sabeti, who was in Tehran, and we drove toward Tehran at 10 P.M. the same night. The following day, around 10 or 11 A.M., we arrived in Tehran. . . . About five P.M. Saidi [another SAVAK superior] telephoned that Seyed Ali Andarzgoo, known as Sheykh Abbas Tehrani, was seen around Iran Avenue close to Haj Akbar's home."

There is not much to the story after this. Agents of the tracing and surveillance team pointed out their target to agents of a SAVAK "shock force." Andarzgoo was machine-gunned, and after he fell to the floor, he pulled out his notebook, tore off some of the pages with writings on them, put them in his mouth and swallowed them, breaking a religious fast with this move. When the agents of the shock force opened fire again, Andarzgoo was killed.

Telephone calls of influential Iranians, high-ranking politicians and military brass were all tapped and recorded by SAVAK. "We had the most modern communications facilities," said a top communications specialist affiliated with SAVAK, referring to the two centers Tehrani spoke about. The communications aide elaborated: "The Shah was always paranoid about a military coup or conspiracy against him by leading politicians, so he ordered us to tap all important calls made by these people."

The specialist recalled one conversation in particular, a conversation that took place between a prominent Iranian politician and the Shah. "The Shah used to call Amini late at night and ask for his suggestions. The Shah would say, 'What more can I do to satisfy the mullahs? I have imprisoned poor Hoveyda, I have also jailed other politicians, furthermore I have promised reforms." The Shah then asked the politician to contact the mullahs as an unofficial mediator. "We did not dare tape the conversations," recalled the specialist, "but because we had Amini's telephone tapped at all times, we could hear the Shah's words."

6

The secret break-in of offices, homes, or the sites of political meetings even in societies where secret police generally advertise their activities is a commonly used tool.

The properly executed break-in can be conducted in the utmost secrecy even in a relatively open society. The security branch of the Royal Canadian Mounted Police—not a type-A secret police force, to be sure—conducted hundreds upon hundreds of illegal break-ins before a scandal broke in the late seventies and the issue of the break-ins became a subject of debate. The break-ins were not individual acts by overzealous agents but were "procedures approved by the force itself," according to Canadian Government Solicitor General Jean-Jacques Blais.

In some cases, homes and offices were broken into in order to install electronic surveillance equipment. In others, they were broken into simply to gather general political intelligence where there was not enough evidence to obtain a search warrant. Operation 300 (or "Haven," as it was also known) began in the mid-fifties and involved break-ins across the face of Canada. One unsurprising such break-in: into the offices of a publisher that in 1971 issued a book titled *The Unauthorized History of the RCMP*.

The commonness of break-ins as an RCMP technique was revealed when some of the security unit's more bizarre activities were uncovered and made public. The activities were stepped up in a campaign against French separatist political groups. The security service became heavily involved in the well-known dirty-tricks business. On one occasion, agents stole dynamite from a construction site and attempted to plant the dynamite on suspected terrorists. Security agents then led Quebec provincial police to the site where the dynamite had been planted in an effort to implicate the Quebec terrorists. In another incident, agents came upon a barn in a section of Quebec that, according to its own intelligence information, would be the site of a planning meeting between Canadian and American political "extremists." Unable to bug the barn for technical reasons, agents decided to burn it down. "The idea was that if we burned the barn," explained former RCMP Staff Sergeant Donald McCleery, "they would have to move somewhere else, where we'd have a better chance of monitoring them." The officer was unembarrassed by the revelation in the press. "Don't get the idea we were a bunch of hoodlums running around and burning barns. I was in the security service for twenty years and there was only one barn burnt." Maybe, but another agent, who worked undercover for the security unit, was surprised by all the commotion that surrounded the revelations about his unit. Responsible for planting a bomb outside the home of a grocery-chain executive allegedly involved in separatist activities, the officer complained that he saw no reason for all the fuss. "I've done worse things for the RCMP," he said.

There is reason to believe him. According to an official RCMP document dated June 11, 1971, the Mounties were encouraged to use "disruptive tactics" in their effort to throw a monkey wrench into the activities of separatist groups. Those tactics included "making use of sophisticated and well-researched plans built around existing situations such as power struggles, love affairs, fraudulent use of funds, information on drug abuse, etc., to cause dissension and splintering of the separatist and terrorist groups." Acting true to its word, security-service agents stole computer tapes from the Parti Québécois headquarters. The tapes contained membership and financial information. After copying, the tapes were later quietly returned. Agents also pilfered files from one left-wing group and planted them with another. The thefts, according to the RCMP's own analysis contained in confidential documents, delivered the "coup de grace" to one organization, which "can no longer enter into contact with members for appeals for financial support," because activities were now disorganized "to such an extent that it was very difficult for them to operate for a long period of time." The theft, said a government spokesman, caused the "loss of research which took them a year and a half to build up." Explaining the Parti Québécois thefts, one security-branch agent noted only that "we were borrowing them more than stealing them; we only borrowed them for a couple of hours." How did the RCMP manage to recruit so many informants in left-wing organizations? Simple, said one official: "We made them an offer they couldn't refuse."

This sort of active surveillance is common to security police all over the world. An American report on methods of surveillance used in Indonesia claims that the Kopkamtib secret police conduct an "anything goes" system that is widespread in scope and mercenary in detail. "The methods include," according to prepared testimony by Professor Benedict O'Gorman Anderson, of Cornell University, for the House of Representatives: ". . . having the houses of people disliked by the regime stoned; sending anonymous letters; intimidation with weapons or less direct means; organizing hoodlums and mafia-type groups to frighten people disliked by those in power; nighttime operations to plant leaflets on people's doorsteps; . . . hiring prostitutes to tail political notables; hiring 'masseuses' to hang around meeting rooms; infiltrating informants into suspicious meetings of Islamic scholars; hiring people to pretend to be reporters taking pictures; ordering military men to pose as rickshaw drivers, roadside food vendors, etc., in the context of 'total intelligence operations.' . . ."

In his famous confession before an Islamic revolutionary court in Tehran, the admitted torturer and SAVAK agent Tehrani told a story not unreminiscent of the sort of surveillance activities that we have witnessed being used by secret police of other countries. He called attention to the so-called Mahan Committee, which was given the responsibility of coordinating operations designed to confuse and divide the Islamic Movement by producing and distributing false leaflets. The Committee was formed on the orders of Lieutenant General Nasser Moghadam, a high SAVAK official, and was situated in a SAVAK safe house in Sultanabad. The famed Joint Committee (of SAVAK, Police, and Gendarmerie, designed to coordinate all antirevolutionary activities) in Tehran coordinated all leaflet activity with the Mahan Committee. Tehrani said that the Committee supervised the printing and distribution of countless leaflets, "the object of which was to create dissension among the so-called religious groups and groups with different ideologies. . . . Our 'subordinates,' that is drivers and guards, distributed them."

The Special Branch of MI6, the British political police, often focuses its undercover and disruptive activities on trade union activity in Great Britain. The line between sincere trade unionism and Communist organizing can be a fine one, but the Special Branch often engages the cooperation of management officials to plant undercover operatives inside the unions, sometimes blurring the line even more by instructing its undercover agents in leadership positions within the union to advocate, and even execute, violent demonstrations. Special Branch also maintains close relationships with employers, who sometimes receive calls from agents about an employee allegedly involved in (to use the jargon of the trade) "hammer and sickle business."

Whether the matter involves hammer-and-sickle or other business, the infiltration of the ranks of the perceived enemy is a very widely used secret police technique. A State Department official says that the Jordanian internal security unit "Mukhabarat" infiltrates agents into all Palestinian guerrilla camps.

7

So far, the secret police have not invaded the suspect's home. They may have listened to phone conversations, infiltrated political groups, spied in the office, or had agents or informants play the role of agent provocateur, but so far the home has remained the citizen's bastion of privacy. But even that territory loses its sanctity during the next phase of the secret police operation: the search.

In most countries where secret police are active, which is to say in most countries, there are two classifications for the house search, or as one Soviet citizen put it, ". . . there are different searches carried out by 'different craftsmen.'" One style of house search is the "white glove" search, where, as in Poland, agents show up at your home, sometimes unannounced, sometimes without a warrant, and putter around for an hour or so, lightly going through the household effects. The point of the search is not to radicalize the target of the search by using brutal investigative methods against him, but to let the potential dissident know who is boss. As one Polish political émigré put it, "The white-glove search would be used when the police were investigating, for instance, the family of an opposition figure if the family itself is not outspoken. To conduct a violent search could possibly turn the rest of the family to the rebel's point of view, a conversion UB agents would like to avoid."

In the Soviet Union, the white-glove search can take the form of a rigid procedure that was fairly common during what dissidents refer to as the "period of lawfulness" (1969–79). According to this procedure, all searches had to be conducted in observance of what dissidents refer to as the "neutral-persons" rule. That is, two non-KGB observers, such as a housekeeper and a neighbor, had to be present during the actual search. It was even possible for the Soviet citizen to request that the KGB make a formal "invitation" requesting permission for the search via an official form through the mail, but not every subject of every search had the gumption to ask the KGB agents standing on their doorsteps, however politely, to come back another day when conditions were more appropriate.

Eli Valk, an activist in the Riga Zionist movement who is now an Israeli citizen, recalls one morning in the early seventies, when he was working in a chemical factory and the head of personnel from the First Department (which was affiliated, of course, with the KGB) called and asked him to report to the personnel office at noon.

Valk was walking toward the office around noon when he noticed two KGB agents standing outside of it.

"Eli Valk?" they asked.

He nodded.

"We want to go to your house," they said.

"Oh, but I must go to Personnel," he told them. "I was summoned there."

"It's okay," the agents told him. "Don't worry about the job." Their tone was reassuring, calm, protective.

Valk had no choice but to say, "All right, let's go."

The agents led him to their car and drove to his house. He didn't have to give them directions, he remembers—they knew exactly where they were going.

Inside the house, before proceeding with the search, they informed him: "You are ordered to give out any materials of anti-Soviet contacts."

"I don't have any," he replied, relying on his own personal (narrow) definition of the meaning of the term "anti-Soviet."

Valk was worried, but not greatly. This was the time of the first Leningrad trial of some dissident Jews and non-Jews accused of attempting to steal a plane and fly to Sweden. The charges, of course, included an attempt to betray the homeland and involvement in anti-Soviet agitation and propaganda. And so, in anticipation of a visit from the KGB, he had taken pains to remove all the papers from the house that he believed might compromise him. Or at least he thought he had. Valk knew he was a disorganized person, and as he had cleared out his house several days prior to this visit by the KGB, there were a few papers that he knew were lying around somewhere, but he couldn't manage to find them.

The KGB agents had no such difficulty. Their expertise in conducting a thorough search clearly exceeded his own. They found the papers in the course of turning the house upside down in an efficient though neat and orderly fashion. Then the agents left his house and searched his mother's place. There they found further evidence of "anti-Soviet" materials: speeches of Zionist leaders, Hebrew records, and books about Israel.

Valk was now in trouble, but during the search he had no fear that physical harm would come to him. It was the "period of lawfulness," and they were, as he had expected, conducting a white-glove search.

The incident reminded him a bit of a search he had witnessed a few years earlier. He had been going to visit a friend who lived in a large communal apartment. Everything seemed normal as he approached the door; there were no extra cars nor were there unusual sounds coming from within the apartment. But when he knocked on the door, a KGB agent answered. "You get a strange feeling when a KGB agent looks at you," he claims. "It was like a sixth or seventh sense. Somehow you just know it's KGB."

Valk looked the agent in the eyes and then said, without missing a beat, "I guess I'll come back later."

Clever, but it did not work. Behind the back of the first agent, appearing out of a room off the hallway, was another KGB agent, whom Valk thought he recognized as one who had once questioned his mother as far back as 1959 or 1960, when she was involved in groups actively promoting the right of Jewish emigration. "Oh, Eli Valk, nice to meet you," this second agent greeted him. He then proceeded to try to impress Valk with his knowledge of Valk's personal affairs. "Why are you not in school?" he questioned. "Your laboratory should be open now." The agents then searched his clothing, asked him a few simple questions, found a brochure on an agricultural exhibition that he had recently attended which was tucked away in his jacket pocket, told him they didn't know that he liked chickens, then told him that he could go home.

The kid-gloves treatment, however, is only half the story. One U.S.S.R. dissident had his house searched by about twenty agents under the command of the procurator. The agents were armed with firearms, portable radios, mine detectors, flashlights, cameras, axes, crowbars, spades, and screwdrivers. The residents of the house were pushed into one room and put under guard. The search began at 8:45 in the morning and ended at 8:15 that night. During the search, the floors were broken up and split, doors were broken down, walls were smashed in, ceilings cracked open, mattresses and pillows torn apart. The agents dug ditches in the yard and under the house. Cesspools were examined with the aid of a magnetic lifting device and other electronic probes.

They discovered the two hiding places in the house. One hiding place was a huge hole in the ground lined with plywood and filled with suitcases containing literature defined as "anti-Soviet." Those who carried out the search left satisfied, and they did not leave their names, nor did they provide documentation of any sort. At one point, the bell rang at the front gate, a number of officials ran out, and when the person who had rung began to walk away, they opened fire. No one was injured, and they went back into the house to continue the search.

This is the type-two search, which dissidents say can be predicted: when more than two agents show up at the house, the search will be exhaustive, trying, and frightening.

But this type of search is not always masterfully, smoothly, and successfully completed, not even by the KGB. This same Soviet couple recall a rather amusing incident that took place when KGB agents searching their home were led by an "expert" apparently trying to conduct a very technical search. The expert went through their shed, running a mine detector along the floor, until something unexpected happened: the mine detector came to life. "A spade!" cried the expert, who then began digging feverishly, only to unearth, however, a gas valve that was lying around the shed earlier but had apparently been buried by the couple's little boy. "What's this?" the expert asked the man's wife, examining the round, red, metallic object with two pipe joints. She remained silent while the expert grabbed the screwdriver and took the valve out to the street, where, with great precaution, he chased some children away from a bench so that he could take the object apart. "So what *is* this?" he asked the woman again. "A gas valve," she finally told him. In a fit of anger, he threw the valve down to the ground. "Why didn't you tell me that before?" he asked angrily.

The Soviet couple, a writer and his wife still living in the Soviet Union, have survived four thorough KGB searches during their career as Soviet dissidents; on the basis of that experience, they offer the following words of wisdom:

"First, no matter how much you expect it, a search will always catch you unawares."

"Second, no matter how much you've cleaned up the house, something will always be found. . . . And, vice versa, no matter how clearly something is lying out in plain sight, it will be left behind without fail. . . .

"Never prepare for a search 'romantically' and don't demonstrate any confidence that you will succeed in pulling it off. Under no circumstances should you make a secret hiding place in bathrooms or door panels. The best thing to do, of course, would be not to keep anything 'impermissible' at home, and if something does turn up, keep it right on your desk. . . . In general, don't have any conversations with them. Don't get involved with them at all. Act as if you're not part of the situation. Don't try to sit with them, observing what they're doing and what they're taking. Don't argue; on the contrary, give them plenty of room to move. This disarms them more effectively. They have gotten used to, if not pleas, then at least requests. Don't relate to them as people, but as programmed robots, or mechanisms.

"The best way to act would be to get a bottle of wine out of the refrigerator and sit down to dinner. . . . As soon as you master this, you'll completely lose interest in every antagonism, and with a sense of immense relief, you'll start looking at them as any bloodhound, garbage picker, or grave robber.

"A search is an impersonal phenomenon. You could say it was irrational and, like any irrationality, illusory—unreal."

But the couple would admit that such advice is easier to give than to follow.

"A search is always stressful. No matter how you have waited for it and prepared for it, it always comes unexpectedly. It breaks in at once, like thunder. It strikes you in the head and knees. . . . Especially when you look at the investigators and know they will find something. And just sit and wait . . . there's another step . . . it's coming closer to that closet . . . closer still.

"But gradually, by the second or third search, this giddiness, which is always accompanied by a certain bravado and a little admiration for your own courage, is exchanged for apathy; for a feeling of inexpressible indifference and disgust at what is happening."

SEVEN

Doctors, Priests, Writers, Human-Rights Organizations, Publishers, Exiles, Defense Attorneys, Students—and Other Enemies of the Secret Police

1

Let us consider the matter of the traditional enemies of the secret police in some perspective.

Last year, the South African Government obtained the conviction of a university professor on charges of economic espionage. Let us leave aside the question of whether or not the evidence was sufficient —or whether the university professor could have been set up by the intelligence apparatus of South Africa. The fact of the matter is that the case did involve some sort of attempt, allegedly on the part of the professor, to obtain detailed blueprints of an obviously important national-security target: the planned Koeberg nuclear power plant, near Capetown. And the convicted professor was intimately involved with the banned African National Congress.

And what is the African National Congress?

It is many things to various people, but in the language of the secret police, the African National Congress is the *enemy*. The possibility that, by virtue of its own repressive actions and policies, the secret police system in effect helped make the African National

Congress what it is today—a disciplined, reasonably well funded, outlawed organization dedicated to the overthrow of the white minority regime—is an interesting question; but the fact of the matter is that the African National Congress is a real, and *not* an imagined, enemy of the secret police.

Consider:

On the night of June 2, 1980, three major South African oil complexes went up in flames. The two huge Sasol plants and the major oil refinery, which were designed to be part of the government's overall plan to make the nation as energy self-sufficient as possible, were also key elements of the government's grand ambition to make South Africa less vulnerable to international economic sanctions.

Precisely because South Africa has a most advanced economy (easily the most advanced in Africa), it also has the most vulnerable energy infrastructure. Like Yugoslavia, South Korea, Taiwan, and the Philippines, with their nuclear power plants, South Africa, with its oil refineries, polyvinyl-chloride plants, rubber factories, and synthetic-fuel complexes, provides enemies of the regime with huge, sitting targets. The Sasol attacks resulted in $1.9 million in physical damage and $5.5 million in fuel losses. But, far more important, the attacks demonstrated anew that, despite having one of the most highly developed internal-security systems in the world, the regime continues to suffer from a serious internal-security problem. The three Sasol plants (situated in Sasolburg, southwest of Johannesburg), were designed to provide almost half the nation's liquid-fuel needs. Unabashedly, the African National Congress—the avowed, outlawed enemy of the South African secret police—took full credit for the sabotage.

Now, the Sasol explosion was not a deep undercover secret police operation. Double agents working as "moles" or agent provocateurs within the African National Congress did not set off the explosions. To be sure, that kind of double-dealing is carried out occasionally by the secret police of many nations, but this was not that kind of phenomenon. In addition to the unacceptably high financial cost of the Sasol explosions, the intelligence network surely would not wish to pay the psychological toll of such self-inflicted wounds. This course would be enormously self-defeating. As the editors of the *World Business Weekly* concluded, "The psychological impact of such actions [as the Sasol explosion] . . . could steadily undermine the morale of the white minority population and lead to a white exodus similar to that of the latter days of the Rhodesian regime. Such a migration would greatly aggravate the already critical shortage of skilled labor, and this could ultimately prove more structurally damaging to the economy than would temporary disruptions resulting directly from terrorism."

No, the secret police have real enemies, not just imagined ones. And incidents such as the Sasol explosion do dramatize, in the minds of many citizens, the need for the state to take strong internal-security measures. Indeed, if enemies of the secret police capable of performing actions violent to the degree of the Sasol explosion did not exist in reality, then the secret police, like any other self-perpetuating government bureaucracy, might have to create them.

But even factoring in the usual degree of institutional cynicism, secret police do not need to fictionalize. The "enemies of the people" are out there. And the secret police do not have to ask themselves whether or not what they are doing is *morally* right. They can rely on the time-honored, indisputable assertion that what they do (at least broadly speaking) is authorized by the state. That is to say, they may be called secret police, political police, internal-security police—but whatever one wishes to call them, they do in fact represent law enforcement, and their work is therefore legitimized in the eyes of government authorities.

Of course, the laws that they enforce may be unjust. Or their values may more exactly reflect those of a ruling elite (as in South Africa, certainly) than the equitable interests of all elements of society. Or their enforcement of the law per se may be quite less than evenhanded in application.

These observations, which may surface in the minds of the more thoughtful and reflective members of the secret police, are, however, irrelevant to their immediate task. That task is twofold:

1. To protect the state from enemies within;
2. To protect the secret police and to survive as an institution of the state.

But these goals do not always coincide perfectly. The secret police agent—suspicious, even paranoid, powerful in his institution's franchise yet hardly always observing the letter of the law himself—tends to develop a siege mentality that overextends even the extreme "state of siege" mentality of the state itself. Like a besieged foot soldier in the front line of a raging battle, the secret police agent develops an *operational* perspective that crushes those terribly important moral considerations. Accordingly, to survey the behavior of dozens of powerful secret police organizations throughout the world is to understand that the enemies of the secret police in any one society tend to be astonishingly parallel to those in an entirely different society.

And so, if we may judge a person or an institution by its avowed or perceived enemies, then, aside from the predictable collection of professional terrorists and other crazies, secret police throughout the world have attracted a strikingly stylized and relatively uniform array of enemies, which suggests something about the generic nature of secret police worldwide.

All of which leads one to ask: does not the very existence of a powerful secret police force *create* enemies as well as remove them? In the case of South Africa, for example, is it prudent for the secret police to treat many "liberal" university professors (or doctors, or priests, or defense counsel) as actual enemies of the state until proved otherwise? And if the secret police must adopt such attitudes in order to survive, doesn't the process create more enemies than might otherwise exist for the regime? Rhetorical questions, or very real ones? An examination of the survival techniques of the secret police force against its perceived enemies should provide some measure of an answer.

2

There are several reasons why the neutralization of a relatively independent and critical press seems to be so central to the operations of a secret police force. A police state, it seems, is a state of mind as much as a state of terror. A critical press threatens the official version of reality by presenting explanations for events as well as alternative policy courses. A police state, it seems, is also an insecure state; a secure society surely should not require such repressive measures to achieve a modicum of stability.

In their extreme sensitivity to any and all criticism of the regime, the secret police reflect that insecurity. And a critical press does not operate within a societal vacuum: bad news tends to travel across international boundaries as the world press picks up the story. Yes, incredible as it may seem, the police state does worry about its image—and in order to survive, it must deal strictly with the press.

Necessarily, a secret police force will tend to monitor foreign press accounts almost as closely as its national press. For example, in Argentina, as in many other military dictatorships, the foreign press is reviewed daily by intelligence experts. They pore over every critical notice, afraid that certain foreign press critics are out to get them. Jacobo Timerman, the former Argentinian publisher who was held prisoner for thirty months by the Argentine Army before severe international pressure triggered his release, has put the matter this way:

"Obsessed with maintaining an image of strength and rectitude, totalitarian governments pay close attention to foreign coverage. . . . A totalitarian government, be it left-wing or right-wing, has a fixed image of itself, a rigid concept of its role in history, and an unshakable concept of its own justice. . . . Why has the military government's violence against journalists reached a magnitude that is, perhaps, even greater than that brought to bear against the nation's terrorists? . . . The only force that can topple this monolithic structure is the press. For only the press can dispute that monopoly on reality which is the sine qua non for the existence of any totalitarian government."

During the days immediately following the 1973 coup that toppled Allende, even the Chilean authorities were from time to time embarrassed by the foreign press coverage of some of the carryings-on of the regime's most zealous agents. When photographs of soldiers burning books in mass fires were smuggled out of the country and reprinted in newspapers around the world, the Interior Minister, at a press conference, admitted that he was thoroughly embarrassed. By the horrible excesses of his agents? No, by the fact that the book burnings had taken place in public, for they had given the junta, in his exact words, a "bad image."

Visits by foreign correspondents, when permitted, must therefore be carefully monitored. A New York *Times* correspondent petitioned Indonesian authorities for permission to visit East Timor. Permission was finally granted, but when he reached the embattled country, he found that all of his interviews were monitored by a third party. The uninvited guest was a major in Indonesian intelligence. "I must stay with you so you get the right information," apologized the major. "My boss told me to go with you wherever you go. If you interview the man in the street, you may get the wrong information."

It seems that foreign correspondents can get entirely out of hand. This is what happened at a press conference held for Russian dissidents in Moscow a few years ago. Western correspondents were handed a proclamation signed by seventy-two dissidents. At the press conference, spokesmen for the dissidents said they had originally visited the offices of the Moscow Procurator, the Presidium of the U.S.S.R. Supreme Soviet, the U.S.S.R. Council of Ministers, and the Central Committee of the Communist Party with their list of grievances, dealing with KGB representatives wherever they presented themselves. (They had been complaining about being denied housing and jobs.) But the dissidents claimed they had gotten the cold shoulder every step of the way and had called this press conference as a last resort.

After that press conference, the petitioners immediately noted a marked change in the KGB officers' attitudes. The dissidents were received very politely, and each individual, in separate interviews, was told that his or her problems would be solved if, among other things, he or she would not schedule any more press conferences. Believing what they were told, the dissidents waited for their cases to be resolved, and did not meet with Western correspondents or compose any more group petitions.*

After a while, however, the petitioners again presented themselves at the KGB office, complaining that they had followed orders but had not had their matters attended to. They were again politely answered by the KGB—but still no action was taken. There was nothing the dissidents could do but go about their daily business as usual. One day, while a good number of them were at the Moscow Central Telegraph Office picking up their mail, they were seized by KGB agents and were either (1) sent to psychiatric hospitals, (2) sentenced to fifteen-day prison terms, (3) expelled from Moscow under armed guard, or (4) made to sign a written promise to leave Moscow (and the international press corps) within three days.

* It is the relationship between the foreign and the national press that deeply worries the authorities. "Pressure from abroad is the only power the dictatorship respects," said a lawyer representing a Paraguayan journalist recently released from prison as a result of an international press campaign orchestrated by the AFL-CIO. But after returning from a well-publicized visit to the United States, the journalist—a columnist for the country's largest newspaper—was jailed anew. "The moment that one journalist gives the remotest reason for whatever functionary to jail him," said the columnist's lawyer, "it happens. As they apply the law as they like, it is not hard to do."

All internal-security organizations, even those operating within democratic societies, closely monitor their press corps. The Security Research Division of Japan's National Police Agency involves itself intimately in "press matters." As one expert put it, "the Security Research officer must be experienced in press work."

Mukhabarat, the intelligence service of Jordan, keeps a very close eye on the press, according to U. S. State Department officials. Says one expert, "It sees that the press doesn't get out of bounds. To criticize the king is unheard of. If you print an article that criticizes the ruling Hashemite family, the intelligence services will want to talk to you. They may even close down your paper for a few days or a couple of weeks." However, the treatment of journalists in Jordan is nothing compared to the approach used by the intelligence services of Syria, a country within which journalists are tortured and frequently disappear from sight entirely. Syrian security personnel operating in Beirut, Lebanon, are especially murderous. In 1980, Reuters' bureau chief was shot and killed; a Syrian journalist living in exile in Beirut was shot in the head; an Arab publisher disappeared near a Syrian-controlled checkpoint (and was found several days later—having been tortured, shot, and mutilated); and the life of a BBC correspondent was threatened, so that he withdrew from Beirut in haste.

Even strict obedience to press laws is no assurance of journalists' immunity from the secret police, who will strike when and if they please. Take the example of an otherwise obscure Catholic priest publishing a newsletter in the Philippines. "I have been keeping the law religiously from the beginning, especially the laws on printing," complained a visibly surprised Father Reuter after they boarded up his office, confiscated his files, and left the building under armed guard. Father Reuter, editor of the tiny weekly *Communicator,* in the Philippines, had had his operation closed down by the secret police after running an exclusive article on a fifty-one-year-old shoemaker who met death at the hands of Metrocom, the Metropolitan Command Intelligence Division of the Philippine Constabulary. "They did not specify the law . . . ," says Father Reuter, . . . "and they never defined subversion. In four years, the government has not defined subversion. They came into my office . . . and in ten minutes, with six colonels and majors . . . they sealed it for 11 days and searched it . . . and then they took all the issues of the *Communicator* and impounded it in one room. . . ." What the priest found difficult to comprehend was the extent to which a small-time operation like his could be perceived as a major threat. He pointed out that the *Communicator* was nothing more than a four-page weekly with a circulation of ten thousand. "And this was accused of being a threat to the security of the state," he said sarcastically.

But, unintentionally or not, the priest was underestimating not only the inherent threat of a free press but also the profound insecurities of states with very aggressive secret police forces working for them. In Haiti, authorities banned a play in 1979 that had the simple title *Presidential Candidates*. The action, of course, represented a cruel logic. In a society in which the people were presented with a president for life and were asked not to bother with the formality of periodic elections, the very existence of a literary work like *Presidential Candidates* was to suggest that maybe there should be some alternative to the one-and-only. Nothing, in fact, had so infuriated Haitian censors in a long time. That very year, the Duvalier government set up a committee for the purpose of reviewing all new films and plays. Then, as if pressing the point home, the regime instituted a new law affecting all journalists. A licensing bureaucracy was established. All this effort was undertaken as if to suggest to Haitian writers that they would have been better off if they hadn't given any of their plays such coy, subversive titles as *Presidential Candidates.*

In a country that relies on an aggressive secret police force to control the population, the press will sooner or later be subject to a full, systematic going-over by that security organization. "It is not just that, in response to the January 1974 riots in Jakarta, the Indonesian government closed down six of the most open-minded and responsible newspapers in the capital," explained Professor Benedict O'Gorman Anderson, associate director of the Cornell University Modern Indonesia Project, "or that many of the newspapers' reporters have been put on unpublicized blacklists so that they cannot find employment in their chosen profession. The fact is that except for a brief flowering in the early New Order period (1967–70), the number of newspapers published has steadily declined to the point that fewer are being published today than in the late Sukarno period, and their content is even more bland and uniform. In a number of provinces no newspapers are published at all."

The campaign waged against the press by the Indonesian secret police throughout the seventies proceeded on six individual fronts. In 1974, Kopkamtib's power to review a publisher's license, previously confined to certain geographical regions of the country, was extended to include all of Indonesia. All press licenses now go through annual Kopkamtib review, and they may be summarily suspended at any time on the authority of a regional Kopkamtib commander. Secondly, a reporter may at any time be summoned to appear before Kopkamtib agents and interrogated. The nature of the interrogation is left to Kopkamtib officials to decide upon, but beatings during such sessions are not uncommon. And the secret police may threaten the reporter's employer with loss of license as well as physical harm. Thirdly, all new publications must have the approval of the Minister of Information (since the 1974 crackdown, only one new license has been issued). Fourthly, all government advertising will be withdrawn, and pressure will be put on private companies to withdraw their advertising, when Kopkamtib officers believe a threat to national security—or government prestige—exists. Fifthly, and by contrast, *government* newspapers, which reflect the official line to the last comma, face no circulation worries: government departments are required to have their personnel subscribe to the official newspapers. Sixthly, Kopkamtib officers hold official briefings for reporters on most matters of national importance (such as the invasion of East Timor, the status of political prisoners, and elections), at which attendance for a reporter is deemed advisable. While these briefings have no formal legal force, in the pervasive climate of intimidation in Indonesia, they of course have the intended effect of ensuring that the Kopkamtib line is clearly conveyed to the public.

Pressures on advertisers serve to curtail the press in South Korea, as well. For many years, the customary editorial policy of *Dong-A Ilbo,* the oldest daily newspaper in South Korea, was to question the domestic policies of the Park Chung Hee government. But, one day, the newspaper clearly went too far; it criticized the secret police. The *Dong-A Ilbo* editors printed some exposés about torture and brutality used by agents against some former opposition national assemblymen. The KCIA, absolutely furious, simply informed the government that it could not possibly operate in such an openly critical intellectual climate. Before long, the government pressured advertisers to pull their accounts out of the paper. And the pressure was not just a one-shot deal. It was unceasing, and as the financial condition of the paper crumbled, the board of directors dismissed and replaced the young journalists who had reported the torture, and subsequent editions of the newspaper were careful not to criticize either the secret police or the regime.

South Korean intelligence tactics used to fight the press can be even more direct than this. In the summer of 1980, after martial law was declared, the "purification squad" of the Standing Committee of National Security Measures, acting under the authority of the Defense Security Command, ordered the country's press organizations to crack down on journalists who offended the regime. The press group was *ordered* to sack all journalists regarded as critics of the government. At the same time, 172 weekly and monthly publications were banned. "We feel like people waiting for sentence at the court," said one political reporter. And before too long, several hundred reporters on the staffs of Seoul's four national dailies were forced to submit resignations.

But direct contact between censors and editors in South Korea has not often been necessary, because there was an implicit understanding on issues such as how far the press could go in reporting American statements and campaign speeches by President Carter. Indeed, army censors, with active cooperation from editors, consistently distorted the views of President Carter and State Department spokesmen on South Korea as they appeared in the press, eliminating virtually all American criticism.

Even in societies that do not have a high literacy level, it is usually only a matter of time until the secret police act against the print media. Take the case of Brazil, which, much to the chagrin of DOPS (one branch of the secret police), lifted direct censorship over newspapers and magazines dealing in public affairs in 1978 (although controls were maintained on other media). Observers of this governmental move pointed out, however, that since the level of literacy in Brazil probably does not exceed 30 percent, and the daily circulation of newspapers throughout Brazil is little more than four million, the millennium of democracy was not exactly at hand. Still, some people obviously didn't like the way things were moving, in a more liberal direction. Before long, right-wing terrorist groups, quite possibly drawn from the armed forces and the police, unleashed a gruesome and violent firebombing counterintelligence attack at newsstands selling the "liberal" literature and newspapers freed for publication by the removal of censorship. "The despair of the fascists in view of the new reality of Brazilian politics is now bordering on psychosis and paranoia," an opposition member of Congress told correspondent ·Warren Hoge, of the New York *Times*. Probably, but the campaign was nonetheless effective. In order to quiet the offended secret police and other right-wing security organizations, legislation was devised that would permit "exercise of the profession in complete freedom, but with responsibility," to use the words of Brazilian President João Baptista Figueiredo. (And this law was to be added to an existing law, which denied the defense of factual accuracy to any reporter or writer who criticized key government officials.)

Control of the press by the secret police all over the world varies in degrees of subtlety. In one communist country, authorities put twelve hundred journalists out of business by the simple expedient of expelling them from the Union of Journalists. It was as simple as that. The year was 1972, and the country was Czechoslovakia. To wrap the matter up neatly, the next year authorities sent all the libraries in the Czechoslovak Socialist Republic a directive ordering them to remove from their shelves the books of some three hundred fifty authors. Again, it was as blunt and simple as that. But, just a few years earlier, the Czech regime had been content to confine itself to a much subtler form of harassment. For example, the editor of a weekly magazine had his publication banned in 1969. Although he was fired from all the jobs he took in order to sustain himself, he continued to publish his tiny weekly. Eventually, he was forced to accept work as a window cleaner.

Once, he was summoned to the local security-police (StB) headquarters, where he was told: "It's a pity that you, a writer, are doing the work of cleaning windows. . . . What if you changed your job . . . ?"

"You don't let me change jobs," he told the officers exasperatedly. (Czech security authorities maintain a list of "troublemakers," which they refer to regularly so as to prevent dissidents from landing worthwhile jobs or gaining promotions.) "What do you want from me?" the man finally asked the authorities.

They told him: "We'll supply you with books written by Czechoslovakians, and also with the books of Czechoslovakian émigrés." They asked him to write reviews of those books favorable to the government's point of view. He refused.

As of this writing, he is still washing windows for a living.

3

What the secret police in many countries do to writers, publishers, and publications may seem incredibly cruel and unnecessarily severe. But, from the standpoint of the regimes, these measures are not irrational acts. The goal of a regime using these stringent measures is control. Accordingly, the regime must monopolize all public voices. The state is not strong enough to listen to any voice other than its own.

Even in Yugoslavia, when, during Tito's era, the secret police were probably less repressive than those operating elsewhere in Eastern Europe, critics—even of Moscow—had to be exceedingly careful. When a Zagreb University literature professor published extracts from his book describing a five-week visit to the U.S.S.R. in terms no more critical of the Russians than Tito himself might have used, the authorities cracked down by arresting the author and confiscating copies of the tiny literary magazine in which it appeared. The actions of the secret police seemed grossly disproportionate to the dimensions of the crime, but Tito didn't view things that way. "Some people think that just because an end was put to the unlawful acts of the Yugoslav security forces," Tito once said, "it means they can do as they please." Tito was referring to the June 1966 purge of the secret police. In that shakeup, thousands of UDBA agents were dismissed and UDBA boss Ranković, the longtime incumbent, was replaced. But what Tito was saying, years later, was that critics of the regime still could *not* do as they pleased—and along with many other writers who thought otherwise, off to jail went the literature professor from Zagreb University, Mihajlo Mihajlov.

Wasn't it odd for the Tito regime to react this way? Literary critic Malcolm Muggeridge offered this astute observation: "This might seem a bizarre offense in Yugoslavia, seeing that Marshal Tito himself has been particularly acerbic at times in his criticism of the Soviet regime and its leadership. It is one thing, however, for the head of an authoritarian state to voice such criticism, and quite another when it comes from an assistant professor of Russian literature at Zagreb University."

A relatively tolerant secret police organization can only afford to go so far. "By mobilizing public opinion," says Chinese playwright

Cao Yu, arrested and detained in China for twelve years because of his critical writings, "it [literature] will have more influence in the long run than just a law or proclamation. Literature is a weapon, though without bullets." The secret police would tend to agree. In Yugoslavia, a 1974 press law prohibits the publication of any press account that causes "the disturbance of public order." In Haiti, journalists who "insult" President Jean Claude Duvalier or his mother—not to mention various key Haitian authorities—face a three-year jail term.

And so, if writers do not know their place in society, they will be put in their place. However, obsequiousness in the service of the secret police is a guarantee of uninterrupted publication. Writers who are critical of the secret police are regarded not as critics but as political enemies. "They [critics] want to weaken the authority of the government in the eye of the people and also influence public opinion outside the country," complained a high official of the Indonesian Internal Security Network after Kopkamtib had banned *Newsweek* magazine in 1976. Perhaps even more to the point, the official was infuriated with *Newsweek* because it "insulted national leadership." The arrest of a journalist and the banning of an Indonesian newspaper sometime later prompted him to expand on his theory of the relations between the press and the police. "We have a heterogeneous society and we cannot allow periodicals that incite the public to continue to appear," he said. After the famous Indonesian poet Willbrodus S. Rendra's fiction and poetry were banned, he found himself arrested by Kopkamtib agents. "Such stuff can lead to unrest and social conflicts," explained a lieutenant colonel in the Indonesian secret police system. "It gives people the wrong picture of development. One must not try to set art up as a force in opposition to the government."

It is probably impossible to overestimate the degree of concern with which many secret police organizations regard the press. "During my time in detention," Steve Biko told the white South African author Donald Woods, now living in exile in London, "they asked me more about you than they asked about me." As Colonel Goosen, of the security police, put it, "It has developed so far that [because of press coverage of security-police activity] South Africans are getting guilt feelings that we might have acted incorrectly."

Or as Prime Minister Indira Gandhi put it when calling for stringent press restraint in 1980, "Is the freedom of the press greater than the interests of the country?"

4

"All I am trying to point out," argues Jacobo Timerman, the former Argentinian publisher, "is the inordinate importance that a totalitarian government gives to its image. . . . In prison, I realized that the press can do more in the struggle for human rights than the pope, the United Nations and Amnesty International. . . . And when I was in prison, I could often ascertain that a few lines in the New York *Times,* an article in *Le Figaro,* or a statement in *Il Corriere della Sera* had immediate repercussions on our living conditions and treatment as prisoners."

Why do the secret police fear those international human-rights commissions? It is the coverage that they receive in the world press —in newspapers, magazines, and books. Without that, one must doubt how much of an impact the findings of the International Red Cross, Amnesty International, or the International Commission of Jurists would have on international public opinion. Why bother with them at all?

One reason: the secret police are concerned with their image. A second reason: some of those organizations (e.g., the Red Cross) are not that difficult to appease.

Let us consider the case of the International Red Cross first.

"I should like to describe for you," a political prisoner in Indonesia wrote to the International Red Cross in a letter that was smuggled out of the country, "the busy activities in preparation for your visits. . . . The following preparations were made. . . .

"1. Pillows, camp beds, plates and mugs have been given to the prisoners, who previously did not have these things.

"2. The chief of the Military Police carried out an inspection.

"3. The tapols [political prisoners] were brought together and told not to say anything that could prove harmful to them.

"4. A loudspeaker relaying music and other things was installed.

"5. The whole place was cleaned up."

Another ex-prisoner, also a fugitive from Indonesia, testified before a U.S. congressional committee in remarkably similar style:

"I submit that when Red Cross teams or other missions enter the prisons to investigate the conditions, strenuous efforts are made to give them a completely false picture. Whenever we received a small portion of egg or meat with our meal, we always knew that someone was coming to investigate the situation. . . ."

Or take this testimony about another human-rights commission given in a U.S. federal court by a former Haitian Tonton Macoutes officer:

Q: "Are you aware of whether or not in approximately 1978 a Human Rights Commission came to Haiti?"

A: "Yes."

Q: "How did you know that?"

A: "Well, because the President issued the order that the Macoutes should not wear their uniforms."

Or, take a look at testimony given before the same U.S. court by a formerly imprisoned Haitian army officer:

Q: "While you were in prison, were you aware of the Human Rights Commission that was in Haiti?"

A: "Yes."

Q: "At the time they visited the prison, were you given any instruction as to what you should say to them?"

A: "Yes. The Commander of the prison came and gave us instructions as to how to talk to them, after which they said they would release us."

Q: "Were any preparations made within the prison itself, in anticipation of the Human Rights Commission coming to the prison?"

A: "Yes. The day before the Commission came, they set up beds, dinner tables; they gave us new clothes and tennis shoes."

Q: "Did the Commission ask you anything about the conditions in prison?"

A: "The Commission didn't question us because they saw that everything was new and everything looked good, *although even the paint wasn't dry yet.*" (our italics)

Visits by international human rights organizations are manageable —from the point of view of the secret police—either by stealth or by co-optation. After all, it is not that difficult for national governments to create conditions that make an independent, outside evaluation exceedingly difficult. Although they have a generally reputable image, representatives of the International Red Cross frequently conduct their investigations into the situation of political prisoners in any given country under conditions so restrictive as to neutralize their effectiveness. It took the International Red Cross until 1979, for instance, to obtain from Israel agreement regarding certain aspects of their visitation rights to Arab prisoners. After considerable negotiation, the agreement shortened the waiting period that Red Cross representatives were forced to observe before being allowed to visit Arab security detainees under interrogation. These visits now occur without witnesses, with no Israelis present. "I wish," said the head of the International Committee of the Red Cross mission in Israel, "we had similar arrangements with other countries, and not only in the Third World."

But any praise for the agreement must be measured, indeed. The waiting period before being entitled to visit Arab detainees undergoing interrogation had been cut down from fourteen days after Red Cross notification of the government to twelve days. And if this compromise seems minimal, consider, too, the loopholes in the agreement reached between Israeli authorities and the Red Cross. The Red Cross can demand to see a prisoner only when it is provided with an official list of prisoners; information provided, let's say from exile sources, does not count. Furthermore, the Israelis can at any time and without offering any explanation deny the Red Cross access on "security grounds." In addition, since the International Committee of the Red Cross is not able to visit prisoners much before the fourteenth day of arrest, and since the alleged torture invariably occurs (on the West Bank or in the Occupied Territories) only during the first few days of detention, the ICRC visits usually are made too late to provide convincing medical evidence to support or contradict the allegations. And finally, any ICRC complaints that are transmitted to authorities are not open to public scrutiny.

The Red Cross is under all these handicaps because it chooses to work *with* national governments, in a quieter manner than some other international relief or human-rights organizations have. The obvious advantage to this cooperative posture is that it results in the attainment of access that is denied other organizations. The disadvantage to this posture is that it results in cooperation with national governments almost wholly on those governments' own terms. Usually those terms are sufficiently restrictive as to raise questions regarding the thoroughness and reliability of the "cooperating" commission's judgments. The chief of the Philippines Constabulary once even went so far as to *request* an inspection by the Red Cross of the detention center at Camp Crame, the Constabulary headquarters. "We have nothing to hide," he said. Maybe, but he refused to permit Amnesty International the same visiting privileges that year as were granted the International Red Cross.

According to the paranoid and Manichean mentality of the secret police, the operative rule is: those who are not for us must be against us. An organization such as Amnesty International, which in essence is not a partisan force, is therefore perceived as an enemy of all secret police systems. "It appears that Amnesty International was all too willing," fumed the solicitor general of the Philippines in 1975, "to accept at face value the claims of the hard-core elements of the local Communist movement, failing to consider that these elements had every reason to exaggerate any form of maltreatment or to fabricate the same in furtherance of their cause. Top-ranking leaders of the local Communist movement . . . confirmed upon their capture earlier this year that the Communist Party of the Philippines hierarchy has carried out as one of its priority programs the utilization of detained members in an intensified agitation propaganda against the government. A linkage between the outside forces and detained members in carrying out such agitation propaganda has been verified." A high official in the Indonesian security forces offered a remarkably similar analysis in 1976: "There are conditions that must be met by Amnesty International in order to be allowed to visit places of detention in Indonesia; namely, it must refrain from adopting a hostile attitude. . . . Amnesty International has been infiltrated by and is being utilized by communist elements. These elements must be cleansed. . . ." And communist countries won't even let Amnesty International close to their prison or psychiatric-ward gates.

The International Commission of Jurists, based in Geneva, is another troublemaker. By 1974, the Commission had gotten around to annoying Uganda's President, Idi Amin, whose State Research Bureau was quickly making its mark as a notoriously brutal secret police organization even by the negative standards of secret police behavior.

In response to severe pressure from the highly respected International Commission of Jurists, Amin set up his own "Commission of Inquiry into Disappearances" in Uganda. He was, he said, both puzzled and furious at the Commission's "outrageous" report, which said that within three years after Amin took power, in 1971, the number of people arbitrarily executed in Uganda "numbered certainly in the thousands and very possibly in the tens of thousands."

So Amin established a presidential commission to delve into the allegations at once. One of those appointed to the group was Mr. Farouk Minawa, who was director of the State Research Bureau!

And Amin was careful to restrict the commission to certain operational rules. While Radio Uganda was instructed to broadcast a call for cooperation with the investigating body, only a few wives of men who had "disappeared" came forward—and those who did were watched so closely and openly by agents of the State Research Bureau that the message was obvious. And when President Amin ordered the commission not to accept testimony offered by witnesses who would not appear before the investigating body in person, all possibilities for considering that person's testimony were closed.

The farce went on in yet other ways. In 1975, the President, calling the commission members to his private command post, asked for a progress report. He was worried despite all the built-in safeguards to the commission's work, and he wanted them to know, he said, that if they felt they had been working too hard, they should certainly feel free to quit. The members of the commission assured Amin that they felt fine. In fact, said the head of the commission (a chief justice personally selected by Amin), the President should feel fine too, because the investigation had not so far uncovered any evidence that linked *him* personally to the disappearances. Quite satisfied, President Amin told them to proceed immediately with their patriotic work. He pointed out that he was under severe pressure because of politically inspired, even racist accusations made by various international bodies, including the United Nations.

The commission dutifully rushed through its work. After the commission issued its report, President Amin declared that if they had come up with evidence connecting him to any of the disappearances, he would have resigned.

The International Commission of Jurists, however, had the last word. "Sources who supplied details to this Commission of Inquiry said there was plenty of evidence to link President Amin directly to many of the killings," it said in a report, "but those with the evidence, including State Research officers and the President's own personal bodyguards, feared for their jobs and their lives if they testified."

5

Lawyers are another source of annoyance to well-established secret police organizations. If their endeavors are not impeded, they can become considerable nuisances. For the secret police, the neutralization of lawyers is not a question of the denial of justice; it is a question of the propagation of security-police effectiveness. From their perspective, legal procedures impede the march toward the achievement of substantive security goals, including, most of all, the containment or functional elimination of the opposition. To this end, the secret police seek the undivided cooperation of the sovereign authorities. It is probably not an overstatement to suggest that an independent judiciary and an independent bar are as threatening to a secret police organization as bomb-throwing revolutionaries, rightwing terrorists, or even a critical press.

In any country dominated by an aggressive secret police force, the role of the defense attorney must be minimized, if not eliminated. In Tunisia in 1978, the government filed a huge case against thirty trade union leaders accused of committing crimes against the government. The defense lawyers were presented with the government's dossier. The file was five thousand pages long. Accordingly, attorneys for the defendants petitioned the court for a two-month adjournment. In its wisdom, the court granted two weeks. The attorneys left the courtroom with two weeks in which to read a dossier of five thousand pages. And then, in another case involving some trade unionists, one defense attorney who waded into a dossier noticed that, presumably by mistake, the clerk of the court had already entered the verdict—and the sentence. And what was written there was exactly what the union leaders wound up getting.

In Egypt, defense attorneys faced similarly trying situations. In one heavy-handed proceeding against almost two hundred alleged political offenders conducted at the famous State Security Court in 1978, defense lawyers found themselves saddled with a colossal government dossier. The charges had been accumulated by the internal-security network. The written allegations concerning the case ran to eleven thousand pages, but, to make matters even more inconvenient, the government insisted that the defense attorneys be restricted to making only three copies—despite the fact that there were almost two hundred defendants. The lawyers protested vehemently to the security court, but the government won the argument. Not only that, but the tribunal censured the lawyers for complaining, levied a stiff fine, and recommended disciplinary action to the Egyptian Bar Association.

A similar attitude of indifference or hostility was common among members of the judiciary in Morocco. In a 1977 trial of the Frontistes,† in Casablanca, the president of the court observed some legal amenities, but not a great many. For instance, he had particular problems with one motion to permit defendants to speak in their own defense. The motion was denied. He ruled that since political statements were banned in Morocco, any statement by defendants would have to be regarded as a political speech.

And in many countries, it is clearly impermissible for a *lawyer* to make a political statement himself, even in the course of defending a client. Dr. Josef Danicz, present during the interrogation of his client by Czechoslovakian security authorities, once brought up the famous Ivan Medić case. He was referring to a 1978 incident when the writer Medić was attacked by unknown persons while leaving a police station.‡ He was deposited in a field after being severely beaten and was discovered the next day by passers-by. For this blasphemous oral recollection, lawyer Danicz was reported to the district prosecutor the next day. Later, the Czechoslovakian security police arrested the lawyer for slandering the state.

South Korean authorities have also manifested hostile attitudes toward defense attorneys. When a South Korean defense attorney involved in an espionage prosecution would apply for permission to call a witness, the court would invariably grant the permission. There would be only one hitch. The KCIA would arrest the witness as a security risk, thereby removing the witness for the defense and giving clear warning notice to other potential defense witnesses. Worse yet, members of the South Korean bar were subject to detention and interrogation by the KCIA and the civilian police— probably not for the primary purpose of eliciting information but mainly as a method of intimidation. And defense attorneys knew that if they pushed the defense of their clients too far, their own

---

† The Frontistes are new-style Mediterranean Marxist-Leninists aiming to create a socialist republic in Morocco. (The original Communist Party in Morocco was banned in 1960, and its leaders have since formed the more moderate Parti du Progrès et du Socialisme.)

‡ Czechoslovakian dissidents believe that StB agents were Danicz's attackers.

families were likely to suffer. A team of lawyers defending opposition leader Kim Dae Jung after his arrest in 1980 were reportedly arrested themselves and were interrogated as part of what Amnesty International described as "an effort to interfere with Mr. Kim's defense. . . ."

The KCIA has always made a big point of keeping tabs on defense attorneys—their mistakes, their extramarital affairs, their vulnerabilities, their clients. It was not unheard of during the seventies for KCIA agents to arrest a defense attorney in the middle of a trial. And when they did this, no judge ever tried to stop them.

In Johannesburg, most lawyers are thoroughly intimidated by the secret police even before a trial starts; a black defendant is lucky even to find a lawyer in time for trial. In Chile, defense attorneys had to cope with the misery of a close working relationship between the College of Lawyers and other bar associations, and DINA. If lawyers were not directly accosted by DINA agents, "peer groups" —acting on DINA's instructions—would initiate disciplinary proceedings as warnings.

Now consider the restrictions often placed on the Moscow lawyer:

• In cases of "especially dangerous crimes against the state," the lawyer is not permitted to take case materials away for study.

• In most political cases, a petition for additional witnesses—or additional investigation—will be denied.

• It is usually during the preliminary proceedings that the state makes the decision as to whether or not the defendant will serve prison time, but the accused person in custody is permitted to consult a lawyer only at the termination of the preliminary proceedings.

• In case of "treason" or "anti-Soviet agitation and propaganda," a lawyer may serve as defense counsel only if his name is on the unofficial KGB list of cleared attorneys; attorneys tend not to remain on that list if they earn a reputation as aggressive defense counsel.

• There are also administrative procedures for arrest and sentencing with trial. Under the "administrative detention" rule, no defense counsel may be present at the hearing. The rule may be invoked for such an offense as "willfully disobeying a police officer."

In the egregious secret police systems that we have studied, contempt of the court system—either by those charged with political crimes or those who bring forward the charges—is an integral part of the psychological atmosphere of the system. And the system is clearly not designed to expedite justice. In Iran under the Shah, the examining magistrate in all cases was in fact a SAVAK employee. Accordingly, SAVAK interrogators rarely had to worry about procedural problems: i.e., inadmissible evidence. Indeed, information elicited during the "questioning" would be placed in a file by interrogators and dispatched to the Joint Committee (See Chapter One, Section 5). It was the Committee that would decide how to proceed with the case. When the decision would be reached, the Joint Committee would forward the file to an examining magistrate (i.e., a SAVAK agent) or a military tribunal. In theory, the magistrate or tribunal would have the option of deciding whether further evidence was required of SAVAK before determining the sentence. But, in practice, further witnesses were rarely required. In fact, in many cases no witnesses were required at all. The examining magistrate would act on the basis of the file provided by SAVAK. The proceedings would be brief; no witnesses would be called. Defense counsel, even when they were present, would have little to do.

In effect, this process was truly significant only at the arrest stage; subsequent to the arrest, the bureaucracy made few actual decisions. The important ones had already been made—by the arresting SAVAK agents or the Joint Committee.

In Indonesia, the secret police carefully control the composition of the public galleries. In the event of an important political trial, visitors' tickets are sometimes issued in bulk to intelligence agents and government officials. "This courtroom is as oppressive as a weapons arsenal being guarded in a time of war," screamed one Indonesian student leader on trial. "Where is the authority of this court?"

In Durban, South Africa, in 1977, twenty students from the University of Zululand were charged under the sabotage act. They were advised that if evidence was given that was satisfactory in the eyes of the prosecution, they might be freed; conversely, detainees who refused to testify would be treated as recalcitrant witnesses, subject to successive three-year terms of imprisonment for contempt of court. One defendant, understandably, had a nervous breakdown in jail while pondering his choices. Another "confessed," then recanted. "My evidence-in-chief," the student had the nerve to tell the judge in open court, "was nothing but a song; thoroughly rehearsed and easily sung."

The procedures of the South African courts in determining causes of death are suspiciously circumscribed. The entire inquest process is tightly restricted to a narrow determination of the primary cause of death. If a detainee is beaten repeatedly by security police but dies of a heart attack, the court accepts a judgment of death by heart attack unless there is evidence as to exactly how the injuries had been inflicted. And it is almost impossible for such evidence to be brought forward. Most expert postmortems are conducted by the authorities before the next of kin have the opportunity to enlist the services of a private pathologist.

Still, there are more rough edges to these open-yet-closed case processes than probably even the South African authorities desire. "The police are just too sloppy in their stories," said a researcher familiar with hundreds of cases on file at the South African Institute for Race Relations in Washington. "Their testimony is filled with contradictory evidence. One policeman will say the hanged man's toes were touching the ground, another that he was swinging high in the air. One will say he hung himself with his shirt, another that he was wearing his shirt."

Whatever the degree of police competence or incompetence in dealing with political detainees, the courts will generally steer clear of getting involved in the process. In the trial of a Palestinian whose lawyer claimed to have observed in Ramallah prison, on the West Bank, one defendant's symptoms of a severe beating, the court was petitioned by counsel to visit the cells. But the Israeli court refused the motion—insisting that counsel had raised an issue not within its competence.

The secret police can also be aided immensely in the judicial process by a careful selection of the presiding magistrates. In Paraguay, matters are so arranged that the majority of the members of the Supreme Court belong to the ruling Colorado Party. They are appointed by the President.

Accordingly, habeas corpus petitions for political detainees are routinely refused. In one notable and hilarious case, a judge dissented when the court denied a petition for the release of Liberal Radical leader Efrén González on grounds that were so obviously incorrect that the judge was simply overwhelmed with embarrassment And so he registered a strong dissent—the first in the memories of court observers. But it may also prove to be the last such dissent. The

Stroessner regime tolerates no dissent, not even from a judge: this judge was severely censured by the ruling Colorado Party and was bounced off the court.

In Sri Lanka, the authorities of the regime and the secret police have also shown contempt for the high court. Twice during a period of five years, an angry government simply abolished the Supreme Court—and constituted an entirely new high court. It also established a Criminal Justice Commission to try politicians and civil rights workers outside the established courts, under rules and procedures "best adapted to elicit the truth concerning the matters that are being investigated," in the government's own words. In South African-controlled Namibia, where all judges and magistrates (and indeed most attorneys and advocates) are selected from the territory's white settler community, no court could invalidate a detention order from the security police, much less order the release of a political detainee after he had been arrested.

In Zaire, the state set up a two-track court system. A special Court of State Security was established in 1972. While the findings of the courts of the first instance can be challenged in both ordinary and political cases by the appeal courts and the Supreme Court, there is no right of appeal from the State Security Court, which deals with cases where the security of the state has been endangered.

It is, then, the enormous power of the agent at work, combined with the relative impotence of the judiciary, that clearly defines the secret police experience in most countries. In South Africa, as in Iran under the Shah, there is scarcely a distinction of significance between the police and the courts. The South African Terrorism Act of 1967 blurs any meaningful distinctions. "No court of law," instructs this legislation, "shall pronounce upon the validity" of any detention order issued under Section 6 of the Act "or order the release of any detainee." General Van den Bergh, the head of BOSS at the time that this Act was established, explained the distinction between the courts and the police as he saw it: "It is not necessary for a *public inquiry* [italics ours] to be held into others [deemed] to be furthering any of the aims of Communism."

In Chile, the head of CNI once explained quite openly and cheerfully that the courts have at most a very restricted jurisdiction over DINA's successor; questions are to be submitted to CNI agents by the courts, but agents are not required to make court appearances.

But that concession is practically generous, compared to the careless contempt of court exhibited by DINA in years before. In one typical incident, a court became so irritated by DINA's failure to respond to its orders that it dispatched a judge to the headquarters of DINA to obtain further information about the case. The judge, however, was refused entry onto the premises. On those rare occasions when a Chilean court had the courage to order the release of a person arrested by the secret police, DINA would simply ignore the order. On one memorable occasion, a court tried to summon DINA agents before it who had carried out a particular arrest. The agents refused to appear, and the Ministry of the Interior backed them up. A Ministry official bluntly informed the magistrate: "The Directorate of National Intelligence is not subordinate to this Ministry, and since the secret services work under conditions of absolute secrecy, it is impossible for them to appear before this Court."

In case the courts did not get the message, the attitude of General Manuel Contreras Sepúlveda, then the director of DINA, must have been instructive. To quote a United Nations report on his position: "For his part, the Director of DINA . . . supported this refusal to appear in a court of justice, not on the basis of any legal provision because, as he has said, there is none, but by stating that this was 'his position'; in addition, he claimed to have received 'express' orders in the matter. For example, in response to the summons by the Court of Appeals which stated that 'whatever the authority to which the Director is subject, he is under legal obligation to provide this Court with information on the above-mentioned circumstances,' he said, 'I must once again reiterate my position that I have to comply strictly with the orders of the President of the Republic and inform you that information of any kind concerning detained persons should be supplied to the courts of justice by the Minister of the Interior, or by the National Service of Detained Persons." That is to say: DINA agents themselves could not be summoned.

President Pinochet, in all candor, actually argues simply that a secret police organization cannot be bound by any normal rules or procedural limitations. Speaking in terms that many other sovereigns might have used, he said: "We have enacted a military code of justice. The ones who are innocent are out of the procedures; but the ones who are guilty, it's being applied what the code says. And we don't need control from anybody on that."

Or, to quote Fidel Castro (the leader of Cuba was speaking in a moment of outrage, for a court had found some political defendants innocent of all charges; Castro instantly ordered a new trial— his justification?) "Revolutionary justice is not based on legal precepts but on moral conviction. . . ."

6

When physicians and scientists do not go along with a regime, a secret police force will often swing into action. The secret police feel threatened by the elite. In addition to its professional and personal sense of superiority to the regime and its minions in the secret service, an educated elite threatens the political system perpetuated in part by the secret police to the extent that they may ideologically oppose the process and the regime even if their posture is a passive one, not to mention actively involve themselves on the side of those whom the regime seeks to neutralize or even eliminate.

Left or right, secret police systems have their own ideas about the proper role of intellectuals and health and science professionals. At a press conference announcing both the arrest of seventeen professors and the "fugitive status" of thirty faculty members of the University of the South, in Argentina, the deputy commander of the Fifth Army Corps proclaimed that "until we can cleanse the teaching area, and professors are all of Christian thought and ideology, we will not achieve the triumph we seek in our struggle against the revolutionary left."

Similar thoughts seem to have inspired Fidel Castro's attitude toward Dr. Marta Frayde. An early enthusiast for Castro, Dr. Frayde was appointed director of the National Hospital, in Havana, shortly after the revolution, and in 1959 Castro awarded her the Order of Lenin. But, eight years later, when she tried to leave Cuba in disillusionment, the G-2 confiscated her passport. After being subjected to years of harassment by G-2, Dr. Frayde was finally arrested and sentenced to twenty-nine years in prison. Leading European and American writers, including Jean-Paul Sartre, Norman Mailer, and Simone de Beauvoir, denounced her trial and sentence as a "sinister judicial farce." Their denunciation had no effect on Castro.*

The justification for such actions is the necessity to curb anti-regime activities. When scores of physicians were rounded up by

---

* But, in December of 1978, Castro set in motion a program to release large numbers of political prisoners. Dr. Frayde was among them.

Chilean police just after the 1973 coup, the regime's justification was that leftist physicians had set up an enormous underground network of clandestine hospitals to treat the poor. Whether or not the regime considered their fieldwork on behalf of residents of Santiago's vast southern working-class district (Barros Lucos), as well as in the western and northern slums of Santiago, as inherently "Marxist" activity is exactly the sort of question raised by any regime's crackdown of this sort. For instance, in Colombia, a young medical doctor working among the peasantry in the regions of Neira and Quinchía was arrested by security officials. But he stoutly denied that he was a member of *any* political organization: "Since as a doctor I have been in close contact with the sufferings of the people, I sympathize with social changes directed toward general welfare, justice, freedom and peace," he said. But, to the regime, that stance was tantamount to communist activity.

The tendency of many states to label health-service activity political activity is widespread. A physician was arrested in 1979 in Colombia on the charge of "having created a medicines cooperative with persons considered to be members of subversive groups, and having provided medical attention to alleged members of guerrilla movements." Similarly, the president of the union of Jordanian doctors was ordered dismissed from his post as head of pediatrics at Ramallah Hospital. The charge was having contacted representatives of the UN's World Health Organization "without permission." The physician had told the World Health Organization that the severe shortage of medical personnel on the West Bank was a consequence of explicit Israeli policy, including the refusal to permit repatriation of many Palestinians who had gone abroad for specialized medical training and wished to return.

The treatment of physicians has been especially brutal in Argentina, where many physicians have simply disappeared. In one testimony to the problem, a woman talked about her treatment at the hands of security authorities: "My husband . . . and I are Argentinian doctors. Because of protests from the medical union to the government concerning the suspension of free medical treatment (in a country with no social security or unemployment benefits); for attending, as a doctor, relatives of detained and disappeared persons; for sending testimonies out of the country concerning the murder and maltreatment of political prisoners, my husband and I were kidnapped by the Army Intelligence Service, at our home in Buenos

Aires on 15 November 1976. My husband was subjected to brutal electrical torture for several days. We were then moved to a large building, where I was kept in one of the boxlike compartments in the floor with a hood over my head, bound hand and foot, hungry and thirsty, with deafening music playing constantly—despite which it was possible to hear the screams of pain of those being beaten. I was released after a month; we have had no news of my husband since then."

To be sure, Chile and Argentina are "special" (particularly egregious) cases. But it is perhaps not irrational to wonder whether, given rapidly changing political and economic circumstances in many countries, Chile and Argentina will prove role models for other regimes. Scientific elites in countries that are comparatively mild must understand that as the security police's definition of what constitutes threatening political activity widens, their personal security diminishes. "Argentina, Brazil, and Chile are of particular concern to scientists because of the large scientific communities in those countries," wrote Earl Callen, Bernard R. Cooper, and John Parmentola, authors of "Science and Human Rights," in a 1980 essay in *Technology Review*. "But perhaps we should use the past tense— in Chile and Argentina, scientific communities hardly exist any more." In Argentina, these scientists write, "intellectual subversion has been defined as a form of terrorism. Freud and Marx have been branded 'ideological criminals,' and psychiatrists, psychologists and mental health workers have been all but wiped out. . . . About 40 per cent of the Argentine Physical Society—some 120 physicists —have been either fired from their jobs or have fled the country."†

† Included on the authors' list of those who died or disappeared in Argentina in the late seventies were (1) a physicist at the National University of Córdoba, kidnapped with her three-year-old son and found dead; (2) a nuclear physicist at the National University of the South, found murdered in jail; (3) a professor of chemistry at the National University of Río Cuarto, Córdoba— arrested and tortured; officials said he committed suicide; (4) a physicist at the National University of Rosario, who disappeared with his wife in 1976 and neither have been heard from since; (5) a physicist at the Argentine Atomic Energy Commission in Buenos Aires and his wife, a computer programmer, detained by the Army in 1976, neither of whom have been heard from since; (6) a physicist at the Atomic Energy Commission in Buenos Aires, taken by police agents in his laboratory; (7) a physical chemist and physicist who headed the plastics-research laboratory of the National Institute of Industrial Technology, taken by police agents in 1978, not seen since; (8) an Argentine physicist formally associated with the Massachusetts

7

According to the point of view of the secret police, ideas are subversive not simply because they may lead to political action but, in the first instance, because they are *considered* political action. To the secret police, there is no such thing as an abstract idea. The familiar intellectual processes of theorizing and model building are interpreted by the secret police as modalities of planning.

Sugama, the chief of staff of Indonesia's Kopkamtib in 1977—who was also in charge of BAKIN, the state intelligence body‡—explained the approach quite nicely in response to a press query in the wake of the arrest of an enormous number of Indonesian students. "These kind of people . . . are not being put away for any political reason—for what they have been saying—but for what they have been planning, or what they are planning to do. And this is different. For that reason . . . the so-called for instance student body, student groups, have been put away for a certain period."

Cornell's Professor Anderson puts the Kopkamtib chief's analysis in a somewhat different perspective: "Freely elected student unions throughout the country were forcibly dissolved by Kopkamtib, and many of their leaders detained on charges of subversion. You may also remember that the students' opposition, which focused on corruption in the Presidential Palace, the rigged 1977 Parliamentary elections, and the unconstitutional means used to ensure Suharto's reelection as president, among other issues—was completely peaceful, limited to seminars, poster campaigns, distribution of leaflets, street parades, and the like." Only severe international criticism in the world press could account for the fact that the 1979 jail sentences pronounced by Kopkamtib were markedly less severe than

---

Institute of Technology, taken by police one night in 1976 and imprisoned without charges (while initially his detention was acknowledged by the Argentine embassy in Washington and the Argentine Atomic Energy Commission, the government later claimed that the original acknowledgement had been in error and that he had never been taken into custody: the physicist has not been heard from since).

‡ These are Sugama's words in describing BAKIN. It is believed that BAKIN is the military intelligence service, while Kopkamtib is civilian-oriented, chiefly.

those meted out in the wake of the 1974 student demonstrations: in 1979 they ranged from "only" eight months to two years in jail.

SAVAK worried about students as much as Kopkamtib or any number of other secret police organizations. It infiltrated student groups in Iran extensively. In its foreign operations, it not only spied on students so closely that at anti-Shah demonstrations, student protestors felt compelled to wear masks over their faces; SAVAK also created its own competing student groups. In Munich, Germany, SAVAK funded and staffed, with its own agents and student informers, the National Unity Group, and it created "cultural societies" in Berlin and Cologne. In England, SAVAK put together the World Confederation of Students, a pro-Shah group designed to counter the proliferation of anti-Shah student organizations in London. According to confidential SAVAK documents, the London office budget in the early seventies for these groups alone amounted to a minimum of ten thousand pounds sterling per year.

The policy of the Egyptian secret police with regard to students is simply more subtle. Working through the Ministry of Education, authorities adjust the length of term; determine when exams are held; hold special exams; and withhold scholarships. If the students are getting restless, for example, exams will be moved up. If a student is an agitator, a scholarship will be withdrawn.

In Taiwan, intellectual critics of the regime are invariably major targets of the Taiwan Garrison Command and the Bureau of Investigation. The regime, for one thing, seems to fear their articulateness as much as anything else. Despite the fact that the anticommunist consensus in that island country remains, on the whole, quite strong, critics appear to worry the authorities immensely, especially when they receive attention in the international press.

One former magazine editor and lecturer at a military academy was imprisoned in 1971 on charges of "subversion." Friends managed to smuggle his stirring court plea out of the country, and the plea subsequently appeared in newspapers abroad. In 1975, former U. S. Congressman Lester Wolff, who has a reputation as one who is concerned with issues involving international human rights, petitioned the Taipei government for the right to visit this prisoner in jail. But the Taiwanese authorities handled this one with impressive finesse. There was one practical complication to the journey, Taipei officials informed the congressman: the driving time from the Taipei airport to the prison that he was interested in was a full three hours, one way. But in fact the drive from Taipei to the prison, even during rush hour, takes at most fifty minutes. The congressman's office naturally took the government at its word, and, unable to make such a major commitment of time, the congressman canceled the trip.

Some years later, this Taiwanese intellectual was permitted to leave Taiwan. His prison sentence had been completed, and the authorities had no stomach for the lecture tour of Taiwan that he planned upon his release. (Nor did authorities have much enthusiasm for imprisoning him again—his case had already attracted too much attention.) So the dissident played his only card: "If you don't give me a passport," said the intellectual, "then I will give the lectures." The negotiations continued. Garrison Command officials took him out to dine at prominent restaurants about once a month, to keep him on a short leash. The dissident held his ground, and the Command finally agreed. This particular individual was obviously less trouble out of the country than in it.

But once abroad, an exiled intellectual or dissident is not, as it were, home free.

Nearly every one of the secret police forces we have studied maintains agents in its foreign embassies. While they may be called "attachés" or some such title, their real job is to keep track of the exiles.

The degree of control of exiles depends in part on the degree of paranoia and insecurity on the part of the controlling authorities. In April of 1980, Colonel Qaddafi, the ruler of Libya, commanded all Libyan exiles to return home instantly or face "liquidation." A few murders perpetrated by the Libyan secret police around the world demonstrated that this was no idle threat.

Qaddafi's approach may be more obvious than that of most other leaders—but it is not unique. As Raúl Manglapus, a former Philippine senator who once had the temerity to run against Marcos for President once put it, "We [exiles] assume we are being watched, that we are under surveillance from various sides. The head of Philippine security has come here several times." Exile in the United States is certainly no assurance of safety, he says. "There is a general threat of intimidation which extends to this country."

This intimidation extends to other exile groups, both within the United States and abroad. In November of 1979, agents from the U. S. Federal Bureau of Investigation called on Mihajlo Mihajlov, the dissident Yugoslavian author, at his home in Arlington, Virginia. The agents told him that they had reliable information that the Yugoslavian secret police were planning to kill him. The FBI agents gave him several phone numbers to call at any time, and one of them offered to supply him with a gun. Mihajlov politely refused the gun. "If the situation arose where the secret police were in a position to do something," he says now, "a gun certainly wouldn't make any difference. How could I expect to defend myself with a gun against the Yugoslavian secret police?"

Mihajlov may have had in mind the case of Mileta Perović, a dissident exile leader. At his 1978 trial in Belgrade, he claimed that he had been kidnapped by UDBA agents in Switzerland in 1977. What was remarkable about UDBA's action was that it took place after Perović had been in exile for fully twenty years. One is inclined, therefore, to speculate that the determination of secret police action in cases involving exiles is not the length of the period of exile but changes in political calculations in the home country; between 1975 and 1978, three other members of Perović's "counterrevolutionary" Cominform groups were also kidnapped by UDBA agents.

Duration of exile is no assurance of safety: the exile's case is always "on file" and can be reactivated at any time. The exiled Chilean Supreme Court judge whose story was recounted in Chapter One was well aware that he was still in the files of Chile's DINA a couple of years after his deportation in 1974. The justice was in exile, teaching law at the University of California at Los Angeles, when, one morning, he discovered that his office had been broken into. Nothing of resale value was taken, but some newspaper clippings that he had placed on top of his typewriter before leaving the previous evening were gone. Conspicuously, at eight o'clock on this morning, the lights were on, and the door was ajar. Whoever had broken in didn't mind if the break-in was apparent. This was typical DINA intimidation, Eugenio insists, to let you know that you were still being watched but not to harm you directly. The next day, he telephoned an FBI agent whom he had met in connection with the Letelier investigation (see below) and who had offered him help anytime he needed it. But the agent recommended that he check in with the Los Angeles office of the Bureau. Eugenio, perhaps not comprehending jurisdictional nuances within the FBI and wondering if he wasn't suddenly getting the cold shoulder, let the matter drop.

Certainly the United States, which harbors more political exiles than any country in the world, and which has no secret police system remotely comparable to those from which these exiles have fled, more often than not maintains a disinterested, hands-off approach. If the U. S. Federal Bureau of Investigation has demonstrated some interest in the problems of political exiles like Mihajlo Mihajlov, it did a poorer job in protecting Orlando Letelier, the Chilean exile who was murdered by DINA agents in Washington in 1976. Letelier had been Defense Minister and ambassador to the United States under Salvador Allende. He was driving a car near Sheridan Circle one morning when a bomb under the car, triggered by remote control, went off. Interestingly, an FBI agent arriving at the scene heard another passenger in the car, the lone survivor of the blast, shouting, "DINA! DINA!" But the agent had no idea what the acronym referred to. His ignorance was as illustrative of the phenomenon of informational compartmentalization within the U.S. intelligence community as anything else. For, as authors John Dinges and Saul Landau point out in their 1980 book *Assassination on Embassy Row,* DINA, the Chilean secret police established in 1973, benefited in its organizational conceptualization and surveillance technology from U.S. expertise in the form of a wide range of aid supplied by the United States Central Intelligence Agency.*

Appropriately, the blast that killed Letelier and a coworker sent shock waves throughout Washington. It demonstrated anew the astonishing degree of freedom that foreign secret agents enjoy in the United States. One has to wonder whether the FBI's evident if belated efforts on behalf of the safety of such exiles as Mihajlo Mihajlov was prompted by this notorious 1976 incident.

For one thing, the subsequent FBI investigation into the Letelier assassination appears to have been a first-rate job, for we have some evidence that even DINA became worried about the probe. A former employee of a well-known international human-rights organization tells this story: FBI agents showed up at her office with some photographs. The subject, she told them, was a Chilean exile who had come to the United States in 1975 as a very recently released

* That aid may have included looking the other way. Although the evidence suggests that George Bush, then CIA director, may have been aware of a DINA operation in the United States against Señor Letelier, there is no evidence that Director Bush sought to discourage DINA.

political prisoner from Chile. At least this was what she thought of him at the time. The FBI had reason to believe otherwise, that the exile was not who he had represented himself to be. The agents explained that the girlfriend of an FBI agent who was deeply involved in the Letelier investigation was traveling on a New York subway one day when she was abruptly approached by a man with a menacing attitude. His message was clear, unmistakable, and thoroughly threatening. He warned the woman to make sure to tell her boyfriend that the FBI had better not proceed too thoroughly with its investigation of the Letelier incident. The man who delivered that threat was the man in the FBI's photograph, the agents said—and he was obviously no "exile."

In short, DINA was warning the FBI. Absurd? DINA threatening the FBI? U.S. citizens would no doubt scoff at the very idea. But if one regards the Letelier assassination as an example of foreign secret police in the United States going too far, this DINA/FBI incident was not a quantum leap in misbehavior but merely a logical outgrowth of generally accepted behavior in the secret police world. For years, after all, KCIA agents roamed the United States more or less at will, shadowing their exiles. Korean residents on the West Coast were so intimidated by KCIA reprisals that they refused to inform American police authorities that KCIA agents here were extorting money from them like Mafia goons. Why should these Korean exiles take the risk by talking? After all, who helped set up the Korean Central Intelligence Agency? And how much police protection did American police authorities provide Iranian students when the Shah was in power? Or Orlando Letelier when he was out of power?

Diane Edwards La Voy, a staff member of a U.S. congressional committee who has studied the matter of cooperation among intelligence and security organizations around the world, explained the relative paralysis of the FBI here at home in this way: "Another factor, more a matter of human nature than of considered policy, may undermine U.S. failure to crack down on friendly agents. That factor is the attitude of U.S. officials toward the foreign dissidents. When officials deal only with the regime in power (its opponents being in prison or otherwise silenced), and actively support that regime against foreign threats and internal 'subversion,' they tend to function according to the simple rule, 'your enemy is my enemy.'"

Another factor at work here is what we would call the unofficial fraternity of secret police cooperation.† In this atmosphere, even ideological differences of the severest kind can be subsumed to the exigencies of police work. If the FBI must respect the working prerogatives of the CIA—and it must—then by what logic can the FBI intervene in the U.S. operations of a foreign secret police agency? Especially when the secret police force in question (such as DINA) has worked so closely with the CIA? The very fact that the FBI involved itself in what many impartial observers regard as a thorough investigation of the Letelier assassination is a startling departure from past procedure—and may help explain the DINA agent's attempted intimidation of an FBI investigator.

Such investigations—performed by one police organization into the work of another—inevitably threaten the logic and continuity of secret police cooperation around the world. The logic is that to maintain the law (such as it is), a secret police force must remain outside the law. Everyone understands this. Therefore, as far as the secret police community is concerned, the only real answer to embarrassing and antifraternal investigations in the aftermath of an operation such as the Letelier assassination is to avoid high-profile operations. Such extreme actions only create problems for all concerned—and put the FBI squarely in the middle, between the time-honored "hands-off" policy and the need to respond to a public outcry.

8

An even more difficult group for the secret police to control than the exiles may be the clergy. Few institutions are better organized than the Church, whether it is Catholic, Moslem, or whatever. But some secret police organizations are better at the job than others.

In Egypt, the state controls religion. The Ministry of Religious Endowments hands out instructions on sermons. Since the state

† In Latin America, that cooperation may not have been all that unofficial. According to John Dinges and Saul Landau, in their book *Assassination on Embassy Row*, a so-called "Operation Condor" served to link a number of Latin American intelligence services. Under the overall direction of Chile's DINA, the consortium (a) exchanged intelligence information, (b) *spied on exiles for one another,* and (c) may even have provided for joint assassination teams to liquidate selected exiles. The Letelier assassination, the authors suggest, may have been a Condor operation.

owns 30 percent of the mosques, the Ministry appoints a mullah in each one of them. If a mullah steps out of line, he faces the prospect of being transferred. The state determines who is behaving and who is not by dispatching police agents into the mosques to monitor the mullahs' sermons.

SAVAK's most conspicuous failure, of course, was its inability to break the mullahs—leading to the rise of the Ayatollah Khomeini. But Iran was hardly the only battleground where governments crossed swords with churchmen who had well-developed social consciences. The police in a wide variety of countries have become conditioned, by the very real strength of clerical opposition, to regard the Church as the enemy.

Opposition on the part of the clergy is not always expressed in high-profile style. A Uruguayan priest who had done nothing more than have coffee with the son of an opposition candidate for the presidency of Uruguay was arrested by the DNII. In his holding cell, the priest, dressed in civilian clothes, was of course extremely nervous, and he asked the guard for a cigarette. The guard granted the request. The priest then asked the guard if he knew what would happen to him. The guard asked the priest if he had done anything wrong. The priest swore that he hadn't, that in fact he was nothing more than a simple priest. The guard spat at him and said, "If I'd known you were a priest, I would never have given you a cigarette. . . . You priests are enemies of the constitution."

The seriousness of this strain between the Church and the police has surfaced all over the world. In 1978, the Argentine Government issued a decree instituting the National Registry of Religions, which requires all religious groups except the Catholic Church to register with the Ministry of Foreign Affairs and Religion. The Romanian Government recognizes fourteen religious communities; but, in Romania in 1948, it recognized sixty. In 1973, about five hundred out of a total of some thirty-five hundred Roman Catholic priests in Czechoslovakia were barred from exercising their ministry. In 1975, seven Czechoslovakian students from the Theological Faculty in Bratislava, after passing their final examinations, were barred from consecration as priests, because they refused to attend a meeting organized by the state-sponsored Pacem in Terris (Peace on Earth). A student of theology was expelled from the faculty for praying in public for arrested nonconformist artists.

The seventies was that kind of decade. In the Philippines, the implementation of martial law in 1972 caused the clergy to rise up, acquiring a social conscience and outspokenness theretofore unmatched in the country's history. At first, says a former Moslem anti-Marcos activist now living in the United States, security police showed some restraints in their treatment of outspoken members of the clergy. He remembers that only months after martial law had been declared in the Philippines, NISA authorities came to a private university-level Catholic school in Davao city to arrest an outspoken critic of Marcos who was scheduled to speak there. The nuns fought off the NISA agents with all the determination of seasoned pros. "How do we know you represent the government?" they asked the plainclothes agents. Stunned by their steely iconoclasm, the agents hurriedly left, only to return later in the day wearing uniforms and led by a commanding officer. Again the nuns resisted, and again the agents left, promising, however, that they would refer the matter to their higher-ups. But, in fact, the agents never reappeared at the school.

In the immediate aftermath of the declaration of martial law, says the former Moslem anti-Marcos activist, incidents revealing this type of uncertainty toward how to treat members of the religious opposition surfaced again and again. NISA agents were not then what they were to become.

But as martial law continued, the arrest and torture of religious opposition leaders became a fact. A prominent clergyman described how, during an interrogation session, officers allegedly played with a .45 and pointed it at the head of a clerical colleague of his who was arrested for his role in support of workers involved in labor disputes.

"This [persecution of the clergy who are socially conscious] is a pattern going on all over our country," says the priest. "In other islands where we are organizing, four of our people are also in jail because of the fact that they are organizing . . . . They have been promised by the constabulary commander that they will get released within two days if they testify that the parish priest is a Communist."

In October of 1976, Maryknoll priests who took part in a demonstration in Manila protesting a referendum to confirm martial law were deported without trial. The following day, the Maryknoll priests' headquarters was raided and their radio station was closed down. And while the police claimed that they acted so harshly because they believed there were links between the Church and the

Communists, the agents seemed to be pressing the point as if only to justify their aggressiveness toward the Church. For example, one bishop's house had been under twenty-four-hour surveillance. When they finally closed down his radio station, he was charged with passing messages to the Communist New People's Army. But when they interrogated him at the radio station, the bishop said there were very few questions asked about his links with the NPA.

Persecution of religious leaders in the Philippines has been extended to far less prominent figures as well. The prime targets of "salvaging" are those who are active in community organizations that are part of the Basic Church Community movement, designed to integrate priests and nuns with their communities in assisting people in developing their lives, according to Sister Mariani C. Dimaranan, chairperson of the Task Force Detainees of the Philippines.

As in the Philippines, persecuting clergymen in Korea throughout the seventies took a number of forms: KCIA surveillance of church sermons and prayer meetings to see whether political matter such as civil rights were discussed, as well as interrogations and detentions of churchmen who had been involved in community work. Three members of the Korean National Council of Churches were arrested on charges of "misuse of church funds," charges thought to relate to church relief work for political prisoners and their families. And the repression was even extended to American missionaries, one of whom was expelled in 1974 after refusing to sign a statement renouncing his criticism of the politics of the Park government, the other one being forced to leave in 1975 after authorities refused to extend his residence permit because the Department of Immigration complained that he had been involving himself in domestic political activity.

While Cuba has attempted a certain degree of accommodation with the Church, various repressive measures continue to be enforced. The government, which makes a strong effort to control all organizations, whether they be social, recreational, or professional, has not exempted religious organizations from its close scrutiny. Therefore, by running programs outside the regime's structures, the Church has become a target of G-2 activity (of late, the government is focusing its repressive activities primarily on the Jehovah's Witnesses).

In Rhodesia, the Catholic Church was a prime target of secret police repression. On February 27, 1973, a Catholic priest received a five-month jail sentence (which was later suspended) for publishing what the prosecution called an "extravagant and rabble-rousing" article in *Moto,* a Catholic newspaper, which described the Rhodesian Constitution as a "mockery of law." The judge criticized the article for not offering practical solutions. "It cannot be emphasized too strongly," he said, "that to harp upon the known problems without offering concrete and practical solutions to them can only exacerbate the situation, and such conduct, if subversive, might well lead to the breakdown in law and order."

History has brought this situation in Rhodesia to a close, but in South Africa there is evidence that persecution of socially active clergy members is accelerating. Bishop Desmond M. Tutu, a leading figure in the Anglican Church who is general secretary of the South African Council of Churches, had his passport seized after he called on parents of mixed ethnic background to support their children in a nationwide boycott of classes that Prime Minister Botha condemned as communist-inspired. But Bishop Tutu does not even consider himself a political activist. "Muzorewa, Makarios and the Ayatollah—all three of them are very good reasons why religious figures should not become political leaders," he said. "But that does not mean that one loses one's political conscience by the fact of ordination. . . . As a Bishop, I'm concerned, inevitably, with the extension of God's kingdom on earth, and that involves opposing laws—any laws, not just the so-called apartheid laws—that offend against Christ's teachings. But I'm strongly opposed to anybody who wants to use the church for political ends, even if they are very good ends." Just three weeks after his passport was seized, Bishop Tutu was for the first time arrested, along with fifty-two other church figures who might have felt less reluctant than he about using the Church as a political vehicle. The arrests occurred after the priests protested the detention of a fellow clergyman who had also offered public support for the nationwide boycott. The Johannesburg minister was detained without trial under the Internal Security Act, which allows the Justice Minister or his representative to hold indefinitely and incommunicado any person considered to be endangering state security or public order. The statute had been used frequently in the late seventies, to restrain opponents of the country's racial laws, but it had rarely been used against churchmen.

The Latin American clergy, however, may win the prize as the most vociferous social critics of the religious establishment throughout the seventies and on into the eighties. So much so that Pope John Paul II cautioned a gathering of Brazilian bishops that in their drive for promoting social progress they were neglecting to spread the gospel. But many Latin American bishops, originally conservative themselves, came to realize that only the Church had the power and moral authority to stand up to repressive regimes. Most Latin American clergy have been involved in fundamentally nonviolent movements to organize landless peasants and poverty-stricken slum dwellers to make effective demands for reform. But even these actions are denounced by some Latin American governments as communist subversion. In Chile, "only the institution of the Church remained independent from the government, capable of acting and expressing itself," to use the words of the chief legal counsel for the Cooperative Committee for Peace, testifying before the U. S. House of Representatives. And so, when, in November of 1975, the news was made public that General Pinochet had demanded that Cardinal Silva dissolve the Peace Committee, it came as no surprise that eleven of its members, including the first executive secretary, were already under arrest. The chief legal counsel himself was detained because he had planned to send Christmas cards to the cardinal and other bishops, in the name of the prisoners. And just weeks after the Bolivian junta seized power in 1980, eleven Bolivian priests had disappeared.

"I believe that an exaggerated emphasis on social questions has led part of the clergy to become involved in harmful political activities," said the head of the intelligence services of Brazil's SNI. "The Church recently produced a document on national security. In the same way, the high command could publish a document on theology."

Retorted Dom Paulo Evaristo Arns, the archbishop of São Paulo, "Perhaps it would not be a bad idea for all the generals to study a little theology."

EIGHT

When the Bizarre
Becomes Commonplace

1

The future of the secret police is made secure by their successes in the past. Secret police forces around the world have proven to be astonishingly effective instruments of control. And in an era in which many states are increasingly insecure, desperate governments are forced to ask the inevitable question: What better method for gluing a society together is there? It is no coincidence, after all, that regimes of both the extreme left and the extreme right, despite all their differences of ideology and political style, select the secret police instrument of societal control time and again. The moral justifications for adopting stringent security measures among regimes of the left and of the right may differ, but the end results are nearly identical: the knocks on the door in the middle of the night; the prolonged and unexplained detentions; the telling marks left on the wrists, the back, or the feet; and the wholesale disappearances of hundreds, and sometimes even thousands, of citizens. These are the telltale signs of a society's reliance on the secret police solution. With the obvious exception of the spread of nuclear weapons, the spread of the secret police solution is as important and troubling a fact of world politics as there is.

The contemporary acceptance of the concept of the secret police solution is obviously related to the brutal simplicity of that option. What could be simpler than eliminating opposition to the government, rather than creating a complex system in which opposition is tolerated if not welcomed? For to achieve a broad and genuine political consensus in a society, so that the governed consent to be governed, is an extraordinarily difficult process that may take years, decades, or even centuries to achieve, and which stands in the way of that instant economic progress that seems so essential in the modern world.

Given these factors, consider anew the secret police solution—immediate, relatively uncomplicated, time-tested, a very accessible "quick fix."

And it often works.

But it does not always work—or it does not work forever. It worked for twenty-one years in Iran, but in the end it failed. Historians can now speculate why. Perhaps it was that SAVAK was more club than brain. Its powers exceeded its talents. And it was betrayed by the carelessness of its sovereign, who permitted SAVAK to become a rallying cry in every household where contempt for the corrupt regime and the heavy-handedness of the secret police prevailed. Compare the Shah's moves to those of Chile's President Pinochet, who put DINA through the blind of the name change; or those of the late Marshall Tito, whose secret police force was (and still is) so secret that few even know its contemporary name and even fewer know how it is organized or how it works. SAVAK was encumbered with one liability that it could not, ultimately, overcome: the miscalculations of the Shah in his struggle with the mullahs, in his moral slackness in the face of growing corruption around his court, and in his relations with his patron, the United States, which in the end pulled the rug out from under the Peacock Throne. A secret police organization cannot succeed in the face of such colossal incompetence.

But, in more competent hands, the secret police can be a terribly effective instrument of control. Their use is a technique that can endure over time. The longevity and consistency of the powers of the KGB are testimony to the grand potential endemic to the secret police solution.

But the secret police solution *itself* is not an adequate basis for governing a society. In the U.S.S.R., the KGB exists alongside a massive and powerful central party structure that has proved its governing abilities and resilience over decades. The KGB also exists alongside a system of massive ideological indoctrination running at fever pitch from cradle to grave. But when the Shah of Iran became the focus of all political hostility, SAVAK was left to stand on its own; there was nothing in the society that the Shah had created to backstop the secret police. The secret police solution, then, cannot be the *whole* solution; even in its most powerful and intimidating forms, there must be other aspects to the organizational plan of a society. The secret police of Communist countries tend to be highly effective not because they are necessarily better, more efficient organizations but because they exist in the context of a much more thoroughly thought-out approach to the problems of governing large masses of people. Call it a totalitarian system or whatever, but in the absence of support from other sectors of government, especially in the area of ideological propaganda, no secret police can go it alone over the very long run.

Even in the short run, the secret police solution creates problems of its own making. It is an engine of social control that has proved in various parts of the world to be difficult to turn off once it is turned on. It develops a momentum of its own so powerful that even the sovereign ruler may live in fear of being destroyed by the machine he himself created; hence the need to have the head of the secret police organization beholden and accountable directly to the sovereign, and the need for a smaller, even more elite group of individuals, closest of all to the sovereign, who are entrusted to keep watch over the main engine.

Any secret police force may develop into a monstrous machine that needs to *create* political problems in order to fuel its own momentum—or to expand its domain. As Joseph Fouché understood, rulers must constantly be reminded of how vulnerable they would be without their secret police. The mad logic of the secret police solution may dictate that the secret police perpetrate the bombing in the public square or other act of terrorism in order to remind everyone of how unstable political life would be without them.

The secret police solution also brings into being in society a massive new political force: the secret police bureaucracy itself. It lobbies for legislation, has the ear of the sovereign, works to control the press, and manipulates public opinion. By making its presence felt in all the decision-making councils of society, the secret police force becomes a coequal in government, not just an errand boy.

Not surprisingly, the secret police organization that is permitted maximum room in which to maneuver can make life every bit as miserable as the antigovernment terrorist. In the presence of a powerful, type-A secret police force, a society changes. A widespread informant system alone tends to foster a paranoid society, in which trust is too risky a virtue. Who is working for the secret police and who is not? No one ever really knows for sure. And everyone is afraid to ask.

This paranoia is compounded by the nagging uncertainty of not knowing when the individual might be designated an enemy of the state—or why. And precisely because this designated power is often left to the secret police force itself, the system permits the secret police to define whole categories of "enemies of the state." Acting as both judge and jury, the secret police force can so expand the definition of what constitutes a spy or a security risk or a communist or a fascist that as its net gets ever wider, its powers expand to the point where even the sovereign ruler may have difficulty controlling it.

This is why the key feature of a type-A secret police force is not its degree of operational sophistication, but the extent of its raw power. A secret police force is sometimes clumsy, sometimes untalented, sometimes slow-footed, and sometimes dim-witted. But it is so powerful that it can usually cover up these failures. And it is only when the secret police have such wide powers that a whole subclass of professional informers and torturers will be created; when the traditional professions of law and medicine and science will be co-opted or eliminated by the secret police; when torture will become a prevalent practice of the state; and when a whole class of "enemies of the state" will be created.

The regime that would avail itself of the type-A secret police solution ought to consider its decision carefully. Even the great Fouché had doubts about the mechanism he perfected, for, in the end, he repudiated his monster: "It is necessary to abandon the errors of a *police d'attaque,* which menaces without guaranteeing and torments without protecting. We must restrict ourselves to the limits of a liberal and positive police." Good advice.

2

To emphasize that which secret police organizations around the world have in common is a way of drawing a general portrait of a universal phenomenon. But in developing that picture of the secret police—whether of the left or of the right, clumsy or sophisticated, small or large—the conclusion is inevitable that there is a specific point at which a type-A secret police force is born: precisely when the state grants it the power to become a state within a state.

This transformation is achieved by the granting of a single power. That power is the power to remove the citizen from his home or place of work or off the street or out of the theater or from his university club or union hall whenever secret police agents wish—and to hold him as long as they wish. Legal scholars call this power the power of *indefinite detention*. This is the essential power of the type-A secret police force.

This is the essential element that precipitates all the other elements into the unique chemistry of a secret police force. After granting the secret police the power of indefinite detention, the torture, the unexplained incarcerations, the disappearances follow in step.

These are the monsters. It is these monstrous institutions that require attention and study, because they offer one very clear way to achieve internal security and stability. At what point does a police institution *snap* into a secret police force? Note these words written by Robert Goldman, professor of law at American University, and Daniel Jacoby, the well-known attorney, in a report, to the Court of Appeals of Paris, describing Mexican police practices:

"Initially, we think it is important to note that similar investigations of torture allegations in other countries by regional and international human rights commissions . . . have established an almost *causal link* [our italics] between, particularly, illegal incommunicado detention and the infliction of cruel treatment on those so detained." But what comes first? The power of indefinite detention? Or the practice of torture? The answer is the power of indefinite detention. As Goldman and Jacoby point out, "Thus, such detention, unlawful in itself, creates a situation which readily invites the use of internationally and domestically proscribed practices against detainees who are effectively stripped of all legal recourse to protest their detention."

This is the chemistry that jolts the monster to life. All else follows logically from this power.

Torture becomes an administrative practice of the secret police precisely because it is a handy technique—an administrative means to a crucial political end. The morality of means will inevitably become sublimated to the overarching morality of ends. To think otherwise is vastly to overestimate the ability of human beings to observe the canons of moral law in the midst of acute political crisis. No more compelling evidence for this proposition can be offered than the behavior of the French in Algeria. Having endured the Gestapo in their own territory while the country was occupied by the Germans, the French just a decade later proceeded to inflict the Gestapo solution on Algiers.

The Algerian experience confirms how a type-A secret police force is born. Torture in Algeria followed logically from the dictates of the Special Powers Law of March 16, 1956, which permitted the Prefect of Algiers to delegate to the military exceptional authority beyond ordinary police powers. As the historian John Talbott has put it: "These powers, as exercised in the circumstances prevailing in Algiers in early 1957, opened the door to the practice of torture. It is not hard to see how this happened. The laws of the Fourth Republic required a suspect to be brought before an examining magistrate . . . within twenty-four hours of his arrest. Such a procedure was one of the safeguards against frivolous arrests and illegal detentions. But in Algiers, the paratroopers arrested and detained for questioning hundreds of men and women suspected of nothing more than possessing useful information. The key provision of the Special Powers Act, and in some respects, the key to much of the controversy over the Battle of Algiers, was the authority to intern suspects, the right of *assignation à résidence*."

This was the chemistry that converted the practices of the 10th Paratroopers Division into secret police practices. "The government had decided to keep Algeria French," noted Professor Talbott. "The soldiers who resorted to torture believed themselves to be meeting the requirements of the government's policy. . . . This is not to say that the military command ever received from the government explicit orders to resort to such methods." It did not have to; the resort to torture as a routine method of interrogation was the inevitable consequence of (a) the deteriorating political situation and

(b) the powers of indefinite detention. "I cannot defend SAVAK's every action," wrote the Shah of Iran in his memoirs, "and will not attempt to do so here. There were people arrested and abused. Unfortunately, this is not a perfect world."

It was the Guy Mollet government in Paris, one must recall, that passed the magic wand to the military; the secret police system did not arise overnight on its own. Like the Shah incorporating SAVAK, or the Pinochet junta enfranchising DINA, "It was the . . . government," according to Talbott, "that sent the Tenth Division into Algiers with orders to put an end to terrorism by whatever means necessary." And like the Shah and Pinochet and Marcos and any number of rulers around the world in recent times, "the civilians did not take back the sweeping powers they had handed to the soldiers, once the crisis passed. They did not think to close the lid on Pandora's box."

Once Pandora's box is opened, can a society ever return to relatively conventional policing?

The government surely won't help return society to normality: having created a monster that is (at least over the short run) exceedingly effective, it is not about to rein in that which is keeping it in power. In any society in which there is violent opposition to the government, the secret police solution can be effective. "The terrorists' campaign," wrote Talbott, "worked [only] as long as the terrorists faced an undermanned and poorly informed police force and benefited from the restraints that civil and criminal law put on the use of state power. The removal of these restraints robbed the terrorists of their anonymity, turned them into hunted men and women, made them informers against each other, stripped them of the protection of their silence." Or, as the Shah put it, "Similar organizations [to SAVAK] exist worldwide, since every country is obliged to protect its populace from subversion."

The general population won't be able to set the clock back. It is naïve to expect the general populace to rise up against the terrorism of the secret police. For one thing, the people will be too terrified— as well they should be—to protest. For another, they may also be privately afraid of what life would be like in the absence of the secret police. In 1980, the government of President Augusto Pinochet, which created the DINA monster, held a plebiscite, albeit under less than entirely ideal conditions. Nevertheless, the Pinochet government obviously was proud of the returns: two-to-one voter approval for an eight-and-one-half-year term. "While the regime . . . remains an international pariah seven years after overthrowing President Salvador Allende Gossens," wrote a New York *Times* correspondent from Santiago, "it has won a wide popular following inside Chile for the tranquility, as well as the economic growth, it has provided." The correspondent quoted one resident of Santiago as saying: "Among the bad, one has to choose the less bad."

To most citizens, freedom that involves instability and chaos will seem too pricey. In response to an article that appeared in a U.S. newspaper beneath the headline "Under Argentina's Sheen, the Terror Goes On," a United States reader wrote in: "The Argentine political system has the same root problems as most of the countries of the world—lack of respect for the law. . . . It would take a hypocrite to say that today seems like anything but a paradise [in comparison to the chaos in Argentina in the early seventies]. The streets of the major cities were battlegrounds and no one was safe. I'm certainly not in favor of unnecessarily heavy-handed tactics from any government—from the right or the left. But I can understand how situations like that one can and do arise in countries where a few 'citizens' take advantage of the general freedom to foment terror for their own idealistic causes. Political stability is the most important ingredient for day to day normalcy."

We must face the fact that the general populace will usually side with the police; and under special circumstances, when the police solution evolves into the secret police solution, it may even side with the secret police—at least at the start. In Britain last year, Scotland Yard recommended to Parliament that new restrictions be placed on the right of assembly. The right of assembly, of course, is one of the cardinal freedoms in a democratic country, and England was history's first. Nevertheless, England may be ready to limit the right of assembly. "Many people side with Scotland Yard," reports one journalist who has lived for some time in London. "After a decade of often violent social conflict, of division and anxiety, many people in Britain think of tranquility as the surest sign that the quality of life as they used to know it will once again be secure. . . . The essence of well-being is the absence of change."

The intellectuals will not succeed in returning a society to normal policing: they can and will do only so much to protest the inevitable consequences of special powers. Indignation, after all, is not an easy emotion to sustain over a long period of time, and the critics will become isolated from the general population as they are increasingly perceived as the enemies of law and order. Before long, the climate of opinion and general indifference will wear out the critics. History, at least in the short run, will not run their way. Writing in her journal in the last full year of the Algerian war, Simone de Beauvoir remarked, "In this sinister month of December 1961, like many of my fellow men, I suppose, I suffer from a kind of tetanus of the imagination. . . . One gets used to it. But in 1957, the burns in the face, on the sexual organs, the nails torn out, the empalements, the shrieks, the convulsions, outraged me."

But the outrage soon passes, and most people find that they can live with the secret police less uncomfortably than they can live with disorder and terrorism. The secret police solution is a terrible price to pay: once a type-A organization comes to life, it is difficult to phase it out of existence.

In the end, of course, citizens will get far more than they bargained for. The tragedy of the secret police solution is that it is such a blunt and crude instrumentality that in the name of preserving paradise it winds up creating hell. It eliminates the (a) communists or (b) fascists, but takes with it all other shades and nuances of political life. And when even the moderate critics of the regime are eliminated, incarcerated, exiled, or intimidated, the secret police machine rolls on—a status-quo machine whose roar is deafening and whose appetite is insatiable. Enemies of the regime will be created even if real enemies have long since ceased to exist. Liberals will be apprehended as communists, traditionalists as fascists. New tasks are essential. Like any other organ of government, the secret police force is a self-perpetuating bureaucracy. It will not fade into the background without a fight.

The secret police solution is not something that can be tried for a short time—like an incomes policy or tax reform—and abandoned overnight. The scars of a Gestapo will remain fresh in people's minds long after the traces of its existence have become practically invisible. In Egypt, the memory of Nasser's concentration camps was surely fresh in Anwar Sadat's mind when, in 1972, he moved to streamline and professionalize the Egyptian security and intelligence services. No one wanted the horrors of Nasser's "Gestapo" to be duplicated. "Sadat remembers that Nasser put many, many people in concentration camps," explains a well-informed U. S. State Department official. "Even those who ran Nasser's camps were sometimes against them. Sadat remembers Nasser's system, and he knows that other people remember that system, too." It is as if the best insurance against choosing a secret police solution may be having had to endure one. But those who have endured such an experience would probably agree that the Gestapo experience is a very high price to pay for attaining the wisdom of not wanting to go through it all over again.

In Iran, the existence of SAVAMA is a painful reality. It is all too reminiscent of SAVAK. One wonders whether the mullahs are repeating the mistake of the Shah. In a famous letter written to an ayatollah on the eve of his execution, a now-deceased SAVAK official explained one of the errors of SAVAK. Tehrani, the SAVAK torturer, urged the mullahs not to repeat the mistakes of the Shah by making SAVAMA into a highly visible Gestapo:

"Availability of news and information in various areas, particularly knowledge of the objectives of the opposition and future plans," Tehrani began, "have always assisted the decision-making of government officials. It is for this reason that the existence of an intelligence unit whose sole function is to gather information of the views of various strata and opposition groups, including Communists, seems to be necessary."

But Tehrani warned the mullahs that there was a wrong way to go about this information-gathering. "However, doing this openly—or announcing the reorganization of the previous SAVAK or anything of this sort—will provide the opposition and the followers of the various ideologies, particularly the Communists, with a suitable propaganda tool."

"For this reason," Tehrani suggested, "the 'intelligence unit' should be organized in a really secret manner and should start its activities under the supervision of a person trusted by the government."

The heavy-handed approach of SAVAK will not, in the long run, defeat communism, asserted Tehrani. "One cannot destroy the Communist groups and the followers of Communist ideology by restricting their freedom, street rights, interruption of their meetings and even pressure," he wrote in his confession. "Because with the continuation of pressure these groups will go underground and then it will be more difficult to fight them."

3

Despite the fact that the FBI and other U.S. internal-security organizations have, at times, extended their franchise unnecessarily and illegally, the United States has never endorsed the concept of an all-powerful executive branch of government.* The courts have always retained enormous powers to review the activities of law-enforcement officers and to levy punishments accordingly. Just last year, two former FBI officials were convicted and sentenced for perpetrating "black bag jobs"—illegal break-ins at the homes of friends and relatives of members of the radical Weathermen during the late sixties. In this climate of judicial authority, what future would an FBI *torturer* have?

But if the past is any guide to the future, it is clear that the seeds of a heavy-handed secret police system lie planted in American culture. The history of this country is marked by extremist tendencies in the pursuit of the maintenance of the status quo, as well as in the pursuit of change. There is a broad historical tendency to rely on law enforcement, rather than other institutions of government, to tackle the problems of social change. The concept of law and order in America is more than a political slogan used frequently by politicians during election campaigns. It is a philosophical outlook that is deeply embedded in the American character.

In terms of the worldwide phenomenon that we have been discussing, there has never been a SAVAK, DINA, or KGB in the United States. Americans may have helped other nations set up their secret police institutions, but they have not allowed a comparable

---

* Perhaps the only major exception to this rule is former President Nixon's "Huston Plan": In July of 1970, an ad hoc Inter-American Committee on Intelligence was set up to make recommendations for increased and improved intelligence-gathering techniques and operations to President Nixon. The Committee, composed of FBI Director Hoover; CIA Director Richard Helms; Lieutenant General Donald Bennet, Director, Defense Intelligence Agency; and Admiral Noel Gaylor, Director, National Security Agency, submitted to the President for approval the "Huston Plan," named after the coordinator of the committee and liaison to the President, Tom Charles Huston. The Plan proposed the use of electronic surveillance, burglary, wiretaps, and mail coverage against violence-prone campus and student-related groups, and any individual or group in the United States that allegedly posed a threat to internal security.

system to be established in the United States—no organization or associated groups that practice, as a general administrative procedure, indefinite detention and interrogation by torture. These are the central defining elements of a type-A secret police system.

However, certain internal-security practices common to a SAVAK or a DINA have been adopted in the United States. Those aspects include extensive surveillance of political activity—in particular, although not exclusively, of the Left; and considerable counterintelligence penetration of left-wing groups, including the employment of agent-provocateur techniques.

In order to achieve a high degree of political surveillance, the United States system of surveillance has operated in a highly decentralized, and to an important degree, unorganized fashion. This disorganization and decentralization derives from the complex political organization of the republic itself, as it operates on at least five levels: federal, state, county, city, and private corporate.

The federal component of this system has included Army Intelligence; the CIA (which is prohibited in theory, but not in reality, from domestic spying); the FBI (practicing the classic variety of surveillance techniques, including surreptitious entry, penetration by informants, and electronic eavesdropping, as well as the usual agent-provocateur and disinformation measures); and the NSA (National Security Agency), with the technological ability to tap telephone conversations and other electronic communications. For a time, the federal Drug Enforcement Agency was a potentially active member of this system, but the Watergate revelations, which resulted in the resignation of President Nixon, curbed that development. At times, other agencies in the mammoth federal government have plugged into this informally organized intelligence system. For instance, in 1967, the Community Relations Service, in theory set up by the 1964 Civil Rights Act to mediate and conciliate racial disputes, was authorized to spy on militant black, antiwar, and radical protest groups.

At state and local levels, a myriad of law-enforcement agencies, with their own intelligence squads, have conducted an astonishing variety of covert infiltration and surveillance operations. In Los Angeles, for example, police officers, operating as undercover agents, have infiltrated and spied on groups ranging from the Soviet Jewry relief organizations to the Los Angeles City Council. In Chicago, the police department's so-called Red Squad investigated and spied on individuals guilty of everything ranging from suspected terrorist activity to speaking out against then-Mayor Richard Daley, fighting pollution, and supporting 1968 presidential candidate Eugene McCarthy. "All the earmarks of a police state"—these were the words used by a Cook County grand jury in 1975, on concluding a six-month investigation into the Chicago Police Department Red Squad's spying operations.

Local police forces in the United States have been quite involved in attempts to curb anti-nuclear-power demonstrations. The Buffalo Police Department has had a standard policy of photographing demonstrators—and routinely placing the results in the Department's antisubversive files. The Los Angeles Police Department assigned a videotaping team to record a 1978 city council hearing on nuclear power. Power companies have even maintained their own security departments (equipping some of them with sophisticated surveillance equipment, including night-time telescopes and wiretapping tools), which have cooperated with government agencies in the identification of anti-nuclear activists because the utility companies partially recruit their security personnel from Army Intelligence, the FBI, the U. S. Treasury Department, and state and local law-enforcement agencies.

This sort of unofficial cooperation among private as well as government law-enforcement agencies has been enhanced by the Law Enforcement Intelligence Unit, a private organization that describes itself as an organization dedicated to promoting "the gathering, recording, investigating and exchange of confidential information not available through regular police channels, concerning organized crime." The LEIU, whose subscribers come from more than 250 state and local law-enforcement agencies, maintains computerized filing systems, while its administrative work is performed by the California Department of Justice's Organized Crime and Criminal Intelligence Branch. But despite its commitment to combatting "organized crime," there is no doubt that LEIU files contain information on political dissidents as well. And that information is sometimes forwarded to LEIU by police department officials attempting to subvert civilian oversight of their intelligence activities. But LEIU is more a tribute to the limitations placed on the U.S. internal-security system than evidence of a SAVAK in the making. The principle of accountability of police intelligence to civilian oversight remains a fearsome reality to law-enforcement officials. The very existence of

LEIU suggests that the existing government political-surveillance system is so inadequate that internal security officers felt it necessary to create an entirely private, nongovernmental organization. LEIU was in fact established, in 1956, by the head of the Los Angeles Police Department's Criminal Intelligence Division as a result of the department's exasperating experience in trying to work with the FBI. (The FBI traditionally insisted on access to local police department files without offering the reciprocity of its files. There was very little real cooperation.) And so, when LEIU was set up, the Bureau immediately targeted it as a threat to its dominance. As a consequence, LEIU, which became a worrisome entity to both rival law enforcement agencies and civilian sectors of society, because it is insulated from civilian oversight, has never produced a very effective instrument of political surveillance.

The theme of noncooperation among United States law-enforcement agencies is common throughout United States history. Had there existed an adequate political-surveillance system within the United States, obviously LEIU would never have had to be created. The fact that there is no such adequate system of surveillance may not, however, be a reason for us to feel complacent about the dangers of the surveillance system ever threatening our civil liberties. Rather, it should help us put into perspective the hysterical claims coming from the more radical sectors of American society with regard to the alleged pervasiveness and supereffectiveness of political surveillance in the United States, or arguments about the existence of a drastically overzealous secret police system in the country.

As long as overlapping federal, state, and local jurisdictions (and rivalries) among police intelligence forces continue to exist, and as long as the processes of judicial and legislative review of police procedures remain a potent force in American politics, nothing approaching a DINA, a SAVAK, or a sophisticated Eastern European secret police system is likely to come into existence in America.

Indeed, one could argue that under the sort of leadership provided by the new director of the FBI, former federal judge William Webster, the likelihood of a full-fledged secret police surveillance system developing in the 1980s in America is diminished. For under Director Webster, programs that have become negatively notorious, such as COINTELPRO, have—if the FBI is to be believed—been disbanded. COINTELPRO was a top-secret FBI program designed along the lines of a department of misinformation, to create confusion among various left-wing groups in the sixties, especially the Black Panthers. And Director Webster's leadership has had a ripple effect throughout the U.S. law-enforcement community. A 1980 survey of police intelligence units in New York, Chicago, Washington, Houston, Atlanta, and Detroit by the Los Angeles *Times* suggest that the heyday of the so-called "Red squads" may be over. "The survey," wrote reporters John J. Goldman and Larry Green, "found that, in general, police departments have sharply cut back on intelligence gathering and have narrowed their activities to combatting terrorism and organized crime. Units have shrunk in size and budgets have been significantly reduced. Often under pressure from courts, city councils and civil liberties groups, police administrators have imposed stringent guidelines on gathering information in some cities."

Despite all this, Americans should not be complacent. We must be aware that, once dismantled, a political police force is easily reassembled, practically overnight. It would be dangerously smug to view the egregious secret police institutions that we have studied as if they represent a look back into a ridiculously primitive past; it may be a look forward into a vision of the future. The fact that it has not happened here does not mean that it won't. The price of liberty is eternal vigilance.

Police authorities, by and large, will insist that they require more power, which is understandable. There are more law-enforcement problems today than ever before. As a high official of the Los Angeles Police Department put it in a moment of exasperation with city-council critics of the department's surveillance operations, "I'll tell you one thing. It's time for the council people to stand up and support the need for intelligence and confidentiality about the intelligence-gatherers, or to announce that they don't want intelligence. If they do that . . . we will be here to pick up the pieces left by the terrorists."

The Los Angeles official, speaking in 1980, did not sound all that different from General Van den Bergh, who in 1969 gave an interview to the *Rand Daily Mail* on the issue of whether the government needed the expansive BOSS Act "to control the situation." Said the head of BOSS: "If you're being attacked by a man armed with an axe, you can hardly be expected to defend yourself with a feather. . . . The police were faced with . . . legal requirements introduced to South Africa via England—long before the world had to begin coping with communism and communist-inspired revolution. They had to caution a suspect that it was not necessary for him to answer any questions or provide any explanations, and if he did so this could be used as evidence in trial. In addition, in accordance with court rulings, no one under arrest could even be questioned by the police. How, under such circumstances, with your hands tied, does one go about fighting a communist-inspired revolution?"

Then the head of BOSS was asked: "Do you think that the wide powers given to the police can be reconciled with the civil freedoms which any individual in a democratic country would like to enjoy?"

Van den Bergh: "Yes, and most definitely. After all, it is just these powers which enable you and me to enjoy freedom in a free and democratic country. Take these powers away from the police, and our freedom—for which we paid dearly—will soon become something of the past. . . ."

Prime Minister Pierre Elliott Trudeau once put the matter only slightly differently: "Even with hindsight, any government has to tread a very narrow line between what would rightfully be denounced as political interference on the one hand, and what would rightfully be denounced as political negligence on the other. We try to meet this general dilemma by exercising general control of the Security Service but keeping out of its day-to-day operations." Defending the Royal Canadian Mounted Police Security Service in the face of allegations of its use of "disruptive tactics" against suspected terrorists, Trudeau snapped: "I'm not a police officer. But when you catch a terrorist because you've opened an envelope, I don't think the bulk of the Canadian people would think that this, even if it is technically a crime, would be something that should bring the RCMP to be put in jail."

There is no question that new areas of the world may be moving toward secret police solutions. If you have any doubt about this, examine the ruminations of a special parliamentary committee in England with regard to the appropriateness of "in-depth" interrogation of suspects in Northern Ireland. In its "Report of the Committee of Inquiry into Police Interrogation Procedures in Northern Ireland," presented to Parliament by the Secretary of State for Northern Ireland in March of 1979, the question was addressed in this way: "The problem is how to supervise and control interrogations so as to minimize the chances of improper behavior and the opportunity of making false allegations, without impairing the efficiency of interrogation in obtaining evidence leading to the conviction of criminals, which the public generally wants and expects."

Another commission of inquiry in Britain,† several years earlier, was not profoundly troubled by the notion that in-depth interrogation of the wrong suspects can and will inevitably occur: "We have also considered the argument that, however careful the selection of detainees for interrogation in depth, it may on occasion involve the interrogation of a man wrongly suspected. It can accordingly be argued that to subject such a man to these techniques is something which should not be tolerated. There is some force to this argument, but it must be remembered that even under normal conditions it is accepted that a person suspected of ordinary crime, who may thereafter be found not guilty, can be subjected to some measure of discomfort, hardship, and mental anxiety. Moreover, interrogation in depth may itself reveal the innocence of the detainee and allow of his release from detention." In consequence, the Parker Committee endorsed the use of interrogation by methods which, by United States standards, would be considered scandalous—the famous "five techniques": wall-standing; hooding; subjecting the victim to irritating high-frequency noises; restricting the victim to a bread-and-water diet; and depriving the victim of sleep. "The true view, it seems to us, must depend on the degree to which the techniques are applied . . . ," concluded the Parker Committee, ". . . on the length of time during which he is deprived of sleep or given a restrictive diet. . . . And all these matters depend upon the medical condition of the detainee." Or, as the Bennett Committee ultimately concluded, "Confessions which are 'voluntary' . . . will, however, only be made in an interrogation procedure with the right atmosphere. They will not be made in the atmosphere of a casual conversation or cosy fireside chat. . . ."

We believe the hard-nosed conclusions of the Bennett and Parker committees would find a sympathetic hearing in practically every country in the world. The tolerance for political disorder and violent terrorism is ever diminishing. Police all over the world will request more power—and probably will get it. Every government needs to adopt methods and powers necessary to achieve internal security. Every government needs a security service.

Our point is simply this: Some security police are worse than others. Much worse.

† Chairman of the committee was Lord Parker of Waddington.

Appendix 1

The Complicated Structure
of the Secret Police

In few states is the internal-security system a simple one. Although notable exceptions exist, the systems tend to be so bureaucratically complicated that one almost needs a road map to figure them out. And of course, no road maps exist. Here are a few examples of the complicated structures of secret police organizations:

The central intelligence agency of the police system in Uruguay is DNII (for Dirección Nacional de Información e Inteligencia)—which seems simple enough. But DNII, even though it operates within a relatively small country, is divided into a myriad of departments—for instance, Department 2 handles trade union problems; Department 3 was designed to combat the Tupamaros (left-wing opponents of the regime, made more famous internationally by the Costa-Gavras film *State of Siege* than they might otherwise have become); and Department 6, which works to prevent and punish "new subversive acts"—i.e., all political opposition. Even the secret police system of a relatively small country will tend to have a complicated bureaucratic structure, sometimes plagued by problems of coordination and control.

The internal-security network of the Philippines illustrates the point again. Despite NISA's (National Intelligence Security Authority) preeminence, the system also takes in Metrocom (The Metropolitan Command Intelligence Division, a subdivision of the civilian constabulary) and ISAFP, the intelligence service of the Armed Forces.

Charito Planas (a well-known opponent of the Marcos regime who, after running opposite President Marcos' wife for office, escaped to the United States with the help of Vice-President Mondale in the late seventies) told us that on one occasion she was arrested, interrogated, and imprisoned by Metrocom, then released a few days later by ISAFP. She added that in the case of two famous Philippine politicians hostile to Marcos (Benigno Aquino, leader of the Liberal Party who was arrested just after martial law was declared in 1972 and released from prison to undergo surgery in the United States in 1980; and Senator Diokno, another prominent Marcos rival), both NISA and the Defense Ministry got into the act, quarreling over which branch of the security apparatus should supervise the politicians' detentions. While NISA seems to be clearly the overlord of the entire system, the overlapping duties of NISA, ISAFP, and Metrocom inevitably invite conflict and competition.

Is this system more of a tribute to President Marcos' Machiavellian talents than to any unwonted bureaucratic overlappings? Although we do not know the answer to that, we do know that it certainly has its advantages. "It is hard to know what you are arrested for," explains Charito Planas. "You may not even know whether the charges are criminal or political." Such a labyrinthian system (reminiscent of the fictional "justice" system portrayed in Franz Kafka's *The Trial*) at least permits the state multifarious options in dealing with the political "dissident," "subversive," "terrorist"—whatever he may be called.

Whether by design or otherwise, this sort of complicated system in the Philippines seems to work well elsewhere in the world. For instance, in Taiwan, according to a number of Taiwanese exiles, it is not unusual to be released by the Taiwan Garrison Command (an internal-security organization) and picked up again by the Bureau of Investigation (another internal-security unit, which is highly competitive with the Command). Or it may even work the other way around, because the competition between the two security agencies is so great that if one or the other intelligence division is interested in your case, they may arrest you without reliable evidence, as if in a hurry to prevent the rival organization from gaining jurisdiction over the case.

It is plausible that such competitiveness is built into a secret police system by design. President Assad, of Syria, created an intelligence structure that is both competitive and complex. The competitiveness, Assad is said to believe, assures that no one intelligence service is able to develop an overwhelming degree of power—or at least not enough to unseat him. The franchises of the various services, which are all poorly designed, add up to a sort of deliberate ambiguity on the part of Assad to establish competing divisions within his sprawling security system. Assad's military intelligence unit focuses its energies primarily on Israel. But it also is assigned to keep a sharp eye upon its own men in military intelligence. Air Force Intelligence is responsible for (1) the security of the President, (2) intelligence against Israel, and (3) monitoring its own organization in much the same way that military intelligence watches its ranks. With one exception, Air Force Intelligence has carte blanche over Assad's other intelligence services. That exception is the Defense Units (or Defense Companies)—made up of twenty thousand tightly knit units under the command of Assad's brother, which are responsible for protecting the regime against coups. And to make matters even more interesting, within the Defense Units structure, there is, according to well-informed sources, an intelligence apparatus of "heavies" who, scouting across the country in Land-Rovers, conduct interrogations at will and engage in covert breaking-and-entering operations ("black-bag jobs") as required.

But the Syrian secret police story does not stop even at this. There is yet another security bureaucracy: the largest civilian-oriented intelligence organization within the country, called the General Intelligence Directorate, which monitors civilians, embassies, and suspected foreign agents, and in addition, it maintains heavy surveillance over all entrances into and exits from the country.

It is not difficult to imagine the difficulties created by the maintenance of such a complex system. The Directorate, which is primarily concerned with the civilian population (but which also has an external section, concerned with espionage), and the Defense Units, which have as their mission to protect the regime against coups, often come into conflict. There is so much competition that it is quite common, sources say, for disputes between representatives of the various services to break out at the scene of a crime, those disputes often becoming so heated that street shootings take place.

Finally, Syria also maintains a National Security Council, headed by a national security adviser, a position once held by the head of the Air Force, who was particularly close to Assad but who was fired after some of Assad's people were mysteriously gunned down. The function of the Council? To coordinate the activities of the intelligence bodies and to try to pool their resources as well.

To some rulers, however, a Kafkaesque system is more trouble than it is worth. King Hussein, of Jordan, it would seem, has no use for Syrian-style rivalry among his intelligence services. Hussein has a strong army, and the regime has been stable for approximately ten years now. Not only does Hussein not require such built-in rivalry, but he probably wouldn't tolerate it if it arose.

In Jordan, the division of labor among the intelligence services is quite clear. Besides the Jordan/Arab Army, there is the Public Security Forces, a paramilitary police force that has jurisdiction over a wide range of matters—from traffic regulation to public order. The Public Security Forces is, in essence, an action arm called upon to curb dissidence within the country. The Public Security Forces is more akin to South Africa's security police than to the National Intelligence Service (formerly called BOSS). The chief internal security and genuine *intelligence* service of Jordan is "Mukhabarat," which puts heavy surveillance on dissidents, especially Palestinians, and which also has an external section that assigns agents to watch foreign embassies—in particular, the embassies of foreign countries whose policies conflict with Jordan's.

Anwar Sadat was yet another Arab leader who appeared to have no need for the type of sharp rivalry and competition among the intelligence services fostered by President Assad, of Syria. Sadat, unlike Assad, did *not* rotate the heads of the intelligence services for political reasons. And Sadat, more like King Hussein, of Jordan, was evidently secure enough not to invite friction: "A bone is not thrown to two or three services at once" was the way one U. S. State Department official neatly put it.

Although there are several intelligence services in Egypt, the division of labor among them seems to be quite clear. Military intelligence (much like its counterpart in Syria) is primarily concerned with spying on Libya and Israel, as well as spying within its own services. GI, or General Intelligence (discussed in Chapter Three, Section 5) as Nasser built it up was still, under Sadat, the largest, most pervasive civilian intelligence organization of Egypt, concerned with all security threats (with the exception of security problems in the armed forces). DGSSI, for General Department of State Security Investigations, is much smaller and not nearly as well equipped as GI, but it is more specialized than the other Egyptian services. While DGSSI itself does not collect information, cases are referred to it for investigation. So, for example, if GI, at the port of Alexandria, uncovers information involving smuggling, the case may very well be turned over to DGSSI for action.

But there is a great deal more to most secret police systems than meets the eye. Perhaps no secret police organization of the seventies received as much publicity as the State Research Bureau—also known as State Research Department, Cabinet Research, or the Research Unit—under former Ugandan President Idi Amin. It is no wonder that the Research Bureau gained so much publicity in the world press. One account by a person familiar with its "security" practices describes the "striker unit," an offshoot of the State Research Department, in rather grim terms:

"The task of the striker unit is elimination. It is directly responsible to President Idi Amin. The pattern of operation is common and well-documented. The vehicle normally used is a Peugeot or BMW; the technique is to drive up to the house or office of the victim. He is arrested; his shoes are removed and those usually remain as a pathetic reminder; he is thrown into the boot of the car; he is driven off; he is unlikely to be seen again."

But the State Research Bureau, despite all the publicity it received, was not the only secret police unit operating within Amin's Uganda. The Military Intelligence Unit, going beyond the mandate suggested by its name, was also responsible for a considerable number of arrests and disappearances that took place during Amin's rule. And the military police, whose headquarters were situated at the notorious government barracks at Makindye, took no back seat to State Research agents with regard to bearing responsibility for brutal killings and tortures, particularly those that took place at Makindye Prison. And finally, the Public Safety Unit, of the regular police of Uganda, which was formed in 1971 to deal with the growing problem of kondoism (armed robbery), headquartered three miles from the city center, at Naguru, was also involved in disappearances and deaths.*

Like the State Research Bureau, of Uganda, Chile's DINA also contracted a monopoly of publicity as the sole antisubversive secret police force of strength within the country.

"It is generally believed that DINA is the only agency responsible for the disappearance of prisoners," said an ex-DINA agent. "This is not so. There are *seven* intelligence services operating in the country. . . . There are five counterintelligence services with clandestine machinery."

Nevertheless, the world press accounts of what was happening inside of Chile were not that far off. For all the competition, General Pinochet, emerging from the 1973 coup that toppled Allende, wanted to create something entirely different. Borrowing freely from all sorts of available models, including Brazil's DOPS (political police),† Pinochet avoided recruiting men into DINA in a way that might limit his control in the future. His technique was classic: divide and conquer; foster competition among the various security agencies.

When DINA was first put together by the junta, President Pinochet drew talent not from the Army and the Air Force, which had their own secret police / intelligence units, but from the Army, Carabineros (uniformed police), and such civilian, nongovernmental groups as Patria y Libertad (a civilian right-wing group staunchly opposed to Allende). By not recruiting from the Air Force and the Navy, competition and a certain degree of jealousy were built into the system, leaving intact, despite DINA's rise to prominence, such units as SIM, the secret service of the military (which was the major clandestine organization working against Allende before the 1973 coup); SIN, the secret service of the Navy (which had the help of the U. S. Navy in carrying out threatening

* And there was, finally, apart from these more or less official security units, an unofficial unit—almost like a Ugandan Brigada Blanca—that operated under a lieutenant colonel who was a member of the Defense Council and who was linked with some of the worst cases of brutality.

† Brazil, like Chile, also had several intelligence services (besides DOPS) in addition to the more or less autonomous organization called OBAN. for Operação Bandeirantes (see Chapter Two, Section 3). OBAN also received a great amount of information from the secret service of the Army, CIE (Centro de Informacões do Exército), and of the Navy, which was the brain center for antiterrorist activities.

maneuvers against the Allende government—SIN had used regular military ships as floating torture centers); SIFA, the secret service of the Air Force (which worked closely with Patria y Libertad, the right-wing group from which Pinochet drew many DINA agents and which developed the technique of using nonmilitary safe houses to conduct interrogations, a ploy later adopted by DINA); SICAR, the secret service of the Carabineros (which developed on a separate track from DINA after the coup and which was placed in charge of guarding the safe houses used for the torture and transportation of prisoners from one safe house to another); and finally, the Bureau of Investigations (which worked closely with SICAR and in the late seventies got assigned to drug-law enforcement).

But, in the case of Chile, only DINA (in 1978 reorganized and renamed CNI, for Center for National Intelligence) reported directly to Pinochet, and there is some evidence that CNI was created as DINA's successor late in the decade precisely to smooth out some of these overlapping and competing units. But, in the few years just after the 1973 coup, until some consolidation of power occurred, the secret police situation in Chile was as labyrinthian as those systems operating in Uruguay and the Philippines, so that one could be arrested by DINA, released, then rearrested by, say, SIM.

When David Ben-Gurion (Prime Minister of Israel, 1948–53 and 1955–63)‡ set up the Israeli intelligence and internal-security system, in the late forties, he proceeded on the basis of what might at first glance appear to be two contradictory principles: one was division of authority and responsibility; the other was coordination, to be effectuated by the Prime Minister's office only.

In Israel today, there are both military and civilian intelligence units. The Information Bureau of the Military is called AMAN. It is staffed entirely by army officers and deals with political and military intelligence (it is not concerned with tracking down subversives or with spying abroad). Then, run directly from the Prime Minister's office, are two civilian intelligence organizations. The first is the Security Department—known as Shin Bet popularly, but officially known as SHABAK (from the contraction of the full name, Sherut Habitachon), for Security Department. Its franchise covers all internal security within Israel and the Occupied Territories.

‡ David Ben-Gurion was also Minister of Defense during both of the times that he served as Prime Minister.

Now we come to an interesting quirk. The average Israeli, or even Arab dissident, for that matter, rarely sees or hears of SHABAK. When an arrest must be made, or a "friendly interrogation" must be conducted, the action proceeds under the aegis of the Department of Special Duties, known as LATAM. This is a division of the Israeli civilian police. Each city has a police headquarters, and within each headquarters there is a LATAM office. As far as the public is concerned, a SHABAK (or Shin Bet) office does not exist. But SHABAK pulls the strings and LATAM performs the required choreography. Unofficially speaking, all LATAM officers are secret agents of SHABAK, who, however, are official agents of LATAM.

Now, once a prisoner is in the custody of a LATAM agent, he may be transferred to the authority of SHABAK (Shin Bet). Jalame Prison, near Kibbutz Yagur, one of the country's biggest kibbutzes, near Haifa, is thought of as the official place for SHABAK, but SHABAK is believed to have a number of nonmilitary safe houses within which it holds detainees. And during the time that the detainee is held by SHABAK (Shin Bet), his place of imprisonment changes frequently.

The elite of this security system is not SHABAK, but MOSSAD. This is another civilian organization dealing with foreign intelligence and counterintelligence throughout the world. Next in the pecking order is not SHABAK, but AMAN, the purely military intelligence service. Then one comes to SHABAK. Why so low on the totem pole? For one thing, SHABAK service offers no glamour of service abroad and no prestigious army uniform and all that comes with it. And for another, the work is not regarded as particularly enviable, since, as one source put it, "90 percent of its targets are Arabs."

Again, SHABAK makes no arrests. In Israel proper, a LATAM agent makes the formal arrest, although sources who have experienced arrest say that plainclothes agents (other than LATAM agents) who remain unidentified sometimes come along to watch, if not to supervise, the process. These agents may very well belong to SHABAK. In the Occupied Territories and the West Bank, military or army police make the arrests, although, again, sometimes other, unofficial agents are reported to be there.

This is an ingenious, semipublic, semiclandestine operational system, which one finds reflected elsewhere in the world.

Alongside of Iran's SAVAK was the Information Bureau of the Police and the Second Branch of the Army—directed toward fighting revolutionaries and controlling one another's actions. Coordinating the system, besides the Shah himself, was the famed Committee. The head of the Joint Committee to Combat Destructive Elements was a civilian police official, but this official was nothing more than a figurehead. The real head of the Committee was, always, a high-ranking SAVAK careerist. The real Committee head thus reported directly to the head of SAVAK. But even among the best-informed revolutionaries, the identity of the real head of the Committee was almost never known. Revolutionaries once assassinated the titular head of the Committee, more as a symbolic act of vengeance than anything else, because they knew full well that the Shah's secret police system presented no easily identifiable targets—except for the Shah himself.

The internal organization of SAVAK was thoroughly complex. One would not have thought an organization as reputedly brutal and in a sense so horridly basic in its aims and methods would have required such a considerable degree of organizational sophistication. With 30 million people, Iran presented a big job, to be sure, but it was no Union of Soviet Socialist Republics, much less even a sprawling Philippines. Still, when we obtained secret documents detailing the internal structure of SAVAK, we were astonished by the elaborate quality of the bureaucracy.

At one level of analysis, SAVAK consisted of three chief segments: (1) the central offices; (2) the main headquarters, in Tehran; and (3) the municipal SAVAK offices around the nation.

At a trial held by the revolutionary court, an accused SAVAK agent who was head of the Supervision and Control Office of SAVAK disclosed the fact that in the SAVAK headquarters in Tehran there were in fact two offices. The first office was composed of five departments, each having a separate jurisdiction: communists, religion, the universities, other educational institutions, and the entire national education system. Office Two also maintained five departments, with jurisdiction over members of city government, the ministries and banks, workers, trade unions, and dissidents in general.

But it was the central offices of SAVAK that encompassed the political landscape of Iran with an even more thorough, paranoid compulsiveness. The First Central Office was the central administrative office. Its duty was to plan and budget for SAVAK operations. The head of this office was the head of all of SAVAK. His deputies ran, among other things, the personnel, communications, operations (clandestine), protocol, and American and British liaison divisions. (The U.S. / Great Britain division was in direct and constant contact with the American embassy.) The First Central Office also had a foreign intelligence division, to coordinate SAVAK's work in that area. Another SAVAK deputy chief was responsible for the training department, which sent some agents to foreign countries for specialized programs in training. A number of agents were trained at military bases in the United States and Israel.

The Second Central Office helped coordinate the informant and informational network of SAVAK, collecting and processing data and transmitting the processed data to the First Central Office.

The Third Central Office was the most important, from the operational standpoint. Known by some as "Internal Security and Action," it was the Shah's defense base, responsible for the domestic security of the regime.

By the mid-seventies, the chairman of the Third Central Office was an accomplished torturer named General Parviz Sabeti, also known popularly as the "kingpin of SAVAK." The head of the Third Central Office, an appointee of the Shah, was also the unofficial head of the Committee.

Now, to make matters even more complicated, the Third Central Office was further divided into four departments, a number of subdivisions, and a secretariat.

Briefly, the departments went as follows: The First Department was put in charge of controlling and suppressing all anti-Shah political and professional organizations both within and outside of the country. And all information pertinent to such individuals and organizations was funneled to the First Department of the Third Central Office. All of SAVAK's staff torturers ultimately reported to the First Department of the Third Central Office. (However, student activity outside of Iran was coordinated by a special envoy who reported directly to the Shah and to the Iranian embassies; it would appear that antistudent intelligence and counterintelligence went forward on a two-track basis: through the special envoy and through the First Department.)

The Second Department had several subdivisions, dealing with workers' organizations, controlled newspapers, farmers' cooperatives, public transportation companies, and so on.

The Third Department kept the files.

The Fourth Department, among other duties, was involved in official censorship and the preparation of training materials for SAVAK agents. It was also through the Fourth Department that the Committee, in conjunction with the Third Central Office, recruited its interrogators.

Now back to the *central offices.* . . . The Fourth Central Office was in charge of the protection and control of SAVAK agents. The Fifth Central Office supervised the technical operations (surveillance equipment) and doled out the supplies. However, the tracing and surveillance teams, once entirely under the control of this office, became too cumbersome and numerous for one office to control, so that each of the central offices with their branches throughout the country began to develop and supervise their own tracing and surveillance teams. This inevitably led to a loss of central control and a tremendous proliferation in the amount of surveillance utilized in Iran.

The Sixth Central Office of SAVAK was a sort of purchasing and detailed budgetary operation. It worried over the budgets of SAVAK offices outside of the country.

The Seventh Central Office sucked in news and political information from public, nonsecret sources, for ultimate collation in the Third Department of the Third Central Office. This Seventh Central Office also provided information and intelligence analyses to the secret police and intelligence services of a number of allies, including NATO countries, Israel, and the United States. The Seventh Central Office especially read and digested information published in the Middle East.

The Eighth Central Office was in charge of spying on, and controlling, foreign embassies and foreign diplomats in Iran.

And finally, the Ninth Central Office controlled the country's passport offices, under the cover of which it investigated targets, applicants for visas, applicants for passports, and so on—for the preparation of SAVAK's comprehensive files. In this capacity, agents assigned to the Eighth Central Office were involved in extensive surveillance, both on-scene and electronic.

SAVAK's Byzantine bureaucracy was not, however, terribly unique in its complicatedness. The most effective secret police organizations, faced with very difficult internal-security problems, seem to expand almost organically into impossibly obscure government bureaucracies. For instance, the secret police system of Yugoslavia may have even more institutional complications than that of SAVAK. It may very well be one of the most sophisticated secret police systems in Eastern Europe, which, if true, would be saying something fairly impressive. Like the country itself, the secret police system is organized along geographical lines. There is a central office in Belgrade, as well as offices in the six republics (Serbia, Croatia, Slovenia, Bosnia, Macedonia, and Montenegro).

Each republic, in essence, has its own UDBA—autonomous yet subject to central control, just like the republics themselves. But Tito apparently played his secret police cards so close to his vest that little is known about UDBA and KOS (military intelligence service) even among well-informed exile circles, not to mention the general Yugoslavian public. Tito, then, succeeded where the Shah failed: although UDBA, like SAVAK, became an uncomfortably familiar name popularized by those arrested, or friends of those arrested, and so on . . . Tito succeeded in keeping the precise organization and operations of UDBA more of a mystery to the public. As Jakša Kušan, publisher of *New Croatia,* or *Nova Hrvastska,* a bimonthly Croatian refugee newspaper based in London, wrote us when we queried him on some fine points of the Yugoslavian police structure, "Due to Western policy of non-interference toward Yugoslavia, there are no defectors from these services to report how they function and what sort of division of labor they have inside. Even the names of these services are not consistent and vary even in official reports." The Federal Secretariat for Foreign Affairs, for example, is usually known under a cover name, the Directorate of Research and Documentation.

At any rate, you can be sure that the names vary in official reports not because the Tito government itself was confused but because the Tito government wanted to create a certain degree of tactical confusion. In Yugoslavia, which Tito held together relatively well for more than two decades, the secret police is precisely as secret as Tito felt it had to be.

Appendix 2

A Torture Glossary

SOME COMMON TORTURE TECHNIQUES

(Used by secret police forces practicing the severest forms of interrogation and repression. Based on a survey of practices used throughout the seventies and early eighties as alleged by former political prisoners from around the world.)

ANAL TORTURES

A variety of instruments will be inserted separately into the anus in order to induce intense physical pain and a sense of humiliation on the part of the victim. Instruments that have been used to this effect are:

Broken bottle.

Broken needle.

Heated iron bar.

Stick.

A *tube* through which water is driven at very high pressure will be inserted into the victim. The water may be boiling hot.

BEATING TECHNIQUES

Varieties (the jargon listed here has been used by both the torturers and the tortured):

Hands and feet of the prisoner will be tied up, and then a very hard piece of wood or a long bar of metal will be placed between the knees so that the prisoner cannot turn left or right. Now immobilized, the prisoner will be beaten.

"The Jap Method": The arms and legs of a prisoner will be bound and a pole will be inserted between the knots. The guards can now lift the prisoner by the pole; or they may put each end of the pole on a table so that the prisoner is suspended between the tables like a carcass. For added effect, a pulley may be attached to the stick and to the movement of a clock to synchronize the beatings: the prisoner will swing like a pendulum from one pair of torturers to another, first to receive a hail of clubs, then to endure a flurry of whips, until the vengeance of the clubbings and whippings becomes insanely timed, like the ticks of a clock.

"Palm Torture": Also known as *el teléfono* (the telephone) or *golpes de campana* (ringing the bell), the palms of the torturer will be used as cymbals to slap the ears of the victim. The slaps begin softly, then increase in strength and number. At the climax, the ears are hit with such force that bleeding results. Deafness often occurs as a result of this torture technique, as well as imbalance and chronic head-shaking if the concussions suffered as a result of the beatings cause the ear canals to break.

"The San Juanico Bridge": The victim will be ordered to lie in a most awkward fashion—with his feet on one bed and his head on a second bed, so that the rest of his body is suspended in midair. Then, whenever he lets his body fall or sag, he will be severely punished with beatings and kicks. In the Philippines, for instance, a bridge constructed by the martial-law administration, connecting the islands of Samar and Leyte, inspired this technique.

"Tea Party": A group of guards enter a cell and beat the prisoner, using fists and clubs. In another version of this technique, prisoners are made to remain standing in the corners of their cells, sometimes on one foot but usually at attention. The prisoner's standing period is interspersed with beatings.

CIGARETTE TORTURES

A lighted cigarette will be applied to some part of the victim's body—arms, chest, face, etc.

Variations:

A cigarette lighter (or gasoline) will be applied to various parts of the body, particularly the toes (and then set alight).

A cigarette-lighter flame will be used to burn the genitals and the pubic hair.

COLD TORTURES

The prisoners will be stored in extremely cold rooms, variously described by prisoners around the world as "cold cells," "cool rooms," "refrigerator cells," etc. Some prisoners mention that air conditioners are obviously used to reduce the room temperatures.

Variations:

Being interrogated in a very cold room while wearing only very light clothing.

Being stripped naked and made to sit or kneel on blocks of ice.

Being stripped naked in sub-zero weather and doused with water.

Being plunged into an ice-cold bath or forced to take an ice-cold shower.

CONFINEMENT

Aside from the obvious—being jailed in tiny, overcrowded cells—prisoners describe being forced into exceedingly small rooms used specifically for torture, or being forced to climb into boxlike structures barely large enough to stand up in.

Variations:

"Special booths," which are smaller than telephone booths—barely large enough to hold one seated person—are used. The prisoner is left in the booth for an indefinite period of time and is taken out periodically for further interrogation and/or torture sessions.

"Small boxes," in which prisoners are kept in total darkness, are used as places of confinement. The prisoner is left without any food, sometimes for several days. Prisoners say the boxes are not big enough for them to stand or move around in. In tropical climates, the boxes are half buried in the ground, so that the ground heat penetrates the boxes, thereby creating ovens.

"Wooden boxes," just large enough for a human body, are stuffed with a prisoner and then propped up at an odd angle so as to produce vertigo; then the box is pounded by the torturers with sticks, so that the wooden box becomes a drum—with the prisoner trapped inside. This torture leaves no observable physical scars, although deafness is commonly induced.

DEPRIVATION OF SLEEP

Prisoners may be deprived of sleep for periods of time ranging from a number of hours up to fifteen days, sometimes even longer.

Variations:

Lights are kept on in the prison cell throughout the night in order to prevent the prisoner from sleeping.

Cold water is thrown on the victim in order to keep him awake.

DOG TORTURES

Dogs will be used to intimidate and attack.

Sometimes dogs are used to commit acts of sexual depravation on prisoners. According to one United Nations report, in one Latin American country there is a torture center at which dogs are specially trained to do precisely that.

One prisoner in a Latin American country testified that she was hoisted by her hair until her feet were above the ground. Then the guards released dogs from a cage. They prowled beneath her, barking menacingly. She fainted and was then revived. After a while the guards let her down to the floor. There the dogs attacked her.

DRUG TORTURES

The most commonly used drugs for torture are the powerful, tranquilizing neuroleptic drugs. Those used most often are: aminazin, haloperidol, triftazin, insulin, and sulphazin. Other drugs that have been applied to political prisoners are tizertsin, sanapax, etaperazin, phrenolong, trisedil, mazjeptil, seduksin, and motiden-depo. These drugs are administered in a variety of forms, including injections by syringes, solvents in solutions for drinking, and in tablet form.

While these drugs have legitimate uses in the treatment of persons suffering from psychiatric disorders, their use must be carefully regulated. These tranquilizers were designed to treat specific disorders, and the application of the drugs to persons not suffering from the specific disorders for which the drugs were intended can cause great harm.

Some side effects of improper use of the drugs are skin disorders, blood disorders, pigmentation disorders, extreme sensitivity of the eyes to light, weight loss or gain, dryness of the mouth, reduced blood pressure, and jaundice. One particularly bad side effect: the so-called "Parkinsonian" disorders, including muscular rigidity, paucity and slowness of body movement, and a constant desire to change the body's position. And while sulphazin was once used in a number of countries to treat schizophrenia and other ailments, it has generally come into disfavor—except at the hands of the secret police, who have noticed that it causes a raging fever so intense that a patient is virtually incapacitated for up to three days after a single injection.

Insulin shock therapy involves increasing the dosage of insulin over a period of days until the patient goes into shock and "hypoglycemic coma." Other drugs allegedly used to obtain confessions are morphine and sodium pentothal. The latter is described by many prisoners as "truth serum." Morphine is administered so that withdrawal symptoms of "patients" will induce them to confess.

ELECTRIC SHOCK

Electric shock is one of the most commonly used torture techniques of the secret police of a wide variety of countries. Electric shock is easy to administer and it often produces instantaneous results (i.e., acute pain leading to confession). Some electric shock units are quite portable and can be taken to the victim's home or place of work. There, while the suspect sits on the sofa, the interrogator simply plugs the unit into the wall socket or uses a portable electric cattle prod.

Variations:

Cranker dynamo: terminals will be tied to various places on the body. For the male prisoner, one terminal will be tied to the penis, the other to the forefinger. The handle of the cranker dynamo will then be turned, producing a flash of current ranging from a low voltage to ninety volts, which jolts the body. The usual dosage: five consecutive jolts lasting about one minute each.

"Dragon chair": a kind of metallic plate used to administer the electric shock.

"The Machine": described by prisoners of one Latin American country as a sort of "loincloth." In one application, the floor under the detainees, who were hung up on ropes with the "loincloth" attached, was wetted down and covered with coarse salt crystals, so that when the victims tried to set their feet on the floor, the current was grounded and the electric shock was set off.

"Parilla": The "grill," as it is called, permits electric shock treatment in this way: the prisoner is tied to a metal bed and current is applied to the body over sessions lasting as long as two hours.

In one electric shock session, a prisoner was submerged in a barrel of superheated oil, then laid out on a mattress to receive electric shock treatment; after he fainted, he was lowered into a bath of icy water to revive.

FALANGA

A very widely used torture technique, "falanga" is the prolonged beating of the soles of the feet with sticks and other blunt instruments, although sometimes just with the hands.

FINGER TORTURES

Variations:

Pencils are placed between the victim's fingers, and then his hands are squeezed.

The hands are tied tightly together and needles are inserted underneath the fingernails. Sometimes a nail will be used.

Fingers will be simply squeezed violently, or hands will be jabbed randomly by needles.

FOOT TORTURES

Variations:

Running barefoot through thorn-covered vegetation.

Being forced to remove one's shoes while police agents place about three grains of gravel in each one. The prisoner is then forced to put his shoes on again and is made to stand on a rock with his hands on his head, so that the gravel eats into the flesh of his heels.

Standing barefoot on the edges of bricks for hours.

Lifting weights above the head for long periods, sometimes while wearing shoes containing pebbles.

Having pins stuck underneath the toenails.

Having a flat, hot iron applied to the soles of the feet.

Having the feet placed in boiling oil.

Having vehicles drive over the hands and feet, causing multiple fractures.

GAGGING TECHNIQUES

Variations:

A filthy rag, sometimes soaked in urine, will be shoved down the victim's throat. During this process, the throat may be grasped so that the windpipe is cut off, thereby inducing violent choking.

Rags soaked in excrement will also be used to induce gagging.

Gasoline and/or hot pepper will be forced into the mouth.

HANGING TECHNIQUES

Variations:

"Parrot's perch"—also known as "the pigeon" and the "swing system." The prisoner is suspended, usually by the wrists or arms and the ankles. An iron bar will be passed under the knees and the whole body left suspended. In this position, the victim will often receive electric shock. In another variation, the prisoner is tied up like this in a tub or pool, and electricity is applied to the water. One victim alleges that while hanging from the "parrot's perch," the end of a reed was placed in his anus and a piece of cotton soaked in gasoline was lit at the other end of the reed.

Other hanging techniques:

In one African country, a separate handcuff was placed on each wrist of the victim, each handcuff was joined to a piece of rope tied to a tree, and the victim was suspended.

"Banana bind": Name given to the technique of being hung up and bound with hands and feet behind the back, then being beaten.

Plain hangings by the hands or the feet from the ceiling.

HOODING TORTURES

Hoods placed over the victim's head can be made of a variety of materials, including rubber, black cloth, a black pillow slip, or a sugar sack. Periods of time as long as ninety-five days, four months, and longer have been used to hood the victim.

Variations:

A rubber hood is used, into which an insecticide is sprayed.

A leather hood is placed over the prisoner's head and is stuck to his face with chemical adhesives.

NAIL TORTURES

The most commonly used nail torture is the *prying apart* of fingernails and toenails—with pliers or whatever.

PSYCHOLOGICAL TORTURES

In addition to the very sophisticated torture techniques involving the administration of mind-distorting drugs and the application of elaborate torture equipment, there are some terribly simple psychological tortures that are designed to do nothing more than steal the prisoner's dignity. Examples:

Being stripped and forced to crawl on the ground and bark like a dog while being beaten.

Being stripped and made to crouch like a rabbit.

Being forced to hop like a frog while being beaten.

The "duck walk": the hands of the victim are handcuffed under his legs, and while in this squatting position, he is made to walk at the same time that he is being beaten.

Threats:

Threats of death and assassination. In several cases, the barrel of a revolver was put in the victim's mouth when he was threatened with death.

Threats of maiming.

Threats of rape.

Threats of electric shock.

Threats of forced injections as well as the forcible intake of a variety of medicines.

Intimidation:

Supplying blankets or bowls marked with a cross to political prisoners, the cross signifying previous use by prisoners with leprosy or tuberculosis.

Intimidation by forcing prisoners to listen to other prisoners' screams. Or moving prisoners to cells within earshot of other prisoners who are being violently interrogated.

Placing political prisoners in cells with mentally defective patients.

Other psychological tortures:

"Cerrojos": Literally translated, "bolts." The technique involves the frequent fastening and unfastening of bolts on the cell doors so as to keep prisoners awake and in fear of being subjected anew to torture sessions at any time.

"Zafarranchos" (from the Spanish verb "zafarse," to run or slip away): The practice of regularly holding a form of maneuvers consisting of a simulated defense of the camp against an imaginary attack from the outside. The mock battles begin with shooting, at which point the prisoners are obliged to keep absolutely still, wherever they are, for a long time, knowing that at the slightest movement the machine guns will open fire; the lights are turned off and the soldiers run about with their loaded rifles aimed at the prisoners.

One detainee was ordered at gunpoint to murder other detainees by hitting them on the head with a hammer, ax, or car axle. Sometimes this was done on a group of detainees who were lined up. The survivor was then shot.

SENSORY DEPRIVATION

The victim is forced to sit facing a white wall for up to six days, sometimes more, with no sleep allowed. After two days, this can cause hallucinations.

Several detainees have reported that they were placed in cells that were painted entirely black, and that some of the furniture was draped in black cloth as well.

High-pitched sounds are piped into a room, causing great irritation to the listener.

SEXUAL TORTURES

The chief form of sexual torture is rape, used on both men and women. Sometimes threats of rape are made, other times rape itself occurs.

Variations:

A man reports having been raped by three guards, and after the assault, police stuck copies of his group's political manifesto into his anus.

Rape with a truncheon or other object inserted into the anus or vagina, twisting and tearing.

Sexual threats:

Threatened castration: A cord is tied around the prisoner's testicles while he lies on his back. The cord is then pulled, forcing him to arch his back.

Threats of sterilization.

Threats of raping the detainee's wife or other female relatives.

Forcing women to lift their skirts up before prison guards.

SIMULATED EXECUTIONS

These are accomplished either by hanging or by firing squad. In the case of the firing squad, the prisoner actually faces the squad, usually blindfolded, and the rifles are fired, but with blanks in them. Sometimes pistols are placed to the victim's head and then blanks are fired.

SITTING TORTURES

Squatting on an imaginary chair until one's muscles collapse.

Squatting with arms held straight out for long periods of time.

Sitting on the edge of a chair, arms outstretched in a forward position and loaded with something heavy to carry. The prisoner is made to maintain this squatting position with a weight on his toes. He must stay in that position sometimes for as long as two hours. When his arms or feet sag or his legs begin to give way, he is hit hard on the shins.

Crouching for one hour with the head and one hand pushed through a small window.

STANDING TORTURES

Victims will be made to stand for long periods of time, sometimes for days.

Variations:

One victim was forced to stand with his legs half bent, arms out-stretched and no other means of supporting himself; in this position he was forced to smoke five cigarettes at once and was not allowed to remove the cigarettes even after his mouth was burnt.

Sometimes the victim will be made to stand against a wall for long periods of time, off balance and with arms outstretched.

SUBMERSION TECHNIQUES

The most commonly used submersion technique involves sub-merging the victim's head under water (often very foul water) until he or she nearly drowns. This may be repeated several times, the du-ration of each submersion being decided according to the victim's pulse.

Variations:

"The *pileta*": the bath. The prisoner will be held under the water of a tank that is filled with human excrement. He will be held by four or five policemen and forced to swallow huge quantities, until the lungs are at the bursting point. This process will be repeated over and over for a period of several hours.

Immersion in water with the head covered by a cloth hood is yet another variation. When the hood becomes wet, it sticks to the nose and mouth, so that when the victim is taken out of the water, breathing is practically impossible.

Total Submersion:

The victim will be tied to a pulley. A heavy stone will be attached to his feet, then he will be immersed in water. A few minutes later he will be pulled up. If he has not already drowned, he will be re-vived, interrogated, and dunked again. A septic tank filled with human excrement and blood may be used, so that the person is cov-ered from head to foot with those substances.

Variations:

In one case, the victim was handcuffed and thrown into a swim-ming pool until almost drowned.

Several countries' prisoners have alleged being buried or half buried in excrement (*not* mixed with water).

WATER TORTURE

Water or some other liquid is forced up the victim's nostrils. Sev-eral liquids may be used, including:

Water.

Gasoline.

Carbonated beverages—called by some prisoners the "7-Up cure." As described by one ex-officer of an Asian country, the torturer shakes the 7-Up bottle, opens it, and pours the contents into the nose at intervals.

Variations:

As described by one former torturer: "To extract information from the victim, he is laid out on a narrow bench to which his hands are tied with wet cloths so as not to show any marks of torture. Then another piece of wet cloth is placed over the mouth and nose. With just three tablespoons of water on the already saturated rag, a man can drown. When he is dead by asphyxiation, he is revived by thumping out the water from his lungs . . . and interrogation continues. . . ."

WARM-UP TORTURES

The purpose of warm-up torture is, literally, to introduce the victim (and perhaps the torturer as well) to the idea that torture is about to occur. It is also believed that if the less severe tortures are applied first, the resulting intimidation will be sufficient to induce confession, and the torture can be stopped. In one country this technique is called *"la calentada,"* which means, roughly, the "heat-up." Some of the techniques of the conventional warm-up session are:

Beating by fists, rifles, and pistol butts.

"El Teléfono" (smashing inward with the palms over the victim's ears, so as to break the eardrums).

Exposure to dehydration in the hot sun.

The 7-Up cure.

Karate blows or blows applied with short sticks.

MISCELLANEOUS TORTURES

Acid burns on the eyes, testicles, vagina, or other parts of the body. Also, burnings by oil or water.

Forced ingestion of vomit; smearing the victim with his own vomit.

Extraction of the teeth with pliers.

The spraying of tear gas into the prisoner's cell.

Plucking the eyebrows or pubic hairs.

Pouring scalding-hot water over the victim, then, immediately after, pouring ice-cold water over him. In one case, the process was allegedly repeated alternately for one half hour.

Sticking a hot iron bar into the victim's nose or eye.

"Wheel torture"—a wheel rim is struck with iron bars while the victim's head is inside it.

Pouring kerosene into the vagina of a woman, then setting it afire.

Forced inhalation of ground chili peppers.

Gouging out the victim's eyes so that they are left hanging out of their sockets.

Slow killing, i.e., shooting a man in the arm, leg, or chest and letting him bleed to death.

Variations:

A body organ is cut off and placed in the dying person's mouth.

Cutting a victim's flesh and forcing him to eat it raw, until he bleeds to death while living on his own flesh; or cutting the flesh, roasting it, and letting the victim feed on it until he dies.

"Immobilization": In its simplest form, this technique consists of strapping the "patient" tightly to his bed and leaving him there.

Variations:

The inmate is tightly wrapped in strips of wet sheeting. The sheeting tightens as it dries, causing great pain. In reported cases, hospital staffs have repeated the process several times on the same patient.

Being chained or handcuffed to pipes.

THIRST TORTURES

Lacing a prisoner's water with soap, or forcing the victim to eat a package of salt, then denying him water.

Rubbing pepper on sensitive areas such as the genitals, nose, and underarms.

INSTRUMENTS OF TORTURE

"Shock baton": This is a rod-shaped instrument, 38 centimeters in length and 750 grams in weight. Within the shaft is a generator, in principle an induction apparatus, which is driven by three 1.5-volt dry cells. At the end of the rod there are two metal electrodes 7 millimeters apart. Each electrode is 10 millimeters in diameter and 2 millimeters high. Two current-bearing metal rings, 1 millimeter thick, are placed on the rod. The rod is activated by pressing a button in the middle of the handle. The intensity of the stimulus is controlled by a voltage divider placed between the rod and the stimulating electrodes, which are a copy of the rod electrodes. According to Amnesty International, this shock baton is manufactured in Minnesota.

Wooden rollers: Often called by prisoners the "roller treatment," rollers are used when the prisoner is forced to lie on a bench to which he is tied by his hands and ankles; a heavy wooden roller is placed across his thighs and rolled over his legs by a policeman standing on the roller.

"Hot Table": An iron frame, like a bed frame, covered with wire mesh that is electrically heated like a toaster. The prisoner is strapped to the table while it is heated, until it becomes red hot.

Whips: A variety of materials may be used in the makings of a whip for the purposes of torture. Some of the materials used are:

Cow's nerve.

Dried hippopotamus skin.

Thongs and lead balls; *El Sargento,* or "The Sergeant," is the name given to this cat-o'-nine-tails whip.

Leather belts.

Wires knotted together.

Rhinoceros whip.

Other Instruments Used for Beatings:

Family-size drink bottle.

Coconut-tree limb.

Pistol.

Wooden hammer.

Plastic or rubber hose.

Long, spiked tail of a tropical fish called the "pari fish."

Firm central rib of the "makalani" palm branch.

Wooden stick, or "lath."

Clubs·

A club wrapped in rubber, with metal bands around it. "National Constitution"—the name given to one favorite club of one department of a Latin American secret police organization.

Canes:

A cane more than one meter long and a little over one centimeter thick. (Sometimes when this cane is used, the prisoner is placed over a trestle that has padding, to prevent accidental injury to the spine. In this position, the prisoner is beaten.)

A rattan one yard long, and thick, "like a man's arm," according to one prisoner, is used to administer the *falanga* torture.

Other Instruments of Torture:

Cattle prods used to administer electric-shock torture.

(Sources for this glossary include reports from the United States State Department, Amnesty International, the International Commission of Jurists, the International League of Human Rights, and court testimony.)

Appendix 3

Human Rights in Foreign Countries and U. S. Foreign Policy

An unacceptable degree of simplemindedness tends to infect most discussions about human rights and foreign policy. For one thing, the issue is often discussed as if Washington were almost solely responsible for the existence of type-A secret police institutions among its allies. That view, of course, resists the idea that our allies possess any substantial degree of independence. It virtually assumes that these internal-security systems are drawn up like new-model cars in Detroit and presented as the latest internal-security models to our customers abroad. Left out of this equation is the possibility that these "customers" have ideas, traditions, and cultural predilections of their own. As Yale Professor James S. Fishbein has wisely put it, to fail to attribute "any substantial independence to countries that are, in some sense, within America's sphere of influence" is to suggest that "the entire burden for all the political crimes of the non-communist world can be brought home to Washington."

Blame heaped on Washington for the occurrence of human-rights violations in allied countries probably comes from a number of sources, but one of them surely is a mistaken and absolutely false analogy between the CIA and the KGB. The mistake arises in not understanding that while the KGB system of internal security will be imposed on a Soviet ally and its maintenance enforced rigorously by Moscow, U.S. policy is far less direct and authoritarian. What SAVAK agents did in Iran is surely better understood as Iranian against Iranian in the broad context of Persian history than as an entirely original imposition of a heinous CIA scheme.

Nevertheless, it would be as fatuous and disingenuous to underestimate Washington's role in the internal policies of allied regimes as to overestimate it. After all, Washington's role can be for the good as well as the bad. The Carter administration's human-rights policy was not without some punch. Human-rights conditions were probably improved by Carter's policy in a number of countries, including the Dominican Republic, Ecuador, Ghana, Nigeria, Peru, Bangladesh, Sudan, Nepal, Guinea, Thailand, and possibly even Cuba. No doubt the dispatching of U.S. observers to political trials in such places as Thailand, South Africa, and the Soviet Union have helped strengthen international pressure. We should continue to include a human-rights component in our foreign policy without jeopardizing national security. We need only to move prudently, slowly, and sensitively, avoiding grand pronouncements that strike most foreigners as either hypocritical or naïve.

But it would be a mistake to overestimate the liberalizing effect of U.S. human-rights policies, just as it would be a mistake to overestimate the influence of the CIA on internal-security institutions. There is a practical limit to U.S. influence as well as ethical reasons for such limits. If the United States cannot be the policeman of the world, and if the United States should not be the secret policeman of the world, then it might also follow that the United States ought not attempt to be the moral policeman of the world. The first responsibility of our government is to ensure the internal security of our own country while maintaining the guarantees of political and human rights.

This task will surely be more difficult in the years to come than it ever has been. Whatever energies our government may have left after it has gotten its own house in order (and we are a long way from that) may perhaps be focused on improving the internal-security practices of other governments. But it must be understood that such an approach will continue to be a lonely one. Most governments will not give a damn about the internal-security policies of other countries. Their concern will focus on national-security and military-security questions. "We deal with Argentina as a country," explained Chinese Vice-Premier Deng Ziaoping, in an interview with Oriana Fallaci, defending China's relationships with such countries as Argentina, Chile, and Cambodia. "We always handle these matters in the interests of our relations with a country and a people. Yes, this is our principle. As for Chile, listen. I know that many progressive friends don't understand our attitude toward Chile but. . . . Let me explain better. . . . When Allende was killed and the democratic forces of Chile got into great difficulties, we studied the question whether we should maintain an embassy there or cut off our relations. Then we thought we should stay. . . . We look reality square in its face."

It is often recommended that the United States withhold support for regimes with repressive secret police systems. But should the United States help set up internal-security mechanisms for regimes that request such help? We have our doubts, because it is probably correct to suggest that the American experience per se may be unique and thus cannot provide an ally with a viable transplant that will reflect well on U.S. intentions as well as provide an ally with an internal-security mechanism that won't create more problems than it was designed to solve (e.g., a SAVAK). On the one hand, the model provided by the United States (CIA/FBI) derives from a society that has many built-in checks and balances that have so far prevented the emergence of a Gestapo-like intelligence unit. But the model is often offered to a society in which no comparable checks and balances exist. The result may be a disaster of distressing proportions. If one talks to government officials in countries where there is a repressive internal-security system, one will hear over and over again that their security systems are *nothing but* their own versions of the FBI/CIA. This is not true, but the assertion is understandable. The American system of policing is practically incomprehensible to many outsiders. Taken as a whole, it is a confusing cacophony of compartmentalized agencies, historical jealousies, political rivalries, and geographic fragmentation. What is surprising about the system is not how poorly it works but that it works at all. But, whatever its positive features, exportability is not one of them.

If the United States has any wisdom at all to offer foreign allies, it is probably a sort of negative wisdom: avoid creating a centralized domestic intelligence agency insulated from political accountability. Even with this advice, the United States would probably be wiser to rely on surrogates, such as the Japanese, to convey the message. With its past history of helping to create SAVAKs and DINAs, Washington, like Moscow, is perhaps better off leaving the business of exporting internal-security mechanisms to allies that are not quite so tainted by the past. In this context, allies with internal-security problems might be better off studying systems like the Japanese rather than the U.S. system of internal security. The Japanese avoid a centralized approach by placing internal-security units within the structure of local police units. These local security bureaus report directly to a national Security Bureau, which is accountable not to a single minister (i.e., no intelligence "czar" here) but to a group of five commissioners who are appointed by the Prime Minister with the consent of both houses of the national Diet.

"It is very important not to have autonomous security police like DINA," said a very high-ranking Japanese security official, interviewed in Washington last year. "If the security police are independent, they will go off recklessly." The only other piece of advice that the United States is in any position to offer anyone is the need for a clear separation between domestic security and foreign intelligence. In this context, Washington might be wise to refer questions from allies to the West Germans, who insist on an inviolable demarcation of internal versus external functions. "This is why the West German system is far more just than the East German system," said one former high CIA official. "In general, the unity of internal and external intelligence is a big negative. It is much better to separate the two."

Chapter Notes

CHAPTER ONE

   1. Mr. Eugenio Velasco told us the story of his arrest and deportation in two separate interviews conducted in Los Angeles on June 28, 1979, at UCLA, where he was teaching law, and in Washington, D.C., on July 17, 1980, where he is now working for a private corporation. In addition to the antigovernment activities we have recounted in this chapter, Mr. Velasco was tried in Chile before the Council of War in 1974: a letter he wrote to the National Association of Chile denounced the human-rights violations that were sweeping the country. The trial lasted nine hours, and the prosecutor was a former law student of his. In the legal maneuvering between the two, the former professor outdueled the former student, who, after consulting with the Minister of the Interior, dropped the case. Mr. Velasco was then released.

   2. Interestingly, the statement by Dwight David Eisenhower about the values of persuasion as opposed to force was used in 1979 by Boyden Associates, Inc., in a newspaper advertisement about leadership qualities around the world.

3. The black South African activist re-created his arrest and imprisonment in an interview on October 19, 1978. He is now living in London, where he is active in the Black Consciousness Movement; he was interviewed on October 19, 1979.

5. Ozra Moini Araghi, mother of Esmail Araghi, who was executed by SAVAK for his revolutionary activities in 1971, briefed us in Los Angeles, where she was visiting other members of her family, on November 19 and 20, 1979. Mrs. Araghi's two sons (besides Esmail) were staunch antigovernment activists under the regime of the Shah. One of her sons was jailed after his participation in the robbery of a bank in Isfahan. The robbery, she says, was politically motivated, but because her son would never admit this to SAVAK authorities, he was sentenced to prison for ten years. The authorities were unable to find conclusive evidence against him, and he was not killed. Imprisoned for eight years, he was freed along with other SAVAK prisoners at the time of the Iranian Revolution, in 1979. Mrs. Araghi's other son was imprisoned because of a bomb explosion in his military garrison, for which, she says, he was blamed simply because, as the brother of two revolutionaries, he was suspect. After a few months' imprisonment, he was tried and released, she suspects, because the real culprit responsible for the bombing in the garrison was found. Mrs. Araghi said to us: "You asked me how I experienced SAVAK? I live with it all of the time. It is in my home. Anytime there are phone calls or the doorbell rings, I think it is SAVAK."

For information on the Committee, see our notes for Chapter Five, Section 3.

6. For a very brief, elementary historical overview of secret police, see William H. Harris and Judith S. Levey, eds., The New Columbia Encyclopedia (New York and London: Columbia University Press, 1975), p. 2466. For a more sophisticated historical overview, see Tom Bowden, Beyond the Limits of the Law (Harmondsworth, Middlesex: Penguin Books, 1978). Of particular interest is Bowden's essay on "Personalized Police Forces," which covers topics including the Oprichina, the personal police of Czar Ivan IV, the political police of Mussolini (OVRA), and on through the contemporary scene.

On Joseph Fouché, Minister of Police under Napoleon, see Tom Bowden, op. cit., pp. 54–57; and Ray Ellsworth Cubberly, The Role of Fouché During the Hundred Days (Madison: Department of History, University of Wisconsin, 1969). Of special interest are the memoirs of Fouché himself: Joseph Fouché, The Memoirs of Joseph Fouché, Duke of Otranto, Minister of the General Police of France, 2 vols. (London: H. S. Nichols, 1896). On the haute police, see Tom Bowden, op. cit., pp. 54–57.

CHAPTER TWO

1. Romy Capulong was interviewed about the agents' search for him and the way in which he managed to escape from the Philippines on March 12, 1980. Mr. Capulong was politically active in a variety of organizations: Lakas ng Bayan (People's Power), an organization of political leaders opposed to martial law; the Interim National Assembly Association, an organization of former members of the House of Representatives and delegates to a Constitutional Convention organized by former President Diosdado Macapagal in 1975; the Liberal Party, one of the two major political parties in the Philippines before the imposition of martial law; and the National Union for Democracy and Freedom, an umbrella organization of opposition groups in the Philippines. In one document relating to his petition for asylum in the United States, Capulong was asked to state what he thought would happen to him if he returned to the Philippines: "I would be arrested, detained without bail indefinitely, held incommunicado and tortured to force me to reveal the names of those who prepared 'Octopus' and those printing and circulating it, to serve as a stern warning to other oppositionists. They would try me by a kangaroo military court and deny my constitutional rights to due process and fair hearing by an impartial tribunal."

2. The exchange between Mr. Sidney Kentridge, barrister for the Biko family, and Colonel Goosen of the South African Security Police, which took place at the inquiry into the mysterious circumstances surrounding Steve Biko's death, appears in Donald Woods, *Biko* (Harmondsworth, Middlesex: Penguin Books, 1979), p. 281.

The SAVAK cables outlining some agents' mishaps, and the subsequent warning to agents to observe certain important precautions in their work, were reprinted by the Confederation of Iranian Students (National Front), in a makeshift document titled *SAVAK: Documents on Iranian Secret Police* (December, 1976), p. 225. The first cable is dated November 19, 1970; the second, February 3, 1976. This document was made available to us by Iranian exiles in the United States, after we tried to obtain it from the Washington embassy of the Islamic Revolutionary Government. But left-wing Iranian exiles, keeping it close to the vest, have been quite selective in permitting access to the document.

The account of the police agent whose murder actually led to the deaths of three other security officials, including two agents from SAVAK, was provided by Dr. Reza Ghanadian, a cancer researcher and former National Front activist during an interview conducted in London on October 9, 1979. The National Front movement was a loose coalition of various small groups led by the liberal democratic leader Mohammad

Mossadegh, who was overthrown by the 1953 CIA-engineered coup. Ghanadian was arrested for his activities in the National Front Movement in 1966 and was sentenced to fourteen months in detention, which he served.

Insight into the enduring competition between agents of the Taiwan Garrison Command and the Bureau of Investigation was obtained from Mr. T. M. Hsieh, in an interview on May 28, 1980. Mr. Hsieh was a magazine editor and lecturer at a military academy in Taiwan when he was first arrested in 1964. In the early seventies, Mr. Hsieh was imprisoned for belonging to organizations the government charged were designed to overthrow the government. In prison, a letter (actually his court plea) that he smuggled out to the United States put him in more hot water. He served six and one half years, from 1971 to 1977, of an almost ten-year sentence. In the end, it was international public opinion that influenced Taiwan authorities—both to release him from prison and to allow him to leave the country, which he did in 1979.

Details on the sometimes counterproductive competition among Syrian security agents came from a confidential source interviewed on July 16, 1980, in Washington, D.C.

3. For more on the testimony of the former DINA agent, see *Private Sociale Mission e.V., Sociedad Benefactora y Educaçional Dignidad,* vs. *Amnesty International, Firma Gruner und Jahr, Henri Nannen (ausgeschieden), und Herrn Kai Herman,* (3 0 123/77), Bonn: Nov. 19, 1979. Reprinted by Amnesty International, West Germany.

On pay and fringe benefits of the black Security Branch policeman in South Africa, we interviewed a confidential source in London on October 19, 1980. This source, banned for five years under the Suppression of Communism Act in February 1973, was then full-time Secretary-General of the black South African Students' Organization (SASO), one of the main organizations of the Black Consciousness movement. He was detained without charge in October 1974 under Section 6 of the Terrorism Act and was held incommunicado for a period of 166 days before being released, in April 1975. He was detained again under the Terrorism Act in August 1977. He is now living in London.

Information on the pay scale of a Philippine internal-security agent comes from interviews with Charito Planas, attorney, LABAN activist, philanthropist, and exile now living in the United States, on July 17, 18, and 19, 1979. For background information on Charito Planas, see *Time* magazine, Apr. 24, 1978, p. 24, and the Winston-Salem *Journal* 1 Dec. 1979, p. 1. Ms. Planas is a member of a very prominent Filipino family. Among the many organizations with which she was involved in the Philippines was the Chamber of Commerce, of which she was the director. As an outspoken critic of the Marcos regime, she was imprisoned for fourteen months, some of that time being spent in solitary confinement. In the spring of 1978 she ran on an opposition slate headed by former Senator Benigno Aquino for a seat in the National Assembly. After the election she went into the Philippine political underground. When Vice-President Walter Mondale was visiting the Philippines, a few months after she lost the 1978 election (which she, of course, maintains was rigged), those who were hiding Ms. Planas asked him if she could come to the United States as a political refugee. Mondale agreed, if she could escape her country undetected. She did and she has been living in the United States since then.

On the pay offered to Romanian agents of the Securitate we interviewed historian Vladimir Georgescu, at the Smithsonian Institution, in Washington, D.C., on March 19, 1980. For more information on Dr. Georgescu, see our notes for Chapter Three, Section 4.

On the special shops designated for Polish military- and security-police officials, see New York *Times*, Aug. 28, 1980, and Los Angeles *Times*, Sept. 2, 1980, Part I, p. 16, which mentions that ". . . key . . . military and police officers have access to their own special shops where high-quality domestic and imported goods are sold."

On privileges awarded to the KGB agent, we interviewed several sources: Mr. Friedrich Nerzansky, Soviet émigré who has worked for twenty-five years in the field of Soviet criminal law, including fifteen years as a criminal investigator in the U.S.S.R. Procurator's Office, January 26, 1980 (for more on Mr. Nerzansky see notes for Chapter Three, Section 3); and Mr. Eli Valk, former Zionist activist now living in the United States, January 24, 1980 (for more on Mr. Valk see notes for Chapter Six, Section 7). We also interviewed other Eastern European exiles who remain in close contact with exiles of the U.S.S.R. with the help of certain human-rights organizations in the United States; and in October of 1979 a former member of the Soviet Academy of Sciences, now living in exile in London.

On the rewards granted to Brigada Blanca agents, of Mexico, and the high-profile style within which they operate, we interviewed Mr. Francisco Fernández Ponte, Washington bureau chief of *Excelsior*, on March 21, 1980 (for more on Mr. Fernández Ponte see notes for Chapter Three, Section 2); Professor Robert Goldman, of American University Law School, on March 18, 1980 (for more on Mr. Goldman see notes for Chapter Three, Section 2); and Mexican journalist Jesús Blancornelas on March 20, 1980 (for more on Mr. Blancornelas see also the notes for Chapter Three, Section 2).

On SAVAK agents' salaries and "perks," we interviewed Dr. Ghanadian on October 9, 1979. It is important to keep in mind that although both salary and fringe benefits granted to secret police agents may be the chief incentive for service, some agents no doubt feel morally and patriotically obliged to serve: See the testimony of the former Tonton Macoutes agent in the case of *Haitian Refugee Center et al., Plaintiff,* vs. *Benjamin Civiletti et al., Defendants,* Vol. 5 (79-2086-Civ-JLK), Miami, Fla., 1980, p. 43: ". . . a Macoutes gives his body and soul to Duvalier. . . . It is not a question of days that I was at the barracks. . . ."

On the free rein to ransom given to Ugandan members of the Air Force, see report of the International Commission of Jurists, *Uganda and Human Rights: Reports to the U.N. Commission on Human Rights* (Geneva: International Commission of Jurists, 1977), pp. 17–18; and Amnesty International, *Human Rights in Uganda* (London: Amnesty International, 1978), p. 12.

On the Triple A death-squad agents of Argentina exercising their "right" to steal, see Inter-American Commission on Human Rights, *Report on the Situation of Human Rights in Argentina* (Washington, D.C.: General Secretariat of the Organization of American States, 1980), pp. 74–75. For the testimony stating that agents sometimes confiscate so much that they transport the goods in vans, ibid., p. 55.

On Brazilian OBAN agents confiscating an artist's work, see U. S. Congress, Senate, *Hearings before the Sub-committee on Western Hemisphere Affairs,* 92nd Cong., 1st sess., 1971. Reprinted by Amnesty International, p. 67.

For the testimony of the Haitian exile on the subject of Tonton Macoutes corruption, we consulted the deposition of a Haitian refugee who arrived in the United States in 1978. The deposition was one of many given to us by Dale Frederick Swartz, Esq., one of the lawyers defending the rights of Haitian refugees in the case of *Haitian Refugee Center et al.* vs. *Benjamin Civiletti et al.* For background information on the subject of Tonton Macoutes corruption, we interviewed Ray Joseph, a *Wall Street Journal* correspondent, on March 13, 1979. (For more on Mr. Joseph see our notes for Chapter Three, Section 2.) And on the former Tonton Macoutes's court testimony see the judge's opinion in the case of *Haitian Refugee Center et al.* vs. *Benjamin Civiletti et al.,* p. 97. The extent of corruption characterizing the Tonton Macoutes is described interestingly by a professor at a New York university, a Haitian who arrived in the United States in 1957, who testified during the proceedings for the case of *Haitian Refugee Center et al.* vs. *Benjamin Civiletti et al.,* pp. 19–26: ". . . the government . . . did not have enough money [to pay the Tonton Macoutes when they originated] . . . So they paid them very little. But they gave them the freedom to ransom the businessmen and to blackmail the businessmen, poor storekeepers in the countryside, the farmers, take their lands, and so on . . . these people were really torturers—at the same time as being economic parasites. . . . It is kind of a Mafia type of relations in the cities, particularly in Port-au-Prince. . . .

". . . If a businessman is going to order 100 bags of wheat . . . one of the Tonton Macoutes will go to him and say, 'Listen, you are going to charge $14. And $4 just for me. . . .' " And it is these circumstances, he contends, that account for the fact that the first Haitian refugees after Duvalier took over, in 1957, were chiefly intellectuals, teachers, and other professional persons who had the means to leave the country: ". . . And then the government discovered that these people could be ransomed, that they could . . . ask them [for] money for giving them . . . the right to leave the country through the embassies, or through the Immigration Service. . . ."

On the statement that "Bribes are a common practice," made by a man now living in the United States who once served in a municipal police department in the Philippines, see Sister Caridad Guidote, "Most Frequently Used Torture Methods of Marcos Police," Philippine *Times*, Aug. 12–18, 1978, pp. 1–6. And on the statement made by the Philippine citizen who spent a long period of time detained by the military in a secret camp, see Concepción Águila, "Detention Camp: Manila," *Bulletin of Concerned Asian Scholars* 6 (Nov.–Dec. 1974): 39–42.

On corruption within the ranks of the Paraguayan spy network, see Penny Lernoux, "Behind Closed Borders," *Harper's Magazine*, Feb. 1979, pp. 20–29.

On corruption in the ranks of the Cuban G-2, we interviewed a group of female Cuban political refugees now living in North Bergen, N.J., on March 15, 1980. Most of these women had been long-term political prisoners.

4. On the typical low-level white South African Security Branch agent's background, we interviewed several sources: a confidential source, a black South African activist imprisoned several times in South Africa, on October 19, 1979; another confidential source, in Berkeley, Calif., on June 13, 1979; and yet another confidential source, formerly a prominent liberal white South African defense attorney, on October 18, 1979.

On the backgrounds of Polish UB agents, we interviewed Polish émigré Irena Lasota Zabludowska on March 11, 1980, and Polish émigré Tadeusz Walendowski, on March 21, 1980. For more on Mr. Walendowski, a prominent figure among Polish rebels and Western journalists in the United States, see our notes for Chapter Three, Section 3.

On the sectors of police life from which Brigada Blanca agents, of Mexico, are recruited, see Robert K. Goldman and Daniel Jacoby, *Report of the Commission on Enquiry to Mexico Submitted to the International League for Human Rights, Fédération Internationale des Droits de l'Homme and Pax Romana* (New York: International League for Human Rights, 1978), pp. 13–14.

On the recruitment of Czechoslovakian StB agents, we interviewed, among others, a former adviser to the Dubček government and former UN official on March 13, 1980.

On the problem of ethnic pluralism in Yugoslavia and the recruitment of secret police agents, we interviewed several sources: Professor Matthew Mestrović, Department of History / Political Science, Fairleigh Dickinson University, on July 21, 1979; several confidential sources, all Croatians, on January 23 and March 15, 1980; and famed dissident Yugoslavian author Mihajlo Mihajlov on March 21, 1980.

On the problems of ethnic pluralism and the recruitment of Syrian secret police agents, we interviewed a confidential source on July 16, 1980. See also Amnesty International, *Syria* (London: Amnesty International, 1979), p. 3.

5. On the recruitment of Chilean DINA agents from among the military ranks, we interviewed a confidential source, a former Chilean Air Force officer, on April 27, 1979. And for the former DINA agent's testimony that illustrates the reluctance of some military men to join the secret police, see *Private Sociale Mission, e.V.*, vs. *Amnesty International*, supra.

On reasons for the establishment of Uruguay's DNII, we interviewed Juan Ferreira, son of the former presidential candidate of Partido Blanco, an opposition party, on May 2, 1979.

On reasons for the creation of the Triple A, we interviewed several sources: three confidential sources, all of whom had experiences with the Triple A, whether directly (i.e., they themselves were arrested), or indirectly (friends or family arrested), at the headquarters of the International League for Human Rights in New York City on March 11, 1980; and attorney Scott Greathead, one of a panel of attorneys who went to Argentina on a fact-finding mission in 1979, at his law firm, Lord, Day & Lord, in New York City, on May 4, 1979. For suggestions that there is collusion between the military and the Triple A, see Amnesty International, *Report of an Amnesty International Mission to Argentina* (London: Amnesty International, 1977), pp. 9–10. Our sources agree with the theory that the Triple A is directly tied in to the Army, that the two organizations often work together, and that very possibly members of the Triple A were recruited from the military.

On the enmity that existed between agents of SAVAK and members of the Iranian Army, we interviewed Mr. Ali Agah, the Iranian chargé d'affaires of the Washington, D.C., Iranian embassy under the Khomeini regime, on July 17 and 19, 1979.

On Papa Doc Duvalier's distrust of the Army, see our notes for Chapter Three, Section 5. For the quote of the Haitian source who defines and describes the duties of the Tonton Macoutes, see the testimony of one "Laraque," *Haitian Refugee Center et al.* vs. *Benjamin Civiletti et al.*, supra, p. 19. He teaches at City College, in New York. For more on him see our notes for Chapter Three, Section 4.

On the hierarchy of the Israeli intelligence services, we interviewed, among others, Dr. Israel Shahak, Professor of Organic Chemistry, Hebrew University, Jerusalem, and president of the Israeli League for Human and Civil Rights in Jerusalem, on March 19, 1980, in Washington, D.C.

6. The American nun working for the Catholic Commission in Rhodesia reconstructed her experience in an interview conducted at her place of work, the Washington Office on Africa, on April 19, 1979.

7. Information on the training of Czechoslovakian agents was provided by a confidential source on March 13, 1980.

Information on the training of Yugoslavian agents, in particular the Faculty for Security and Social Self-Protection, appears in *Tanjug in English*, 1318 GMT, Dec. 1, 1977.

On the "KGB School," we interviewed Friedrich Nerzansky on January 26, 1980, and a confidential source on March 13, 1980; and Larisa and František Silnitsky, authors of *Communism in Eastern Europe*, on January 27, 1980. For Czech StB defector Frolik's description of the KGB-controlled upward-mobility system of education and training, see Josef Frolik, *Špión Vypovídá* (Cologne: Index, 1979), pp. 268–80. Frolik was a member of State Security (StB) from December 1952 to June 1969, at which time he defected. Upon leaving Czechoslovakia, on July 21, 1969, Frolik went to Bulgaria for a vacation, then to Turkey, where he was debriefed by U.S. intelligence officials. He arrived in the United States in July of 1969.

On the training of Cuban G-2 agents in the Soviet Union, see Pepita Riera, *Servicio de Inteligencia de Cuba Comunista* (Miami: Florida Typesetting of Miami, Inc., 1966).

Information on the International Police Academy and on foreign police training in the United States is extensive and variegated. Some of the information on the International Police Academy was obtained from human-rights organizations' collections of materials originally gathered together by former Senator James Abourezk, who actively investigated the issue of foreign police training in the United States during the mid-seventies. See, for example, a letter sent by Matthew J. Harvey, assistant administrator for legislative affairs, Department of State, Agency for International Development, to Senator James Abourezk, U. S. Senate, in May of 1974. The letter was a reply to the Senator's request concerning (1) contracts for police training and related programs, (2) the scope of activities of the Office of Public Safety, and (3) the termination of police programs. The letter includes several tables, listing, for example, "International Police Academy operating expenses FY 75."

See also another letter written to Senator Abourezk in September of 1973 by Matthew Harvey in response to Abourezk's letter to Lauren Goin, Director of the Office of Public Safety, Agency for International Development, requesting information on specific courses taught at the International Police Academy, as well as on the relationship of the IPA to police facilities at Fort Gordon, Georgia; it also includes an attached list of numbers of agents trained at IPA, on a country-by-country basis. Especially interesting information on the IPA is the text of a lesson plan for the course "Interviews and Interrogations," taught at the International Police Academy—the lesson plan appears in notes taken by an unidentified source (found in the files of the research organization known as the Human Rights Internet, Washington, D.C.) whom we know, however, accompanied Diane Edwards La Voy, U. S. Intelligence Committee, U. S. Congress, on an interview with Lauren Goin, director, Office of Public Safety. The interview notes are dated July 26, 1974.

For additional background information on the International Police Academy, see Michael Klare and Nancy Stein, "Secret U. S. Bomb School Trains Third World Police Agency," *American Report*, November 26, 1973; Michael Klare and Daniel Schechter, "International Police Academy: The 'State of Siegers' Besieged," *Real Paper*, June 26, 1974; Michael Klare, "The Reality Behind 'State of Siege'," *The Nation*, Dec. 10, 1973, pp. 619–23; the report issued by the Office of Public Safety, *International Police Academy Graduates for FY 69–73* (date of the release of this memo is unknown); and Center for National Security Studies, "Foreign and Secret Police: CIA's Global Legacy," *CIA's Covert Operations* vs. *Human Rights* (Washington, D.C.: Center for National Security Studies, undated issue), p. 9.

For the quote by the Mauritian graduate of IPA, see Alexandrina Shuler, *Front Lines*, September 26, 1974, p. 2.

For comments about the IPA appearing in a Greek newspaper, see an issue of *Avghe* that appeared in 1975 (no further date available).

For statements made by the commanding officer of the U. S. Army Institute for Military Assistance at Fort Bragg, North Carolina, expressing his aversion to torture, see Fayetteville *Observer* and Fayetteville *Times*, 26 Nov. 1978, p. 1.

For additional information on other United States schools that helped to train foreign police, see John Marks and Taylor Branch, "Tracking the CIA," *Harper's Weekly Newspaper*, Jan. 24, 1975, reprinted by the Center for National Security Studies in Washington, D.C., an article about International Police Services, Inc. (INPOLSE), a school very similar to the IPA, according to CIA defector Philip Agee. The authors of this article say that INPOLSE operated for nearly twenty-three years as an arm of the CIA under cover as a private firm.

For some more general surveys of various schools that were involved in training foreign police, see Daniel Kagan, "Cold War Colonialism: U. S. Schools for Dictators," *Hustler*, Mar. 1978, pp. 60, 80, 110–15, an article that names and describes five schools at which foreign military personnel were believed to be trained in the United States: U. S. Army School of the Americas (USARSA), Fort Gulick, C.Z.; U. S. Army Infantry and Ranger School, Fort Benning, Ga.; John F. Kennedy School of Military Assistance, Fort Bragg, N.C.; U. S. Army Command and General Staff College, Fort Leavenworth, Kan.; and Inter-American Defense College, Washington, D.C. See also the report of the U. S. Defense Security Assistance Agency, *Training Facilities / Institutes That Provide Training to Foreign Military Personnel,* Nov. 1975; and a report by the North American Congress on Latin America, Latin America and Empire Report, *Pentagon's Protégés,* Vol. X, No. 1, Jan. 1976. For a description of NACLA see bibliographic notes.

See also Jeffrey Stein, "Grade School for Juntas," *The Nation,* May 21, 1977, pp. 621–24, on the Fort McNair School known as the Inter-American Defense College; and "Inter-American Defense College," *Military Review,* Apr. 1970, pp. 20–27.

On foreign police training at Fort Bragg, see a letter written by representatives of Friends of the Filipino People, a United States-based human rights group opposed to the rule of Ferdinand Marcos, Carolina Chapter, sent to representatives of the U. S. Department of the Army, Institute for Military Assistance, Fort Bragg, N.C., Dec. 1978, re a Freedom of Information Act request filed Nov. 8, 1978, asking for a list of course titles taught at the John F. Kennedy Center, especially the psychological-warfare training courses. See also a letter written by representatives of the Friends of the Filipino People, Carolina Chapter, Durham, N.C., to Congressman Ike Andrews, demanding an end to the type of foreign police training they allege has been taking place at Fort Bragg, Sept. 18, 1979.

See also Amnesty International, *Campaign for the Abolition of Torture,* May 1976, Vol. III, No. 5, p. 1, which reports on a school in Warner Springs, Calif., known as the Survival, Evasion, Resistance and Escape School, and which reportedly teaches naval personnel how to resist torture if taken prisoner of war (the school came to light in March of 1976 when a naval officer sued the U. S. Government for assault and battery in connection with injuries he sustained, allegedly, while he was a participant in the program).

See also the report of the Argentine Commission for Human Rights, *U. S. Military Training for Argentina* (Washington, D.C.: May 1977).

On the United States Army School of the Americas, otherwise known as USARSA, see a report issued by the Department of the Army, Head-quarters of the U. S. Army School of the Americas, Fort Gulick, C.Z., Feb. 25, 1975, a personnel-strength report and a list of courses taught there.

On training of foreign police at Fort Leavenworth, see New York Times, Nov. 1, 1970, p. A1.

For more general information on the Office of Public Safety, see the New York Times, Feb. 20, 1975, p. A1, on the Defense Department's report that government and private teams were training military personnel in thirty-four countries under contracts worth $727 million: "The department said that the programs were not new but were part of a pattern set in the nineteen fifties, and were increasingly being conducted by commercial organizations rather than by U.S. military advisers." See also U. S. Congress, House, Report of the Special Study Mission to Latin America on: I. Military Assistance Training and II. Developmental Television (Committee Print. A Resolution Authorizing the Committee on Foreign Affairs to conduct thorough studies and investigations of all matters coming within the jurisdiction of such committee) 91st Cong., 2nd sess., May 7, 1970.

On the intent of U.S. aid given to Iranian intelligence officials for the development of SAVAK, we interviewed a retired general of the Iranian Army now living in Beverly Hills, Calif., Aug. 28, 1980.

On the Federal Police Academy, in Brazil, established with U.S. aid in 1968, see a report of the North American Congress on Latin America, Command and Control: U. S. Police Operations in Latin America, Jan. 1972, p. 15. See also New York Times, Aug. 14, 1980, p. A12.

On Bolivian officers educated at the Brazilian school, see New York Times, Aug. 14, 1980, p. A12.

On U.S. aid to the Philippines under the auspices of the International Narcotics Control Program, see Richard P. Claude, Human Rights in the Philippines and United States Responsibility, a working paper. (College Park, Md.: Center for Philosophy and Public Policy, University of Maryland, 1978), p. 18. See also Walden Bellow and Severina Rivera, eds., Logistics of Repression and Other Essays: the Role of U. S. Assistance in Consolidating the Martial Law Regime in the Philippines (Washington, D.C.: Friends of the Filipino People, 1977), pp. 31–32. On the similarities between the Office of Public Safety program and that of the U.S. DEA, see the text of a speech delivered by Nancy Stein, of the North American Congress on Latin America, at the Amnesty International Regional Conference, Malibu, Calif., Oct. 16, 1976. Consult also Edward Jay Epstein's Agency of Fear (New York: G. P. Putnam's Sons, 1977).

Information on the private school in the United States offering a special course designed to train foreign officers as well as Americans in the techniques of combatting terrorism is taken from notes on an interview with the school's director, July 5, 1979.

8. For excerpts of SAVAK torturer Tehrani's confession with regard to training he received in Israel, see "Israeli-SAVAK Connection," *Iran Voice*, Vol. 1, No. 11, Aug. 13, 1979, p. 1.

On training offered by the Malaysians to some of the most sophisticated intelligence officers of the Philippines and Thailand, see Los Angeles *Times*, June 11, 1980, p. A1. Information on the East Germans helping the Angolans, Yemenis, and Ethiopians in establishing their security services comes from an interview with a former high official of the CIA, July 15, 1980. On the passing of information between the Iranian intelligence services under the Shah and the Egyptian security police, we interviewed a confidential source at the U. S. State Department, Aug. 12, 1980. On cooperation between the CIA and the security section of the Royal Canadian Mounted Police, see Robert Justin Goldstein, "Mounties on the Loose," *Worldview*, Nov. 1978, p. 5. Goldstein is assistant professor of science at Oakland University, Rochester, Mich.

On the assassination of former Chilean Ambassador Orlando Letelier, in Washington, D.C., see John Dinges and Saul Landau, *Assassination on Embassy Row* (New York: Pantheon Books, 1980).

On cooperation between Uruguayan and Brazilian police as exemplified in the case uncovered by a Brazilian magazine editor and a photographer, see the report issued by La Fédération Internationale de l'Homme and Le Secrétariat International des Juristes pour l'Amnistie en Uruguay, *Complaint Alleging the Violation of Human Rights in Uruguay and Brazil presented to the Chairman, Inter-American Commission on Human Rights, Organization of American States*, Washington, D.C., Aug. 2, 1979.

On cooperation (with regard to liquidating political enemies) carried out by DINA agents of Chile and Triple A agents of Argentina, see Secretaria Ejecutiva de Solidaridad de la Izquierda Chileana para America, *Chile Informative 102: La DINA en Chile* (Mexico City: Casa de Chile, 1976).

On the Chilean leftist who fled to Paraguay and was subsequently returned to Chile by Paraguayan police, see information on the case of Jorge Fuentes Alcarón, in Amnesty International, *A Selection of Case Histories and Lists of Disappeared Prisoners by Occupation* (London: Amnesty International, Mar. 1977), p. 27.

On the openness of SAVAK files to the CIA and other Western intelligence services, as well as MOSSAD, see *SAVAK: Documents on Iranian Secret Police* [*Confederation of Iranian Students* (*National Front*)], Dec. 1976.

For information on the Foreign Broadcast Information Service shared by British and American intelligence officials, see Ray S. Cline, *Secrets, Spies and Scholars* (New York: Acropolis Books, 1976), pp. 75–76.

On Interpol, see Michael Fooner, *Interpol* (Chicago: Henry Regnery, 1973). In addition, the National Commission on Law Enforcement and Social Justice has done a number of investigative reports, including: *The Central Intelligence Agency - Interpol Connection* (Los Angeles: National Commission, 1977); *Recent Findings on Interpol* (Los Angeles: National Commission, 1977); and *The Victimization of American Citizens by Interpol Abuse* (Los Angeles: National Commission, 1977). While the editorial point of view of some of these reports may perhaps be slanted negatively against Interpol, other portions of the reports are neutral and valuable, because they consist of an informative series of clippings from reliable newspaper sources on the subject of allegations against Interpol.

On the importance of computer technology in the effort of the Argentinian security police to help General García Meza plan his 1980 coup in La Paz, Bolivia, see Los Angeles *Times,* Aug. 3, 1980, p. 3; and *The Economist,* Aug. 23, 1980, p. 37.

On the computerized files of West Germany's criminal and internal-security police, see New York *Times,* Apr. 2, 1980, p. A3.

On Clodo, the Comité Liquidant et Détournant les Ordinateurs, see *The Economist,* Apr. 18, 1980, p. 46.

9. On the Eleventh Department of the First Chief Directorate of the KGB, see John Barron, *KGB: The Secret World of Soviet Secret Agents* (New York: Reader's Digest Press, 1974), pp. 79–80.

For information on the way in which the KGB controls the security services of other East European nations and other burgeoning secret police systems, such as those of Yemen and Angola, we interviewed a former high official of the CIA, July 15, 1980. According to author John Barron, cooperation between the U.S.S.R. and other East European countries works both ways; that is, the intelligence officials of the satellite countries help the U.S.S.R., just as the U.S.S.R. helps the satellite countries. He cites the example of the Czech intelligence officers who, during the 1964 American presidential campaign, printed tens of thousands of pamphlets containing fictitious quotations and false information on Barry Goldwater. Says Barron: "To the Czech contributions must be added those from the clandestine services of East Germany, Poland, Hungary, Bulgaria, Romania, and, most recently, Cuba. At negligible expense to the Soviet Union, they greatly enlarge the operational capabilities of the KGB and sometimes enable it to achieve objectives that it could not easily attain on its own." The Cuban DGI, however, may be the most valuable to the Soviet Union, says Barron. "Aside from their [DGI's] proximity to the U.S. the Cubans possess a glamour which gives them an entrée to Latin America and the Third World that no other Soviet-bloc nation enjoys." See John Barron, *KGB: The Secret World of Soviet Secret Agents,* supra, pp. 143–44 and 147.

On cooperation between President Nguema Biyogo Macie and the "Communist camp," see Los Angeles *Times,* Aug. 7, 1979, p. 10.

10. On the time of day (or night) when the secret police of Czechoslovakia make their arrests, see Josef Frolik, *Špión Vypovídá* (Cologne: Index, 1979), pp. 268–80. For further information, we also interviewed a confidential source, Mar. 13, 1980.

According to the testimony of a former Tonton Macoute, some arrests in Haiti were especially designated to be kept *very secret.* See the testimony of the former Macoute in the case of the *Haitian Refugee Center et al.* vs. *Benjamin Civiletti et al.,* supra, p. 24: ". . . The orders went through from President Duvalier to the Commander of the Macoutes, all persons entering Haiti were to be arrested and to be sent to Fort Dimanche [prison]. But the order was through the ways of the national radio, all people coming from foreign countries were to be liberated and sent home; but secretly the order was given for them to be arrested."

On Polish UB agents' style of arrest, we interviewed Polish émigrés Zabludowska, Mar. 11, 1980, and Walendowski, Mar. 21, 1980. On the arrest style of Romanian agents of the Securitate, we interviewed historian Vladimir Georgescu, Mar. 19, 1980, whose manuscript *Politics and History,* smuggled into the United States, led to his arrest in 1977.

On the arrest procedures followed by UDBA agents, of Yugoslavia, we interviewed famed Yugoslavian dissident author Mihajlo Mihajlov, Mar. 21, 1980, Professor Matthew Mestrović, of Fairleigh Dickinson University, July 21, 1979, and several other Yugoslavian exiles.

On the theory that Chile's DINA eliminated the need for itself, we interviewed a confidential source, a former Intelligence Service Chilean Air Force officer, Apr. 27, 1979. It is important, however, to keep in mind that in the aftermath of the July 23, 1980, assassination of the head of the army intelligence school, the government started to crack down again. See New York *Times,* Aug. 5, 1980, p. A4, and New York *Times,* July 10, 1980, p. A2: "Mounting pressure on President Augusto Pinochet to restore constitutional government in Chile is being met with a resurgence of repression against critics of the Government." For further discussion of this topic, see notes for Chapter Three, Section 5, on reasons why DINA was allegedly disbanded and replaced by an organization called CNI.

On the arrest style of the secret police in Cuba today, we interviewed (Mar. 15, 1980) a group of Cuban exiles who had been political prisoners for varying lengths of time.

On the arrest style predominant in Israel and the West Bank and Occupied Territories, we interviewed Dr. Israel Shahak, professor of organic chemistry, Hebrew University, Jerusalem, and president of the Israeli League for Civil and Human Rights in Tel-Aviv, in Washington, D.C., Mar. 19, 1980; and former Vice-Consul Alexandra Johnson, stationed in Jerusalem Feb. 1977 to Jan. 1979, in Sacramento, Calif., June 19, 1980. For a general overview of some procedures common to arrests taking place in Israel, the West Bank, and the Occupied Territories, see "Israel and Torture," *Journal of Palestine Studies 34*, No. 2 IX (Winter 1980): 76–118.

On the smooth arrest that took place in Afghanistan in the late seventies, see Los Angeles *Times*, Jan. 16, 1980, p. 1.

11. On the style of Argentinian arrests, we interviewed several confidential sources at the International League for Human Rights headquarters in New York City, Mar. 11, 1980. One of the interviewees, a ship welder, was arrested by the military during a labor strike, and later on was arrested by agents of Triple A. Another source was not arrested himself, although his wife disappeared in Argentina in 1977.

Information on the way in which Argentinian authorities determine the odds and set their goals for conducting arrests was taken from an interview with Scott Greathead, of the law firm of Lord, Day & Lord, in New York City, May 4, 1980. He was one of several attorneys who went to Argentina on a fact-finding mission in 1979. They issued the report *Materials on Human Rights and the Situation of Defense Lawyers and Judges in Argentina* (New York: Lawyers Committee for International Human Rights, 1979).

Juan Ferreira, son of the former presidential candidate of a major opposition party in Uruguay, described his arrest by Uruguayan authorities in an interview on May 2, 1979.

The description of the arrest style of a Philippine torturer operating in the rural provinces appears in a report by the Task Force Detainees of the Association of Major Religious Superiors in the Philippines, *Political Detainees of the Philippines, Book Three* (Manila: Task Force Detainees, 1978), pp. 118–20. According to our sources, the torturer worked on contract to the military and was a sergeant in the Philippine Constabulary. The arrests in the rural areas generally tend to be more violent than those conducted in the middle of the city. For example, the rough manner in which the ASSO forms (arrest, search, and seizure orders) are handed out to the poor peasants, who are often illiterate, have led to heart attacks in the older victims.

On the general demeanor of Brigada Blanca agents in Mexico, we interviewed the Washington bureau chief of *Excelsior*, Mar. 21, 1980; Mexican journalist Jesús Blancornelas, Mar. 20, 1980; and Professor

Robert Goldman, of American University Law School, Mar. 18, 1980. For an excellent distillation of relevant individual rights and guarantees in the Mexican constitution, see Robert K. Goldman and Daniel Jacoby, *Report of the Commission of Enquiry to Mexico*, supra, pp. 6–12.

On the arrest style of DINA agents, see Amnesty International, *Disappeared Prisoners in Chile* (London: Amnesty International, 1977), pp. 9–10. We also interviewed several Chilean exiles who described their arrests by DINA to us: Eugenio Velasco, former Chilean Supreme Court justice and attorney, June 28, 1979 and July 17, 1980; José Zalaquett, former Chief Legal Counsel for the Cooperative Committee for Justice and Peace in Chile, Apr. 26, 1979 (for more information on Mr. Zalaquett, see later Chap. Two note); and a confidential source, a former SIFA officer, Apr. 27, 1979.

Information on the pseudonyms used by DINA agents appears in United Nations, Economic and Social Council, Ad Hoc Working Group on the Situation of Human Rights in Chile, 31st sess., *Protection of Human Rights in Chile* (A/31/253), Oct. 8, 1976, pp. 93–96, paras. 357–66. For more on the anonymity upheld by DINA agents, see the report of the Secretaria Ejecutiva de Solidaridad de la Izquierda Chileana para América, *Chile Informative 102, La DINA en Chile*, supra.

For the full text of the deposition of a former DINA agent on the subject of anonymity maintained by DINA agents, see United Nations, Economic and Social Council, Human Rights Commission, 36th sess., *Question of Human Rights in Chile* (E/CN.4/1381), Jan. 9, 1980, pp. 61–63, annex.

12. The Chief Legal Counsel to the Chilean Peace Committee was José Zalaquett, who was interviewed on Apr. 27, 1979, at Woodstock Theological Center, on the Georgetown University campus, where he teaches. Mr. Zalaquett is also chairman of the International Executive Committee of Amnesty International.

On the arrest of Charito Planas, we interviewed her in Washington, D.C., on July 17, 18, and 19, 1979.

CHAPTER THREE

2. For the judge's opinion with regard to the power of the security forces operating within Haiti, see *Haitian Refugee Center et al., Plaintiff*, vs. *Benjamin Civiletti et al., Defendants*, Vol. 5, (79-2086-Civ-JLK), Miami, Fla.: 1980, p. 104.

On the early stages of the formation of the Tonton Macoutes, see Nancy Gordon Heinl and Robert Deb Heinl, *Written in Blood: The Story of the Haitian People, 1492–1971* (Boston: Houghton Mifflin, 1978), pp. 596–97. See also *U.S. News & World Report*, Sept. 10, 1962,

p. 77; *Time,* Jan. 26, 1962, p. 38; *Time,* May 12, 1961, p. 25; *Atlantic Report,* Aug. 14, 1961; and *Look,* July 3, 1962, pp. 39–40. On the beginnings of the Tonton Macoutes we also interviewed Ray Joseph, *Wall Street Journal* staff writer and editor of *Haiti Observateur,* a newspaper published by Haitians living in New York, on Mar. 13, 1980.

On the evolution of SIFA, the Chilean Air Force Intelligence Service, we interviewed a confidential source, a former SIFA officer now living in Washington, D.C., on Apr. 27, 1979. For more on the development of SIFA, see "Organization of Torture and Murder," *Counterspy,* Vol. 3, Issue 2, Winter 1976, pp. 69–71; and the report of the Secretaria Ejecutiva de Solidaridad de la Izquierda Chileana para América, *Chile Informative 102, La DINA en Chile:* (Mexico City: Casa de Chile, 1976).

On the evolution of SAVAK, see a report by William J. Butler and Georges Levasseur, *Human Rights and the Legal System in Iran* (Geneva: International Commission of Jurists, 1976), p. 32, for the list of articles incorporating SAVAK; and for background information on the other internal-security organizations that operated alongside of SAVAK, see Fred Halliday, *Iran: Dictatorship and Development* (Harmondsworth, Middlesex: Penguin Books, 1979), pp. 75–78.

On the relationship of the Communist Party to the Czechoslovakian secret police, we interviewed a former adviser to the Dubček cabinet and former United Nations official on Mar. 11, 1980. For Czech StB defector Frolik's testimony, see Josef Frolik, *Špión Vypovídá,* supra, pp. 268–80.

On conditions leading to the formation of the Potgieter Commission, in South Africa, see London *Observer,* Oct. 31, 1971; for comments on the formation of the commission by Mr. Michael Mitchell, member of the South African Parliament, ibid.; and for comments by Mr. Colin Eglin, leader of the Progressive Party, ibid. For more samples of popular opinions on the establishment of the Potgieter Commission, see the Johannesburg *Star,* Sept. 6, 1969; for commentary from the media on the formation of the commission, see *Rand Daily Mail,* Aug. 2, 1972.

The opening passage of the report of the Potgieter Commission clarifies the reasons why the commission was established: "Taking into consideration—(a) the potential threat of conventional and unconventional war against the Republic; (b) the threat of terrorism and potential guerrilla war on our frontiers and in the interior; (c) the continual possibility of internal subversion; (d) the necessity of the Government's being fully informed and kept abreast of matters relating to security; (e) the security set-ups of other comparable democratic countries; and (f) the security of the State in general whatever its nature and from whatever direction it is threatened. . . ." See South Africa, *Report of the Commis-*

sion of Inquiry into Matters Relating to the Security of the State, 1971, p. 1. See also the report of the International Defense and Aid Fund for Southern Africa, *BOSS: The First Five Years* (London: International Defense and Aid Fund, 1975). See also Republic of South Africa, *Government Gazette,* No. 2520, Vol. 51; and of course, see the report of the Potgieter Commission itself, *Report of the Commission of Inquiry into Matters Relating to the Security of the State,* 1971.

For Prime Minister Vorster's comments on the powers of BOSS, see Parliamentary Debates, Apr. 21, 1971, reprinted in International Defense and Aid Fund for Southern Africa, *BOSS: The First Five Years,* supra, p. 21. For Van den Bergh's comments that the Potgieter Commission had issued an excellent report, see International Defense and Aid Fund for Southern Africa, *BOSS: The First Five Years,* p. 22.

On the present status of the State Security Council of South Africa, see the London and Manchester *Guardian* (American edition), Apr. 20, 1980, p. 8.

For additional background information on the structure of the South African intelligence system, chiefly the Bureau for State Security and the Security Branch, see *Rand Daily Mail,* Feb. 12, 1972, p. 9; and on the "special nature" of BOSS as evidenced by the Public Service Amendment Act, which made it clear that BOSS was to be controlled directly by the Minister and not by the public service commissioners, as are other state departments, and as evidenced by the fact that according to the Security Services Special Account Act, BOSS was financed by a special account of its own, *not* subject to usual Treasury control, see Johannesburg *Star,* July 19, 1969, p. 15. For further clarification of the powers of BOSS and the Security Branch, we interviewed a professor at the Georgetown Center for Strategic Studies, a confidential source, on Apr. 25, 1979; and, another confidential source, a white South African exile now living in Berkeley, Calif., on June 13, 1979.

On the wide variety of private armies and other security services operating in Mexico, we interviewed Francisco Fernández Ponte, Washington bureau chief of *Excelsior,* the largest-circulation newspaper in Mexico City, Mar. 21, 1980, in Washington, D.C., and Professor Robert Goldman, acting dean of law, American University, at the time, Mar. 18, 1980. Professor Goldman has done extensive work investigating violations of human rights in Mexico, having coauthored with Daniel Jacoby *Report of the Commission of Enquiry to Mexico Submitted to the International League for Human Rights, Fédération Internationale des Droits de l'Homme and Pax Romana* (New York: International League for Human Rights, 1978).

On the subject of the Brigada Blanca, we also interviewed Mr. Jesús Blancornelas, editor and publisher of the Mexican newspaper *ABC* (initials B and C stand for Baja California; the newspaper was situated in Tijuana). Blancornelas, however, ran into trouble after his newspaper published a series of investigative articles on corruption in government. He was, says an *Excelsior* correspondent in Washington, D.C., "run out of his paper." Apparently the government sent in outside agitators to stage a union dispute and, according to our sources, also attempted to buy out various reporters, many if not all of whom, however, refused to accept the bribes to report favorably on the government. Mr. Blancornelas was then charged with "mishandling funds" and was forced to leave the country. His case in Sonora has been stalled.

On Argentina's Triple A, see Amnesty International, *Report of an Amnesty International Mission to Argentina* (London: Amnesty International, 1976), pp. 9–10. See also John Dinges and Saul Landau, *Assassination on Embassy Row* (New York: Pantheon Books, 1980), pp. 140, 154.

On Brazil's death squads, in particular the one known as "White Hand," see Los Angeles *Times,* "Rio to Crack Down on 'Death Squads,'" Mar. 6, 1980, p. 11; Washington *Post,* "Police Hero Held in Brazil Killings," Feb. 23, 1978, and "Movie Prompts Investigation of Brazilian Death Squads," June 17, 1978; and New York *Times,* "Death Squad Is Spreading Terror in Rio Shanty Towns," Apr. 5, 1980, p. 11. On death squads in Latin America in general, see *Newsweek,* Apr. 20, 1970, pp. 61–62.

On the expansion of the KCIA, we interviewed Donald Ranard, former director of the Office of Korean Affairs, in the State Department (1970–74) and Political Counselor in the American Embassy in Seoul (1959–62), currently director of the Center for International Policy, in Washington, D.C., July 16, 1980. Mr. Ranard has also written several magazine articles on the present situation in Korea: "Park's Clone in South Korea," *The Nation,* June 23, 1980, pp. 776–77; and "Seoul Brothers," *The Nation,* Jan. 19, 1980, pp. 36–37.

3. On the struggle between former Interior Minister and Łódź secret police official Moczar and the Polish Communist Party during the late sixties, we interviewed Irena Lasota Zabludowska, Polish émigré now living in New York City, on March 10, 1980; Zabludowska points to this conflict as an example of classic Communist Party / secret police conflict; and Tadeusz Walendowski, another Polish émigré, on March 21, 1980. Since 1979, Mr. Walendowski has been associated with the Committee for Social Self-Defense, which served as the major liaison between striking Polish workers and Western journalists during the 1980 strikes that spread over Poland. Mr. Walendowski has been active in the underground publishing movement in Poland for some time, acting as a coeditor of an unofficial Polish quarterly, and he is also the founder of Poland

Watch Center, in the United States. For more background information on this conflict between the Party and Moczar, see New York *Times*, Sept. 28, 1980, p. A5, an article printed before Moczar's appointment to the Polish Politburo, which, however, projects that Moczar will return to the Polish political scene, and Dec. 3, 1980, p. A1, which confirms that Moczar has been appointed to the Politburo.

On the struggle between the KGB, the MVD, and the procuracy to gain jurisdiction over political cases, Friedrich Nerzansky, a graduate of the Moscow Institute of Law who has worked for twenty-five years in the field of Soviet Criminal law, including fifteen years as a criminal investigator in the U.S.S.R. procurator's office, was interviewed on January 26, 1980. Nerzansky immigrated to the United States in 1977. He is the author of a book soon to be published by Harper & Row, *Land of Crime*.

On the idea that one of Yuri Andropov's chief ambitions is to restrain the secret police from gaining the power they wielded during Stalinist times, see *Time*, June 23, 1980, p. 30.

For John Barron's comments on the relationship of the Communist Party to the KGB, see John Barron, *KGB: The Secret World of Soviet Secret Agents* (New York: Reader's Digest Press, 1974), p. 73.

On the reluctance of the Party to appoint a KGB head President or Chairman of the Party, we interviewed a former member of the Soviet Academy of Sciences, in October of 1978, who while in Moscow had been a specialist in U.S. foreign policy.

The story about the procurator's run-in with the KGB on a particular case was learned during our interview with Mr. Nerzansky, January 6, 1980.

It is interesting to note that apparently, at one point in Czechoslovakia's history, the secret police actually spied on the Party and the Committee as part of police policy guidelines. Writes Frolik in his book *Špión Vypovídá*, supra, pp. 368–80: "Third Department of State Security [political counterintelligence]. . . . This was the actual police, responsible for the majority of the crimes perpetrated in the fifties. . . . It covered all the parties making up the National Front, professional and trade organizations and up to the year 1955 this did not even exclude the Communist Party of Czechoslovakia and its Central Committee. The unit given responsibility over the Party was called 'unit for the struggle against enemies within the Party.' . . ."

4. On the S.D. (Service Detectives), the secret police who watch over the other secret police units in Haiti, see *Haitian Refugee Center et al., Plaintiff,* vs. *Benjamin Civiletti et al., Defendants,* supra, testimony of an ex-army officer of Haiti, p. 74. For more on this subject we interviewed *Wall Street Journal* correspondent Ray Joseph on March 13, 1980.

On NISA, the secret police unit that watches over the other secret police units in the Philippines, we interviewed Romy Capulong, patent attorney and LABAN activist now living in the United States, Mar. 11, 1980—see notes for Chapter Two, Section 2, for more information on Mr. Capulong, whom we also interviewed on the subject of the origins of NISA, information that appears later in this chapter. We also interviewed Jerry Jumat, a former Moslem anti-Marcos activist now living in Washington, D.C., Mar. 19, 1980, on the subject of NISA. According to our sources, NISA is considered the *brains,* such as they are, of the Philippine security services. The Constabulary and ISAFP, the intelligence service of the Armed Forces, are considered the *action* forces, or dispatch forces.

On the Egyptian General Intelligence Service penetrating the military intelligence service of the country, we interviewed a confidential source, a U. S. State Department official, Aug. 12, 1980.

On the Iranian Special Bureau, which watched over the other security units in Iran, see Fred Halliday, *Iran: Democracy and Dictatorship,* supra, p. 77.

On the Inspector's Office of the Ministry of the Interior, in Czechoslovakia, see Josef Frolik, *Špión Vypovídá,* supra, pp. 345-70.

On Cuba's G-5, we interviewed Raúl Chibas, Mar. 14, 1980, in New York City. Señor Chibas actively fought the Machado and Batista dictatorships, only to be disappointed in the outcome of Cuba's revolution, much like the famed prisoner Huber Matos, who was released after spending twenty years in prison and who once also fought alongside of Castro. We also interviewed (Mar. 15, 1980) a group of Cuban women now living in New Jersey, one of whom was recently released after serving a twenty-year sentence.

5. On the Romanian Securitate reporting directly to President Ceausescu, we interviewed Vladimir Georgescu, a dissident historian and author who, when his book *Politics and History* was smuggled into the United States, was imprisoned, in 1977. But his close association with Zbigniew Brzezinski (a friendship formed when Mr. Georgescu was a professor at Columbia University, in New York—the same time Brzezinski was teaching there) and his contacts with other American politicians and influential individuals contributed to his release after a relatively short period of time in prison.

On Duvalier's fear of the Army usurping his power, see *Haitian Refugee Center et al., Plaintiff,* vs. *Benjamin Civiletti et al., Defendants,* supra, p. 94, for the judge's opinion on Duvalier's attitude. See also the judge's opinion, p. 104. For more on Duvalier's relationship to the Army, see the testimony of Laraque, who left Haiti in 1957, pp. 12-14.

On the streamlined structure of the Tonton Macoutes, we interviewed Ray Joseph, *Wall Street Journal* correspondent, Mar. 13, 1980; see also the testimony of Laraque, *Haitian Refugee Center et al., Plaintiff*, vs. *Benjamin Civiletti et al., Defendants*, supra, p. 22; and see the testimony of a former Tonton Macoutes himself, ibid., pp. 24–26.

On the supremacy of NISA, in addition to Mr. Capulong and Mr. Jumat we also interviewed Charito Planas, attorney, former LABAN official and exile now living in the United States, on July 17, 18, and 19, 1979, in Washington, D.C.

On President Assad's caution in making sure that the Defense Companies remain close and loyal to him, we interviewed a confidential source in Washington, D.C., on July 16, 1980. See also Amnesty International, *Syria* (London: Amnesty International, 1979), p. 3.

On King Hussein's resolution to make sure that the security services are loyal to him, we interviewed another confidential source at the State Department on July 18, 1980.

On President Nasser and his expansion of General Intelligence into an intelligence organization not too dissimilar to the U. S. Central Intelligence Agency, we interviewed a confidential source, a State Department official, in Washington, D.C., Aug. 12, 1980. For more on Nasser's use of concentration camps to imprison his enemies, in particular Egyptian Marxists, see Jean Lacouture, *Nasser: A Biography* (New York: Alfred A. Knopf, 1973), pp. 228–29. On the smaller intelligence services of Egypt, we also interviewed this same confidential State Department source and another confidential source in Washington, D.C., on July 16, 1980.

On the beginnings of DINA, we interviewed (Washington, D.C., Apr. 26, 1979) José Zalaquett, former Chief Legal Counsel of the Committee of Cooperation and Peace in Chile (see our notes for Chapter Two), professor at Woodstock Theological Center and chairman of the International Executive Committee of Amnesty International. For more of Mr. Zalaquett's views on this subject, see U. S. Congress, House, Subcommittee on International Relations, *Chile: The Status of Human Rights and Its Relationship to U. S. Economic Assistance Programs*. 94th Cong., 2nd sess., 1976. Former Supreme Court justice and attorney Eugenio Velasco, whose story is recounted in Chapter One, was also interviewed, in Los Angeles, on June 28, 1979, and in Washington, D.C., on July 17, 1980. See also John Dinges and Saul Landau, *Assassination on Embassy Row* (New York: Pantheon Books, 1980), p. 33.

On the internal structure of DINA, see John Dinges and Saul Landau, op. cit., pp. 133–37; "Organization of Torture and Murder," *Counterspy*, Vol. 3, Issue 2, pp. 69–71; and Secretaria Ejecutiva de Solidaridad de la Izquierda Chileana para América, *Chile Informativo 102, La DINA en Chile* (Mexico City: Casa de Chile, 1976).

On DINA's inner circle, see John Dinges and Saul Landau, op. cit., p. 138.

On BOSS answering solely to the Prime Minister, see *Rand Daily Mail*, Feb. 12, 1972, p. 9; on SAVAK answering directly to the Shah, see Fred Halliday, *Iran: Democracy and Dictatorship*, pp. 78–79.

On the prevalence of distrust within most authoritarian dictatorships, we interviewed (Washington, D.C., July 16, 1980) Donald Ranard, former director of the Office of Korean Affairs, in the State Department.

6. Ambassador Knox's appearance on "Face the Nation" was recalled by Joseph, March 13, 1980. On the reasons why Duvalier felt compelled to change the name of the Tonton Macoutes, see the testimony of Laraque, *Haitian Refugee Center et al., Plaintiff,* vs. *Benjamin Civiletti et al., Defendants,* supra, p. 18.

On the Leopards, the organization that replaced the Tonton Macoutes in the Haitian cities, see again the testimony of Laraque, op. cit., p. 18; and see esp. testimony of Edward McKeon, consul officer in Haiti, June 1976 to July 1978; McKeon was assigned to the embassy and worked in the Consular Section in Port-au-Prince (pp. 20–21). McKeon's testimony is valuable because it confirms the testimony in this court case of so many of the exiles, refugees, and political opponents of the Duvalier regime.

For the testimony on the familiar image of the Tonton Macoutes of Haiti wearing dark glasses as a uniform, and the point of view that only in the cities has this flagrant form of repression disappeared, see excerpts of the testimony of Marc Romulus, one of the allegedly "last" political prisoners of Haiti, gathered together by the Haitian Refugee Center, in Washington, D.C. Unfortunately, dates and a proper bibliographic citation do not appear on the pages presented by the Refugee Center.

For more on the idea that the Volunteers for National Security, which "replaced" the Tonton Macoutes, are virtually indistinguishable from the Macoutes, see the testimony of a Haitian refugee who came to the United States in March of 1980. See *Haitian Refugee Center et al., Plaintiff,* vs. *Benjamin Civiletti, et al., Defendants,* p. 1307. The twenty-one-year-old told the court that she was arrested "because we spoke badly of the government and things like that." On the judge's opinion that the Macoutes and the VSN's are virtually identical, see *Haitian Refugee Center* vs. *Benjamin Civiletti,* pp. 93–97.

On the speculation with regard to why Chilean President Pinochet felt obligated to change the name of DINA to CNI, we interviewed a confidential source, a former SIFA officer, in Washington, D.C., Apr. 27, 1979, and Eugenio Velasco, July 17, 1980, and June 28, 1979. The documentation in support of their point of view that the name change is virtually insignificant, however, is extensive: see United Nations, Economic and

Social Council, *Protection of Human Rights in Chile* (A/33/331) Oct. 1, 1978, pp. 31–35, paras. 120–44; New York *Times*, "Dissolution of Chile's Police Agency a 'Farce,'" Sept. 7, 1977; United Nations, Economic and Social Council, *Question of Human Rights in Chile* (E/CN.4/1362), Jan. 9, 1980, pp. 34–36, paras. 83–91; report of the Chile Committee for Human Rights, *Newsletter No. 17* (London: Chile Committee for Human Rights, Aug. 1977), pp. 1–2; and "Chile: After DINA," *Newsweek*, Sept. 12, 1977, p. 50.

On the name change of the Czechoslovakian secret police, see Josef Frolik, *Špión Vypovídá*, pp. 268–80. For further information we interviewed a confidential source, March 13, 1980; and Larisa and František Silnitsky, editors of *Communism and Eastern Europe: A Collection of Essays* (New York: Karz Publishers, 1979), Jan. 27, 1980.

On the name change of the Polish secret police, we interviewed Zabludowska, Mar. 11, 1980, and Walendowski, Mar. 21, 1980.

On the name changes of the Yugoslavian secret police, we interviewed a Yugoslavian refugee living in Los Angeles, on Feb. 10, 1980, who wrote in a letter accompanying a sketch of the intelligence services of Yugoslavia: "Despite the fact that the government wanted this name change, it was common practice to refer to SDS as UDBA." (Again, evidence of the frequency of name changes of the Yugoslavian secret services is the fact that former Yugoslavian citizens do not agree on the names of the services—some use the initials SDS, some SDB, etc.) On this subject we also interviewed Mihajlo Mihajlov, in Washington, D.C., Mar. 21, 1980; and we wrote some questions with regard to name changes to Mr. Jakša Kušan, publisher of *New Croatia*, or *Nova Hrvastska*, a bimonthly newspaper based in London and a refugee publication that has been in existence for twenty-two years.

According to a report written by Matthew Mestrović in the North American Newspaper Alliance, distributed by Universal Press, Tito may have kept the nature of his intelligence services such a secret that entire organizations may have existed about which few citizens know: "Aside from UDBA and KOS, there is a third much smaller and elite secret service, headquartered in Tito's presidential office. This service, about which little is known, is for Tito's personal use, but its function is probably to obtain high-level intelligence and to keep an eye on the UDBA and the KOS, rather than organize anti-exile operations. . . ." See North American Newspaper Alliance report, Nov. 4–5, 1978.

It is important to add that some Yugoslavian citizens do not believe that Ranković's overthrow meant anything. In fact, one Yugoslavian refugee wrote to us: "Contrary to the proclamations of the regime, the overthrow of Ranković did not change UDBA's character. Instead its files, which were never destroyed, were reopened and greatly augmented after 1971. . . ."

On Brezhnev's concern that the KGB had gotten to look too much like a Gulag, leading to the transferral of many political crimes that previously would have been under KGB jurisdiction to MVD jurisdiction, we interviewed Friedrich Nerzansky, Jan. 26, 1980; see also Amnesty International, *A Chronicle of Current Events: Journal of the Human Rights Movement in the USSR, No. 49* (London: Amnesty International, 1978), p. 3; and Amnesty International, *Prisoners of Conscience in the USSR*, 2nd ed. (London: Amnesty International, 1980), pp. 66–67.

On the changing of the name of the South African intelligence service from BOSS to DONS, see Johannesburg *Star*, June 24, 1978; and for background on the information scandal, which is believed to be related to the name change, see "Secret Funds Scandal Shakes White Confidence," *Southern Africa*, Feb. 16, 1979, pp. 16–17 (*Southern Africa* is a liberal magazine published by the Southern Africa Committee of New York), and *South Africa Namibia Update*, Vol. 3, No. 5, Apr. 11, 1979, p. 1 (*South Africa Namibia Update* is a publication that monitors economic and political developments in South Africa and Namibia, and is published by the Africa Policy Information Center of the African-American Institute at UN Plaza, in New York).

On the changing of the name of the Italian intelligence service, see "SID into SIS," *The Economist*, Nov. 6, 1976, p. 60.

On the perilous status of the KCIA due to negative publicity and the need for transferrals of power to the Army Security Command, see New York *Times Magazine*, Oct. 19, 1980, pp. 112–13; Michael Chinoy, "Chun Purifies South Korea," *The Nation*, Oct. 25, 1980, p. 403; and New York *Times* issues: May 19, 1980, p. A3; Jan. 21, 1980, p. A3; and May 29, 1980, p. A3. For further clarification on these points, we interviewed Ranard, July 16, 1980.

On Castro's reappointment of Ramiro Valdés as Minister of the Interior, see New York *Times*, June 8, 1980, p. A1. For further clarification, we interviewed Chibas, Mar. 14, 1980, and a group of Cuban women exiles who remember reading and hearing about the reinstatement, Mar. 15, 1980.

Information on DIER, the precursor to G-2, comes from an interview with Raúl Chibas, Mar. 14, 1980, who, as a Sierra Maestra fighter and rebel alongside of Castro during the revolution, was in a position to know such privileged information.

On the demonstration of the SAVAK agents for jobs, see *Kayhan International*, Mar. 1, 1979, p. 2; and *Time*, Feb. 19, 1979, p. 32.

On the change of SAVAK into SAVAMA we interviewed a retired

Iranian general living in Beverly Hills, Aug. 28, 1979. See also *The Economist*, Feb. 23, 1980, p. 29.

7. On the size of SAVAK, see Fred Halliday, *Iran: Dictatorship and Development*, p. 80.

On the size of NISA, we interviewed several Philippine exiles, in particular Romy Capulong, Mar. 12, 1980, a major figure in the distribution of the radical publication *Octopus* (see Chapter Two, Section 1), which was composed partially of government documents that had been smuggled by infiltrators of government and private corporations.

On the size of the KGB, see *Time*, June 23, 1980, p. 23.

On the cumbersome size of the Czechoslovakian secret service, see Josef Frolik, *Špión Vypovídá*, pp. 268–80.

For South African Prime Minister Vorster's refusal to be specific with regard to the size of BOSS, see Johannesburg *Star*, July 19, 1969.

CHAPTER FOUR

2. On the work schedule of the Paraguayan interrogator, see Amnesty International, *Deaths Under Torture and Disappearance of Political Prisoners in Paraguay* (London: Amnesty International, 1977), p. 8. Although torture sessions for any victim may last days, it is believed that teams of torturers in Paraguay take turns interrogating. Those turns usually last for approximately one hour only, according to a confidential source we interviewed in Washington, D.C., Apr. 25, 1979. The source is a professor of Latin American studies who recently spent two years living in Paraguay. We also interviewed this source on the description of the interrogation of the professor performed by the student, which appears later in the chapter, and on mistakes made by Paraguayan torturers practicing "submarine" torture.

On the work shift of the typical South African interrogator, we interviewed several sources. On Oct. 15, 1979, we interviewed an Indian woman now living in London who was detained and interrogated by members of the Security Branch in the late sixties. According to her, the interrogators usually work in four-hour shifts. On Oct. 19, we interviewed two other sources, both black South African exiles now living in London and actively working for the Black Consciousness movement. One was once active in the black South African Students' Organization (SASO). According to him, interrogators work from the morning until, roughly, four o'clock in the afternoon. And, he adds, it is during the course of the night that the real torture takes place, for it is those who are not officially on duty who then come to the prison and perform such work, thereby protecting themselves from doing the work on the record.

For more on this subject, see Donald Woods, *Biko* (London: Paddington Press, 1977), p. 13: "Detainees with personal experience of Security Police methods say the day interrogation teams specialize in coordinated questioning, psychological tactics and verbal abuse, but that the night teams are the assaulters, beating up detainees to 'soften them up' for the day teams. . . ." We also interviewed Malefe Pheto, whose story is recounted in Chapter One, Section 3. For more on interrogations performed by the South African Security Branch, see Hugh Lewin, *Bandiet: Seven Years in a South African Prison* (Harmondsworth, Middlesex: Penguin Books, 1976), memoirs of a white ex-prisoner.

On the Paraguayan interrogators' intake of amphetamines, see Amnesty International, *Deaths Under Torture*, p. 8.

On the use of Argentinian relief teams during lengthy interrogation sessions, see Amnesty International, *Prison Conditions in the Unidad Penitenciaria No. 1 Cárcel de Coronda* (London: Amnesty International, 1979), p. 3.

On the interrogation session during which Security Branch officers left their victim and went on a coffee break, we interviewed Malefe Pheto. We also interviewed Mr. Pheto on the subject of gymnastic equipment situated at John Vorster Square, and on the buddy system of South African interrogators. The Indian woman whom we interviewed on South African interrogators' work shifts also described the buddy system in our interview conducted on Oct. 15, 1979: she told us that when she told one of her interrogators that what he and his partner were doing to people like herself was similar to the persecution of six million people in Germany that once happened, he said, "So what?" The other interrogator immediately attempted to cover up the callousness of his partner's remark, adding that it wasn't just Jews who were killed, but also Russians and Communists!

On the pattern of larger teams interrogating high-level black-power detainees such as Steve Biko, see Donald Woods, *Biko*, p. 303.

On the number of interrogators used to interrogate Arab political prisoners on the West Bank, see "Israel and Torture," *Journal of Palestine Studies 34*, No. 2 IX (Winter 1980): 99–100.

On the process whereby British interrogators working within the Crime Squad, the Criminal Investigation Department and the Special Branch (working on suspects in Northern Ireland) work in pairs of two, furnishing their notes to the pair of interrogators following them, see Great Britain, "Report of the Committee of Inquiry into Police Interrogation Procedures in Northern Ireland," Cmnd. 7497, *Report, 1979*, para. 55, p. 18.

On the practice of Chilean torturers working in separate detention and interrogation teams, see *Report on the Use of Detention Centers*, p. 15;

this list, otherwise unmarked, was found in the files of the Human Rights Internet, in Washington, D.C., an information clearinghouse and international network fostering communication among scholars, activists, etc.

On the practice of guards at the military unit Fusileros Navales wearing cloth hoods all the time, see Ricardo Vilaro, *Testimony on Prison Conditions in the Navy Barracks, Fusileros Navales (FUSNA)* (London: Amnesty International, 1979).

On the former prisoner's observation that ESA torturers were far more vicious when they worked in groups than when they worked alone, see Amnesty International, *Torture in Greece: The First Torturers' Trial* (London: Amnesty International, 1975), p. 40.

In numerous countries, some of the most heinous incidents of alleged torture occurred when the torturers/interrogators appeared to be under the influence of alcohol. For example, a U.S. prisoner tortured in Greece said: "On the Sunday they wanted me to know that in the evening, drunken soldiers would enter my cell and that I would have trouble. And at midnight they actually came. . . . What I went through in the next hours was a real hell. . . ." See Amnesty International, *Torture in Greece*, p. 40. Similarly, consider this testimony of a Filipino victim: "He said that when the officers got drunk they fired shots in the air and abused him." See Amnesty International, *Report of a Mission to the Republic of the Philippines* (London: Amnesty International, 1976), p. 38. And finally, consider this testimony, which appeared in a report by the International Commission of Jurists, *Uganda and Human Rights: Reports to the U. N. Commission on Human Rights* (Geneva: International Commission of Jurists, 1977), p. 128: "The people doing the killings seemed to get enjoyment from them. They were delighted when someone was going to die. First they would drink a lot of waragi: a local gin. I recall that Oola, when he knew someone was going to die, would come to the prison that night and say, 'Leo iko kazi . . .' (Swahili meaning 'Today there is work'). Then he would go and drink himself to death. He would come back at night: that was when they killed people, at 8 P.M. at night. Oola does all the shootings."

On the Greek torturer who told a prisoner that ESA men relegated the human factor to second place, see Amnesty International, *The First Torturers' Trial*, p. 44.

3. On instructors at DGS (Portuguese security police) headquarters relying on films so as to instruct pupils in the fine art of torture, see "Torture Films Found at Police HQ," New York *Times*, May 3, 1974. See also Earl M. Cooperman, "Doctors, Torture and Abuse of the Doctor-Patient Relationship," 116 *Canadian Medical Association Journal*, Apr. 1977, p. 2.

On the Uruguayan torture center where *"el flaco"* was used as a human guinea pig, see Amnesty International, *El Infierno* (*Hell*): *Life Inside an Uruguayan Torture Center, A Testimony* (London: Amnesty International, 1977), p. 4.

On the KESA training center at which detainees were beaten and converted into torturers in the service of ESA, see Amnesty International, *Torture in Greece*, p. 38.

On the ESA officer's confession (at the Greek torturers' trial) that it was easy to deliver blows since he had suffered them himself, ibid., p. 38.

On the Greek ex-prisoner's analysis of this rationale of ESA officers to beat their detainees, ibid., p. 47.

4. For the full text of the Muñoz Alarcón (former DINA agent) confession, see United Nations, Economic and Social Council, 33rd sess., *Protection of Human Rights in Chile* (A/33/331), annex XVII, Oct. 3, 1976.

5. On the recruitment of Paraguayan interrogators as torturers, we interviewed, Apr. 25, 1979, the confidential source mentioned previously in these notes, a professor of Latin American studies who lived in Paraguay for two years and is now a human-rights activist living in Washington, D.C.

On the recruitment of young men into Department Six of Uruguay's DNII, we interviewed Juan Ferreira, son of a former presidential candidate of the Partido Blanco, at the office of the International League for Human Rights in New York, May 2, 1979. On the woman tortured at "El Infierno" who claims that she saw the shoes and pants legs of her torturers when she peeked out underneath her hood, see Amnesty International, *El Infierno* (*Hell*), p. 3.

On the rise of SAVAK torturers Naseri and Naji, we interviewed Dr. Reza Ghanadian in London, Oct. 9, 1979. For more information on Dr. Ghanadian, see our notes for Chapter Two, Section 1.

On Cambodian torturer Brother Deuch, see *Newsweek*, Sept. 8, 1980, p. 42.

On the youthfulness of torturers at a particular prison in Argentina, see testimony of Dr. Samuel Falicoff, Inter-American Commission on Human Rights, *Report on the Situation of Human Rights in Argentina* (Washington, D.C.: General Secretariat of the Organization of American States, 1980), p. 78.

On the prisoner's statement that Argentinian torturers often only beat prisoners who are blindfolded, see Amnesty International, *Prison Conditions in the Unidad Penitenciaria No. 1 Cárcel de Coronda*, p. 3.

On the recruitment of hard-core criminals into the ranks of Indonesian torturers, see U. S. Congress, House, Subcommittee on International Organizations of the Committee on International Relations, *Human Rights in Indonesia and the Philippines*, 94th Cong., 2nd sess., 1976, p. 13. The technique of co-opting convicted criminals as torturers has apparently taken place in the U.S.S.R. as well. See Amnesty International, *Prisoners of Conscience in the USSR* (London: Amnesty International, 1980), p. 166, which discusses allegations of "how criminal prisoners were employed to beat other prisoners."

On the use of alleged "goon syndicates" for torturing political detainees in the Philippines, see Sister Caridad Guidote, "Most Frequently Used Torture Methods of Marcos Police," Philippine *Times*, Aug. 12–18, 1978, pp. 1–2.

On the list of torturers serving the junta during the early years of DINA's existence, see report of Chile Democrático, *List of Torturers at the Service of the Fascist Junta in Chile* (Rome: Secretariat of Solidarity, Rome, 1974). Chile Democrático is an international association formed after the 1973 establishment of the military dictatorship The list was compiled on the basis of testimonies made by the first persons to testify about such atrocities before both the United Nations and Chile Democrático.

6. On Iranian Colonel Zamani's making a mockery of the moment of silence staged by inmates of the Qasr prison, see "From the Torture in Qasr Prison . . . ," *Keyhan*, Mar. 4, 1979.

On the relative leniency of one of the most famous generals of the Philippine Constabulary, we interviewed Charito Planas, attorney, activist, philanthropist, and exile now traveling across the United States, in Washington, D.C., July 17 and 18, 1979.

7. For the full text of the interview with Lieutenant Julio César Cooper, see Amnesty International, *Interview with Lieutenant Julio César Cooper* (London: Amnesty International, 1979). The confession of an Indonesian torturer made in 1969 is strikingly similar to Lieutenant Cooper's. For example, one incident that sparked this torturer's ultimate abandonment of his job was a somewhat personal experience, as was Cooper's. Wrote the torturer, Usamah: "The memory that he was our family doctor, the one from whom I usually sought help, the doctor who had succeeded in curing my aunt's chronic asthma, inhibited my desire not to be sentimental. This inner conflict was accompanied by feelings of irritation and rage. If only, yes, if only he had been someone else, he would have been 'worked over' right at the start. . . ." In addition, this same Indonesian torturer was forced to exercise brutal authority over a classmate of his, just as Cooper was forced to do so over a boyhood friend of his: "Sri was a classmate of mine. . . . I didn't have a chance to explain to her that I was only on duty at the guardhouse, under orders and forced to carry them out. . . . I wanted to cry out. . . ." For the full text of the confession, see Usamah, "War and Humanity: Notes on Personal Experience," which originally appeared in the 1969 issue of the

Jakarta literary magazine *Horizon;* this translation is taken from the Apr. 1970 issue of *Indonesia,* published by Cornell University's Modern Indonesia Project.

8. On the Iranian torturer who said he never expressed personal hatred toward his victims but was interested only in doing a job, see *Los Angeles Times,* June 22, 1979; and on the other SAVAK torturer who made a practice of stuffing a slipper into his victims' mouths so as to stifle their screams, ibid.

On the confessed Greek torturer's statement at the 1975 torturers' trial that he was just doing a job, see Amnesty International, *Torture in Greece,* p. 31.

On the Argentinian torturer at La Coronda Prison who told one of his prisoners that all he wanted was to earn a good rest, see Amnesty International, *Prison Conditions in the Unidad Penitenciaria No. 1 Cárcel de Coronda,* pp. 2–3; and on the indoctrination of Argentinian torturers, ibid., p. 2.

On the Uruguayan torturer who explained his motivations for "going after" a 19-year-old Communist Party member, we interviewed (May 2, 1979) Juan Ferreira, son of the former presidential candidate of the Partido Blanco, himself arrested several times.

On the Uruguayan torturer at "El Infierno" who uttered staunchly anticommunist statements to a line of prisoners, see Amnesty International, *El Infierno,* p. 1.

On the Greek ESA torturer who spoke out against the upper-middle classes while torturing his victim, see Amnesty International, *Torture in Greece,* p. 31.

On the arrest of the Chief Legal Counsel for the Chilean Cooperative Committee for Peace, we interviewed José Zalaquett, Apr. 26, 1979. For more on Mr. Zalaquett, see our notes for Chapter Two, Section 12.

On Ben Eliezer's despair over the educational, intellectual, and moral values of some of the Israeli soldiers, see *The Christian Science Monitor,* Apr. 4, 1979, p. 27.

On the ESA torturers who believed they were the "greater Greeks," see Amnesty International, *Torture in Greece,* p. 29.

On the UDBA man who boasted of having killed Ivo Masina, see Bruno Bušić, *UDBA Archipelago* (Arcadia: Croatian Information Service, 1976), p. 7.

9. On Major Harold Snyman, the officer who was in charge of the now-deceased Steve Biko, see Donald Woods, *Biko,* p. 264.

On Kopkamtib's enlistment of the services of physicians to design tests aimed at determining the political persuasions of detainees, see bulletins issued by TAPOL-U.S., *Campaign for the Release of Indonesian Political Prisoners* (Montclair, N.J.: TAPOL), Nos. 16 and 17, Nov. 1978, p. 11, for a list of allegations of doctors' involvement in designing the test, summarized from *Feiten en Meningen*, Vol. 5, Nos. 1–2, July 1978, pp. 5–10; Bulletin No. 33, Apr. 1979, p. 6, for excerpts of an interview with a commander of Kopkamtib, with Dutch journalist Wecher Hulst (*Haagse Pos*, Feb. 10, 1979); and Bulletin No. 14, Apr. 1978, p. 11, for excerpts of another interview with a high Kopkamtib official.

The psychological tests apparently consist of no fewer than four hundred questions, all of which must be answered in the political prisoner's own words. According to one source, a typical question is, "What will you do if you find that you do not agree with the government's policy?" And according to an article in *Kompas*, Jan. 5, 1978, written by another former prisoner who went to Buru, some questions reported by another tapol were: Do you agree with nationalism or internationalism? Do you like to read newspapers that report about crime or about mountain expeditions? Which do you prefer, kissing women or eating in a restaurant? (For more on this, see TAPOL *Bulletin No. 14*, Apr. 1978, p. 9.)

For General Sumitro's information on the psychological tests, see New York *Times*, Apr. 26, 1978, reprinted in TAPOL *Bulletin No. 15*, June 1978, p. 15.

10. On the role of doctors who helped to measure the levels of fear and anxiety plaguing Chilean political prisoners, see United Nations, Economic and Social Council, 31st sess., *Protection of Human Rights in Chile* (A/31/253) Oct. 8, 1976, pp. 84–85, para. 314. And on the doctor at the prison Cuatro Álamos, known as "el Brujo," ibid., p. 89, para. 335.

On the Chilean woman who was taken to a CNI clinic, see United Nations, Economic and Social Council, 36th sess., *Question of Human Rights in Chile* (E/CN.4/1362) Jan. 29, 1980, pp. 23–25, para. 60.

On the Greek doctor who became known among prisoners as the "orange juice doctor," see Amnesty International, *Torture in Greece*, p. 17.

On the Polish physician nicknamed Dr. Mengele by inmates of Rakowiecka Street Prison, we interviewed Irena Zabludowska, Polish émigré now living in New York City, Mar. 11, 1980.

For the testimony of the Argentinian prisoner who claims to have heard her husband's torturers consulting a doctor during a torture session, see the testimony of Estela Cornalea, who, along with her husband, Alberto, was detained without charges by the Argentine military, Nov. 25, 1976, Amnesty International, *Testimony of an Argentine Prisoner* (London: Amnesty International, n.d.), p. 12.

On the doctor at the Uruguayan torture center who advised torturers on how to proceed, see Amnesty International, *El Infierno*, p. 5.

On the doctor on hand to supervise torture sessions at the central police station in Bilbao, see Amnesty International, *Report of an Amnesty International Mission to Spain* (London: Sept. 1975), p. 10.

On the Brazilian prisoner who claims that he felt a doctor's stethoscope on his chest during his torture session, see Fred B. Morris, "In the Presence of Mine Enemies," *Harper's Magazine*, Oct. 1975, p. 64.

On the political prisoner held in a camp in Manila who describes the negative attitude shared by doctors and nurses at the camp toward political detainees, see Concepción Águila, "Detention Camp: Manila," *Bulletin of Concerned Asian Scholars* 6 (Nov.–Dec. 1974): 42.

On the physician present during a hunger strike at a camp in Perm Colony VS3933135, see Amnesty International, *Prisoners of Conscience in the USSR* (London: Amnesty International, 1980), p. 122.

11. On the role of the MVD in administering cases involving political prisoners between the times of release and of confinement, ibid., pp. 178–79. For more on Soviet psychiatric hospitals, see *Time*, June 23, 1980, p. 64.

On the Serbsky Institute, see Alexander Podrabinek, *Punitive Medicine: A Summary* (London: Amnesty International, Aug. 1, 1977). See also Amnesty International, *Prisoners of Conscience*, pp. 21, 130, 131, 177, 186, 200–1.

On the prominence of MVD personnel in running the special psychiatric institutions, see Alexander Podrabinek, op. cit., p. 18.

On the doctor who told a patient in a Soviet psychiatric hospital that patients' conditions are evaluated solely according to the diagnoses offered by members of the KGB, see Amnesty International, *Prisoners of Conscience*, pp. 188–89.

On the doctor who told a patient that his "disease is dissent," ibid., p. 135.

12. On the persecution of Chilean doctors who were opposed to the junta, see New York *Times*, Jan. 13, 1974, p. 3.

On the doctors who treated Steve Biko, see Donald Woods, *Biko*, pp. 321–44.

On the collusion between SAVAK and the coroner's office in Iran, see *Kayhan International*, 1979 (no further date verification available).

On the shooting of nine revolutionaries whom authorities later said were shot while trying to escape, see *Iran Voice*, July 9, 1979, p. 6, for excerpts of Tehrani's confession; and see Reza Baraheni, "Special Report: the SAVAK Documents," *The Nation*, Feb. 23, 1980, pp. 193–202.

On the analysis of how physicians are sometimes caught unwittingly in the torture process, see Drs. Albert Jonsen and Leonard Sagan, "Medical Ethics and Torture," *New England Journal of Medicine* 294 (June 1976): 631–40.

On the RCMP's making use of physicians' prescription lists, see report of the Civil Liberties Association, National Capital Region, *A Partial*

Listing of Facts and Allegations Regarding Security Operations in Canada (undated), p. 3. On Operation Featherbed, ibid., p. 4.

For the full text of the Parker Committee report, see Great Britain, Northern Ireland Office, Parliament. Parliamentary Papers (Commons), 1971–72, Vol. 18, Cmnd. 4901, "Report of the Committee of Privy Counsellors Appointed to Consider Authorized Procedures for the Interrogation of Persons Suspected of Terrorism," Mar. 1972.

On Dr. Earl Cooperman's views on the dangers of the medical profession's becoming merely another state agency, see Earl M. Cooperman, "Doctors, Torture and Abuse of the Doctor-Patient Relationship," *Canadian Medical Association Journal* 116 (Apr. 1977): 707, 709–10.

For more on the views of Professor Alfred Heidjer and Dr. Herman van Geuns with regard to the responsibility of the medical profession vis-à-vis inhibiting the practice of torture whenever possible, see Herman van Geuns and Alfred Heidjer, *Professional Codes of Ethics* (London: Amnesty International, 1976).

On the doctor's statement that the interests of security in South Africa supersede the terms of the Hippocratic oath, see Donald Woods, *Biko*, p. 338.

13. On the Milgram experiment, see Stanley Milgram, "Behavioral Study of Obedience," *Journal of Abnormal Social Psychology* 67 (1963): 371–78; and Stanley Milgram, "Some Conditions of Obedience and Disobedience to Authority," *Human Relations* 18 (1965): 57–76.

CHAPTER FIVE

1. Information on the lesson plan for the course "Interviews and Interrogations," taught at the International Police Academy, comes from notes taken by an anonymous source who, in the company of Diane Edwards La Voy, Intelligence Committee, U. S. Congress, interviewed Lauren Goin, director, Office of Public Safety, AID, July 26, 1974.

The term "School for Torturers" was used to describe the International Police Academy in the Greek left-wing newspaper *Avghe* (undated), abridged and provided by the Library of Congress, Washington, D.C., for Senator James Abourezk, Sept. 1975.

For an excellent distillation of country-by-country estimates of torture in terms of its systematic or sporadic application, consult Amnesty International sources: *Report 1978* (London: Amnesty International, 1978); *Report 1979* (London: Amnesty International, 1979); and *Report 1980* (London: Amnesty International, 1980).

The Chilean attorney's analysis of the role of torture as practiced by DINA comes from our interview with José Zalaquett, former Chief Legal

Counsel of the Committee of Cooperation and Peace in Chile, Apr. 26, 1976.

Contradictory points of view on the motivation for torture were expressed by several Chilean sources who suggested that, in addition to the political motivations for practicing torture, sadism on the part of agents played a major role as well. This point of view was expressed by Eugenio Velasco, former Chilean Supreme Court justice and former defense attorney (specializing in cases involving disappeared persons), in an interview conducted at the University of California, Los Angeles, June 28, 1979—and reinforced by an interview (Apr. 27, 1979) with a confidential source, a former SIFA officer once sentenced to death by Chilean authorities, now living in exile in Washington, D.C.

For background information on the subject of torture in Chile, see: testimony of José Zalaquett before the U. S. Congress, House, Committee on International Relations, *Chile: The Status of Human Rights and Its Relationship to U. S. Economic Assistance Programs,* 94th Cong., 2nd sess., 1976; and the following United Nations reports: Economic and Social Council, 31st sess., *Protection of Human Rights in Chile* (A/33/331), Oct. 8, 1976; Economic and Social Council, 36th sess., *Question of Human Rights in Chile* (E/CN.4/1381), Jan. 9, 1980; Economic and Social Council, 34th sess., *Protection of Human Rights* (A/34/583, add. 1), Nov. 21, 1979; Economic and Social Council, 33rd sess., *Protection of Human Rights in Chile* (A/33/331), Oct. 1, 1978; and Economic and Social Council, 36th sess., *Question of Human Rights in Chile* (E/CN.4/1362), Jan. 29, 1980. See also Report of the Secretariat for Solidarity in America with the Chilean People, *Chile Informative 104, 141, Assassination of Letelier: The Actors in a Sinister Plot and Crisis in the Cabinet: An 'Intervened' Pinochet?* (Toronto: Chile Informative, 1978); and a report issued by Casa de Chile, *Chile Informative No. 102, La DINA en Chile* (Mexico City: Casa de Chile, 1976). Also, a report by Konrad Ege and Martha Wenger, . . . *The Embassy of the Federal Republic of Germany and Torture in Chile* (Washington, D.C.: Washington Area Clergy and Laity Concerned, 1977); and Amnesty International, *Disappeared Prisoners in Chile* (London: Amnesty International, 1977). On the shift from arbitrary and massive repression under DINA to selective repression under CNI in Chile, see Los Angeles *Times,* May 18, 1979, Part II, p. 7. This article, focusing on the "new crackdown" in Chile as part of President Pinochet's response to mounting pressure to restore a constitutional government, states: "The Chilean Human Rights Commission, a private group, reported an increase in rights violations during the first half of this year compared with last year, *including charges of torture of prisoners by the security police* [emphasis ours]." This statement draws an important distinction between torture a la DINA and a la CNI. Note the observation expressed in this article by a liberal Chilean lawyer about the commonly made statement that torture in Chile is now selective, rather than massive: "Torture is more sophisticated now, they don't leave marks and people don't disappear as they did before."

2. On the various styles and methods of torture and interrogation implemented by Singapore secret police, see Amnesty International, *Singapore* (London: Amnesty International, 1978), pp. 10–11.

On this particular beating by Haitian security forces, see the testimony of a Haitian refugee in the case of *Haitian Refugee Center et al., Plaintiff*, vs. *Benjamin Civiletti et al., Defendants*, Vol. 5 (79-2086-Civ-JLK), Miami, Fla., 1980, p. 4. This court case contains numerous allegations and descriptions of torture at the hands, primarily, of the Tonton Macoutes. For additional information of this nature, we used the series of depositions and affadavits prepared by Dale Frederick Swartz, Esq., director, Alien Rights Law Project, in conjunction with the Haitian Refugee Center case against Benjamin Civiletti.

The poet and Iranian ex-prisoner Reza Baraheni offered an analysis of the general style of torture practiced by SAVAK agents, in "Special Report: The SAVAK Documents," *The Nation*, Feb. 23, 1980, pp. 193–202.

For more on torture in Iran, see: William J. Butler and Georges Levasseur, *Human Rights and the Legal System in Iran* (Geneva: International Commission of Jurists, Mar. 1976), p. 22; Amnesty International, *Iran* (London: Amnesty International, Nov. 1976), p. 8; Amnesty International, *Human Rights in Iran, Testimony by Brian Wrobell Before the Subcommittee on International Organizations of the Committee of International Relations* (London: Amnesty International, 1978), p. 63; the following issues of *Iran Voice*, the weekly newssheet published by the Iranian embassy in Washington, D.C., under the Khomeini regime: Vol. 1, Nos. 1–5, June 4 to July 2, 1979; the following issues of *Iranian People's Struggle*, a left-wing newspaper published in Iran: Vol. 1, Nos. 1–5 (1975), Vol. 2, Nos. 1–3 (1976), and Vol. 2, No. 5, Aug. 1977; and the following issues of the *Iranian National Front Bulletin* (bulletin of a liberal left-wing group in Iran that has since dissolved): Vol. 1, Nos. 1–4 (1972), and Vol. 2, No. 2, Aug. 1974.

For an astonishing variety of revealing information on all aspects of SAVAK, including torture, see the document compiled by the Confederation of Iranian Students (National Union), *SAVAK: Documents on Iranian Secret Police* (Geneva: 1976). The document was compiled by students who raided the Geneva, Switzerland, headquarters of SAVAK and confiscated confidential memos, a number of which we have had translated from the Farsi.

Congressman Andrew Maguire's discussion of the importance and prevalence of electric shock torture to the South African Security Branch appeared in *The Christian Science Monitor*, Aug. 2, 1978. Other sources, however, contradict Congressman Maguire's view about the importance of electric shock torture. One confidential source, a white South African exiled author living in London, whom we interviewed on October 12, 1979, argues that due to scandalous incidents in which it became apparent that South African police were using electric shock, authorities have adopted other, less "obvious" torture techniques (by less obvious, we assume that our source means the adoption of torture techniques that don't leave marks on victims). Another confidential source, a prominent South African attorney now living in London, whom we interviewed on October 18, 1979, made a similar point. According to this attorney, the Lenkoe trial serves as evidence of the point that the authorities have been forced to steer clear, at least to some degree, of applying electric shock torture. A renowned pathologist and authority on burns, Dr. Alan Richards, was called in from the United States by the defense to testify that electric shock *had* in fact been applied to James Lenkoe, a thirty-five-year-old Lesotho national who died five days after his arrest, on the night of March 5, 1965. (One Security Branch official testified that electric shock was in fact not used—but his testimony seemed unconvincing after Dr. Richards' appearance.)

According to our sources, when electric shock torture, along with sexual harassment, is used, it is applied chiefly to black detainees and suspects.

On torture in South Africa in general, as well as electric shock in particular, see: "Torture in South Africa?" *Proveritate*, Dec. 15, 1972, pp. 11–12. *Proveritate* was a publication issued by the Christian Institute in South Africa; the Institute was banned, Oct. 1977. The opposition group sponsoring *Proveritate* was multiracial. See also Hilda Bernstein, *South Africa: The Terrorism of Torture* (London: International Defense and Aid Fund, 1972); Amnesty International, *Political Imprisonment in South Africa* (London: Amnesty International, 1978); and the following newspaper stories written by June Goodwin, of *The Christian Science Monitor:* "A South African Teen-ager Tells of Ordeal with Police," Aug. 9, 1978; "Another Detainee Dies in South Africa," July 12, 1978; "South Africa Strives to Soften Police State Image," Aug. 1, 1978; and "Police Torture of Blacks Charged," Aug. 2, 1978.

On the subject of blacks and torture, it is interesting to note that a confidential source, a white South African exile living in Berkeley, whom we interviewed on June 13, 1979, stated that uniformed officers immediately become violent at the prisons upon the arrival of the security police, suggesting, therefore, that they are responding to pressure from their "superiors."

On the South African Government's reply to Amnesty International's report on torture, see Amnesty International, *Political Imprisonment in South Africa*, p. 56.

The Philippine Government's reply to Amnesty International's allegations of torture appears in the report of Amnesty International, *Report of an Amnesty International Mission to the Republic of the Philippines*, 1975 (London: Amnesty International, 1977), p. 8.

The former member of the Quezon City Police Department was interviewed by the Philippine *Times*, a United States-based publication, Aug. 12–18, 1978, p. 6.

The analysis of the impact of torture is taken from the testimony of José Zalaquett, U. S. Congress, House, *Chile: The Status of Human Rights and Its Relationship To U. S. Economic Assistance Programs*, 1976, p. 61.

Information on KGB interrogation procedures comes from an interview with Eli Valk at the National Conference of Soviet Jewry in New York City, Jan. 24, 1980. On this subject, Aishe Seytmuratova, a Crimean Tatar activist imprisoned from 1971 until 1974 for her role in the movement advocating the return of the Tatar people to their homeland in the Crimea, was interviewed in New York, Jan. 25, 1980.

On the KGB's and MVD's use of psychiatric hospitals and isolation cells as a means of silencing political protestors, see report by Amnesty International, *Prisoners of Conscience in the USSR: Their Treatment and Conditions*, Chap. 7, "Compulsory Detention in Psychiatric Hospitals" (London: Amnesty International, Apr. 1980), pp. 172–203.

For details on drug tortures applied in Soviet psychiatric institutes, see Alexander Podrabinek's *Punitive Medicine: A Summary* (London: Amnesty International, Aug. 1, 1977); and S. Alexeyeff, "Abuse of Psychiatry as a Tool for Political Repression in the Soviet Union," *Medical Journal of Australia* 1 (5) (31 Jan. 1976): 122–23.

On the categories of drugs administered in the Soviet special psychiatric hospitals, see Amnesty International, *Prisoners of Conscience in the USSR*, pp. 172–203.

The pain and paralysis of Leonid Ivanovich is vividly described in Amnesty International's *Prisoners of Conscience*, p. 198. On allegations of drug torture of a similar sort being used in South Africa, see Manchester *Guardian*, Aug. 3, 1980, p. 22.

For more-detailed information on the effects of drug treatments on detainees, with special emphasis on the countries in which physicians apply them, see the source notes for Chapter Four, Sections 8–11.

3. The description of the interrogation of a black South African activist by South African Security Branch officers at John Vorster Square comes from a confidential interview (Oct. 19, 1979) with a black South African exile now living in London who is an active member of London's

Black Consciousness movement. Another interesting personal testimony on interrogation by security police, not included in this chapter, came from an interview with an Indian South African woman, conducted in London, Oct. 15, 1979. Strikingly, she described being interrogated about her dreams—and being forced to stand for six days without sleep during her imprisonment.

In the South African magazine *Proveritate*, Dec. 15, 1972 (no longer in existence, since the banning of the Christian Institute, which issued it), there is an interesting discussion of reasons why it is so difficult to prove allegations of torture. Among the observations made: the detainee is held incommunicado, so that the prisoner's story becomes a matter of his word against that of two or more policemen; there is no truly independent visitor to detainees—a magistrate may visit once a fortnight, but "to whom does he render report, and who acts? After all due respect has been accorded to magistrates, they are still essentially in the employ of the Minister of Justice"; unless a detainee is well supported by an efficient lawyer, he may die in detention and there may be a delay in informing the next of kin, and the next of kin may have difficulty securing the services of a private pathologist to observe the usually prompt post-mortem; the private pathologist may only observe and ensure that prescribed procedures are in fact carried out by the district surgeon; people who do in one way or another glean information regarding the treatment of detainees tend to seal their lips out of fear of banning, withdrawal of passports, and being detained themselves.

On the Arab who claimed to be tortured by security police but who did not issue a formal statement against his interrogators, see "Special Feature: Israel and Torture," *Journal of Palestine Studies 34*, No. 2 IX (Winter 1980): 107. In support of this, according to a cable issued by Alexandra Johnson (and reprinted in this "Special Feature"), former U.S. vice-consul stationed in Jerusalem who was eventually dismissed by the State Department, "He [a local attorney] said that he contested the validity of the confession only in cases where the accused might be sentenced to imprisonment for life or a very long term of years. . . . In all other cases . . . he advised his clients to affirm their confessions in court, regardless of whether they had been extracted by force." See p. 106 of *Journal of Palestine Studies 34*. For more on allegations of torture and mistreatment applied to Arab detainees primarily on the West Bank and in the Occupied Territories, see two bulletins issued by the Palestine Human Rights Campaign, Bulletin No. 17, Apr. 1979, and Bulletin No. 5, Feb. 1978 (Washington, D.C.); Amnesty International, *Report and Recommendations of an Amnesty International Mission to the Government of the State of Israel* (London: Amnesty International, 1979); and the report of the Israeli League for Human and

Civil Rights, *Second Collection on Torture and Police Brutality in Israel* (Tel-Aviv: Apr. 30, 1979); and for background information on some women detainees, see Soraya Antonius, "Prisoners for Palestine: A List of Women Political Prisoners," *Journal of Palestine Studies 35*, No. 3 IX (Spring 1980): 29–80.

On the Israeli practice of holding a "trial within a trial," a process in which a defendant argues that he was coerced to confess, see Amnesty International, *Report and Recommendations to the Government of the State of Israel*, pp. 33–35.

On interrogation by the KCIA, see Amnesty International, report of an *Amnesty International Mission to the Republic of Korea* (London: Amnesty International, 1977), pp. 36–37. For more on interrogation by the KCIA, see Amnesty International, *Ali Lameda: A Personal Account of the Democratic People's Republic of Korea* (London: Amnesty International, 1979).

On techniques of interrogation as practiced by SAVAK authorities at the famed Joint Committee facility, see *Iranian People's Struggle*, Vol. 1, No. 5 (Nov. 1975), p. 3. On the Joint Committee, see also: International Commission of Jurists, *Human Rights and the Legal System in Iran*, p. 20; and *Iran Voice*, Vol. 1, No. 6 (July 9, 1979), p. 1. In this issue of *Iran Voice*, executed SAVAK torturer Tehrani is quoted: "The Committee was very successful early in its activities, to discover and make recognition of several armed political groups engaged in anti-Shah activities. Among these were the 'Siahkal Group' and the 'People's Guerrillas Organization.' After this initial success, which incidentally coincided with the terror of General Farsio, and the attack on the Gholhak Police Station, the 'joint committee' was reorganized on the basis of some similar committees existent in Latin America."

On the interrogation in 1979 of a Taiwanese dissident by security police, see a report by Hsiung Lin-yi, *On Being Detained* (Leucadia: Formosan Association of Human Rights, 1980). Hsiung was (at the time that he issued this report) Taiwan Provincial Assembly member, elected 1977, a lawyer, editor, legal adviser of *Formosa* magazine, and commissioner of the Opposition Campaign Committee.

Taiwanese authorities, however, do not often admit using violent techniques in interrogations. At the trial of the eight dissidents associated with *Formosa* magazine, the court introduced a letter from the Bureau of Investigation, the agency responsible for the interrogation of a Mr. Lee, stating that *no improper means were used*. See New York *Times*, Apr. 26, 1980, p. A3.

A point of view that diverges from the allegations of the left-wing opponents of the current regime in Taiwan was expressed by Alice Kao. a Taiwanese reporter for the *United Daily News*, on a 1980 tour through the United States aimed at countering the claims, specifically, of Linda Arrigo Shih, whose husband was arrested and hunted down after the famed Kaohsiung riots; Kao was interviewed in Los Angeles on February 23, 1980. According to Ms. Kao, the Taiwan Garrison Command does use violence: "[I] wouldn't deny they use violence . . . but conditions have improved." They use "force," she said, correcting herself, *not* violence. Ms. Kao's definition of violence is "asking questions in a harsh way."

For more on allegations of torture in Taiwan, see Amnesty International, *Taiwan* (London: Amnesty International, 1976), p. 9; and the following stories from the New York *Times:* Mar. 17, 1980, p. A6; Mar. 27, 1980, p. A4; and Mar. 25, 1980, p. A8.

On the careful style of interrogation practiced by the head of Nokorbal, the Cambodian secret police, see *Newsweek,* Sept. 8, 1980, p. 42.

For the full text of the Uruguayan defector's interview, see Amnesty International, *Interview with Lieutenant Julio César Cooper Made in Stockholm* (London: Amnesty International, Jan. 17, 1979. On the South African interrogator's relentless pursuit of information from the detainee, regardless of whether or not the information obtained is factually correct, see Donald Woods, *Biko* (Harmondsworth, Middlesex: Penguin Books, 1978), p. 313. For more on the alleged harassment of Woods by South African security officers, see New York *Times,* Dec. 13, 1977; and for more on the response of the South Africans to charges of beating Steve Biko, see New York *Times,* Nov. 14, 1979.

Testimony of a Greek ex-prisoner in 1975 was extracted from a report by Amnesty International, *Torture in Greece: The First Torturers' Trial* (London: Amnesty International, 1977), p. 17. A strikingly similar bit of testimony appeared in a collection of documents provided for us by Richard P. Claude, of the Center of Philosophy and Public Policy, University of Maryland, regarding the case of *People of the Philippines, Complainant,* vs. *Trinidad Gerrilla,* ^d*Trinidad Herrera,* ^d*Norma Salvador,* ^d*Clara Banez, Respondent.* (SPI. No. 77-1272), 1977. Trinidad Herrera, leader of the military organization ZOTO, of the Philippines, said in her counter affidavit of June 14, 1977: "I readily complied with their order insofar as the papers and pamphlets really owned and possessed by me were concerned. However, I refused to sign or initial those which I know are neither owned nor possessed by me. The interrogators insisted that I sign even those. I finally agreed to do so, but only when they said that I could write anything I wanted on said materials, provided I affix my signature thereon. And so, before affixing my signature on those documents and pamphlets, I wrote something to this effect: 'This was supposedly taken from my room.' I noticed that this angered the interrogators. I presume that this was one of the reasons why they tortured and maltreated me."

NOTES TO PAGES 175–79

The description of the interrogation of a Taiwanese dissident was excerpted from Hsiung Lin-yi, *On Being Detained*, pp. 2–3.

On the technique of interrogators obtaining two confessions from detainees, see "Special Feature: Torture in Israel," *Journal of Palestine Studies 35*, p. 105.

On the interrogation techniques of Chinese Public Security agents, see Amnesty International, *Political Imprisonment in the People's Republic of China* (London: Amnesty International, 1978), pp. 45–46 and 50–52; and Los Angeles *Herald-Examiner*, May 7, 1979, p. A5. Specifically, on the interrogation of Zhang, see Amnesty International, *Political Imprisonment*, pp. 46–49.

4. On Decree 187, requiring arrested persons to be examined by medical authorities before entering a place of detention and at the time of release, see the testimony of José Zalaquett, U. S. Congress, House, *Chile: The Status of Human Rights and Its Relationship to U. S. Economic Assistance Programs*, 1976, p. 63.

On the collaboration of U. S. Drug Enforcement Administration agents with the Mexican Federal Judicial Police in the techniques of interrogation, see the allegations in *The Village Voice*, June 4, 1979, pp. 11–15. On torture in general in Mexico, see Robert K. Goldman, professor of law, American University, Washington, D.C., and Daniel Jacoby, lawyer before the Court of Appeals of Paris, France, *Report of the Commission of Enquiry to Mexico* (New York: International League for Human Rights, Dec. 1978), pp. 16–19.

On the two phases of torture practiced by Greek ESA officers with regard to their perception of the desirability of leaving marks on their victims, see Amnesty International, *Torture in Greece*, p. 11.

On the testimony of the South African prisoner subjected to torture, allegedly by the administration of electric shock, see Amnesty International, *Political Imprisonment in South Africa*, p. 66.

For the full testimony of the Chilean woman on the subject of being subjected to electric-shock torture by secret police agents, see United Nations, Economic and Social Council, 36th sess., *Question of Human Rights in Chile* (E/CN.4/1362), Jan. 29, 1980, p. 25, para. 60.

Testimony alleging torture and the playing of loud music by secret police agents appears in the Organization of American States, Inter-American Commission on Human Rights, *Report on the Situation of Human Rights in Argentina* (Washington, D.C.: General Secretariat, 1980), p. 79. For more allegations of torture in Argentina, see: Amnesty International, *Report of an Amnesty International Mission to Argentina* (London: Amnesty International, 1977), pp. 36–40; Amnesty International, *Prison Conditions in the Unidad Penitenciaria No. 1 Cárcel de Coronda* (London: Amnesty International, 1979); Amnesty International, *Testimony on Secret Detention Camps in Argentina* (London:

Amnesty International, 1980); Amnesty International, *Visit Beautiful Argentina* (London: Amnesty International, 1978); report of the Lawyers Committee for International Human Rights, *Materials on Human Rights and the Situation of Defense Lawyers and Judges in Argentina* (New York: Lawyers Committee, Mar. 1979); and the following articles: New York *Times*, Sept. 16, 1979, p. A11; and *The New York Review of Books*, "Argentine Terror: A Memoir," Oct. 11, 1979, pp. 13–14.

Further allegations of torture were made to us in an interview (New York, Mar. 11, 1980) at the office of the International League for Human Rights, with three confidential sources. See our notes for Chapter Two, Section 11.

Testimony of the Indonesian prisoner alleging torture techniques and the role of music in the torture process of the secret police appears in U. S. Congress, House, Subcommittee on International Organizations of the Committee on International Relations, *Human Rights in Indonesia and the Philippines*, 94th Cong., Dec. 18, 1975, and May 3, 1976, p. 13.

On torture in Indonesia in general, see Amnesty International, *Indonesia* (London: Amnesty International, 1977), pp. 59–88; and U. S. Congress, House, Committee on Foreign Affairs, *Human Rights in Asia: Noncommunist Countries*, 96th Cong., 2nd sess., 1980. See also issues of the organization TAPOL-U.S., Campaign for the Release of Indonesian Political Prisoners, bulletins: No. 1, Oct. 1975; No. 5, June 1976; No. 6, Aug. 1976; No. 7, Oct. 1976; No. 8, Dec. 1976; No. 11, June 1977; No. 13, Oct. 1977; No. 14, Apr. 1979; No. 15, June 1978; Nos. 16 and 17, Nov. 1978; No. 31, Dec.–Jan. 1978–79; No. 33, Apr. 1979. (Montclair, N.J.: TAPOL).

On the torture center in downtown Asunción, see bulletin of the Inter-American Association for Democracy and Freedom, *Hemispherica*, Vol. XXVIII, No. 2 (Feb. 1979), p. 3. On torture in Paraguay in general, see Amnesty International, *Paraguay* (London: Amnesty International, 1978), pp. 8–9; Amnesty International, *Deaths Under Torture and Disappearance of Political Prisoners in Paraguay* (London: Amnesty International, 1977).

On torture and the role of music in the torture process at Infantry Battalion ⚡13, in Uruguay, see Amnesty International, *El Infierno (Hell): Life Inside an Uruguayan Torture Center* (London: Amnesty International, 1977), p. 3. On torture in Uruguay in general, see Amnesty International, *Deaths Under Torture* (London: Amnesty International, 1978); Amnesty International, *Conditions of Detention for Political Prisoners in Uruguay* (London: Amnesty International, June 1979); Amnesty International, *Uruguay: The Cases of 14 Prisoners of Conscience* (London: Amnesty International, Mar. 1979); Amnesty International, *Political Imprisonment in Uruguay* (London: Amnesty International, June 1979);

and Ricardo Vilaro, *Testimony on Prison Conditions in the Navy Barracks, Fusileros Navales (FUSNA)* (London: Amnesty International, 1979).

On the Philippine Constabulary detention center "Production Room," see Amnesty International, *Report of an Amnesty International Mission to the Republic of the Philippines* (London: Amnesty International, 1976), p. 37.

On the "Operation Room" at the Interior Ministry in Kabul, Afghanistan, see New York *Times*, Sept. 16, 1979, p. A13; and on torture in general in Afghanistan, see Amnesty International, *Violations of Human Rights and Fundamental Freedoms in the Democratic Republic of Afghanistan* (London: Amnesty International, 1979), pp. 13–16; New York *Times*, Sept. 16, 1980, p. 13; and Los Angeles *Times*, May 18, 1979, Part II, p. 7.

On Argentina's "Club Atlético," see Amnesty International, *Testimony on Secret Detention Camps in Argentina* (London: Amnesty International, 1980), pp. 4–5.

On the "House of Bells," see *Newsweek*, Mar. 31, 1975, p. 51.

On the SIFA "Scream Room," see *Newsweek*, Mar. 31, 1975, p. 51.

On "Palace of Laughter," see United Nations, Economic and Social Council, Ad Hoc Working Group on the Situation of Human Rights in Chile, 31st sess., *Protection of Human Rights in Chile* (A/31/253) Oct. 8, 1976, p. 92, para. 354.

On former Ugandan President Idi Amin's nicknaming of his torture chambers, see International Commission of Jurists, *Uganda and Human Rights* (Geneva: International Commission of Jurists, 1977), pp. 28–29. For more on torture in Uganda, see Amnesty International, *Human Rights in Uganda* (London: Amnesty International, 1978), pp. 13–22; and the following newspaper stories: Los Angeles *Times*, May 11, 1979, Part I, p. 21; and Sept. 20, 1979, Part I, p. 16.

On the nicknaming of torture techniques and instruments used by Paraguayan security police, see Inter-American Association for Democracy and Freedom, *Hemispherica*, Vol. XXVIII, No. 2 (Feb. 1979), p. 3.

On Brazil's "dragon chair" see U. S. Congress, Senate, Committee on Foreign Relations, *Communist Threat to the United States Through the Caribbean*, 2nd Cong., 1st sess., 1971, p. 7. It is important to point out that, according to the Western press, Brazil has released its "last" political prisoners. See New York *Times*, Feb. 10, 1980, p. 3.

On Malawi's "electric hat" torture, see Amnesty International, *Malawi* (London: Amnesty International, 1976), p. 7.

5. The description of the appearance and purpose served by safe houses in the Philippines, written by a former prisoner detained by the military for a lengthy period of time, appears in Concepción Águila, "Detention

Camp: Manila," *Bulletin of Concerned Asian Scholars* 6 (Nov.–Dec. 1974): 39. According to one report, torture conducted at safe houses in the Philippines is extremely violent, perhaps even more violent than it usually is at detention centers. "Mr. Tayag was taken blindfolded to a NISA safe house . . . when he was handed back to the Fifth CSU, the beatings were less severe than those at the safe house." See Amnesty International, *Report of a Mission to the Republic of the Philippines*, p. 24.

The testimony of two religious figures on the subject of safe houses in the Philippines appears in U. S. Congress, House, Committee on International Relations, *Human Rights in Indonesia and the Philippines*, p. 63.

Information on the use of Mexican safe houses comes from an interview (Mar. 21, 1980) with Francisco Fernández Ponte, Washington bureau chief of *Excelsior*.

On the appearance of Indonesian dwellings believed to be used as safe houses, see U. S. Congress, House, *Human Rights in Indonesia and the Philippines*, p. 43.

On the private farm allegedly used by DINA for purposes of torturing political detainees, see United Nations, 31st sess., *Protection of Human Rights in Chile*, p. 97, para. 371.

On clandestine torture facilities in Zaire, see Amnesty International, *Human Rights Violations in Zaire* (London: Amnesty International, 1980), p. 18.

On the remote camp at which a black South African claims to have been detained, see Amnesty International, *Political Imprisonment in South Africa*, p. 62.

6. For the full testimony of Bertha Alicia López García de Zazueta, the Mexican woman whose family was tortured along with her, see the *Statement of Mrs. Zazueta to the Mexican Committee to Defend Political Prisoners* (undated), provided courtesy of the Council on Hemispheric Affairs, Washington, D.C.

Information on the Paraguayan family of four generations arrested all at one time comes from an interview with a confidential source, an author and professor of Latin American history and human-rights activist living in Washington, D.C., Apr. 25, 1979.

On the South African Security Branch agents' technique of continually shifting the whereabouts of prisoners, see *The Christian Science Monitor*, Apr. 24, 1978, p. 6.

Mrs. Esmail Araghi was interviewed twice during her visit to Los Angeles, Nov. 20 and 21, 1979.

The story of Father Hagad was learned during an interview (Mar. 19, 1980) with Jerry Jumat, a former Moslem anti-Marcos activist now living in Washington, D.C. Further mention of Father Hagad's case appears in John M. Swomley, "Inside Marcos' Concentration Camps," *The Christian Century* 91, Nov. 13, 1974, p. 1067.

7. On the "good-cop bad-cop" interrogation technique, we interviewed (Apr. 27, 1979) a confidential source, a former SIFA officer.

On the Chilean SIFA torturer known as the "gentleman of torture," see James Pringle, *Newsweek,* Mar. 31, 1975, p. 51.

On good-guy techniques used during interrogation sessions by Israeli authorities, see Palestine Human Rights Campaign, *Israel and Torture: An Insight Inquiry* (Walnut Bottom, Pa: Palestine Human Rights Campaign, 1977) (reprint of a London *Sunday Times* study).

On the factors exempting detainees of the Philippines from being subjected to torture, see Amnesty International, *Report of an Amnesty International Mission to the Republic of the Philippines,* supra, p. 7. Sometimes, apparently, torture will be halted in order to prevent great damage to the victim: "He was then interrogated and tortured continuously for three months until July 1974, when they stopped to let his wounds heal" (ibid., p. 27). For more on torture in the Philippines, see the report of the Task Force Detainees, *Quarterly Report* (Philippines: Sept. 1979), which includes a listing of all political detainees by region within the entire country, as well as lists of arrests and releases, many of which were conducted in an atmosphere of terror and torture. See also Task Force Detainees of the Philippines, *Political Detainees of the Philippines, Book 3* (Manila: Task Force Detainees, 1970); William J. Butler, *The Decline of Democracy in the Philippines* (Geneva: International Commission of Jurists, 1976); U. S. Congress, House, *Human Rights in Asia: Noncommunist Countries,* supra, 1980; U. S. Congress, House, *Human Rights in Indonesia and the Philippines,* supra, 1976; Richard P. Claude, *Human Rights in the Philippines and United States Responsibility,* a working paper (College Park, Md.: Center for Philosophy and Public Policy, University of Maryland, 1978); and Sister Caridad Guidote, "Most Frequently Used Torture Methods of Marcos Police," *Philippine Times* (Washington, D.C.), Aug. 12–18, 1978, pp. 1–6.

On conditions of detention of Benigno Aquino, see Hong Kong *Standard,* Nov. 27, 1978; and Amnesty International, *Report of a Mission to the Philippines,* supra, p. 40.

Information on conditions of detention at Camp Crame was learned during an interview with Philippine student leader Jerry Barrican in Washington, D.C., July 19, 1979. In 1969, Barrican was elected chairman of the University of the Philippines Student Council. He was granted permission to go abroad in the late seventies.

Information on the interrogation of the former Dubček-regime official was told to us (Mar. 13, 1980) by the official himself, a confidential source.

Privileged treatment of a Haitian associate of a former U.S. consular official appears in the testimony of Edward McKeon, in the case of *Haitian Refugee Center* vs. *Benjamin Civiletti,* supra, p. 16.

The Chilean defense attorney who was Chief Legal Counsel of the Cooperative Committee for Peace in Chile, José Zalaquett, was interviewed (Apr. 26, 1979) at the Woodstock Theological Center of the Georgetown University campus.

Information on Polish UB agents' light-handedness, relatively speaking, with regard to their style of interrogation, comes from interviews with Polish exiles now living in the United States. For instance, we interviewed (Mar. 11, 1980) Irena Zabludowska, a Polish émigré now living in New York City, and (Mar. 21, 1980) Tadeusz Walendowski, a Polish political activist now living in the United States. (For more on Mr. Walendowski, see our notes for Chapter Three, Section 3.) In support of this theory of light-handedness, a story that appeared in the New York Times, Mar. 31, 1980, p. A3, is worth reading: The article speaks about ". . . dissidents who are regularly harassed but rarely imprisoned with long sentences." See also an article in the New York Times, Apr. 10, 1980, the story of a UN employee by the name of Alecja Wesolowska, who at the time of this writing is being held by police in Poland. "In contradiction to fragmentary reports in the Western press, which said that she had spent an arduous time in solitary confinement and suggested that she might have been brutalized to produce a confession, her treatment in prison was reasonably good. She shared a cell with three other women and was permitted to exercise and receive carefully supervised visits from her immediate family." It is important to understand the cruelty, however, of this light-handedness, despite the absence of physical torture: " 'She wasn't physically mistreated,' one source said. 'She was well treated and because of that she was probably misled. She was preparing to leave the jail. *It was the way they approached her to open her up* (i.e., confess).' " (our emphasis)

The Romanian historian who was granted "class A" treatment during his arrest, interrogation, and detention was interviewed at the Smithsonian Institution, Washington, D.C., Mar. 19, 1980.

For information on torture in Romania, see Amnesty International, *Romania* (London: Amnesty International, 1978); and Amnesty International, *Romania* (London: Amnesty International, 1980). Both reports detail the treatment of political dissidents in psychiatric hospitals, which is the chief form of torture used by many secret police forces of Soviet-bloc countries.

8. Information on medical treatment of former prisoners of Chile comes from several UN reports: Economic and Social Council, 36th sess., *Question of Human Rights in Chile* (E/CN.4/1362), supra, pp. 23–25, paras. 60, 61; and Economic and Social Council, 31st sess., *Protection of Human Rights in Chile* (A/31/253), supra, p. 97, para. 370 (n).

Information on medical treatment administered to Greek former prisoners appears in Amnesty International, *Torture in Greece,* supra, p. 19.

On the structure of the DINA prison Cuatro Álamos. we interviewed (Apr. 26, 1979) José Zalaquett, who was once a prisoner there. On DINA agents using Cuatro Álamos as a place of physical rehabilitation after torture, see United Nations, Economic and Social Council, *Protection of Human Rights in Chile* (A/31/253), supra, p. 47, para. 154.

On Tehrani's description of poisoning captives with cyanide capsules, see Reza Baraheni, "Special Report: the SAVAK Documents," *The Nation,* Feb. 23, 1980, pp. 193-202; and excerpts from the confession of SAVAK torturer Tehrani that appeared in *Iran Voice,* July 19, 1979, p. 6. On SAVAK agents' cover-up concerning the shooting of nine prisoners outside of Evin prison, ibid., pp. 4 and 6.

The "art" of falsifying causes of deaths of political prisoners was not peculiar to Iran. There is evidence, for example, that such falsification has been practiced by Israeli authorities as well. Consider this statement made by Israeli attorney Felicia Langer, which appears in the report of the United Nations General Assembly, 31st sess., Oct. 1, 1976, *Report of the Special Committee to Investigate Israeli Practices Affecting the Human Rights of the Population of the Occupied Territories* (A/31/218), p. 24, para. 95: "A fifty-year-old who had recently been released from Nablus prison, not long after his release and on the way to Tulkarm where he was to be interrogated, was so severely beaten by the police that he died. An official announcement attributed the causes of death to a heart attack, but at the postmortem it was revealed that there were no traces of a heart attack or stroke."

For information on a similar discrepancy between allegations of torture and official reports (in this case, not involving death), see a bulletin issued by the Friends of the Filipino People, *Response to the State Department Annual Human Rights Review* (Washington, D.C.: Friends of the Filipino People, Mar. 1979), p. 2: "For example, in investigating the case of a UCC ministe who was severely tortured, the government panel said that the minister, "because of thirst and by his own volition, drank his own urine."

For the full testimony of the former DINA agent on the subject of how DINA agents would mark their detainees' fates on their cards in the DINA files, see the case of *Private Sociale Mission, e.V., Sociedad Benefactora y Educacional Dignidad,* gegen. *Amnesty International, Firma Gruner und Jahr, Henri Nannen (ausgeschieden), und Herrn Kai Hermann,* Bonn, Nov. 19, 1979, reprinted by Amnesty International. Sektion der Bundesrepublik, Deutschland, e.V., publisher. Amnesty International has been accused of libel by a German colony in central Chile as a result of an Amnesty International booklet alleging the occurrence of torture of political detainees at the camp. This case represents one of the rare instances in which someone has challenged an Amnesty International report and attempted to prevent the organization from publishing. On May 23, 1977, a court in the Federal Republic of Germany decided that Amnesty International would *not* be allowed to publish and distribute the brochure anymore. The ultimate disposition of this case, at the time of this writing, is still to be determined.

On the disappearance of political prisoners as a worldwide phenomenon, see:

ARGENTINA: New York Provisional Commission for Disappeared Persons and Political Prisoners in Argentina, *Missing in Argentina: the Desperate Search for Thousands of Abducted Victims* (New York: Amnesty International, 1980); Amnesty International, *The Missing Children of Argentina* (London: Amnesty International, 1979); Inter-American Commission on Human Rights, *Report on the Situation of Human Rights in Argentina* (provisional version) (Washington, D.C.: General Secretariat of the Organization of American States, 1980); Jacobo Timerman, "The Bodies Counted Are Our Own," *Columbia Journalism Review* 19, May–June 1980, p. 32; and *The Village Voice*, Apr. 2, 1979, p. 26.

CHILE: Secretariat for Solidarity in America with the Chilean People, *Chile Informative 104, 141* (Toronto, Ontario: Chile Informative, 1978); report of the Secretaria Ejecutiva de Solaridad de la Izquierda Chileana para América, *La DINA en Chile* (Mexico City: Casa de Chile, 1976); Office for Political Prisoners and Human Rights in Chile, *Chile Report ⅟4* (New York: Aug. 1978), pp. 9–11; and Los Angeles *Herald-Examiner*, May 20, 1979, p. 6.

EL SALVADOR: Los Angeles *Times*, June 11, 1980, Part II, p. 7; and Amnesty International, *Press Release on El Salvador*, July 16, 1980.

ETHIOPIA: Amnesty International, *Human Rights Violations in Ethiopia* (London: Amnesty International, 1978), p. 14.

GUATEMALA: Amnesty International, *Guatemala* (London: Amnesty International, 1979), p. 15; and *Amnesty Action*, Dec. 1979 (New York: Amnesty International, 1979), p. 5; and Peter Strafford, "Anarchy in Central America," *Spectator*, June 23, 1979, p. 11.

HAITI: *Haitian Refugee Center et al.*, vs. *Benjamin Civiletti et al.*, supra, see the testimony of Marc Romulus, one of the alleged "last" political prisoners of Haiti, p. 3; see also the testimony of Laraque, ibid., pp. 2–29.

MALAWI: Amnesty International, *Malawi* (Aug. 1976), pp. 7–8.

MOZAMBIQUE: "Human Rights End at Mozambique Border," *To the Point*, Aug. 25, 1971, p. 31.

NICARAGUA: Amnesty International, *Republic of Nicaragua* (London: Amnesty International, 1976), p. 35.

PARAGUAY: Amnesty International, *Deaths Under Torture and Disap-*

pearance of Political Prisoners in Paraguay (London: Amnesty International, 1976).

URUGUAY: Amnesty International, *Political Imprisonment in Uruguay* (London: Amnesty International, June 1979), p. 7; and Amnesty International, *Uruguay: Deaths Under Torture* (London: Amnesty International, 1978).

On the Philippine practice of "salvaging," defined and described by Sister Mariani C. Dimaranan, chairperson of the Task Force Detainees of the Philippines, see *Philippine Times*, Vol. 9, No. 14, Apr. 28, to May 4, 1978, pp. 1, 6–7.

For the full text of Rep. James M. Jeffords' (R-Vt.) comments on the upswing of disappearances in the Philippines, see "Message to Marcos," *Asian-American News*, Apr. 1–15, 1980, pp. 5 and 15.

The analysis of secret police rationale for utilizing the practice of disappearances of political enemies was expressed by Professor Robert Goldman, American University Law School, Mar. 18, 1980.

On Amnesty International's complaint about DINA's attempt to make the organization believe that missing individuals do not exist, see Amnesty International, *Disappeared Prisoners in Chile* (London: Amnesty International, Mar. 1977), p. 3.

On the torment caused by disappearances to the victims' families and friends, see the report of the Inter-American Commission on Human Rights, *Report on the Situation of Human Rights in Argentina* (provisional version), p. 21. On disappearances as a form of nullification of legal standards established in some countries, ibid., p. 21. On the "normal" disappearance procedures that occurs in Argentina, ibid., p. 55. On the confiscation of appliances by Argentinian secret police in the process of accomplishing a disappearance, ibid., p. 55. On the abductions of children, ibid., pp. 60 and 64–65.

9. Excerpts from the government prosecutor's speech at the 1975 torturers' trial in Greece appear in Amnesty International, *Torture in Greece*, supra, p. 14.

On the Colombian security officer's defense of the interrogator's use of moral or physical coercion to obtain a confession, see the unpublished speech of Nancy Stein, of the North American Congress on Latin America, at the Amnesty International Regional Conference held in Malibu, Calif., Oct. 16, 1976.

On the same subject as it has been defended by a Nepalese inspector, ibid.

On Gabriel Bach's (Israeli state attorney) condemnation of the use of torture by security police, see *The Christian Science Monitor*, Apr. 4, 1979, p. 27. The Israeli Government, however, generally does not concede that torture is practiced. According to the Los Angeles *Herald-Examiner*, May 1, 1979, p. A4: "The Israeli government has repeatedly and strenuously denied that torture of Arab prisoners from the Occupied Territories is systematic or widespread. Minister of Justice Schmuel Tamir has told Parliament that the Red Cross investigated 1300 cases last year in which mistreatment was suspected and found that six percent of them warranted further inquiry."

One of the more interesting defenses offered by government authorities on the subject of harsh interrogation techniques practiced by security forces can be attributed to British officials. See Jack Holland, "The Secret Torturers," *The Nation,* Sept. 8, 1979, pp. 174-75: the European Commission on Human Rights, at Strasbourg, in 1976, investigated British security officials' use of the "five techniques": hooding, forcing the victim to stand spread-eagled against a wall for periods of up to sixteen hours at a stretch, depriving the victim of sleep, depriving the victim of food, and piping high-pitched "white noise" into the victim's cell. The government admitted using the five techniques and noted that they had borrowed the techniques from the Russian KGB, adding that the five techniques had been in use in all of Britain's colonial wars since the late 1940s, but until the revelation of their use in Northern Ireland, the practice had remained a well-kept secret.

Furthermore, a British commission offered the following defense of the interrogation techniques practiced by security forces (see Great Britain, Home Office, "Report of an Enquiry into Allegations Against the Security Forces of Physical Brutality in Northern Ireland arising out of Events on the 9th of August, 1971, Cmnd. 4823. *Report, 1972,* p. 13, para. 48): "Requiring detainees to stand with their arms against a wall but not in a position of stress provides security for detainees and guards against physical violence during the reception and search period and whenever detainees are together outside their own rooms. . . . It also assists the interrogation process by imposing discipline. . . ." "These methods have been used in support of the interrogation of a small number of persons arrested in Northern Ireland who were believed to possess information of a kind which it was operationally necessary to obtain as rapidly as possible in the interest of saving lives, while at the same time providing the detainees with the necessary security for their own persons and identities. . . ." (Ibid., para. 52.)

For more on the interrogation techniques used by British security forces in Northern Ireland, see: Great Britain, Northern Ireland Office, *Report of the Committee of Inquiry into Police Interrogation Procedures in Northern Ireland,* Mar. 1979, Cmnd. 4797, *Report, 1979;* Great Britain, Parliament, *Parliamentary Papers, 1971-72* (Reports, Vol. 18), Cmnd. 4901, "Report of the Committee of Privy Counsellors Appointed to Consider Authorized Procedures for the Interrogation of Persons Suspected of Terrorism"; Great Britain, Northern Ireland Office, *Report of a Committee to Consider, in the context of Civil Liberties and Human*

NOTES TO PAGES 198–201

Rights, Measures to Deal with Terrorism in Northern Ireland, Cmnd. 5847, *Report, January 1975;* and Great Britain, Home Office, *Enquiry into Allegations Against the Security Forces Arising out of Events on the 9th of August, 1971,* Cmnd. 4823, *Report, 1972.*

On South African General Van den Bergh's explanation for the rash of detainee deaths by suicide, see Johannesburg *Star,* July 3, 1977.

On South Korean General Lee Hi Song's opinion that Kim Dae Jung, former contender with Park Chung Hee for the presidency, whose death sentence was commuted due to international pressure, was tortured while in prison, see New York *Times,* July 24, 1980. See also New York *Times,* Sept. 14, 1980, p. 2: At his trial in South Korea, Mr. Kim himself said: "I was confined in a basement for sixty days and experienced an ordeal beyond description. I went through an ordeal that made me lose my mind altogether. I could hear someone moaning in the cell next to mine. I was stripped naked, and forced to wear battered army fatigues and threatened with torture. . . ." See also New York *Times,* Aug. 20, 1980, p. A12.

On the opinion voiced by the chief constable of the Royal Ulster Constabulary, in Northern Ireland, on the subject of self-inflicted wounds manufactured by terrorists, see Amnesty International, *Report of an Amnesty International Mission to Northern Ireland* (London: Amnesty International, 1978), pp. 4–6.

On Philippine Defense Secretary Juan Ponce Enrile's opinion on terrorists who inflict wounds on themselves, see Richard P. Claude, *Human Rights in the Philippines and United States Responsibility* (College Park, Md.: Center for Philosophy and Public Policy, University of Maryland, 1978), p. 13.

On a former SAVAK official's reaction to allegations that a revolutionary had been severely tortured, see *Time* magazine, Feb. 19, 1979, p. 32.

.10. For clear definitions of gradations of maltreatment and torture, see Great Britain, Northern Ireland Office, "Report of the Committee of Inquiry into Police Interrogation Procedures in Northern Ireland," supra, p. 29, para. 81. The so-called Parker Committee Report here cites the definitions presented in the Report of the European Commission of Human Rights, 1976, in the case of Ireland against the United Kingdom: "inhuman treatment"—at least such treatment as deliberately causes severe suffering, mental or physical (which in the particular situation is unjustifiable); "torture"—often used to describe inhuman treatment that has a purpose, such as the obtaining of information, or confession, or the infliction of punishment, and is generally an aggravated form of inhuman treatment; "non-physical torture"—the infliction of mental suffering by creating a state of anguish and stress by means other than bodily assaults;

and "degrading treatment—treatment or punishment of an individual may be said to be degrading if it grossly humiliates him before others or drives him to act against his will."

On the extent of torture occurring on the West Bank and Occupied Territories, see the testimony of Dr. Israel Shahak, U. S. Congress, Senate, Committee on the Judiciary, *The Colonization of the West Bank Territories by Israel*, 95th Cong., 1st sess., 1977, p. 93; and Palestine Human Rights Campaign, *Bulletin 8*, June 1978, supra, p. 8. Chiefly, we interviewed two sources with contradictory points of view on a number of key issues related to this subject. We interviewed (Washington, D.C., Mar. 19, 1980) Dr. Israel Shahak, Professor of Organic Chemistry, Hebrew University, Jerusalem, and President, Israeli League for Human and Civil Rights, in Tel-Aviv. We also interviewed (June 19, 1980) Alexandra Johnson, former vice-consul in Jerusalem Feb. 1977 to Jan. 1979, now living in Sacramento, Calif. Dr. Shahak draws a fine yet important line between torture and maltreatment, arguing that torture cases occurring in the Occupied Territories are very rare, or few relative to the population. The problem, he says, is day-to-day brutal maltreatment, such as, for example, picking people up in demonstrations, or establishing roadblocks, etc. And he points out that these daily cases of maltreatment are accomplished on the initiative of local orders *only*. According to Ms. Johnson, however, there is the possibility that torture cases are far more frequent and systematic than Dr. Shahak suggests. See *Journal of Palestine Studies 35*, supra, p. 103: "The practices described by the ten [visa] applicants," writes Ms. Johnson, "run strongly counter to any explanation of physical abuse during interrogation as merely the aberrant behavior of an occasional 'rogue cop.'" To further assess Ms. Johnson's opinions, it is important to see the article by Victor Cygielman, "Most Israelis Outraged at Claims of Systematic Ill-Treatment," *The Christian Science Monitor*, Apr. 4, 1979, p. 27.

For the full text of the *Sunday Times* series of articles on the subject of torture in Israel, the West Bank, and the Occupied Territories, see Palestine Human Rights Campaign, *Israel and Torture: An Insight Inquiry*, supra.

For general estimates on the systematic or unsystematic nature of torture from country to country, see Amnesty International, *Report 1978*, supra, *Report 1979*, supra, and *Report 1980*, supra.

On torture of Provisional IRA members by security forces of the Royal Ulster Constabulary, see *Report of an Amnesty International Mission to Northern Ireland* (London: Amnesty International, June 1978).

For the wisdom of the South African court commenting on the conditions of detention in the country as compared to those characteristic of Northern Ireland, see Johannesburg *Star*, Nov. 14, 1974.

On the question of how systematic or unsystematic the use of physical torture on the part of Cuban secret police agents may be, see Hugh Thomas, "Castro Plus 20," *Of Human Rights,* Spring 1979, Vol. 2, No. 2 (Georgetown University), p. 16; on the case of Huber Matos, celebrated hero of the Cuban revolution who became a twenty-year-long prisoner of Castro's regime, see Inter-American Association of Democracy and Freedom, *Hemispherica,* Vol. XXVIII, No. 10, Nov. 1979, p. 2; for more on Huber Matos, see New York *Times,* Feb. 4, 1980, p. A4; and on torture in Cuba in general, see publications of the Inter-American Association, *Hemispherica,* Vol. XXVI, No. 6 (June–July 1977), p. 1; and Vol. XXVII, No. 7 (Aug.–Sept. 1978), p. 1.

For a contrasting point of view, see Frank Calzón, *Castro's Gulag* (Washington, D.C.: Council for Inter-American Security, 1979), pp. 17, 25–28. Calzón argues that "the use of sophisticated torture and prisoner abuses comparable to those characteristic of the Soviet [gulag] has been documented for several years." He also says, "In the Mazona G-2 prison, for example, the use of electric shock torture has been revealed." In addition to these allegations of severe physical torture, Calzón quotes a study released by the Inter-American Commission on Human Rights (June 1976) pointing out that some female political prisoners were kept naked in lightless cells without water; see p. 43.

On the evolutionary nature of the process of torture vis-à-vis SAVAK, we interviewed Dr. Reza Ghanadian, Iranian cancer researcher now living in London, Oct. 13, 1979. For more on Dr. Ghanadian, see our chapter notes for Chapter Two, Section 2.

On the prosecution of torturers in Greece, see Amnesty International, *Torture in Greece,* supra, pp. 61–71.

On the trial of a few SAVAK torturers by the Islamic revolutionary government in 1978, we consulted numerous foreign and American newspaper articles on the trial of SAVAK torturer Tehrani. For more on this, consult our bibliography.

On investigations into allegations of torture in Peru, see Amnesty International, *Peru* (London: Amnesty International, 1979), p. 11.

On halfhearted attempts to bring Portuguese torturers to trial, see Amnesty International, *Torture in Greece,* supra, p. 62.

For additional information on other countries where torture trials have been held or where officers have been otherwise disciplined, see Amnesty International, *Report of an Amnesty International Mission to India* (London: Amnesty International, 1979), p. 52. And see *Amnesty Action Bulletin* (Dec. 1979) (New York: Amnesty International, 1979), p. 4, for discussion of disciplining of Israeli officers alleged to have used torture.

On the Philippine Air Force colonel's reluctance to report charges of torture on the part of the Metropolitan Military Command agents against his pregnant daughter, see the files of the Friends of the Filipino People for the year 1978 (this piece of information appeared in a newspaper article Xeroxed and kept in the FFP files—the source name, however, was unidentifiable).

CHAPTER SIX

1. The 1971 confidential SAVAK memo was extracted from a book comprising a series of confidential memos obtained by students who raided the Geneva, Switzerland, headquarters of SAVAK in 1976. See Confederation of Iranian Students, National Union, *SAVAK: Documents on Iranian Secret Police* (Frankfurt: National Union, 1976), p. 177. All other SAVAK memos included in this chapter are also extracted from this book. For more information on this book, see our notes for Chapter Two, Section 2.

On domestic political espionage conducted in the United States by the National Security Agency, and on the alliance of Britain's Post Office with the NSA as part of a spying plan (i.e., telephone tapping), see Frank J. Donner, *The Age of Surveillance* (New York: Alfred A. Knopf, 1980), p. 276. On NSA's eavesdropping center in northern England, see *New Statesman*, July 17, 1979, p. 43.

On Iran's Joint Committee as the receptacle for all secret reports of all security sections of a wide variety of government and private organizations, see *Iran Voice*, July 9, 1979, p. 3. The Committee had a big job, but it apparently succeeded quite well in its efforts. Said SAVAK torturer Tehranı (now executed): "General Nasser Moghadam was the chief of the third office of SAVAK, and he was given the task of forming the 'joint committee' by the order of the Shah. The 'committee' was then formed with the help of the Army and Gendarmerie and was primarily responsible for combatting all antigovernment activities in the universities, and by doing so eradicate the leaders and frontrunners of student groups. . . . The Committee was very successful, early in its activities. . . ." For more on the Committee, in particular how it was formed, see William J. Butler and Georges Levasseur, *Human Rights and the Legal System in Iran* (Geneva: International Commission of Jurists, 1976), p. 20. See also *Iranian People's Struggle*, Vol. 1, No. 5, Nov. 1975, p. 3.

Information on the number of informers situated at all Iranian universities comes from an interview with a retired general of the Iranian Army living in Beverly Hills, Aug. 28, 1979. On the number of informers and the various departments within which they operated at the University of Tabriz, see *Jomhuriyeh Eslami*, June 17, 1979. For more on informers in Iran, see Fred Halliday, *Iran: Dictatorship and Development* (Harmondsworth, Middlesex: Penguin Books, 1979), p. 80: "Estimates of those who work for SAVAK vary from 3,120 (the Shah, 1976), to 30,000–60,000 (*Newsweek*, 1974); but while there is uncertainty about the number of full-time employees, no one denies that SAVAK has a far larger army of part-time informers spread throughout Iran and Iranian communities abroad. *Newsweek* claimed in 1974 that up to three million Iranians acted in one way or another as SAVAK informers, and in a rare public statement a SAVAK official in 1971 confirmed that this latter category included 'workers, farmers, students, professors, teachers, guild members, political parties and other associations.' "

On informers working for DINA, see John Dinges and Saul Landau, *Assassination on Embassy Row*, supra, p. 134. On the radio taxis that routinely monitored the conversations of passengers, see the report of the Secretaria Ejecutiva de Solidaridad de la Izquierda Chileana para América, *La DINA en Chile*, supra; see also excerpts of the confession of the deceased former DINA agent Juan Muñoz Alcarón, United Nations, Economic and Social Council, 33rd sess., *Protection of Human Rights in Chile* (A/33/331), Oct. 1, 1978, Annex XLVII, pp. 1–3: "Captain Jorge Luchino is chief of the labour section of the Tacna Regiment, second department, and is responsible for all the industries in Greater Santiago and its environs. This organization exists to persecute, remove, dismiss and terrorize all workers in general. . . . This labour apparatus comprises a veritable army of informers who enable the intelligence services to detain, interrogate, torture and, as I have already said several times, kill people for showing dissatisfaction or acting against the Government. It is enough to say one word against the Government for a man to lose his job. . . ."

On the screening system for Chilean informants, we interviewed a confidential source, a former SIFA officer, in Washington, D.C., Apr. 27, 1979.

2. On Paraguayan informants, we interviewed (Apr. 25, 1979) a confidential source, a Latin American history professor who has written numerous articles (sometimes under a pseudonym)—see Alberto Cabral, "Political Murder in Paraguay," *America*, Apr. 22, 1977, pp. 376–78. On "pyragueismo" as a subindustry in Paraguay, see Penny Lernoux, "Behind Closed Borders," *Harper's Magazine*, Feb. 1979, p. 28.

On informers in Mozambique, see "Human Rights End at Mozambique Border," *To the Point*, Aug. 28, 1978, p. 31.

On the number of informants working for PIDE, Portugal's secret police, during the early seventies, see *The Economist*, Nov. 2, 1974, p. 32. See also *The Economist*, May 18, 1974, p. 31: "The PIDE's strength has been generally overestimated: its records show about 950 officers and full-time agents plus around 600 technical, administrative and other employees, some of whom also acted as agents, and *2,000 informers* [our emphasis]."

Furthermore, as reported in the Nov. 2 issue of *The Economist,* many informers were not caught and disciplined: "Of the PIDE's many informers (now said officially to number 20,000), fewer than 40, specifically accused of causing suffering, have been arrested." For a sense of just how paranoid the average citizen and foreigner living in Portugal might have become in the early seventies, we interviewed (Oct. 13, 1979, in London) a confidential source, a foreigner who lived in Portugal during that time. This source remembers the case of a rich Englishman, a playboy, who went to Portugal to retire, but lost all of his money, as he was used to "living very well." She remembers that PIDE officials knew he was accumulating debts. (Furthermore, the Englishman could not work, as foreigners were not permitted to; most foreigners were living there to save taxes.) And so, PIDE officials approached him to inform, but the man claims that he told them he wanted "no part of politics," and claimed that they let him go. Says this confidential source: "I never knew what freedom (in other countries) was until I came to Portugal," so confining and intimidating it was to feel that those around you might be informing on you.

On the sophisticated network of informants operating within South Africa, see *The Economist,* June 21, 1980, p. 25. And on Prime Minister Vorster's comments with regard to the importance of the police informer to South African law, see Cape *Times,* Feb. 27, 1977. According to a report in the London *Sunday Times,* Jan. 10, 1978, security police were attempting to recruit ministers of the South African NG Sendingkerk, a religious organization, as informers. Although the chief of security police in Cape Town denied the allegations, Sendingkerk members insist that a minister was asked to act as an informant on the actions of black delegates shortly before the beginning of the synod, and that attempts to infiltrate this church had taken place before.

On the system of informants maintained throughout East Germany, see New York *Times,* Oct. 18, 1980, p. A3.

On the informant system and the First Departments throughout the Soviet Union, we interviewed several sources, including (Jan. 26, 1980) Friedrich Nerzansky, a graduate of the Moscow Institute of Law who has worked for twenty-five years in the field of Soviet criminal law, including fifteen years as a criminal investigator in the U.S.S.R. procurator's office. Nerzansky's wife, who at one time worked for the Ministry of Industrial Construction, learned that someone called the First Department of this Ministry of Industrial Construction and asked questions about her. The person who called identified himself as an employee of the Department of Visas and Permissions—otherwise called OVIR. Mr. Nerzansky says that in each large business there is one office where a "Special" or "First" Department employee will work, and there is usually one person working in each "special" or "first" department. Mr. Nerzansky says that the KGB recommends certain people to work in these offices, but their salary is not determined by the KGB.

On the informant system penetrating all sectors of life in Czechoslovakia, we interviewed a former legal adviser to Dubček's cabinet on Mar. 13, 1980. Czech StB defector Josef Frolik's statements with regard to the Fifth Administration of the secret police, which plays a major role in the analysis and recruitment of informers, appear in his book *Špión Vypovídá*, pp. 345–70.

On the difficulty of recruiting informants within the East Timor society, we interviewed (New York, Mar. 13, 1980) a confidential source who has helped several individuals escape the country.

On the difficulty of recruiting informers from the Basque population, see Amnesty International, *Report of an Amnesty International Mission to Spain* (London: Sept. 1975), p. 10.

On the infiltration of student circles in Indonesia, see U. S. Congress, House, Committee on International Relations, *Human Rights in Indonesia and the Philippines*, 94th Cong., 2nd sess., 1976, p. 19.

On the paranoia characteristic of most citizens of the U.S.S.R. due to the widespread informant system, we interviewed Eli Valk, at the headquarters of the National Conference on Soviet Jewry, New York City, Jan. 24, 1980. Mr. Valk is an Israeli journalist originally from Riga, Latvia, U.S.S.R., and he is currently coordinator of the Soviet Jewry Research Bureau of the National Conference on Soviet Jewry. He belongs to the "first generation" of Soviet Jewish refusenik activists. In 1971, Valk, after acting for many years as a leader of the Riga Zionist movement, was granted permission to emigrate with his family. Since 1972, Valk has been working with the Israel Broadcasting Authority in the Russian Language Department as a senior news editor.

On Taiwanese informants and their penetration of all institutions, resembling the KGB informant system, we interviewed Mr. T. M. Hsieh, on a visit to Los Angeles, May 28, 1980. Mr. Hsieh was a magazine editor and lecturer at a military academy in Taiwan when he was first arrested. We also interviewed Ms. Alice Kao, a reporter for the Taiwan newspaper *United Daily News*, on her 1980 swing tour through the United States, Feb. 23, 1980. It is both an "obligation" and a "privilege" to inform for the Taiwan Garrison Command, she says.

On the twenty-one-year-old student leader in South Africa who confessed to informing for BOSS, see the London *Sunday Times*, Aug. 22, 1976.

On payment of Iranian informers and the story of the young man who refused to cooperate with SAVAK, we interviewed Dr. Reza Ghanadian, cancer researcher now living in London, Oct. 9, 1979. For more on Dr. Ghanadian, see our notes for Chapter Two, Section 2. See also the report by William J. Butler and Georges Levasseur, *Human Rights and the Legal System in Iran,* supra, p. 20: "All government employees are subjected to a general review by the SAVAK before employment. It maintains extensive files on individuals, including government employees."

On the payment of Haitian informers, we interviewed *Wall Street Journal* correspondent Ray Joseph, Mar. 13, 1980. (For more on Mr. Joseph, see our notes for Chapter Three, Section 2.)

Information on the French system of informants was learned during interviews with a former high CIA official on July 15, 1980, and in New York, Aug. 14, 1980.

On informants' involvement in barter in the southern Philippines, we interviewed Jerry Jumat, a former Moslem anti-Marcos activist from the southern Philippines now living in the United States, on Mar. 19, 1980.

On the rewards for informing for the Yugoslavian secret police, we interviewed two confidential sources, Jan. 25, 1980, and Mar. 15, 1980; we also interviewed Fairleigh Dickinson Professor Matthew Mestrović, July 21, 1979.

On the rewards for informing for the Romanian Securitate, we interviewed historian Vladimir Georgescu at the Smithsonian Institution, Washington, D.C., Mar. 19, 1980.

On the Nicaraguan informer who said he was forced to inform, see New York *Times,* Feb. 3, 1980.

On the confession of Iranian informer Iraj Jahangiri before the revolutionary court, see "Top SAVAK Torturer Held While Escaping," *Kayhan International,* 1979 (no further date verification available in UCLA library files).

The memorandum entitled "Guidance of the Sources" appeared in *SAVAK: Documents on Iranian Secret Police,* supra, p. 186. The memo is dated Feb. 21, 1972.

3. On the recruitment of KGB informers, we interviewed Eli Valk, Jan. 24, 1980. Often, says Valk, a KGB agent will meet with a dissident and prospective informant in a highly visible place, such as a café, so that other dissidents will see that someone they know is collaborating with an agent and will either be encouraged to do so themselves or will wonder who else among them is also collaborating. Another common pitch, he says, is for the KGB agent to say to a dissident who wants to emigrate: help us by informing and we'll help you emigrate.

The story of the Czechoslovakian woman who was approached by StB agents was told to us by a confidential source in New York, Mar. 13, 1980.

On the sentencing of a Taiwanese citizen to seven years for failing to report a communist spy or falsely reporting a communist spy, see U. S. Congress, House, Hearings Before the Subcommittee on Asian and Pacific Affairs on International Organizations of the Committee on Foreign Affairs, *Human Rights in Asia: Noncommunist Countries*, 96th Cong., 2nd sess., 1980, p. 271.

On the techniques used by Canadian G-4 agents to recruit informers, see Gerard F. Rutan, "Watergate North: How the Mounties Get Their Men," *Civil Liberties Review* (New York: American Civil Liberties Union, July/Aug. 1978), pp. 18–19.

On the co-optation of Cuban children to inform, we interviewed (Feb. 23, 1980) a confidential source, a young Cuban refugee who arrived in the United States in 1971.

On the G-2 agents who continually appeared at the home of a former political prisoner during the time of the International Festival of the Communist Party, July 1978, we interviewed a Cuban woman in New Jersey, Mar. 15, 1980.

On the recruitment of voodoo priests to act as informers in Haiti, we interviewed *Wall Street Journal* correspondent Ray Joseph, Mar. 13, 1980. For background information on voodoo and Haitian society, see Nancy Gordon Heinl and Robert Deb Heinl, *Written in Blood: The Story of the Haitian People, 1492–1971* (Boston: Houghton Mifflin, 1978), pp. 669–90.

On the recruitment, of Chilean "rehabilitated former delinquents," to inform, see the report of the Committee for the Defense of Human Rights in the Southern Cone, *Clamor*, Issue No. 4, Dec. 1978, p. 7.

On the confession of the Iranian who claimed to have informed on both lowly and important individuals, see *Kayhan International*, June 25, 1979.

On the recruitment of a Canadian informer to carry out specific tasks —such as infiltrating certain bookstores—see Ottawa *Citizen*, Nov. 23, 1977, and on the former employee of the Egyptian embassy in Ottawa wiretapping telephone conversations of Arab diplomats, see Ottawa *Citizen*, Nov. 19, 1977; these allegations were compiled in a report prepared by the Civil Liberties Association, *A Partial Listing of Facts and Allegations Regarding Security Operations in Canada* (National Capital Region: undated), p. 5; and on the gamut of informers ranging from janitors upward, see Toronto *Globe and Mail*, Nov. 10, 1977, also included in the report of the Civil Liberties Association, p. 4; and on payment of the top-notch informer, see New York *Times*, Nov. 11, 1977, p. 8.

The information on the white South African informer comes from an interview with a former BOSS employee, conducted by a reporter working for South Africa Morning Newspapers in London, on July 7 and 8 of 1979. The interview, however, was never published. There is considerable debate among liberal South African circles in London with regard to the level at which the employee was working for BOSS. The veracity of the employee's claim that he worked as an *agent* for BOSS is doubted by some who claim that they believe he worked only as an *informant*. But there is consensus on the point that the employee was at the very least an informant, if nothing else. His confession to having been a spy for BOSS was made in early July, 1979. See Desmond Blow, ". . . the Spy Who Sold Out His Chief," *Sunday Express,* July 8, 1979. Gerard Ludi, the police agent who infiltrated the liberal *Rand Daily Mail,* mentions the employee in this article: "When I investigated anyone I would inform Van den Bergh (former BOSS chief) of the facts. But not [him]. He would exaggerate because the better the information he gave, the better the money he was paid."

4. On the Seventh Directorate of the KGB, see John Barron, *KGB: The Secret World of Soviet Secret Agents* (New York: Reader's Digest Press, 1974), p. 87. Barron also refers to this directorate as the Surveillance Directorate.

On comments by A. Alan Borovoy, general counsel for the Canadian Civil Liberties Association, see Gerard F. Rutan, "Watergate North: How the Mounties Get Their Men," op. cit., p. 25.

On the type of surveillance conducted by members of the Brigada Blanca, we interviewed Mr. Francisco Fernández Ponte, Washington bureau chief of *Excelsior,* Mar. 21, 1980; and, Mar. 20, 1980, Jesús Blancornelas, editor and publisher of the Mexican newspaper *ABC,* who, after publishing a series of articles on corruption in government, was charged with "mishandling funds" and was forced to flee the country. Finally, on March 18, 1980, we interviewed Professor Robert Goldman, of American University Law School and coauthor of a report on Mexico submitted to the International League for Human Rights. (For more on these three individuals, see our notes for Chapter Three, Section 2.)

On the purposefully obvious form of surveillance practiced by Taiwanese security authorities, see page two of the report of a Taiwanese-American whose brother had major problems with Taiwanese secret police authorities, the repercussions of which were felt by the family. The report, prepared and presented by the Formosan Association for Human Rights, in Leucadia, Calif., is neither officially titled nor dated as presented by the Association.

On surveillance techniques of the South Korean law enforcement agencies in the mid-seventies, see Amnesty International, *Report of an Am-*

nesty International Mission to the Republic of Korea (London: Amnesty International, 1977), p. 27.

On South Korean agents telephoning their targets of surveillance and asking them their plans for the day, see U. S. Congress, House, *Human Rights in Asia: Noncommunist Countries,* 1980, supra, p. 39.

Yugoslavian author Mihajlo Mihajlov jokingly talked about the sense of security afforded by the large number of agents following him in Yugoslavia during an interview conducted on March 21, 1980. Mihajlov says that, later on, sometime after his release from prison in 1970, agents stopped being so obvious in conducting their surveillance and began to follow him far more clandestinely. The purpose of this more secretive manner of conducting their business, he says, is to "really know where you are going."

On the Polish UB agents' surveillance technique of blockading, we interviewed Irena Zabludowska, Polish émigré living in New York, on March 11, 1980.

5. On Cuban G-2 agents who appear at their targets' places of work, we interviewed a group of women who are Cuban refugees now living in North Bergen, N.J., on March 15, 1980. See also the report of the organization Of Human Rights, "Ex-Prisoners and Their Families Live as 'Pariahs' in Cuba," *Of Human Rights,* Vol. 2, No. 2 (Georgetown U., Spring 1979), pp. 17–18. This information first appeared in a story by Bonnie M. Anderson and Fernando Villaverde, of the Miami *Herald,* on December 31, 1978.

On the issue of Kopkamtib, a branch of the Indonesian internal security network, affecting the employability of citizens, see Amnesty International, *Indonesia* (London: Amnesty International, 1977), pp. 28–30: "Special screening teams employing large numbers of army officers operate in every region under the supervision of the central screening office in Jakarta. The amended 1969 instructions provided the basis for a major campaign which involved screening the staff of all departments and units, and this process was again initiated in 1974. There were many reports in 1974 and 1975 of regional and local departments, such as post offices, medical and educational institutions, being purged of large numbers of suspects. In some cities, entire government offices lost more than half their personnel following the screening of the staff." See also the bulletin of the organization TAPOL: U. S. Campaign for the Release of Indonesian Political Prisoners (Montclair, N.J.: TAPOL), *Bulletin No. 35,* Aug. 1979, p. 3, for a copy of a form that families of released prisoners in East Java have been required by Kopkamtib to sign, which states, among many things, "When at any time my husband/wife/child/relative is confined by the authorities to house or town arrest, I promise: (1) To supervise . . . so that (s)he will not engage in political activities which are forbidden by the Government of the Republic of Indonesia." See also TAPOL *Bulletin No. 6*, Aug. 15, 1976, p. 3, and TAPOL *Bulletin No. 15*, June 1978, p. 6: "Until very recently government regulation required anyone seeking employment to provide a letter from his/her village head or the police stating that the person had not been involved in the 1965 coup attempt." The bulletin goes on to say, however, that even though this restrictive regulation has been rescinded, such letters are often demanded by employers both out of habit and out of fear. Furthermore, Professor Benedict O'Gorman Anderson, of Cornell University, testified in 1980: "Employment in any branch of the government, including the vast state educational system, as well as in what the government calls 'vital enterprises' (covering most of the modern sector of the Indonesian economy) is barred to former prisoners." See U. S. Congress, House, Subcommittee on International Organizations, and the Subcommittee on Asian and Pacific Affairs of the Committee on International Relations, *Human Rights in Indonesia and East Timor*, 1980, p. 3 (reprinted by the organization TAPOL): "What is given us is freedom on loan. It could be taken from us at any time," Anderson quotes one ex-prisoner.

On the powers of the Federal Office for the Protection of the Constitution, in West Germany, with regard to employment in government sectors, see Los Angeles *Times*, Nov. 13, 1978, Sec. I, p. 1.

Juan Ferreira told us about harassing telephone calls he received in Uruguay from police during an interview conducted in New York on May 2, 1979.

For exiled South African author Donald Woods's statements that Security Branch officers monitored all his phone calls, particularly those to Steve Biko, see Donald Woods, *Biko* (London: Paddington Press, 1978), p. 110.

Information on telephone harassment practiced by South Korean secret police was provided by Donald Ranard, former director of the Office of Korean Affairs in the State Department and former Political Counselor in the American Embassy, on July 16, 1980.

The story about the disconnection of the telephone of the former adviser to the Dubček regime was told to us by the adviser himself in an interview on March 13, 1980.

On the way in which the Egyptian secret police work with whatever authority is in control of the phone service, we interviewed a confidential State Department source on August 12, 1980.

Information on telephone surveillance practiced by the French was given to us by a former high official of the CIA on August 14, 1980.

On the comprehensive telephone surveillance system that operated in

Iran under the Shah's regime, see excerpts of the Tehrani confession that appeared in *Ettela'at*, June 24, 1979. The story of the SAVAK agents who pursued and ultimately killed a rebel also appeared in *Ettela'at*, June 24, 1979.

On the Czechoslovakian "flying squads," see Josef Frolik, *Spión Vypovídá*, supra, pp. 345–70.

On the tapping of telephones of influential Iranians, see *Kayhan International*, Mar. 12, 1979.

6. On illegal break-ins conducted by the RCMP, see Gerard F. Rutan, "Watergate North: How the Mounties Get Their Men," *Civil Liberties Review*, supra, pp. 17–26; Robert Justin Goldstein, "Mounties on the Loose," *Worldview*, Nov. 1978, pp. 4–7; Geoffrey Stevens, "New Tales of the Royal Canadian Mounted Police," *Inquiry*, May 29, 1978, p. 9; *Maclean's*, Jan. 1978, p. 43; and the following newspaper stories: New York *Times*, Dec. 2, 1977, p. A12; New York *Times*, Nov. 11, 1977; Toronto *Globe and Mail*, Mar. 21, 1978; Ottawa *Today*, Mar. 20, 1978; and Washington *Star*, Nov. 26, 1977. For an interesting discussion of the issues of national security and violations of individual liberties, see Canada, Parliament, *Parliamentary Debates* (Commons), 3rd sess., Vol. 121, No. 9, (1977).

On methods of surveillance used in Indonesia, see the testimony of Professor Anderson, U. S. Congress, House, *Human Rights in Indonesia and East Timor*, supra, p. 8.

For information on the Mahan Committee provided by executed SAVAK torturer Tehrani to the Islamic revolutionary court in Tehran, see *Ettela'at*, June 24, 1979.

On the activities of the Special Branch, the British political police, see Mary Holland, "The Special Branch's Speciality," *New Statesman*, Apr. 26, 1974, pp. 568–69.

On infiltration of the Palestinian guerrilla camps achieved by Mukhabarat, the Jordanian internal security unit, we interviewed a confidential source at the State Department on July 18, 1980.

7. On the "white gloves" search as it takes place in Poland, we interviewed Polish émigré Irena Lasota Zabludowska, Mar. 11, 1980.

On the "period of lawfulness," we interviewed Eli Valk, Jan. 24, 1980.

On the more violent type of search carried out by KGB agents, see Viktor Nekipelov and Nina Komarova, "Selections from 'About Our Searches'" (Russian), *Freedom Appeals*, Issue No. 1 (New York: Freedom House, Sept.–Oct. 1979), pp. 4–10.

Violent searches are by no means confined to the KGB. The following description of a search that went on in Nicaragua during the Somoza regime is one of many examples of a wide variety of countries that could be used to illustrate the universality of the phenomenon of the violent search: ". . . There have been night searches in all of the houses. . . . At about 1 A.M., security agents present themselves at all homes of the 'suspicious.' They gather together all of the family in one room—women, children and old people included—and make them sit on the floor, with guards pointing their rifles at them to intimidate them. . . ." See a report by Amnesty International, *The Republic of Nicaragua, including the findings of a Mission to Nicaragua* (London: Amnesty International, 1976), p. 36.

CHAPTER SEVEN

1. On the bombing of a South African oil refinery and two huge Sasol plants on June 2, 1980, see "Where South Africa Is Most Vulnerable," *World Business Weekly*, June 16, 1980, p. 7.

2. For Jacobo Timerman's comments on the Argentine security authorities and their fear of negative press coverage, see Jacobo Timerman, "The Bodies Counted Are Our Own," *Columbia Journalism Review* 19, May–June 1980, pp. 29–33.

On Chilean security personnel's burning of allegedly controversial reading materials shortly after the 1973 coup, see the report by the Chile Committee for Human Rights, *Newsletter*, Vol. 3, No. 1 (Washington, D.C.: Chile Committee for Human Rights, Jan. 1978), p. 3.

An ad hoc working group in Chile in 1978 encountered a number of incidents that, to the minds of those on the commission, prove that the press in Chile has indeed been muzzled. According to a United Nations Report, Economic and Social Council, 34th sess., *Protection of Human Rights (Chile)* (A/34/583, add. 1), Nov. 21, 1979, p. 73, para. 2: "They [members of the Commission] stated that it had been impossible to secure publication in Chilean newspapers of the list of missing persons and that it was only through the hunger strike of 1977 that the public at large had even been acquainted and confronted with the problem of missing persons by the press. . . . in a recent communication . . . on the question of the fate of missing persons in Chile, the Association of the Relatives of Missing Detainees reports that although press conferences had been held recently with the attendance of representatives from all of the media, the content of the press conference has not been published. . . . Reliable evidence of the disappearance of detainees in Chile has existed since September 1973. The failure of the Chilean mass media to reflect this evidence was certainly a factor which permitted the disappearances of detainees to continue."

On the incident in which Indonesian authorities followed a foreign correspondent around in the country, see U. S. Congress, House, Subcommittee on International Organizations, and the Subcommittee on Asian and Pacific Affairs of the Committee on International Relations, *Human Rights in Indonesia and East Timor*, 1980, p. 15. (Reprinted by the organization TAPOL-U.S.)

On the arrest, imprisonment, expulsion and forced depositions of dissidents in Moscow who contacted the Western press, see Khronika Press, *A Chronicle of Current Events in the USSR, No. 35* (New York: Khronika Press, July–Sept. 1979), pp. 11–12.

Information on the Security Research Division, of Japan, comes from an interview with a confidential source, a high-level security officer of Japan, on July 17, 1980.

Information on Mukhabarat, the intelligence service of Jordan, was learned during an interview with a confidential source at the State Department, on July 18, 1980.

On the persecution of journalists and publishers in Syria, we interviewed a confidential State Department source (July 18, 1980) and another confidential source (July 16, 1980). For more on the persecution of journalists in Syria, see New York *Times*, July 30, 1980, p. A6.

On the closing of the weekly newspaper *Communicator*, in the Philippines, we listened to the tape *Collision Course*, a documentary on the persecution of religious leaders in the Philippines, which was created by a group of Maryknoll fathers and produced by BBC in 1977.

On the banning of the play *Presidential Candidates* in Haiti, see the testimony of *Wall Street Journal* correspondent Ray Joseph in the case of *Haitian Refugee Center et al., Plaintiff*, vs. *Benjamin Civiletti et al., Defendants*, Vol. 5, (79-2086-Civ-JLK), Miami, Fla., 1980, pp. 65–68: ". . . you had before the Duvalier regime, a press that was able to criticize certain things of the government. . . . After a few months of turbulence, came the Duvalier regime. They . . . decided to systematically crush the press, including the major Catholic newspaper. They tore down the presses and burned the buildings and most of the newsmen had to escape Haiti. Since then, you have not had a free press in Haiti. . . . The Duvalier family is not to be criticized. The Tonton Macoutes should not be criticized. . . ." Joseph says that *Presidential Candidates* was not the first play to be censored by the government. On May 9, 1979, the government began censoring a variety of plays and films, including a play set in Brooklyn, New York, about a Haitian political and economic refugee. For more on the censoring of the press in Haiti, see *The Guardian*, Sept. 21, 1979; and the Miami *Herald*, Oct. 12, 1979, one of many newspaper articles reprinted and given to us by Dale Frederick Swartz, Director, Alien Rights Law Project, Washington, D.C. Mr. Swartz was involved in the *Haitian Refugee Center* case, filed against Attorney General Civiletti in 1980.

On the persecution of the press in Indonesia, as outlined by Professor

Anderson, see U. S. Congress, House, Subcommittee on International Organizations, *Human Rights in Indonesia and East Timor*, supra, pp. 72–73; and on the process whereby Kopkamtib officials curtail commentary of a negative nature, ibid., p. 73.

On the persecution of the staff of *Dong-A Ilbo*, see Amnesty International, *Report of an Amnesty International Mission to the Republic of Korea* (London: Amnesty International, 1975), p. 29. On the "purification squad" of the Standing Committee of National Security Measures, acting under the authority of the Defense Security Command in South Korea, see New York *Times*, Aug. 1, 1980, p. A3. And on the implicit understanding between security police and press representatives on the limits to which the press can go, see New York *Times*, Sept. 4, 1980, p. A9.

On the supposed lifting of censorship in Brazil, see New York *Times*, Aug. 24, 1980, p. A3.

On the expulsion of Czechoslovakian journalists from the Union of Journalists in 1972, see Amnesty International, *Czechoslovakia* (London: Amnesty International, 1977), p. 11.

For the story of the editor of the weekly magazine that was banned in Czechoslovakia in 1969, we interviewed, on March 13, 1980, a confidential source.

3. On the arrest in 1965 of the Yugoslavian author who published in a magazine extracts of his book on the subject of his visit to the U.S.S.R., we interviewed famed dissident Yugoslavian author Mihajlo Mihajlov on March 21, 1980. For more on Mihajlov's arrest, see Mihajlo Mihajlov, "My Spiritual Experience," *Religion in Communist Dominated Areas* (*RCDA*), Vol. 17, Nos. 7 and 8 (New York: RCDA, 1978), pp. 102–3, in which the author recounts his entire experience: ". . . on my way in [to his office on campus] I noticed that students and colleagues were looking at me oddly. I went into the men's room to check whether something was wrong with my clothing. It turned out that they had simply read the papers, and I didn't. That day the newspapers published Tito's speech to prosecutors whom he reproached for not having noticed that the literary magazines were publishing all sorts of things, for example, my series of articles entitled 'Moscow Summer.' . . . According to Tito, they were 'slandering a fraternal socialist country,' that is, the Soviet Union." For Tito's comments about restrictions on citizens despite reforms supposedly made in UDBA, the secret police, see Mihajlo Mihajlov, "My Spiritual Experience," op. cit., p. 104. And for the full text of literary critic Malcolm Muggeridge's comments on Mihajlo Mihajlov, see Muggeridge's introduction to Mihajlov's book *Unscientific Thoughts*, transl. V. Mihajlov (London, Ont.: Zaria Publishing, 1979).

On security authorities' fear of negative literary commentary on them in the People's Republic of China, see New York *Times*, Feb. 20, 1980, p. A6.

On the Yugoslavian 1974 press law prohibiting "the disturbance of public order," see the report of the Committee in Defense of Soviet Political Prisoners, *A Dossier on Repression in Yugoslavia* (London: Committee in Defense of Soviet Political Prisoners, 1977), p. 2.

For the high official's comments on the reasons behind the banning of *Newsweek* in 1976 in Indonesia, see TAPOL: U. S. Campaign for the Release of Indonesian Political Prisoners, *Bulletin No. 8* (Montclair, N.J.: TAPOL, Dec. 15, 1976), p. 7; for comments with regard to the harassment of another journalist, see TAPOL *Bulletin No. 5*, June 15, 1976, p. 4; and on comments made by an Indonesian lieutenant colonel with regard to the banning of the works of Willbrodus S. Rendra, see TAPOL *Bulletin No. 15*, June 1978, p. 3. After a number of newspapers were closed down in 1978, a high Kopkamtib official remarked, "We are in no mood to be tolerant." See TAPOL *Bulletin No. 14*, Apr. 1978, p. 6.

For Steve Biko's comments on the interest the security police showed in author Donald Woods, see Donald Woods, *Biko* (London: Paddington Press, 1978), p. 130. On Colonel Goosen's statement at the Biko inquest that antisecurity police press coverage is affecting South Africans, ibid., p. 303.

For Prime Minister Indira Gandhi's statements in support of stringent press restraints in 1980, see New York *Times*, Aug. 19, 1980, p. A3.

4. For Argentine publisher Jacobo Timerman's analysis of the reason why the human-rights commissions have become of great concern to the secret police (publicity by the press), see Jacobo Timerman, "The Bodies Counted Are Our Own," op. cit., pp. 30–33.

For the former prisoners' analyses of the ways in which the Indonesian security authorities cover up the deplorable quality of prison conditions for the sake of the visiting commissions, see TAPOL *Bulletin No. 11*, June 15, 1977, p. 5; and U. S. Congress, House, Subcommittee on International Organizations of the Committee on International Relations, *Human Rights in Indonesia and the Philippines*, 1976, supra, p. 10.

On the testimony of the former Tonton Macoutes officer with regard to cover-ups for the benefit of a visiting human-rights commission to Haiti, see the case of *Haitian Refugee Center et al., Plaintiff*, vs. *Benjamin Civiletti et al., Defendants*, supra, p. 33; and see the testimony of a former army officer, ibid., pp. 85–87.

On the agreement reached by Israeli authorities and the International Red Cross, see Amnesty International, *Report and Recommendations of an Amnesty International Mission to the Government of the State of Israel* (London: Amnesty International, 1980), pp. 27–28; Amnesty International, *Report 1979* (London: Amnesty International, 1979), pp. 163–64; Amnesty International, *Report 1980* (London: Amnesty International, 1980), p. 28; and *The Christian Science Monitor*, Apr. 4, 1979, pp. 27–28.

On the chief of the Philippine Constabulary who invited the Red Cross to inspect the detention center at Camp Crame, see Dr. John Swomley, Jr., "Inside Marcos' Concentration Camps," *The Christian Century* 91, Nov. 13, 1974, pp. 1066–67; and for the full text of the solicitor general's comments with regard to an Amnesty International report, see Amnesty International, *Report of an Amnesty International Mission to the Republic of the Philippines* (London: Amnesty International, 1976), p. 84.

For the full text of the high official's reply to a report that was critical of the plight of political prisoners in Indonesia, see TAPOL-U.S., *Bulletin No. 7*, Oct. 15, 1976, pp. 6–7.

On the ludicrously pro-Amin commission of inquiry into disappearances that was set up in Uganda in 1974, see International Commission of Jurists, *Uganda and Human Rights: Reports to the U. N. Commission on Human Rights* (Geneva: International Commission of Jurists, 1977), pp. 121–24.

5. On the persecution of Tunisian lawyers, see Amnesty International, *Tunisia: Imprisonment of Trade Unionists in 1978* (London: Amnesty International, 1978), pp. 5, 12, and 13.

On the persecution of Egyptian defense attorneys, see Amnesty International, *Report 1979* (London: Amnesty International, 1979), p. 155. For more information about other cases in which lawyers' access to dossiers was impeded, see Amnesty International, *Report 1978* (London: Amnesty International, 1978), p. 254.

On the persecution of Moroccan defense attorneys, see Amnesty International, *Morocco* (London: Amnesty International, 1977), p. 8.

On the persecution of Czechoslovakian attorney Josef Danicz, who contested the StB authorities, we interviewed a confidential source on March 13, 1980. See also the *Bulletin of the Center for the Independence of Judges and Lawyers*, Vol. 2, No. 1 (Geneva: International Commission of Jurists, 1979), p. 9.

On the persecution of South Korean defense attorneys, see Amnesty International, *Report of an Amnesty International Mission to the Republic of Korea* (London: Amnesty International, 1975), pp. 21–25, and pp. 41–42 for information on a specific trial involving eight members of the People's Revolutionary Party, in which it was alleged that no foreign journalists were allowed to be present, because, as the Prime Minister put it in a National Assembly speech in October of 1974, "There was too great a risk they might misunderstand and misrepresent what happened in court." And on the persecution of South Korean attorneys defending opposition leader Kim Dae Jung, see an Amnesty International press release, Aug. 5, 1980.

On the fact that black defendants have difficulty finding attorneys to represent them in South Africa, see *The Christian Science Monitor*, Aug. 1, 1978. An additional problem for many black detainees in South Africa relates to a language barrier they encounter with those who are supposed to defend them. See Amnesty International, *Political Imprisonment in South Africa* (London: Amnesty International, 1978), pp. 27-29: "Since many of those brought before South Africa's courts are defended on a 'pro deo basis' [by the Defense counsel appointed by court] and their parent tongue is neither English nor Afrikaans, the official languages of the court, this innovation in judicial procedure appears to make it almost inevitable that many defendants will incriminate themselves, thus jeopardizing their defense case during this pretrial interrogation."

On the persecution of Chilean lawyers by the College of Lawyers and other bar associations, see *Bulletin of the Center for the Independence of Judges and Lawyers*, pp. 5-6; and Secretaria Ejecutiva de Solidaridad de la Izquierda Chileana para América, *Chile Informative 102: La DINA en Chile* (Mexico City: Casa de Chile, 1976).

For information on restrictions placed upon lawyers in Moscow, see Amnesty International, *Prisoners of Conscience in the USSR* (London: Amnesty International, 1980), pp. 65-86.

On SAVAK agents as employees of the judicial system in Iran, see Amnesty International, *Human Rights in Iran* (London: Amnesty International, 1978), pp. 4-6. For more information on the Joint Committee, see notes for Chapter Five, Section 3.

On the oppressive atmosphere of courtrooms in which political prisoners in Indonesia are tried, see TAPOL-U.S., *Bulletin No. 33*, Apr. 1979, pp. 2 and 4.

On the trial in South Africa of twenty students from the University of Zululand, in 1977, see Amnesty International, *Political Imprisonment in South Africa* (London: Amnesty International, 1978), pp. 30-31.

On the circumscribed procedures followed by South African courts in determining causes of death, see New York *Times*, Nov. 29, 1977.

On the refusal of the court to visit the cells on the West Bank where a defendant was allegedly beaten, see United Nations, General Assembly, 33rd sess., *Report of the Special Committee to Investigate Israeli Practices Affecting the Human Rights of the Population of the Occupied Territories* (A/31/1218), Oct. 1, 1976, p. 30.

On the selection of Judges in Paraguay, see Amnesty International, *Paraguay* (London: Amnesty International, 1976), p. 12.

On the abolishment of the Supreme Court of Sri Lanka, see *Bulletin of the Center for the Independence of Judges and Lawyers,* pp. 27–31; and on the establishment of a Criminal Justice Commission to try politicians and civil rights workers outside the established courts, see Amnesty International, *Report of an Amnesty International Mission to Sri Lanka* (London: Amnesty International, 1976), pp. 24–28.

On the inability of a court to invalidate a detention order from the security police in South African-controlled Namibia, see Amnesty International, *Political Imprisonment in South Africa,* pp. 27–29.

On the two-track court system of Zaire, see Amnesty International, *Human Rights Violations in Zaire* (London: Amnesty International, 1980), p. 7; and on the South African Terrorism Act of 1967, see Amnesty International, *Political Imprisonment in South Africa,* pp. 27–29. For General Van den Bergh's statement rejecting the need for a public inquiry to be held into the aims of alleged Communists, see *Proveritate,* Sept. 15, 1972, pp. 13–14.

On CNI agents' exemption from the requirement of having to appear in court, see United Nations, Economic and Social Council, 33rd sess., *Protection of Human Rights in Chile* (A/33/331), Oct. 1, 1978, pp. 37–38, paras. 157–61. On the DINA agents who refused a judge entry into the premises of DINA headquarters, see *Bulletin for the Center of Independence for Judges and Lawyers,* p. 6. For background information on the statement made by the Minister of the Interior to the effect that DINA agents are not required to appear before the court, see United Nations, Economic and Social Council, *Protection of Human Rights in Chile,* 1978, pp. 37–38, paras. 157–61. And for the direct quote of General Manuel Contreras Sepúlveda, former DINA director, on the subject of agents appearing in court, ibid. For President Pinochet's defense of the Chilean judicial system, see the text of an interview with General Pinochet, Oct. 21, 1973, broadcast of "Issues and Answers" (interviewers: Charles Murphy, ABC News' Miami Bureau Chief, and Geraldo Rivera, newsman, WABC-TV, New York). The interview with General Pinochet was taped in Santiago Oct. 6. The junta reviewed the program and censored a thirty-second portion of the interview concerning prisoners held in the National Stadium. In the interview, President Pinochet appeared to be rather unabashed about the procedures of the courts in Chile and quite sharply critical of international public opinion with regard to Chile:

"Interviewer: Would you not consider, then, a representative panel of international jurists to attend one of these tribunals [military tribunals] as witnesses?

"Pinochet: If you were the ones who were being in our situation you would not permit such a thing.

"Interviewer: How does the General react to the action taken by the

United States Senate in unanimously voting to withhold almost all aid to Chile until there is a restoration of human rights in this country?

"Pinochet: I can tell to the members of the Senate that, regrettably, it has been the influence of international Communism on them, that's the truth that we're saying. . . ."

For more on Fidel Castro's defense of the Cuban court system, see Frank Calzón, *Castro's Gulag: The Politics of Terror* (Washington, D.C.: Council for Inter-American Security, 1979), p. 25.

6. On statements made by the deputy commander of the Fifth Army Corps at a press conference focused on the subject of the "fugitive status" of thirty faculty members, see New York *Times*, Jan. 7, 1978, p. A3.

On Dr. Martha Frayde, of Cuba, see Of Human Rights, *Of Human Rights*, Vol. 2, No. 2 (Georgetown U., Spring 1979), pp. 1, 10–11.

On the arrest of scores of Chilean doctors just after the coup, see New York *Times*, Jan. 13, 1974, p. A3.

On the Colombian doctor who was persecuted for sympathizing with the poor, see Amnesty International, *Amnesty Action* (New York: Dec. 1979), p. 3.

On the president of the union of Jordanian doctors who was dismissed from his post, see Palestine Human Rights Campaign, *Palestine Human Rights Bulletin No. 14* (Washington, D.C.: Feb. 1979), pp. 1–2.

For the full testimony of the Argentinian woman doctor who is married to a doctor, both of whom were arrested by security authorities in 1976, see Inter-American Commission on Human Rights, *Report on the Situation of Human Rights in Argentina* (Washington, D.C.: General Secretariat of the Organization of American States, 1980), pp. 74–84.

For comments made by Drs. Earl Callen, Bernard R. Cooper, and John Parmentola, see "Science and Human Rights," *Technology Review*, Dec.–Jan. 1980, pp. 21–29.

7. For excerpts of the interview with the chief of staff of Indonesia's Kopkamtib, see TAPOL-U.S., *Bulletin No. 31*, Dec.–Jan. 1980, p. 10.

For more of Professor Anderson's testimony with regard to the rigged student elections, see U. S. Congress, House, *Human Rights in Indonesia and East Timor*, 1980, supra, p. 7.

On the formation by SAVAK of the "cultural societies" in Berlin and Cologne, see Confederation of Iranian Students (National Union), *SAVAK: Documents on Iranian Secret Police* (Geneva, 1976), p. 15.

On the way in which Egyptian security authorities manipulate student politics by manipulating the educational system, we interviewed a confidential source at the U. S. State Department, Aug. 12, 1980.

Mr. T. M. Hsieh, the Taiwanese magazine editor and lecturer at a military academy who was imprisoned from 1971 to 1977, told us his story on his visit to Los Angeles on May 28, 1980.

On Colonel Qaddafi's command that all Libyan exiles return home or face liquidation, see *Manchester Guardian Weekly,* Apr. 20, 1980, p. 3.

For comments made by former Philippine Senator Raúl Manglapus on the subject of exiles in the United States being watched by secret police, see Nicholas Daniloff and John Maclean, "Bang, Bang, You're Dead," *Washingtonian,* July 1979, pp. 50–66.

Mihajlo Mihajlov told us how he was approached by FBI agents in an interview conducted on March 21, 1980, in Washington, D.C.

Information on Yugoslavian exiles who were taken prisoner by Yugoslavian secret police agents many years after they had left their native country comes from Amnesty International, *Report 1978,* supra, p. 247.

Mr. Eugenio Velasco, former Chilean Supreme Court justice, whose full story is recounted in Chapter One, told us about his experiences with DINA agents after he came to this country, in an interview conducted on July 17, 1980.

For additional information on the Letelier assassination, see Saul Landau and Ralph Stavins, "This Is How It Was Done," *The Nation,* Mar. 26, 1977, p. 358; and on the trial of some Cuban exiles involved in the Letelier murder, see New York *Times,* Jan. 9, 1979, p. A4, New York *Times,* Jan. 10, 1979, p. A6, New York *Times,* Jan. 23, 1979, p. A10, and New York *Times,* Jan. 11, 1979, p. A10.

Information on DINA agents harassing members of the FBI who were involved in the investigation into the Letelier murder was told to us by Wendy Turnbull, former employee of Amnesty International headquarters in San Francisco, on June 8, 1979.

Information on the presence of foreign secret police agents in the United States harassing exiles here is taken from Diane Edwards La Voy, "Foreign Nationals and American Law," *Society* 15, Nov.–Dec. 1977, pp. 58–64.

8. On state-controlled religion in Egypt, we interviewed a confidential source at the U. S. State Department on August 12, 1980.

On the Uruguayan priest who was harassed because of his relationship with an opposition activist, we interviewed Juan Ferreira, son of the former presidential candidate of the Partido Blanco, on May 2, 1980.

On the 1978 Argentine decree instituting the National Registry of Religions, see Amnesty International, *Visit Beautiful Argentina . . .* (New York: Amnesty International, 1978), p. 2.

On the Romanian Government's recognition of only fourteen religions, see Amnesty International, *Romania* (London: Amnesty International, 1978), p. 29.

On the persecution of religious leaders in Czechoslovakia, see Amnesty International, *Czechoslovakia*, supra, p. 12.

On the shift in attitude toward leading religious figures of the opposition on the part of the security police in the Philippines, we interviewed Jerry Jumat, a former Moslem anti-Marcos activist from the Philippines, Mar. 19, 1980.

Information on the escalation of religious persecution in the Philippines is presented in the Maryknoll fathers' television production *Collision Course*, supra.

For additional information on salvaging in the Philippines, see our notes for Chapter Five, Section 7.

On the persecution of South Korean religious figures, see Amnesty International, *Report of an Amnesty International Mission to the Republic of Korea*, supra, p. 31.

On the persecution of religious opposition figures in Cuba, see Frank Calzón, *Castro's Gulag*, supra, pp. 31–33.

On the persecution of the Catholic Church in Rhodesia in the early seventies, see International Commission of Jurists (with the Catholic Institute for International Relations), *Racial Discrimination and Repression in Southern Rhodesia* (London: International Commission of Jurists, 1976), p. 40.

On the persecution of figures of the religious opposition in South Africa, see New York *Times* issues: May 4, 1980, p. A3; and May 27, 1980, p. A3.

On the Latin American clergy as vociferous social critics, see Los Angeles *Times*, July 11, 1980, Part II, p. 6.

For the full text of the testimony of the Chief Legal Counsel for the Cooperative Committee for Peace in Chile, see U. S. Congress, House, Subcommittee on International Relations, *Chile: The Status of Human Rights and Its Relationship to U. S. Economic Assistance Programs*, 94th Cong., 2nd sess., 1976.

On the persecution of religious political activists in Bolivia, see New York *Times*, July 25, 1980, p. A5.

On the antagonism felt between Brazilian clergy who are politically active and leading politicians, see Amnesty International, *Brazil: Background Paper* (London: Amnesty International, 1978), p. 4.

CHAPTER EIGHT

2. On the relationship of illegal incommunicado detention and the infliction of torture, see Robert K. Goldman and Daniel Jacoby, *Report of the Commission of Enquiry to Mexico Submitted to the International League for Human Rights, Fédération Internationale des Droits de*

l'Homme and Pax Romana (New York: International League for Human Rights, 1978), p. 17.

On the development of the practice of torture in Algeria, see John Talbott, *War Without a Name: France in Algeria, 1954–62* (New York: Alfred A. Knopf, Inc., 1980), p. 86.

On the Shah of Iran's admission that SAVAK agents were occasionally guilty of abusing their powers, see Mohammad Reza Pahlevi, *Answer to History* (New York: Stein & Day, 1980), p. 158.

On soldiers in Algeria resorting to torture, see John Talbott, op. cit., p. 86.

On the Shah of Iran's defense of the practices and the general style of SAVAK agents, see Mohammad Reza Pahlevi, op. cit., pp. 156–69.

On the British public's overall acceptance of the politics and practices of Scotland Yard, see Jamie Kitman, "A Nerve Gas We Can Love," *The Nation*, July 5, 1980, p. 12.

On Simone de Beauvoir's description of becoming hardened to the fact of torture going on in Algeria, see John Talbott, op. cit., p. 93.

The analysis of Anwar Sadat's reasons for streamlining the intelligence structures of Egypt was learned in an interview with a confidential source, a U. S. State Department official, in Washington, D.C., Aug. 12, 1980. For more on President Nasser's use of concentration camps for imprisoning his political enemies, specifically Egyptian Marxists, see Jean Lacouture, *Nasser: A Biography* (New York: Alfred A. Knopf, 1973), pp. 29–35.

On the security service that has replaced the Shah of Iran's SAVAK, we interviewed a former general of the Iranian Army, now living in Beverly Hills, Aug. 28, 1979. For more on SAVAMA, see "A Year After," *The Economist*, Feb. 23, 1980, pp. 29–35.

For more on Tehrani's recommendations to the ayatollah on how to structure an efficient clandestine internal-security service, see *Iran News*, July 2, 1979, p. 5.

3. For a good distillation of the Huston Plan, see report of the Center for Research on Criminal Justice, *The Iron Fist and the Velvet Glove: An Analysis of the U. S. Police* (Berkeley, Calif.: Center for Research, 1975), pp. 100–1.

For a review of some specific cases as well as some general overviews of past abuses committed by United States intelligence officials, see New York *Times*, Feb. 17, 1980, p. 1, on the alleged cover-up by the FBI's chief paid informer inside the Ku Klux Klan on FBI agents' involvements in violent attacks on blacks, civil rights activists, and journalists in the early sixties; New York *Times*, Feb. 18, 1980, p. A1, on the same case; Los Angeles *Times*, May 13, 1980, p. 1, on the recent Supreme Court revision of the legal standard for police treatment of people in custody, the Court deciding that in some instances law enforcement officials may be found to have improperly interrogated their subjects; and Fred Barbash, Washington *Post*, July 21, 1980, p. A1, on the important case *Rhode Island* vs. *Innis*, in which it was decided that police wrongly played on a suspect's conscience in order to obtain his confession: "The Baltimore police call it the 'no-good SOB case.' A man was arrested for a shooting. While he was at the station, a Baltimore policeman sauntered in and announced, 'I'd like to shake the hand of the guy who shot that no-good SOB.' The suspect stood up, introduced himself, accepted congratulations and was later convicted on that evidence." See also Los Angeles *Times*, Sept. 19, 1980, Part I, p. 12, on the case of W. Mark Felt, former No. 2 FBI man, and Edward S. Miller, former FBI domestic intelligence chief, both convicted of conspiring to violate the rights of citizens for their role in authorizing illegal break-ins, during the early seventies, into the homes of fugitives of the radical organization known as the Weather Underground. See also Kenneth O'Reilly, "The FBI—HUAC's Big Brother," *The Nation*, Jan. 19, 1980, pp. 42–45, on the FBI's alleged efforts over two decades to harass and discredit critics of the government; and see the report of the American Friends Service Committee, *The Police Threat to Political Liberty* (Philadelphia: American Friends Service Committee, 1979), which includes a detailed discussion of U.S. intelligence attempts to subvert the rebellions of the sixties, an analysis of the status of domestic intelligence during the seventies, and analyses of the domestic intelligence activities of the police departments of Los Angeles, Philadelphia, Baltimore, Seattle, and Jackson, Mississippi.

On the structure of the American intelligence community, see Edward J. Epstein, *Agency of Fear* (New York: G. P. Putnam's Sons, 1977), pp. 47, 65, 240–41.

On the Cook County grand jury's six-month investigation into the Red Squad's spying operations in Chicago, see Los Angeles *Times*, May 15, 1980, Part I, pp. 1, 22–23. For more on Chicago Police Department surveillance operations, see Center for Research and Criminal Justice, *The Iron Fist and the Velvet Glove*, supra, pp. 119–20.

On the practices of the Buffalo Police Department in terms of surveillance and spying, see Norman Solomon, "Nuclear Big Brother," *Time Bomb: A Nuclear Reader from the Progressive* (Madison, Wis.: Progressive Foundation, 1980), p. 13.

On surveillance techniques of the Los Angeles Police Department and on the practice of power companies maintaining their own security departments, see Norman Solomon, op. cit., p. 13. For additional information on the collusion of private and government organizations in order to spy on citizens, see the report of the American Friends Service Committee, *The Police Threat to Political Liberty*, supra, pp. 96–102.

On the LEIU, see Linda Valentino, "The LEIU: Part of the Political Intelligence Network," *First Principles,* Vol. 4, No. 5 (Washington, D.C.: Center for National Security Studies, Jan. 1979). For more on the LEIU, see American Friends Service Committee, *The Police Threat to Political Liberty,* supra, pp. 81–94; George O'Toole, "America's Secret Police Network," *Penthouse,* Dec. 1976, pp. 77–82 and 194–206; Center for Research and Criminal Justice, *The Iron Fist and the Velvet Glove,* supra, pp. 116–18; and *Time,* June 25, 1979, p. 22.

On COINTELPRO, see Los Angeles *Times,* May 23, 1980, p. 1; and American Friends Service Committee, *The Police Threat to Political Liberty,* supra, pp. 12, 16–17.

On the 1980 survey of police intelligence units in New York, Chicago, Washington, Houston, Atlanta and Detroit conducted by the Los Angeles *Times,* see Los Angeles *Times,* May 15, 1980, pp. 1, 22–23.

On the Los Angeles Police Department official who argues in favor of the need for intelligence and confidentiality about the intelligence-gatherers, see Los Angeles *Herald-Examiner,* May 13, 1980, p. A3.

For the full text of the interview with former BOSS chief General Van den Bergh, see "BOSS Man on Terrorism Act," *Rand Daily Mail,* Nov. 22, 1971.

Many state leaders have used words as harsh as those used by General Van den Bergh in this interview when asked to defend the practices of their security services. Marshal Tito himself once said, "We must take measures which, according to our constitution and our laws, we have a right to do. . . . Otherwise it would be interpreted as a sign of weakness. We are afraid of no one and nothing." For more of Tito's comments, see Washington *Post,* Dec. 24, 1978, p. A12. See also the report of Amnesty International, *Malawi* (London: Amnesty International, Aug. 1976), p. 2, for some comments made by Dr. Hastings Banda, who became President for Life in July 1971: "If, to maintain political stability and efficient administration I have to detain 10,000, 100,000, I will do it. I want nobody to misunderstand me. I will detain anyone who is interfering with the political stability of this country. . . ."

For Canadian Prime Minister Trudeau's opinion on the need to curb terrorism and his rationale in defense of some of the allegedly extreme day-to-day operations of the RCMP Security Service, see Gerard F. Rutan, "Watergate North: How the Mounties Get Their Men," *Civil Liberties Review,* July–Aug. 1978, p. 24. Solicitor General Francis Fox made some defensive statements in support of the RCMP activities that are quite similar to those made by Trudeau. See Canada, Parliament, *Parliamentary Debates* (Commons), 3rd sess., Vol. 121 (1977). Fox, quoting from the 1969 report of the Royal Commission on Security, said: "A security service is unavoidably involved in activities which run counter to the spirit, if not to the letter of the law, and in illegal or other activities which may seem to infringe upon individual rights." Canadian Chief Superintendent Donald Cobb, former senior officer of the elite national police force, was even more blunt about the range of illegal activities performed by the RCMP. See New York *Times,* Jan. 14, 1978: "'We were used to living with certain illegalities,' he said, adding, 'They were so commonplace that they were no longer thought of as illegal.'"

For Trudeau's comments on mail openings accomplished by RCMP officers, see Washington *Star,* Nov. 19, 1977, p. A4.

On the Bennett Committee findings with regard to the importance of supervision during an interrogation session, see Great Britain, "Report of the Committee of Inquiry into Police Interrogation Procedures in Northern Ireland," Cmnd. 7497, *Report, 1979,* p. 14, para. 42; on the Parker Committee rationale in defense of severe interrogation techniques, despite the worry that frequently used techniques of that sort could lead to the interrogation of innocent detainees, see Great Britain, Northern Ireland Office, Parliament. Parliamentary Papers (Commons), 1971–72, Vol. 18, Cmnd. 4901, "Report of the Committee of Privy Counsellors Appointed to Consider Authorized Procedures for the Interrogation of Persons Suspected of Terrorism," Mar. 1972, p. 7, para. 33; on the Parker Committee conclusions with regard to the importance of considering the *degree* to which the "five techniques" of interrogation are applied as well as the medical condition of the detainee, see Parker Committee Report, supra, p. 6, para. 29; and on the Bennett Committee statement that "[The confessions] will not be made in the atmosphere of a casual conversation or cosy fireside chat," see the Bennett Committee Report, supra, p. 13, para. 37.

Bibliography

BIBLIOGRAPHIC NOTES

Extremely thorough interviews were conducted with exiles, refugees and émigrés from around the world. The interviews took place, often under circumstances of considerable confidentiality, in London, New York, and Washington—three of the main exile centers of the world. The sources came from the following countries:

Argentina, Chile, Cuba, Czechoslovakia, East Timor, Egypt, Haiti, Indonesia, Iran, Israel (West Bank and Occupied Territories), Japan, Korea, Mexico, Paraguay, Philippines, Poland, Portugal, Romania, Rhodesia, South Africa, Soviet Union, Syria, Taiwan, Uruguay, and·Yugoslavia.

In addition, the resources of a number of nonprofit, nongovernmental organizations were made available to us. Some of these organizations are listed below:

American Friends Service Committee: This organization, established by the Religious Society of Friends, is dedicated to the search for nonviolent solutions to human problems. Founded by a group of Philadelphia Quakers in 1917, it works to provide relief and rehabilitation in areas of political tension or disaster.

Amnesty International: This is a worldwide organization working for the release of individual prisoners of conscience and on special campaigns directed against countries it considers to be violators of human rights.

Formosan Association of Human Rights: This organization, formally organized in 1976, opposes numerous procedures of the government of Taiwan: detention of political prisoners, the perpetuation of martial law, the application of torture to political prisoners, and the violation of civil rights of Taiwanese living abroad, among others.

Freedom House: This organization maintains year-round programs designed to defend and strengthen free institutions both in the United States and abroad. Freedom House aims at analyzing political rights all over the world, for the benefit of United States businessmen, officials, scholars and members of the news media.

Inter-American Association for Democracy and Freedom: Since its creation, in 1950, this organization has functioned in support of democratic forces in the Western hemisphere, including the support of democratic leaders both in power and in exile. The IADF also serves as a center for Latin American refugees and intervenes on behalf of political prisoners in Latin America by securing political asylum for them whenever possible.

International Commission of Jurists: This organization, headquartered in Geneva, Switzerland, draws support from judges, law professors, attorneys, and other members of the legal community and their associations. The national sections of the ICJ, working in over fifty countries, supply the International Secretariat with relevant information. The ICJ also privately intervenes on behalf of political prisoners and sends missions to various parts of the world to observe political trials.

Khronika Press: This organization, headquartered in New York, publishes documents and books of the Soviet human-rights movement in both Russian and English, with topics ranging from historical to contemporary viewpoints on human rights.

North American Congress on Latin America: This research organization, founded in response to the U.S. invasion of the Dominican Republic, has been devoted to analyzing the impact of U.S. strategies in Latin America.

PEN American Center: The initials of this organization's name stand for poets, playwrights, essayists, editors, and novelists. PEN American Center is an international association of writers, its main concern being to promote cooperation among men and women of letters.

Task Force Detainees of the Philippines: The Task Force, a project of the Association of Major Religious Superiors, is a religious monitor of human-rights abuses in the Philippines. The Association of Religious Superiors is a coalition of about eighty-four heads of various religious orders in the Philippines.

A (T) after a cited work means that we commissioned a translation into English from the native-language publication or document.

SELECTED BIBLIOGRAPHY

I. Books

Barron, John. *KGB: The Secret World of Soviet Secret Agents.* New York: Reader's Digest Press, 1974.

Becker, Harold K. *Police Systems of Europe: A Survey of Selected Police Organizations.* Springfield, Ill.: Charles C. Thomas, 1973.

Bellow, Walden; and Rivera, Severina, eds. *Logistics of Repression and other Essays: The Role of U. S. Assistance in Consolidating the Martial Law Regime in the Philippines.* Washington, D.C.: Friends of the Filipino People, 1977.

Bowden, Tom. *Beyond the Limits of the Law.* Harmondsworth, Middlesex: Penguin Books, 1978.

Bunyan, Tony. *The History and Practice of the Political Police in Britain.* London: Quartet Books, 1977.

Castro, Orlando-Hidalgo. *Spy for Fidel.* Miami: E. A. Seemann Publishing, Inc., 1971.

Cline, Ray S. *Secrets, Spies and Scholars.* New York· Acropolis Books, 1976.

Cubberly, Ray Ellsworth. *The Role of Fouché During the Hundred Days.* Madison, Wis.: Department of History, University of Wisconsin, 1969.

Deacon, Richard. *A History of the Russian Secret Service.* London: Muller, 1972.

Dinges, John; and Landau, Saul. *Assassination on Embassy Row.* New York: Pantheon Books, 1980.

Donner, Frank. *The Age of Surveillance.* New York: Alfred A. Knopf, 1980.

Elliff, John T. *The Reform of FBI Intelligence Operations.* Princeton, N.J.: Princeton University Press, 1979.

Epstein, Edward Jay. *Agency of Fear.* New York: G. P. Putnam's Sons, 1977.

Fitch, Herbert Trevor. *Traitors Within· The Story of the Special Branch, New Scotland Yard.* London: Hurst & Blackett, 1933.

Fooner, Michael. *Interpol.* Chicago: Henry Regnery, 1973.

Fouché, Joseph. *The Memoirs of Joseph Fouché, Duke of Otranto, Minister of the General Police of France,* 2 vols London: H. S. Nichols, 1896.

Frolik, Josef. *Špión Vypovídá.* Cologne: Index, 1979. (T)

Halliday, Fred. *Iran: Dictatorship and Development.* Harmondsworth, Middlesex: Penguin Books, 1979.

Heinl, Nancy Gordon; and Heinl, Robert Debs. *Written in Blood: The Story of the Haitian People, 1492–1971.* Boston: Houghton Mifflin, 1978.

Hingley, Ronald. *The Russian Secret Police: Muscovite, Imperial, Russian and Soviet Political Security Operations, 1565–1970.* London: Hutchinson, 1970.

Hollis, Rex. *A Documented Exposure of Secret Police in New Zealand.* Auckland, N.Z.: Wilson Printery, 1966.

International Police Association. *International Bibliography of Selected Police Literature.* London: M and W Publications, 1968.

Lacouture, Jean. *Nasser: A Biography.* New York: Alfred A. Knopf, 1973.

Levytski, Borys. *The Uses of Terror: The Soviet Secret Police, 1917–1970.* New York: Coward, McCann & Geoghegan, 1972.

Moorehead, Caroline. *Hostages to Fortune.* New York: Atheneum, 1980.

Myagkov, Aleksei. *Inside the KGB.* New York: Arlington House, 1976.

Pahlavi, Mohammad Reza, the Shah of Iran. *Answer to History.* New York: Stein & Day, 1980.

Pelikán, Jiří. *The Czechoslovak Political Trials, 1950–1954: The Suppressed Report of the Dubček Government's Commission of Inquiry, 1968.* London: MacDonald & Co., 1971.

Riera, Pepita. *Servicio de Inteligencia de Cuba Comunista.* Miami: Florida Typesetting of Miami, 1966. (T)

SAVAK: Documents on Iranian Secret Police. Confederation of Iranian Students (National Front). December 1976. (T)

Slussen, Robert M.; and Wolin, Simon, eds. *The Soviet Secret Police.* New York: Frederick A. Praeger, 1957.

Talbott, John. *The War Without a Name: France in Algeria, 1954–62.* New York: Alfred A. Knopf, 1980.

Vogelgesang, Sandy. *American Dream, Global Nightmare.* New York: W. W. Norton, 1980.

Woods, Donald. *Biko.* London: Paddington Press, 1978.

Zubek, John P., ed. *Sensory Deprivation: Fifteen Years of Research.* New York: Appleton-Century-Crofts, 1969.

II. Foreign Government and Police Documents

Canada. *Official Secrets Act.* Ottawa, 1970.

Canada. Parliament. *Parliamentary Debates* (Commons), 3rd sess., Vol. 121 (1977).

Canada. Parliament. *Parliamentary Debates* (Commons), 3rd sess., Vol. 121 (1978).

Canada. *Protection of Privacy Act.* Ottawa, 1974.

Canada. Royal Canadian Mounted Police, "H" Division, Province of Nova Scotia. *Annual Report.* 1976.

Army of Chile, Military Institutes Command. *Circular to Regulate the Functioning of the Educational Establishments of Greater Santiago.* Aug. 12, 1974.

Chile. Diario Oficial, No. 23.879, de 18 de Junio de 1971. "Decreto Ley No. 521." (T)

Council of Europe. European Commission of Human Rights. *Ireland Against the United Kingdom of Great Britain and Northern Ireland* (5310.71). Report of the Commission Adopted on Jan. 25, 1976.

Great Britain. Home Office. "Enquiry into Allegations Against the Security Forces Arising Out of Events on the 9th of August, 1971." Cmnd. 4823. *Report, 1972.*

Great Britain. Northern Ireland Office. "Report of a Committee to Consider, in the Context of Civil Liberties and Human Rights, Measures to Deal with Terrorism in Northern Ireland." Cmnd. 5847. *Report, January 1975.*

Great Britain. Northern Ireland Office. "Report of the Committee of Inquiry into Police Interrogations Procedures in Northern Ireland." Cmnd. 4797. *Report, 1979.*

Great Britain. Northern Ireland Office. Parliament. Parliamentary Papers (Commons), 1971–72, Vol. 18. Cmnd. 4901, "Report of the Committee of Privy Counsellors Appointed to Consider Authorized Procedures for the Interrogation of Persons Suspected of Terrorism." Mar. 1972.

Great Britain. Parliament. Parliamentary Papers (Commons), 1975–76, Vol. 39. Cmnd. 6630, "The Feasibility of an Experiment in the Tape-recording of Police Interrogations."

Japan. Metropolitan Police Department. *Keishicho.* Tokyo: Public Relations Section, Administrative Division of the Metropolitan Police Department, 1980.

Japan. National Police Agency. *Summary of the Police White Paper, Fiscal 1978 Edition, by the National Police Agency.* Foreign Press Center, 1978.

Japan. Supreme Court of Japan. *Outline of the Japanese Judicial System.* 1975.

Yamamoto, Shizuniko, Commissioner General. *The Police of Japan.* Tokyo: National Police Agency, 1977.

South Africa. *Government Gazette.* No. 2520. Sept. 17, 1969.

South Africa. *Report of the Commission of Inquiry into Matters Relating to the Security of the State.* 1971.

Yugoslav Federal Assembly Session, *Report on Security.* By Draško Jurišić. June 23, 1975.

III. UNITED STATES GOVERNMENT DOCUMENTS

CONGRESSIONAL TESTIMONY

U. S. Congress. House. *Chile: The Status of Human Rights and Its Relationship to U. S. Economic Assistance Programs. Hearings before the Subcommittee on International Relations*, 94th Cong., 2nd sess., 1976.

U. S. Congress. House. Foreign Affairs Committee. *Foreign Assistance Legislation for FY 80–81. House Foreign Affairs Committee, International Security and Scientific Affairs Subcommittee on Foreign Military Training*, 96th Cong., 1st sess., 1979.

U. S. Congress. House. Foreign Affairs Committee. *Human Rights and the Detention of Andrei Sakharov: Update. Hearings before the Subcommittee on International Organizations of the Committee on Foreign Affairs*, 96th Cong., 2nd sess., 1980.

U. S. Congress. House. Foreign Affairs Committee. *Human Rights in Asia: Noncommunist Countries. Hearings before the Subcommittee on Asian and Pacific Affairs on International Organizations of the Committee on Foreign Affairs*, 96th Cong., 2nd sess., 1980.

U. S. Congress. House. Foreign Affairs Committee. *Review of the 36th Session of the United Nations Commission on Human Rights. Hearings before the Subcommittee on International Organizations of the Committee on Foreign Affairs*, 96th Cong., 2nd sess., 1980.

U. S. Congress. House. Committee on International Relations. *Human Rights in Indonesia and the Philippines. Hearings before the Subcommittee on International Organizations of the Committee on International Relations*, 94th Cong., 2nd sess., 1976.

U. S. Congress. Senate. Committee on Appropriations. *Review of Factors Affecting U. S. Diplomatic and Assistance Relations with Haiti.* Committee on Appropriations, 95th, Cong., 1st sess., 1977.

U. S. Congress. Senate. Committee on Foreign Relations. *Hearings before the Subcommittee on Western Hemisphere Affairs*, 92nd Cong., 1st sess., 1971. Reprinted by Amnesty International.

U. S. Congress. Senate. Committee on the Judiciary. *The Colonization of the West Bank Territories by Israel. Hearings before the Subcommittee on Immigration and Naturalization of the Committee on the Judiciary*, 95th Cong., 1st sess., 1977.

U. S. Congress. Senate. Committee on the Judiciary. *Communist Threat to the United States Through the Caribbean. Hearings before the Subcommittee to Investigate the Administration of the Internal Security Act and Other Internal Security Laws*, 91st Cong., 1st sess., 1969.

U. S. Congress. Senate. Select Committee on Ethics. *Korean Influence Inquiry. Adlai E. Stevenson, Chairman. Hearings before the Select Committee on Ethics*, 95th Cong., 2nd sess., 1978.

UNITED NATIONS DOCUMENTS

United Nations. Economic and Social Council, 31st sess. *Protection of Human Rights in Chile* (A/31/253), Oct. 8, 1976.

United Nations. Economic and Social Council, 33rd sess. *Protection of Human Rights in Chile* (A/33/331), Oct. 1, 1978.

United Nations. Economic and Social Council, 34th sess. *Protection of Human Rights (Chile)* (A/34/583, add. 1), Nov. 21, 1979.

United Nations. Economic and Social Council, 36th sess. *Question of Human Rights in Chile* (E/CN.4/1381), Jan. 9, 1980.

United Nations. Economic and Social Council, 36th sess. *Question of Human Rights in Chile* (E/CN.4/1362), Jan. 29, 1980.

United Nations. Economic and Social Council, 36th sess. *Question of the Violation of Human Rights and Fundamental Freedoms in Any Part of the World, with Particular Reference to Colonial and Other Dependent Countries and Territories* (E/CN.4/1382), Dec. 27, 1979.

United Nations. General Assembly, 31st sess. *Report of the Special Committee to Investigate Israeli Practices Affecting the Human Rights of the Population of the Occupied Territories* (A/31/1218), Oct. 1, 1976.

OTHER U. S. GOVERNMENT DOCUMENTS:

United States Army Institute for Military Assistance. *Précis of Courses FY 76.* Fort Bragg, N.C., n.d. Provided courtesy of the Institute for Policy Studies, Washington, D.C.

United States Defense Intelligence School. *Bibliography of Intelligence Literature,* 6th ed., Apr. 1969.

United States Defense Security Assistance Agency and Deputy Assistant Secretary (of Security Assistance), OASD/ISA, "Technical Assistance and Training Teams Currently in Foreign Countries," July 1975; and "DOD Civilian and Military Personnel Involved in In-Country Training of Foreign Military Personnel," Mar. 1977.

U. S. Defense Security Assistance Agency. *Training Facilities / Institutes that Provide Training to Foreign Military Personnel.* Nov. 1975.

United States Department of the Army. *Graduates of USARSA as of 5 September 1975* (undated).*

United States Department of the Army Headquarters, U. S. Army School of the Americas, Fort Gulick, C.Z. *Personnel Strength Report and Courses Offered for Calendar Year 1975* (undated).

United States Department of Commerce. Exchange of letters between Michael Klare, Visiting Fellow of the Center for International Studies, Princeton University, and Rauer H. Meyer, Director of the Office of

* USARSA stands for United States Army School of the Americas.

Export Administration, United States Department of Commerce, Bureau of East-West Trade, regarding Klare's request for information on the sale of U.S. computers to foreign police forces, under the Freedom of Information Act, 1976.

U. S. Department of Justice. *FBI Guidelines on the Use of Informants that Attorney-General Edward H. Levi ordered into Effect.* Jan. 5, 1977.

United States Department of State. Agency for International Development. *Project Implementation Order/(to the Philippines) Commodities, Delivery Periods: 11/30/75 and 3/31/75* (undated). Provided courtesy of Richard P. Claude, Center for Philosophy and Public Policy, University of Maryland.

United States Department of State. Agency for International Development. Reply letter of Matthew J. Harvey, Assistant Administrator for Legislative Affairs, Department of State, Agency for International Development, to Senator James Abourezk, concerning the Technical Investigation Course and other police training conducted and sponsored by the Office of Public Safety. Sept. 25, 1973.

U. S. Department of State. Agency for International Development. Reply letter to Senator James Abourezk from Matthew J. Harvey, Assistant Administrator for Legislative Affairs, on the subjects of: contracts for police training and related programs; the scope of activities of the Office of Public Safety; the termination of police programs. May 1974.

U. S. Department of State. *Country Reports on Human Rights Practices for 1979: Report Submitted to the Committee on Foreign Affairs, U. S. House of Representatives, and Committee on Foreign Relations, U. S. Senate.* 96th Cong., 2nd sess., 1980.

United States Department of State. Office of Public Safety. *International Police Academy Graduates, FY-69 to FY-73* (undated). Provided courtesy of the Institute for Policy Studies, Washington, D.C.

United States Department of State. Office of Public Safety. *Report of the Drug Law Enforcement Project of the USAID/La Paz Safety Program,* Apr. 1970.

IV. MAJOR JOURNALS AND MAGAZINES

Águila, Concepción. "Detention Camp: Manila," *Bulletin of Concerned Asian Scholars* 6 (Nov.–Dec. 1974): 36–42.

Alexeyeff, S. "Abuse of Psychiatry as a Tool for Political Repression in the Soviet Union." *Medical Journal of Australia* 1, Jan. 1976, pp. 122–23.

Allende, Hortensia. "The Coup in Chile: A Short Chronology," *Counterspy,* Spring/Summer 1975, pp. 42–47.

Antonius, Soraya. "Prisoners for Palestine: A List of Women Political

Prisoners," *Journal of Palestine Studies 35*, No. 3 IX (Spring 1980): 29–80.

Bill, James A. "Iran and the Crisis of '78," *Foreign Affairs*, 57, Winter 1978/79, pp. 323–42.

Brittain, R. P. "The Sadistic Murderer," *Medical Science and the Law* 10, Oct. 1970, pp. 198–207.

Britton, Peter. "Indonesia's Neo-Colonial Armed Forces," *Bulletin of Concerned Asian Scholars* 7, July–Sept. 1975, pp. 14–21.

Bro-Rasmussen, F.; and Rasmussen, O. V. "Falanga Torture. Are the Sequelae of Falanga Torture Due to the Closed Compartment Syndrome in the Feet?" *Ugeskrift for Laeger* 140, Dec. 1978, pp. 3197–3292.†

Callen, Earl; Cooper, Bernard R.; and Parmentola, John. "Science and Human Rights," *Technology Review*, Dec./Jan. 1980, pp. 21–29.

Chomsky, Noam. "East Timor: The Press Cover-up," *Inquiry*, Feb. 19, 1979.

Cohn, J.; Jensen, R.; Severin, B.; and Stadter, H. "Torture in Argentina, Syria and Zanzibar," *Ugeskrift for Laeger* 140, Dec. 1978, pp. 3202–6.

Cooperman, E. M. "Doctors, Torture and Abuse of the Doctor-Patient Relationship," *Canadian Medical Association Journal* 116, Apr. 1977, pp. 707, 709–10.

Dam, A. M.; Nielsen, I. L.; and Rasmussen, O. V. "Torture: An Investigation of Chileans and Greeks Who Had Previously Been Submitted to Torture," *Ugeskrift for Laeger* 139, May 1977, pp. 1049–53.

Daniels, M. "Pathological Vindictiveness and the Vindictive Character," *The Psychoanalytic Review* 56 (1969): 169–96, Issue No. 2.

Davison, G. C. "Elimination of a Sadistic Fantasy by a Clinet-Controlled Counterconditioning Technique: A Case Study," *Journal of Abnormal Psychology* 73, Feb. 1968, pp. 84–90, Issue No. 1.

Dyhre-Poulsen, P.; Rasmussen, L.; and Rasmussen, O. V. "Undersøgelse af et instrument til elektrisk tortur," *Ugeskrift for Laeger* 139, May 1977, pp. 1054–56.

Ege, Konrad. "West German Cultist Concentration Camp in Chile," *Counterspy*, Dec. 1978, pp. 43–53.

Genefke, I. K.; and Kjaersgaar, A. R. "Tortur i Uruguay og Argentina," *Ugeskrift for Laeger* 139, May 1977, pp. 1057–59.

Goldsmith, J.; and Siomopoulos, V. "Sadism Revisited," *American Journal of Psychotherapy* 30, Oct. 1976, pp. 631–40.

Gribbin, Peter. "Brazil and the CIA," *Counterspy*, Apr./May 1979, pp. 4–11.

† *Ugeskrift for Laeger*, roughly translated, means *Weekly for Doctors*.

Holland, Mary. "The Special Branch's Specialty," *New Statesman*, Apr. 1974, pp. 568–69.

Jonsen, A.; and Sagan, L. A. "Medical Ethics and Torture," *New England Journal of Medicine* 294, June 1976, pp. 1427–30.

Kassim, Anis. "National Lawyers Guild Report (a review)," *Journal of Palestine Studies 36*, No. 4 IX (Summer 1980): 142–46.

Klare, Michael T. "The Reality Behind 'State of Siege,'" *The Nation*, Dec. 10, 1973, pp. 619–22.

———; and Schechter, Daniel. "The International Police Academy: The 'State of Siegers' Besieged," *The Real Paper*, June 26, 1974, pp. 15–16.

La Voy, Diane Edwards. "Foreign Nationals and American Law," *Society* 15, Nov.–Dec. 1977, pp. 58–64.

Mihajlov, Mihajlo. "Impressions of America," *The New Leader*, Apr. 23, 1979, pp. 9–27.

Milgram, Stanley. "Behavioral Study of Obedience," *Journal of Abnormal Social Psychology* 67 (4) (1963): 371–78.

———. "Some Conditions of Obedience and Disobedience to Authority," *Human Relations* 18 (1) (1965): 57–76.

Morris, Fred B. "In the Presence of Mine Enemies," *Harper's Magazine*, Oct. 1975, pp. 57–67.

Nowland, D. "Measuring Man's Inhumanity," *Irish Medical Journal* 70, Sept. 1977, p. 375.

O'Toole, George. "America's Secret Police Network," *Penthouse*, Dec. 1976, pp. 77, 194–203.

Peck, Winslow. "Apartheid's Corporate Covert Action," *Counterspy*, Spring 1976, pp. 46–55.

Pogebrin, Letty Cotlin. "The FBI Was Watching You," *Ms.*, June 1977, pp. 37–44.

Pringle, James; and Willey, Fay. "Chile: Gentlemen of Torture," *Newsweek*, Mar. 31, 1975, p. 51.

Ranard, Donald. "Park's Clone in South Korea," *The Nation*, June 23, 1980, pp. 776–77.

———. "Seoul Brothers," *The Nation*, Jan. 19, 1980, pp. 36–37.

Ridenour, Ron. "Interpol: The International Kingdom of Police Spies," *Coast*, Jan. 1977, pp. 22–28.

Rouleau, Eric. "Khomeini's Iran," *Foreign Affairs* 59 (1) (1980): 2–20.

Rubinfine, David L. "On Beating Fantasies," *International Journal of Psychoanalysis* 46 (3) (1965): 315–22.

Rutan, Gerard F. "Watergate North: How the Mounties Get Their Men," *Civil Liberties Review*, July/Aug. 1978, pp. 17–26.

Severin, B.; Jeks, P.; and Rasmussen, O. V. "Cerebral Asthenopia in a Torture Victim," *Ugeskrift for Laeger* 140, Dec. 1978, pp. 3206–7.

Spengler, A. "Manifest Sadomasochism of Males: Results of an Empirical Study," *Archives of Sexual Behavior* 6, Nov. 1977, pp. 441–56.

Stein, Jeffrey. "Grad School for Juntas," *The Nation*, May 21, 1977, pp. 621–24.

Stevens, Geoffrey. "New Tales of the RCMP," *Inquiry*, May 29, 1978, pp. 9–12.

Swomley, Dr. John, Jr. "Inside Marcos' Concentration Camps," *Christian Century* 91, Nov. 13, 1974, pp. 1066–68.

Timerman, Jacobo. "The Bodies Counted Are Our Own," *Columbia Journalism Review* 19, May–June 1980, pp. 29–33.

Usamah. "War and Humanity: Notes on Personal Experiences," *Indonesia*, Apr. 1970, pp. 1–10.‡

V. MAJOR MAGAZINE AND JOURNAL ARTICLES, UNAUTHORED

ARGENTINA:

"En Kendt Argentinsk Sygeplejerske Er SporLøst Forsundet," *Dansk Sygeplejerad*, Jan. 23, 1980, p. 7. (T)

CHILE:

"Chile: After DINA," *Newsweek*, Sept. 12, 1977, p. 50.

"The Organization of Torture and Murder," *Counterspy*, Winter 1976, pp. 69–71.

"Special Forces of the 'Ejército de Chile,'" *Armed Forces*, Jan. 1979, pp. 11–13.

IRAN:

"New Characteristics of the Iranian Army," *Islamic Revolution; Dimensions of the Movement in Iran*, Vol. 1, No. 1 (Apr. 1979), pp. 5–7.

"The SAVAK-CIA Connection," *The Nation*, Mar. 1, 1980, pp. 229–30.

MOZAMBIQUE:

"Human Rights End at Mozambique Border," *To the Point*, Aug. 25, 1978, p. 31.

PORTUGAL:

"A PIDE to Catch a PIDE?" *The Economist*, Nov. 2, 1974, pp. 31–32.

"How Not to Run Your Secret Police," *The Economist*, May 18, 1974, p. 31.

‡ *Indonesia* is a publication of the Cornell University Modern Indonesia Project.

SOUTH AFRICA:

"Another AID Study Takes Aim at Shaping Southern Africa," *Southern Africa*, Feb. 1979, p. 12.

"Secret Funds Scandal Shakes White Confidence," *Southern Africa*, Feb. 1979, pp. 16–17.

"Torture in South Africa?" *Proveritate*, Dec. 15, 1972, p. 12.

"The View from BOSS," *Newsweek*, Oct. 25, 1976, p. 53.

VI. FOREIGN NEWSPAPERS, NEWSLETTERS

IRAN:

"Confession of Bahman Naderipour (Tehrani)," *Ettela'at*, June 24, 1979. (T)

"Dismissal of Fourteen People of the Corrupt Regime of Tabriz University," *Jomhuriyeh Eslami*, June 17, 1979. (T)

"Excerpts from the Confession of Tehrani," *Ettela'at*, June 23, 1979. (T)

"Fifth Session of the Trial of Tehrani," *Keyhan*, June 19, 1979. (T)

"From the Torture in Qasr Prison . . . ," *Keyhan*, Mar. 4, 1979. (T)

Iranian National Front Information Bulletins:

No. 1, Vol. 1 (June 1972); No. 2, Vol. 1 (Oct. 1972); No. 3, Vol. 1 (Nov. 1972); No. 4, Vol. 1 (Dec. 1972); No. 2, Vol. 2 (June 1976); No. 5, Vol. 2 (Aug. 1977).

Iranian People's Struggle Bulletins:

No. 1, Vol. 1 (Apr. 1975); No. 2, Vol. 1 (May 1975); No. 3, Vol. 1 (July 1975); No. 4, Vol. 1 (Oct. 1975); No. 5, Vol. 1 (Nov. 1975); No. 1, Vol. 2 (Apr. 1976); No. 2, Vol. 2 (June 1976); No. 3, Vol. 2 (Oct. 1976); No. 5, Vol. 2 (Aug. 1977).

"Revolutionary Court Has Begun the Trial of Eight More SAVAK Agents," *Keyhan*, June 29, 1979. (T)

"SAVAK Agent Naderipour's letter to Ayatollah Taleghani before his Execution: Organize SAVAK for the Fight Against Communists," *Iran News*, July 2, 1979, p. 5. (T)

"Slaughter of the Pahlavi Regime," *Ettela'at*, Feb.–Mar. 1979 (imprecise date). (T)

"Three SAVAK Torturers Have Been Executed," *Keyhan*, May 25, 1979. (T)

"A Tunnel of Torture Discovered under the Swimming Pool of Qasr Prison," *Keyhan*, May 24, 1979. (T)

PHILIPPINES:

Bonifacio, Gillego. "The Anatomy of a Dossier," Manila *Chronicle*, Mar. 2, 1972, p. 11.

SOUTH AFRICA:

"BOSS Man on Terrorism Act," *Rand Daily Mail*, Nov. 22, 1971.

"BOSS: The Official Facts," Johannesburg *Star*, Sept. 6, 1969.

"Has Prime Minister Bowed to Criticism?" Johannesburg *Star*, Sept. 6, 1969.

"Interrogators Deny Claims of Assault," *Rand Daily Mail*, Nov. 8, 1974.

"Winter, the Spy Who Sold Out His Chief," *Sunday Express*, Aug. 8, 1979.

YUGOSLAVIA:

"Security and Self-Defence Faculty," *Tanjug in English*, 1318 GMT, Dec. 1, 1977.*

"Umro Je Branko Štih," *Večernýi líst*, June 27, 1979.†

Večernýi líst. Dec. 5, 1975.

VII. Major Newspaper Stories Published in the United States

AFGHANISTAN:

"Legacy of Afghan Prison: Brutality, Torture, Death," Los Angeles *Times*, May 18, 1979, Part II, p. 7.

CHILE:

"A Misplaced Complacency Toward Repression," Los Angeles *Times*, May 18, 1979, Part II, p. 7.

Oakes, John B. "Pinochet in No Rush," New York *Times*, May 3, 1979, p. A23.

HAITI:

"Horrors of Haitian Jails Echo in Miami Courtroom," Los Angeles *Times*, July 4, 1980, Part I, p. 18.

IRAN:

Iran Voice:
   Vol. 1, No. 1 (June 4, 1979); Vol. 1, No. 3 (June 18, 1979); Vol. 1, No. 4 (June 25, 1979); Vol. 1, No. 5 (July 2, 1979); Vol. 1, No. 11 (Aug. 13, 1979).‡

* Tanjug is a Yugoslavian news agency that works with many leading news services around the world.

† *Večernýi líst* is the afternoon newspaper of Zagreb, the capital of Croatia.

‡ *Iran Voice* was the weekly newssheet of the Iranian Embassy in Washington, D.C., under the early Khomeini regime.

KOREA (SOUTH):

"New Repression in South Korea," New York *Times*, May 29, 1980, p. A3.

"Seoul Vows New Restrictions Won't Delay Democracy," New York *Times*, May 19, 1980, p. A3.

PEOPLE'S REPUBLIC OF CHINA:

"Deng: A Third World War Is Inevitable," Manchester *Guardian*, Sept. 28, 1980, p. 17.

PHILIPPINES:

Guidote, Sister Caridad. "Most Frequently Used Torture Methods of Marcos Police," Philippine *Times*, Aug. 12–18, 1978, pp. 1–6.

"Message to Marcos: Testimony of Rep. James M. Jeffords (R-Vt.) before the U. S. Congress," *Asian-American News*, Feb. 21, 1980, pp. 5–15.

Monteclaro, Eddie B. "Salvagings Reported," Philippine *Times*, double issue of Apr. 21–27 and Apr. 28 to May 4, 1978, pp. 1, 6–7.

YUGOSLAVIA:

Mestrović, Mate, "War over Croatia," North American Newspaper Alliance, Nov. 4–5, 1978.

UNITED STATES:

"U.S.A.I.M.A.—Controversy and Foreign Soldiers," Fayetteville *Observer* and the Fayetteville *Times*, Nov. 26, 1978, Sec. I, p. 1.

"U. S. Teams Train Forces in 34 Lands," New York *Times*, Feb. 20, 1975.

VIII. HUMAN RIGHTS PUBLICATIONS

AFGHANISTAN:

Amnesty International. *Violations of Human Rights and Fundamental Freedoms in the Democratic Republic of Afghanistan.* London: Amnesty International, 1979.

ARGENTINA:

Amnesty International. *Argentina: Action for the Disappeared. Information and Actions on 22 Missing Persons.* London: Amnesty International, 1979.

———. *Argentina: Military Aid, Trade and Investment Transfers.* London: Amnesty International, 1978.

———. *Missing Children of Argentina.* London: Amnesty International, 1979.

———. *Prison Conditions in the Unidad Penitenciaria No. 1 Cárcel de Coronda.* London: Amnesty International, 1979.

———. *Report of an Amnesty International Mission to Argentina.* London: Amnesty International, 1976.

———. *Testimony on Secret Detention Camps in Argentina.* London: Amnesty International, 1980.

———. *Visit Beautiful Argentina.* . . . New York: Amnesty International, 1978.

Inter-American Commission on Human Rights. *Report on the Situation of Human Rights in Argentina* (provisional version). Washington: General Secretariat of the Organization of American States, 1980.

Lawyers Committee for International Human Rights. *Materials on Human Rights and the Situation of Defense Lawyers and Judges in Argentina.* New York: Lawyers Committee, Mar. 1979.

Provisional Commission for Disappeared Persons and Political Prisoners in Argentina. *Missing in Argentina: The Desperate Search for Thousands of Abducted Victims.* New York: Provisional Commission, 1980.

BANGLADESH:

Amnesty International. *Report of an Amnesty International Mission to Bangladesh.* London: Amnesty International, 1978.

BRAZIL:

Amnesty International. *Brazil: Background Paper.* London: Amnesty International, June 1978.

La Fédération Internationale de l'Homme et Le Secrétariat International des Juristes pour L'Amnistie en Uruguay. *Complaint Alleging the Violation of Human Rights in Uruguay and Brazil Presented to the Chairman, Inter-American Commission on Human Rights, Organization of American States.* Washington, D.C., Aug. 2, 1979.

CANADA:

Civil Liberties Association, National Capitol Region, *Partial Listing of Facts and Allegations Regarding Security Operations in Canada.* Toronto: Civil Liberties Association, n.d.

Law Union of British Columbia. *Brief Presented to the Commission of Inquiry Concerning Certain Activities of the RCMP,* Established under Order-in-Council, P.C. ⅜1977-1911, July 6, 1977.

CHILE:

Amnesty International. *Disappeared Prisoners in Chile.* London: Amnesty International, 1977.

Chile Committee for Human Rights. *Newsletter ⅜17.* London: Chile Committee for Human Rights, 1977.

Chile Committee for Human Rights. *Newsletter,* Vol. 3, No. 1 (Jan. 1978).

Chile Democrático. *List of Torturers at the Service of the Fascist Junta in Chile.* Rome: Secretariat for Solidarity, 1974.

Chile Informativo 102: elaborado por la Secretaria Ejecutiva de Solidaridad de la Izquierda Chileana para América. *La DINA en Chile.* Mexico City: Casa de Chile, 1976. (T)

Ege, Konrad; and Wenger, Martha. *The Embassy of the Federal Republic of Germany and Torture in Chile.* Washington, D.C.: Washington Area Clergy and Laity Concerned, 1977.

Landau, Saul. *They Educated the Crows: An Institute Report on the Letelier-Moffitt Murders.* London and Amsterdam: Transnational Institute, 1978.

Office for Political Prisoners and Human Rights in Chile. *Chile Report ※4.* New York: Office for Political Prisoners, Aug. 1978.

Secretariat for Solidarity in America with the Chilean People. Chile Informativo 140, 141. *Assassination of Letelier: The Actors in a Sinister Plot.* Toronto: Chile Informative, 1978.

COLOMBIA:

Amnesty International. Press Release, *Recommendations to the Colombian Government,* Apr. 17, 1980.

CUBA:

Calzón, Frank. *Castro's Gulag: The Politics of Terror.* Washington, D.C.: Council for Inter-American Security, 1979.

Inter-American Association for Democracy and Freedom. *Hemispherica:* Vol. 26, No. 6 (June–July 1977); Vol. 27, No. 7 (Aug.–Sept. 1978); Vol. 28, No. 1 (Jan. 1979); Vol. 28, No. 4 (Apr. 1979); Vol. 28, No. 5 (May 1979); Vol. 28, No. 6 (June–July, 1979); Vol. 28, No. 10 (Nov. 1979); Vol. 29, No. 2 (Feb. 1980).

CZECHOSLOVAKIA:

Amnesty International. *Czechoslovakia.* London: Amnesty International, 1977.

EASTERN EUROPE, GENERAL:

Center for Appeals for Freedom. *Freedom Appeals.* New York: Freedom House:
No. 1 (Sept.–Oct. 1979); No. 2 (Nov.–Dec. 1979); No. 4 (Mar.–Apr. 1980); No. 5 (May–June 1980).

Silnitsky, Larisa. *Recollections of Bratislava.* New York: Radio Liberty Special Report, 1974.

EAST TIMOR:

Chomsky, Noam. *East Timor-CALC Foreword*. Clergy and Laity Concerned, 1980 (place of publication unspecified).

Fretilin Delegation. *Statement by the FRETILIN Delegation to the Fourth Committee During Discussions on the Question of East Timor*. New York: Fretilin Delegation, 1979.

Gilbert, C.; Heading, M.; and Waddingham, J. *East Timor: How Many People Are Missing?* No. 28. Victoria, Australia: Timor Information Service, Feb. 1980.

EL SALVADOR:

International Commission of Jurists. *Republic of El Salvador*. New York: International Commission of Jurists, 1978.

ETHIOPIA:

Amnesty International. *Human Rights Violations in Ethiopia*. London: Amnesty International, Nov. 1978.

FEDERAL REPUBLIC OF GERMANY:

Amnesty International. *Amnesty International's Work on Prison Conditions of Persons Suspected or Convicted of Politically Motivated Crimes in the Federal Republic of Germany: Isolation and Solitary Confinement*. London: Amnesty International, 1980.

GREAT BRITAIN:

Amnesty International. *Report of an Amnesty International Mission to Northern Ireland*. London: Amnesty International, 1978.

GREECE:

Amnesty International. *Torture in Greece: The First Torturers' Trial, 1975*. London: Amnesty International, 1977.

GUATEMALA:

Amnesty International. *Guatemala*. London: Amnesty International, 1978.

HAITI:

Friends of Haiti. *Haiti Report*, Vol. 1, Nos. 1 and 2 (fall/winter 1976). New York: Friends of Haiti.

Haitian Refugee Project. *Newsletter*, Vol. 1, No. 1 (Feb. 1980). Washington, D.C.: Haitian Refugee Project.

INDIA:

Amnesty International. *Report of an Amnesty International Mission to India*. London: Amnesty International, 1979.

INDONESIA:

Amnesty International. *Indonesia*. London: Amnesty International, 1977.
Sudisman, General Secretary of the Indonesian Communist Party. *Analysis of Responsibility: Defense Speech of Sudisman at his trial before the Special Military Tribunal*. Jakarta: July 21, 1967.
TAPOL: U. S. Campaign for the Release of Indonesian Political Prisoners. Montclair, N.J.: TAPOL-U.S.*
Bulletins:
  No. 1 (Oct. 1, 1975); No. 5 (June 15, 1976); No. 6 (Aug. 15, 1976); No. 7 (Oct. 15, 1976); No. 8 (Dec. 15, 1976); No. 11 (June 15, 1977); No. 13 (Oct. 15, 1977); No. 14 (Apr. 15, 1978); No. 15 (June 15, 1977); Nos. 16 and 17 (Nov. 1978); No. 27 (Apr. 1978); No. 31 (Dec.–Jan. 1978–79); No. 33 (Apr. 1979).

IRAN:

Amnesty International. *Human Rights in Iran. Testimony on behalf of Amnesty International by Brian Wrobel, LL.B., before the Subcommittee on International Organizations of the Committee on International Relations, House of Representatives*. London: Amnesty International, 1978.
————. *Iran*. London: Amnesty International, 1976.
————. *Law and Human Rights in the Islamic Republic of Iran*. London: Amnesty International, 1980.
Butler, William J.; and Levasseur, Georges. *Human Rights and the Legal System in Iran*. Geneva: International Commission of Jurists, 1976.
Committee for Artistic and Intellectual Freedom in Iran. Bulletins. New York: CAIFI. Issues of Mar. 28, 1978, and Nov. 16, 1978.
Halliday, Fred. *After the Shah* (issue paper). Washington, D.C.: Institute for Policy Studies, 1979.
Iranian Students' Association. Bulletin, Aug. 1, 1978.
Marwick, Christine M. "The Intelligence Failure in Iran: The Report of the House Subcommittee on Intelligence Evaluation," *First Principles*, Vol. 4, No. 6. Washington, D.C.: Center for National Security Studies, 1978.

* TAPOL is an Indonesian contraction for *tahanan politik*, meaning political prisoner.

ISRAEL:

Amnesty International. *Report and Recommendations of an Amnesty International Mission to the Government of the State of Israel*. London: Amnesty International, 1979.

Israeli League for Human and Civil Rights. *The Israeli Involvement in the Protection of Latin American Dictatorships*. Tel-Aviv: Israeli League for Human and Civil Rights, 1978.

――――. *Second Collection on Torture and Police Brutality in Israel*. Tel-Aviv: Israeli League for Human and Civil Rights, 1979.

Palestine Human Rights Campaign. *Israel and Torture: An Insight Inquiry*. Walnut Bottom, Pa.: Palestine Human Rights Campaign, 1977 (reprints of a study done by the London *Sunday Times*).

――――. *Palestine Human Rights Bulletins*. Washington, D.C.: PHR Campaign:
No. 2 (Aug. 1977); No. 4 (Dec. 1977); No. 5 (Feb. 1978); No. 8 (June 1978); No. 10 (Nov. 1979); No. 14 (Feb. 1979); No. 16 (Mar. 1976); No. 17 (Apr. 1979); Nos. 19–20 (June–July 1979); No. 22 (Sept. 1979); No. 23 (Nov. 1979); No. 24 (Jan. 1980).

JAPAN:

Citizens Crime Commission. *Tokyo: One City Where Crime Doesn't Pay!* Philadelphia: Citizens Crime Commission, 1975.

KOREA (NORTH):

Amnesty International. *A Personal Account of the Experience of a Prisoner of Conscience in the Democratic People's Republic of Korea*. London: Amnesty International, 1979.

KOREA (SOUTH):

Amnesty International. *Report of an Amnesty International Mission to the Republic of Korea*. London: Amnesty International, 1975.

LAOS:

Amnesty International. *Political Prisoners in the People's Democratic Republic of Laos*. London: Amnesty International, 1980.

LATIN AMERICA, GENERAL:

Arriagada, Genaro. *Ideology and Politics in the South American Military*. Princeton, N.J.: Woodrow Wilson International Center for Scholars, Mar. 21, 1979.

North American Congress on Latin America. *Command and Control: U. S. Police Operations in Latin America*, Jan. 1972.

————. *Foreign Graduates of U. S. Military Schools, Fiscal Years 1970–75*, Jan. 1976.

————. *The Inter-American Defense College* (reprinted from *Military Review*), New York: NACLA, Apr. 1970.

————. *Latin America and Empire Report, "The Pentagon's Protégés; U. S. Training Programs for Foreign Military Personnel,"* Jan. 1976.

PEN American Center. *Latin America: The Freedom to Write.* New York: PEN, 1980.

MALAWI:

Amnesty International. *Malawi.* London: Amnesty International, 1976.

MALAYSIA:

Amnesty International. *Malaysia.* London: Amnesty International, 1976.

MEXICO:

Goldman, Robert K.; and Jacoby, Daniel. *Report of the Commission of Enquiry to Mexico Submitted to the International League for Human Rights, Fédération Internationale des Droits de l'Homme and Pax Romana.* New York: International League for Human Rights, 1978.

Héctor Marroquín Defense Committee. *Héctor Marroquín Defense Newsletter*, Vol. 1, No. 2. New York: Héctor Marroquín Defense Committee, Fall 1978.

Marroquín, Héctor. *My Story.* New York: Héctor Marroquín Defense Committee, 1978.

Statement of Mrs. Bertha Alicia López García de Zazueta to the Mexican Committee to Defend Political Prisoners (undated).

MOROCCO:

Amnesty International. *Morocco.* London: Amnesty International, 1977.

NAMIBIA:

Amnesty International. *Namibia.* London: Amnesty International, 1977.

NICARAGUA:

Amnesty International. *The Republic of Nicaragua, including the findings of a Mission to Nicaragua.* London: Amnesty International, 1976.

PARAGUAY:

Amnesty International. *Deaths Under Torture and Disappearance of Political Prisoners in Paraguay.* London: Amnesty International, 1976.

————. *Paraguay.* London: Amnesty International, 1978.

PEOPLE'S REPUBLIC OF CHINA:

Amnesty International. *Political Imprisonment in the People's Republic of China.* London: Amnesty International, 1978.

PERU:

Amnesty International. *Peru.* London: Amnesty International, 1979.

PHILIPPINES:

Amnesty International. *Report of an Amnesty International Mission to the Republic of the Philippines.* London: Amnesty International, 1976.

Butler, William J., Esq., chairman. *The Decline of Democracy in the Philippines.* Geneva: International Commission of Jurists, 1976.

Claude, Richard P. *Human Rights in the Philippines and United States Responsibility,* a working paper. College Park, Md.: Center for Philosophy and Public Policy, University of Maryland, 1978.

Friends of the Filipino People. Letter sent by Friends of the Filipino People representatives to Congressman Ike Andrews, U. S. House of Representatives, demanding an investigation into the role of the John F. Kennedy School of Military Assistance, at Fort Bragg, N.C., in the training of military personnel for repressive regimes. Sept. 18, 1978.

Task Force Detainees of the Association of Major Religious Superiors in the Philippines. *Political Detainees of the Philippines,* Book 3. Manila: Task Force Detainees, 1978.

———. *Quarterly Report of the Task Force Detainees of the Philippines on Political Detainees.* Manila: Task Force Detainees, 1979.

RHODESIA:

Amnesty International. *Rhodesia/Zimbabwe.* London: Amnesty International, 1976.

Anti-Apartheid Movement. *Zimbabwe Briefing No. 6: Guardians of White Power (the Rhodesian Security Forces).* London: Anti-Apartheid Movement, 1978.

International Commission of Jurists (with the Catholic Institute for International Relations). *Racial Discrimination and Repression in Southern Rhodesia.* London: International Commission of Jurists, 1976.

ROMANIA:

Amnesty International. *Romania.* London: Amnesty International, 1978.
———. *Romania.* London: Amnesty International, 1980.

SINGAPORE:

Amnesty International. *Singapore.* London: Amnesty International, 1978.

SOUTH AFRICA:

Africa Policy Information Center of the African-American Institute. *South Africa/Namibia Update*, Vol. 3, No. 5. New York: Apr. 11, 1979.

Amnesty International. *Political Imprisonment in South Africa*. London: Amnesty International, 1978.

————. *Political Imprisonment in South Africa: An Update to an Amnesty International Report*. London: Amnesty International, 1979.

Bernstein, Hilda. *South Africa: The Terrorism of Torture*. London: International Defense and Aid Fund for Southern Africa, 1972.

Cronjé, Suzanne. *Witness in the Dark; Police Torture and Brutality in South Africa*. London: Christian Action, 1964.

Episcopal Churchmen for South Africa. "BOSS." New York: Episcopal Churchmen, Aug. 3, 1977.

International Defense and Aid Fund for Southern Africa. *BOSS: The First Five Years*. London: International Defense and Aid Fund for Southern Africa, 1975.

————. *South Africa: The BOSS Law*. London: International Defense and Aid Fund for Southern Africa, 1971.

Program for Social Change. *Second Report on Arrests, Detentions and Trials of Members and Supporters of: South African Students Organization (SASO), Black People's Convention (BPC), Black Allied Workers Union (BAWU), Theatre Council of Natal (TECON), and Black Community Programs (BCP)*. Braamfontein: Program for Social Change, Dec. 23, 1974.

Rieke, Professor Luvern V. *The Trial of Ravan Press: Report to the Lawyers' Committee for Civil Rights Under Law*. Seattle: School of Law, University of Washington, n.d.

Sachs, A. *South Africa: The Violence of Apartheid*. London: International Defense and Aid Fund for Southern Africa, 1971.

SPAIN:

Amnesty International. *Report of an Amnesty International Mission to Spain*. London: Amnesty International, 1975.

SRI LANKA:

Amnesty International. *Report of an Amnesty International Mission to Sri Lanka*. London: Amnesty International, 1976.

SYRIA:

Amnesty International. *Syria*. London: Amnesty International, 1979.

TAIWAN:

Amnesty International. *Taiwan*. London: Amnesty International, 1980.
Formosan Association for Human Rights. *Human Rights in Taiwan*. New York: Formosan Association, n.d.
Lin Yi-hsiung. *On Being Detained*. New York: Formosan Association for Human Rights, 1980.
"To Heal, Not to Hate: A Report on the Kaohsiung Incident" (reprinted from *Free China Review*). Taipei: Kuang Hwa Publishing Co., Feb. 1980.

TUNISIA:

Amnesty International. *Tunisia: Imprisonment of Trade Unionists in 1978*. London: Amnesty International, 1978.

TURKEY:

Amnesty International. *Turkey*. London: Amnesty International, 1977.

UGANDA:

Amnesty International. *Human Rights in Uganda*. London: Amnesty International, 1978.
International Commission of Jurists. *Uganda and Human Rights: Reports to the U. N. Commission on Human Rights*. Geneva: International Commission of Jurists, 1977.

UNITED STATES:

American Friends Service Committee. *The Police Threat to Political Liberty*. Philadelphia: American Friends Service Committee, 1979.
Campaign for Political Rights. *Organizing Notes*, Vol. 3, No. 2 (Mar. 1979). Washington, D.C.: Campaign for Political Rights.
Center for Research on Criminal Justice. *The Iron Fist and the Velvet Glove: An Analysis of the U. S. Police*. Berkeley, Calif.: Center for Research on Criminal Justice, 1975.
National Commission on Law Enforcement and Social Justice. *The Central Intelligence Agency - Interpol Connection*. Los Angeles: National Commission, 1977.
———. *Recent Findings on Interpol*. Los Angeles: National Commission, 1977.
———. *The Victimization of American Citizens by Interpol Abuse*. Los Angeles: National Commission, 1977.

URUGUAY:

Amnesty International. *Conditions of Detention for Political Prisoners in Uruguay*. London: Amnesty International, 1979.

————. *Interview with Lieutenant Julio César Cooper.* London: Amnesty International, 1979.

————. *Life Inside an Uruguayan Torture Center: A Testimony.* London: Amnesty International, 1977.

————. *Political Imprisonment in Uruguay.* London: Amnesty International, 1979.

————. *Testimony on Prison Conditions in the Navy Barracks. Fusileros Navales (FUSNA).* London: Amnesty International, 1979.

————. *Uruguay: The Cases of Fourteen Prisoners of Conscience.* London: Amnesty International, March 1979.

————. *Uruguay: Deaths Under Torture.* London: Amnesty International, 1978.

USSR:

American Enterprise Institute, *Studies in Political and Social Processes. A Conversation with Vladimir Bukovsky.* Washington, D.C.: American Enterprise Institute, 1979.

Amnesty International. *A Chronicle of Current Events: Journal of the Human Rights Movement in the U.S.S.R.* London: Amnesty International. Issues Nos. 43, 44, 45 (1979); No. 49 (1978); No. 50 (1979).

————. *Prisoners of Conscience in the USSR.* London: Amnesty International, 1980.

Khronika Press. *A Chronicle of Current Events in the USSR.* New York: Khronika Press. Issues No. 34 (Apr.–June 1979); No. 35 (July–Sept. 1979).

Podrabinek, Alexander. *Punitive Medicine: A Summary.* London: Amnesty International, 1977.

YUGOSLAVIA:

Babić, Col. Ivan. *U. S. Policy Towards Yugoslavia.* New York: Croatian National Congress, 1979.

Bušić, Bruno. *UDBA Archipelago: Prison Terror in Croatia.* Arcadia: Croatian Information Service, 1976.

Committee to Aid Democratic Dissidents in Yugoslavia. Bulletin No. 1 (July 10, 1980).

Committee in Defense of Soviet Political Prisoners. *A Dossier on Repression in Yugoslavia.* London: Committee in Defense of Soviet Political Prisoners, 1977.

Croatian Information Agency. *Naked Island—Goli Otok.* Toronto: Croatian Information Agency, 1978.

Croatian Information Service. *Question of Yugoslav Agents in U. S. Surfaces at Trial.* New York: Croatian Information Service, 1977.

Croatian National Congress. *Violation of Human and National Rights in Croatia.* New York: Croatian National Congress, July 21, 1980.

Marković, Vladimir, letter sent from a Cultural Reformatory Home in Yugoslavia, as an appeal to readers for freedom. Nov. 1979.

ZAIRE:

Amnesty International. *Human Rights Violations in Zaire.* London: Amnesty International, 1980.

IX. HUMAN RIGHTS PUBLICATIONS, GENERAL

Amnesty International. *Evidence of Torture: Studies by the Amnesty International Danish Medical Group.* London: Amnesty International, 1977.

————. *Handbook.* London: Amnesty International, 1977.

————. *Report of the Medical Committee National Advisory Board.* San Francisco: Amnesty International, 1978.

————. *Report on Torture.* New York: Farrar, Straus & Giroux, 1973, 1975.

————. *Report 1978.* London: Amnesty International, 1978.

————. *Report 1979.* London: Amnesty International, 1979.

————. *Report 1980.* London: Amnesty International, 1980.

Amnesty International Medical Seminar. *Violations of Human Rights: Torture and the Medical Profession.* London: Amnesty International, 1978.

Bulletin of the Center for the Independence of Judges and Lawyers. Geneva: International Commission of Jurists, 1979.

Clergy and Laity Concerned. *SAVAK: DINA: KCIA.* Washington, D.C.: CALC, n.d.

Geuns, Herman van; and Heijder, Alfred. *Professional Codes of Ethics.* London: Amnesty International, 1976.

Klare, Michael T. *Supplying Repression.* Washington, D.C.: Institute for Policy Studies, 1977.

Of Human Rights, Vol. 2, No. 2. Washington, D.C.: Georgetown University, Spring 1979.

X. LEGAL DOCUMENTS

Affidavit of Romeo T. Capulong, State of New York, City of New York, Mar. 5, 1980; and Addendum to Form I-589. Development of Information on Romeo T. Capulong Application for Political Asylum.

Haitian Refugee Center et al., Plaintiff, vs. *Benjamin Civiletti et al., Defendants,* Vol. 5 (79-2086-Civ-JLK). Miami, Fla., 1980.

Private Sociale Mission e.V., Sociedad Benefactora y Educacional Dignidad vs. *Amnesty International, Firma Gruner und Jahr, Henri Nan-*

nen (*ausgeschieden*), *und Herrn Kai Herman* (3 0 123/77). Bonn:
Nov. 19, 1979. Testimony of a former DINA agent, reprinted by Amnesty International in Germany. (T)

XI. BROADCAST REPORTS

Maryknoll Fathers. *Collision Course,* a documentary on the persecution of religious leaders in the Philippines. BBC Production, 1977.
Murphy, Charles, ABC News Miami bureau chief; and Rivera, Geraldo, newsman WABC-TV New York, interviewers. *Issues and Answers.* Guest: General Augusto Pinochet, President of Chile's military junta. Santiago, Chile: Oct. 6, 1973.

Index